THE CHILDHOOD OF EDWARD THOMAS

D1344614

also by Edward Thomas

★

COLLECTED POEMS

The Childhood of
EDWARD THOMAS

a fragment
of autobiography

with a preface by
ROLAND GANT

FABER AND FABER
London · Boston

First published in 1938
by Faber and Faber Limited
3 Queen Square London WC1N 3AU
First published in this edition 1983
Printed in Great Britain by
Redwood Burn Ltd, Trowbridge, Wiltshire
All rights reserved

© Diary, Myfanwy Thomas, 1971, 1977 and 1983
© Preface, Roland Gant, 1983

British Library Cataloguing in Publication Data

Thomas, Edward
The childhood of Edward Thomas.
1. Thomas, Edward
I. Title
941.082′092′4   DA566.9.T/
ISBN 0–571–13046–1

Library of Congress Data has been applied for

PREFACE

*

In a letter dated 5 December 1913 to the writer Eleanor Farjeon[1] Edward Thomas spoke of having 'written a book on Keats[2] and begun one . . . no less than an autobiography, not a chronological and geographical history of E. T. but an attempt to put on paper what he sees when he thinks of himself from 1878 to about 1895'. When reviewing work became scarce after the outbreak of the Great War in August 1914 Thomas concentrated on *A Literary Pilgrim in England*,[3] originally commissioned as *Homes and Haunts of Writers* and referred to by its author as ' 'Omes and 'Aunts'. In addition to this bread-and-butter writing he set down memories of his early years. When he showed the manuscript to Chapman and Hall, the publishers 'complained that it was difficult to read in manuscript', as he told Eleanor Farjeon in a letter dated 2 May 1915. Eleanor, a devoted friend, typed it out, but owing to war conditions and Thomas's death in 1917 the memoirs did not appear until 1938, published by Faber and Faber, who two years previously had brought out Edward Thomas's *Collected Poems*, introduced by Walter de la Mare.[4]

[1] Farjeon, Eleanor, *Edward Thomas: The Last Four Years*. Oxford University Press, London, 1958.

[2] Thomas, Edward, *Keats*. T. C. & E. C. Jacks, London, 1916.

[3] Thomas, Edward, *A Literary Pilgrim in England*. Methuen, London, 1917.

[4] Thomas, Edward, *Collected Poems*, with an introduction by Walter de la Mare. Faber & Faber, London, 1936.

PREFACE

The Childhood of Edward Thomas[5] included a preface by Edward's brother Julian, as true and moving now as when it was written. He described the style as belonging to

> Edward's later period, when he had shed all preciosity and began to write the simple prose which he finally decided was the best of all—prose, as he said to me shortly after he had finished his critical study of Walter Pater, 'as near akin as possible to the talk of a Surrey peasant'. He was thinking, no doubt, of George Sturt's Bettesworth. In the pages that follow will be found the self-drawn portrait of 'the opinionated savage youngster he once was, fishing, fighting, paper-chasing, bird's nesting, consorting with vagabonds and at last finding sanctuary with the books of Richard Jefferies. . . . Edward was happy neither at home nor at school. Like all his brothers [there were five of them] he was the despair of his parents, a mystery to both mother and father.

Edward's father was the P. H. T. to whom he addressed the poem that begins:

> I may come near loving you
> When you are dead
> And there is nothing to do
> And much to be said. . . .

Julian Thomas believed that

> To my father he owed more than he would ever admit, in especial the art of reading aloud, and through

[5] Thomas, Edward, *The Childhood of Edward Thomas: a Fragment of Autobiography*, with a Preface by Julian Thomas. Faber & Faber, London, 1938.

this the appreciation of poetry. One pleasant memory at least I have of the painful Sunday afternoons that he describes—my father's reading aloud from *Hiawatha*, which began when he at last realized the failure of 'improving' literature to arouse any interest whatsoever in any of us. Only one more musical voice have I heard, and that was Edward's own. . . . He read in an almost unaccented monotone, slowly, clearly, so that not one word, not one shade of meaning was lost. Many years later he read aloud his first poems to me: and then, all too soon, that voice was stilled.

Edward Thomas's inner voice is very clear in both *The Childhood* and *The Diary*.[6] Of the people in the South London suburbs where he grew up there is this portrait of the woman who came over from Lambeth to do his mother's washing and whose 'great red arms and . . . clean rapid ways awed me, her glass of beer and plate of bread and cheese in the middle of the morning awed and delighted me'. Among schoolmasters, 'there was a strict sardonic one with ginger hair, a mild incalculable black-haired one with a ridiculously mild voice, and an altogether humorous one with bulging eyes and an amused unastonishable look who managed the top form with a smile. . . .' A particular schoolfellow was 'puny and skinny, his face screwed up with quick Cockney malice and amusement. He had several sisters very much like him, always pattering and grinning. The family was a cheerful one, excellent at Christmas parties, just what our family was not. . . .'

[6] Thomas, Edward, *Diary of Edward Thomas 1 January–8 April 1917*, with a Foreword by Myfanwy Thomas and an Introduction by Roland Gant, woodcuts by Hellmuth Weissenborn. The Whittington Press, Andoversford, Gloucestershire, 1977.

But 'a thousand times better' was Swindon, where Edward spent holidays with his grandmother, uncle and aunt.

My uncle was a fitter in the Great Western Railway works . . . tall, easy-going, and had a pipe in his mouth and very likely a dog at his heels. I was proud to be with him as he nodded to the one-legged signalman and the man with a white apron and a long hammer for tapping the wheels of all the carriages. . . . The variety of staid men and jaunty men, old men and boys, tall and stocky men, the frowners and the smilers, fascinated me with endless indolent inarticulate half-conjectures; and suddenly out of the multitude my uncle—or for a moment once or twice a man extremely like him. Straight out of that mysterious pageant, the one positively and entirely living one, he used to come into the house, into the kitchen, into his chair and begin to eat.

A quarter-century—much of it spent in toiling at reviewing and commissioned books in conditions of near-poverty—had elapsed between those visits and the sharp evocation of them. The same clarity is apparent in the spare, acute observation of his surroundings entered day by day in his diary of the Western Front. On 12 February 1917:

Taylor says (as he makes my bed and as usual asks if he does it right): 'I am not proud, but I likes to be comfortable. I have been domesticated since I joined the Army.' Nothing to do all morning, afternoon at our position—hare, partridges and wild duck in field S.E. of guns. I feel the cold—the morning sun turns to a damp thaw wind. . . . Some grass showing green through melting snow. Thorburn worries because he can't laugh at silly low talk. Evening censoring letters and reading Sonnets; others writing—when I begin to talk to Rubin, the Captain said 'You get on with your Sonnets' and then all was silent. Awful fug.

In this entry made less than two months before his death in action the writer, who had recalled so vividly his boyhood in the fragment of autobiography left behind in England, was a near-secret poet who signed his work 'Edward Eastaway' and, to those around him, an elderly —at thirty-eight—subaltern liked and respected by his men and gently mocked by his superior officer for his outlandish choice of reading. Thomas's distinctive voice, 'clear . . . not one shade of meaning lost', comes through in his description of those other mutely courageous men crammed with him into the misery of the trenches and dugouts and in his notice of the grass and fellow-creatures who, like some of the men, survive the bombardments.

After Edward Thomas was killed on Easter Monday, 9 April 1917, by the vacuum caused by an unexploding shell, his kitbag of personal possessions was forwarded to his widow Helen. His youngest child, Myfanwy, described how after her brother Mervyn's death in 1965 his son found among some papers Edward Thomas's diary. This grandson, also called Edward, transcribed the diary, which had been kept in a minute and closely written hand. After careful checking, it was typed by the poet's daughters. 'The reading of the diary's curiously ridged pages—like the scallops of a sea-shell—so truthful, poignant and full of his minute observation, was a most moving and disturbing experience for Bronwen and me,' Myfanwy Thomas wrote in her Foreword to a

limited edition of the *Diary* which had originally
appeared in the Autumn 1971 issue of the *Anglo-Welsh
Review* with an introduction by Professor George
Thomas, official biographer of Edward Thomas. Pro-
fessor Thomas included the *Diary* in his edition of
Edward Thomas's *Complete Poems.*[7]

The Childhood, long out of print, and *The Diary*, which
lay unpublished for over fifty years, are brought together in this volume. His London and Wiltshire boyhood contributed much to Edward Thomas's outlook
and eventual literary achievement, and his *Diary* is rich
in images and notes that might have been used in poems
that remained unwritten.

ROLAND GANT

[7] Thomas, Edward, *Complete Poems*, edited, with Introduction and Notes, by R. George Thomas. Oxford University
Press, London, 1977.

CONTENTS

*

I

INFANCY

*

When I penetrate backward into my childhood I come perhaps sooner than many people to impassable night. A sweet darkness enfolds with a faint blessing my life up to the age of about four. The task of attempting stubbornly to break up that darkness is one I have never proposed to myself, but I have many times gone up to the edge of it, peering, listening, stretching out my hands, and I have heard the voice of one singing as I sat or lay in her arms; and I have become again aware very dimly of being enclosed in rooms that were shadowy, whether by comparison with outer sunlight I know not. The songs, first of my mother, then of her younger sister, I can hear not only afar off behind the veil but on this side of it also. I was, I should think, a very still listener whom the music flowed through and filled to the exclusion of all thought and of all sensation except of blissful easy fullness, so that too early or too sudden ceasing would have meant pangs of expectant empti-ness. The one song which, by reason of its repetition or

13

of some aptitude in me, I well remember, was one combining fondness with tranquil if peevish retrospection and regret in a soft heavy twilight. I reach back to it in that effort through a thousand twilights lineally descended from that first one and from the night which gave it birth. If I cried or suffered pain or deprivation in those years nothing remains to star the darkness. Either I asked no question or I had none but sweet answers. I was at peace with life. Indoors, out of the sun, I seem never to have been troubled by heat or cold strong enough to be remembered. But out of doors, somewhere at the verge of the dark years, I can recall more simply and completely than any spent indoors at that time one day above others. I lay in the tall grass and buttercups of a narrow field at the edge of London and saw the sky and nothing but the sky. There was some one near, probably a servant, necessary but utterly insignificant. I was alone and happy to be so, just as indoors I was happy among people and shadows between walls. Was it one day or many? I know of no beginning or end to it; but an end I suppose it had an age past.

Then I entered the lowest class of a large suburban board school. There were some boys and more girls whom I desired and sometimes struggled to sit next; and at least two whom I avoided. One a poor dirty girl without eyelashes who came from an old hovel at the top of one of the poorer and older streets, and has lent a certain disrelish ever since to the name of 'Lizzie'; the

other was a boy whom I had seen charging at his desk
with his head lowered, like a bull. Of the mistresses I
can see a tallish one, with pink complexion, high cheekbones and sleek light brown hair, whose home was a
confectioner's shop, so that it happened that she gave
away sweets for slight merits; one dark and shorter,
more likeable and hateable; and a stout, short, bustling
head mistress in whom I never knew of anything but
her appearance to prove her common humanity with
the children and other teachers. I learnt easily: perhaps
my memory would record the sweets I earned but not
the punishments, nor yet the morning and afternoon
labours, whether well or ill performed, of five days in
the week. I had no elder brother, and the younger ones
of three and one were not yet old enough to accompany
me; if I had any friend with whom I walked or trotted
home, embraced and embracing as I see children now, I
have forgotten. Not that I was lonely, but that I was
stung with no intense delight by company, nor with
pain by lack of it. I knew boys and girls in several of the
streets parallel to ours or crossing it. One or more of
them was with me when I found myself somehow on
the forbidden side of a black fence which divided the
back gardens of one street from a meadow and cut
short another street; there were trees and cows in the
meadow, and a small pond not far from the fence.
With one of these friends, a girl, I went home once and
in her back garden I first saw dark crimson dahlias and

smelt bitter crushed stalks in plucking them. As I stood with my back to the house among the tall blossoming bushes I had no sense of any end to the garden between its brown fences: there remains in my mind a green-ness, at once lowly and endless. Why some children, whether my equals or old enough to protect me, were pleasant, and how, I cannot say. Their faces are invis-ible to me all except one: I can say only that some were fat and the eyes narrow, and that some girls had dark hair, others fair. The one that I can see has black curly hair, dark eyes and cherry lips; and she is smiling: her name was Tottie Armour. We picked sorrel leaves and ate them among the gorse bushes on Wandsworth Common. A railway ran across the Common in a deep bushy cutting, and this I supposed to be a natural valley and had somehow peopled it with unseen foxes. The long mounds of earth now overgrown with grass and gorse heaped up at my side of the cutting from which they had been taken were 'hills' to us, who wore steep yellow paths by running up and down them. Equal to them in height and steepness, and almost equal as play-ing grounds, were the hills of snow lining Northcote Road, the principal street, one winter. I remember the look of many of the streets, but as not a year has since gone by without my seeing them it is probably not their very early look, save in perhaps a few cases. The first was when I stood by the beerhouse at the bottom of one of them and watched what was happening fifty yards up in the roadway. A mad dog had run into one of the narrow front gardens and lay just inside the railings; a man on the other side with a pickaxe was about to kill the dog; and a small crowd had collected in the roadway. I do not know that I saw the blow struck, but the idea of sharp heavy steel piercing the shaggy hair, flesh and bone of a living creature has remained horrible and ineffaceable ever since. Another street which I seem to recall as it was then and as it soon afterwards ceased to be was one leading to Clapham Junction Station. It consists of a low inn with a red painted board up and a row of old dark small cottages mostly with longish front gardens and low wooden fences and a rustic outmoded look inspiring a sort of curiosity and liking as well as some pity or contempt.

If I cannot call up images of most of the streets as they were then, because I have witnessed the gradual development since, perhaps the reason is the same for my being unable to call up images of my father and mother or of my brothers. No. I have only one clear early glimpse of my father—darting out of the house in his slippers and chasing and catching a big boy who had bullied me. He was eloquent, confident, black-haired, brown-eyed, all that my mother was not. By glimpses, I learnt with awe and astonishment that he had once been of my age. He knew, for example, far more about marbles than the best players at school. His talk of 'alley-taws'—above all the way his thumb drove the marble out of the crook of his first finger, the speeding sureness of it—these betokened mastery. Once or twice I spent an hour or so in his office in an old government building. The presence of a washstand in a sitting-room pleased me, but what pleased me still more was the peculiar large brown carraway biscuit which I never got anywhere else. My father at this time gave or was to have given lessons to Lady Somebody, and he mentioned her to me once when we were together in his office. She became connected somehow with the carraway biscuit. With or without her aid, this rarity had a kind of magic and beauty as of a flower or bird only to be found in one wood in all the world. I can hear but never see him telling me for the tenth or hundredth time the story of the Wiltshire moonrakers hanging in a chain over a bridge to fetch the moon out, which they had mistaken for a green cheese, and the topmost one, whose hold on the parapet began slipping, crying out, 'Hold tight below while I spit on my hands,' and many another comic tale or rhyme. My mother I can hardly see save as she is now while I am writing. I cannot see her but I can summon up her presence. She is plainest to me not quite dressed, in white bodice and petticoat, her arms and shoulders rounded and creamy smooth. My affection for her was leavened with lesser likings and with admiration. I liked the scent of her fresh warm skin and supposed it unique. Her straight nose and chin made a profile that for years formed my standard. No

hair was so beautiful to me as hers was, light golden
brown hair, long and rippling. Her singing at fall of
night, especially if we were alone together, soothed and
fascinated me, as though it had been divine, at once the
mightiest and the softest sound in the world. Usually
perhaps there was a servant, but my mother did everything for us in the house, made many of our clothes and
mended them, prepared and gave us food, tended us
when sick, comforted us when cold, disappointed, or
sorrowful. The one terrible thing I witnessed as a small
child was my mother suddenly rising from the dining-
table with face tortured and crying, 'I am going to die.'
My father took her on his knee and soothed her. I had
and have no idea what was the matter. For her younger
sister I felt a similar affection and admiration, though
less, and far less often exercised, for her visits were
neither long nor frequent. The grace, smoothness and
gentleness of her voice and movements gave me pleasure. My first conscious liking for the female body was
at sight of her sitting less than half dressed in a chair,
her head bent and one foot on to which she was pulling
a stocking lifted from the floor. Years afterwards I used
to think of this from time to time to envy the privilege
of early childhood. She sang livelier songs, e.g. from
Patience, than my mother ever did. But she did not
know our ways and her complaints or corrections were
harsh by comparison with my mother's.

Not long after I began to attend school I went away

alone with my mother for a long holiday. We spent a week here and a week there in different friends' houses. We stayed at Much Birch Vicarage in Herefordshire. It had a shrubbery, a carriage gate. I ate custard out of a custard glass; once I agreed to have a second helping of something if I could have a clean plate, and this made people laugh and look at one another. . . . In a house, probably at Newport, Monmouthshire, that had a tower or was higher than its neighbours, and in a very light many-windowed room, I sat among grown-up people and asked for mustard with my mutton. . . . I walked up a steep street in Newport, looking at the houses on the right-hand side and thinking of a school-friend of my mother's, named Lucy, whom I had never seen. . . . At Newport also I saw the dark damp-looking oldish house on a hill, with trees and iron railings round it, where my mother as an orphan lived unhappily for many years with two maiden aunts. Then I went to Caerleon upon Usk to see another and blameless great-aunt named Margaret. I see small houses and gardens on one side and the Usk on the other between steep banks. An idiot passes with boys following him. My aunt's house was the last, as if you could go no farther on account of a bend in the river. There were beautiful great rosy apples in the garden, and a well with a broad stone over it, and ivy and snails on the narrow paths. Then for the first time I thoroughly understood what wells, apples, and snails were. Indoors there were more great apples: it was not always possible to finish what was so happily begun. A smoked salmon hung up in a whitewashed kitchen or pantry, and I think I should know the taste again if I could ever meet anything so delicious, but I no longer expect to find it under the name of smoked salmon. There also I first learnt what a river was, having previously seen nothing better than the Thames, almost as broad as it was long at Westminster. The Usk was not too broad; it was winding; I heard the sound and felt the flood of it. Also I was told that a certain islet or peninsula or level meadow half encircled by the water was the site of King Arthur's Round Table. Either ideas suggested by 'King Arthur' and 'Round Table' even then vibrated in my brain or they remained there until, a very short time afterwards, they did so undoubtedly when united with the stories of love and battle in *The Adventures of King Arthur and his Round Table*. One day, moreover, a porpoise came up the river, and men rowed a small boat hither-thither, and shouted and lifted up their oars and struck heavy blows on the water, not (I think) on the porpoise. And in memory I see all together the riverside street old and rustic and an idiot coming up it, the Usk and the men hunting the porpoise in the bend round King Arthur's Round Table. Away from the river rose a green hill and a stone farmyard wall athwart its slope and I saw black pigs hustling through the gateway at the end of the wall. My mother was with me.

Afterwards we had some days at Swansea with a great-aunt Mary and I saw the sea and the Gower cliffs and rocks. I collected shells and pebbles that took my fancy, especially one rounded one like a Bath bun which we took back to the garden at Swansea, where it remained for twenty years and more. I have loved flat or round seaworn pebbles ever since, and can never carry away as many as I wish from a new coast or hillside where I am walking.

This holiday gave me the most definite and most pleasant of my very early memories, together with some less definite ideas associated with Caerleon and Wales which afterwards increased, I might almost say magically, by the aid of things heard in home talk or read in books, and of a visit several years later.

Until that visit I can discern no landmarks. My waking life was divided between home, school and the streets and neighbouring common. Glimpses of the outer world I had few. But I remember General Gordon's death at Khartoum, and, whether from a picture in a newspaper or from imagination, I retain an image of a soldier in a fez and armed with a revolver standing with his back to a portico, facing the enemies who swarmed up the steps below and being struck at by one from the side.

Our street like three or four others parallel to it was in two halves, running straight up the opposite sides of a slight valley, along the bottom of which ran the principal street of mixed shops and private houses. Our house was low down in the half which ran up west-wards to Bolingbroke Grove, the eastern boundary of Wandsworth Common. These little semi-detached one-storied pale brick houses in unbroken lines on both sides of the street had each, even then when they were new, something distinguishing them and preventing monotony. The people in them made them different. In addition, some were beginning to be draped in creepers. Some gates stood open, some were shut. One had bushes in the garden, another had flowers, another nothing but dark trodden gravel. The house above ours, in the next pair, was presumably meant for a doctor, and possessed a coach house which looked almost as if it belonged to us. That was our outward distinction. Inside from the front door to the back of the house there was as long a passage as possible, the rooms opening out of it. The staircase ran up to a room with an opaque glass window in the door, a second room, and two others connected by a door. The rooms downstairs I hardly remember at all. But in one of them my great-uncle James Jones lay asleep after dinner, a red handkerchief covering his face and trembling in the blast of his snoring which we called 'driving the pigs to market'. Through the open window of another, one Mayday, Jack-in-the-Green bounded in to beg a penny, showing white teeth, white eyes, black face, but the rest of him covered and rippling with green leaves. The passage was a playground when it was too wet or too dark to be out of doors. Here, when I had at any rate one brother—probably three or four years old when I was five or six—who could run, we two raced up and down the passage to be pounced upon by the servant out of a doorway and swallowed up in her arms with laughter. Upstairs the room with the glass door was at long intervals occupied by a visitor, such as my father's uncle James or my mother's sister, and I think cards were played there. Except relatives I think there were few visitors to the house. Sometimes the old red-faced gent next door, a court usher, came in: and once as he laid his hand on a large sheet of printed matter, perhaps at an election time, he said impressively, 'I am a staunch Liberal, staunch.' Once a young couple had tea with us and everyone laughed at some cheerful remark about the lady's name being about to be changed. . . . I and at least one brother slept in one of the two connected bedrooms. I had no night fears and few dreams. Several times some shapeless invisible thing threatened me at the end of the bed and I lay in terror, trying vainly to scream for help. On Christmas morning I used to wake up in the dark and smell the oranges and feel my presents, and guess at them and begin an apple and go on to sweets, especially those contained in a cardboard box scented curiously, loaf-shaped, and coloured like a top of a bun, which came from a cousin of my mother's at the Much Birch Vicarage. When I and a brother were recovering from scarlet fever we lay or sat up in our cots, while our father in the other room read aloud the *Cuckoo Clock*. Not a shred of the story is left to me, but I seem to see my father—though I could not see him at the time—sitting in an arm-chair bent over the book. He also read at least the opening chapters of *Great Expectations,* with such effect that, though I have never since looked at them, I have an indelible impression of a churchyard in cold and misty marshland and out among the stones a convict in clanking chains, and a tiny feeble boy with the absurd and as it were enfeebling name of Pip. I do not know whether I read *Robinson Crusoe* or had it read aloud to me. I loved it entirely, and a faint spice of amusement was added to my love by the repetition of 'says I'. Two scenes most impressed me. The first was the picture of men tumbling savages over the sides of a ship by means of brushes like a sweep's dipped in tar. The second was where wolves are pursuing a doomed riderless horse over the snow. But I cannot remember the act of reading this or any other book at home. *Fairy Know-a-bit* by A.L.O.E. was read to me. The fairy in it was created for the purpose of imparting facts about things in everyday use. The facts though not distasteful passed rapidly through my brain, and the fairy, though probably an inartistic invention, fascinated me and attained such a measure of reality for me that I used to fancy it possible for him to appear from between the leaves of some big old book as he did in the story. To my mind the book would have been a certain cookery book with pictures of flesh, fish, and fowl, or dishes. There were, I suspect, invented fairies in another book which had and has a charm impossible for me either to communicate or, I fear, to make credible. It was my first school prize. The words, 'The Key of Knowledge', occurred in its title or they stood out somewhere else. It was illustrated by coloured pictures. But it disappeared, I never had any idea how, before I had read far into it, and I never saw it again. From time to time down to the present day I have recalled the loss, and tried to recover first of all the book, later on the thread of its story, something that would dissipate from its charm the utter darkness of mystery. For example, fifteen years ago in Wiltshire two strangers passed me and I heard one of them, a big public schoolboy, say to the other, a gamekeeper, 'What do you think is the key of knowledge?' and back again came the old loss, the old regret and yearning, faint indeed, but real. There were times when I fancied that the book had held the key to an otherwise inaccessible wisdom and happiness, and the robbery appeared satanically sinister.

I was not much at other boys' houses except for Christmas or birthday parties. We met either in the street or in the back gardens, where some had swings fixed. Most of them lived in the same street, but their parents and mine were not as a rule on terms of more than distant acquaintanceship. The chief party was the doctor's, some time soon after Christmas. There was a great crowd of strange boys and girls whom I got to like and hate, or be indifferent to, for a few hours, and probably never saw or thought of for another twelve months. Most were older than myself; some, I was conscious, had parents who were richer or of different class; we were restrained and suspicious of one another, and the only unquestionably good things there were the mince pies, jellies, sausage rolls. . . . Now and then we visited friends in Lambeth, where my father and mother had lived from their marriage up to the time of their removal to Wakehurst Road when I was about two. I remember the girls faintly, not so as to describe them, but well enough to wish that I could see them again to revive their images. In most houses I had at least a preference for one of the girls and liked to be teased afterwards for having kissed her in a game of forfeits, or for shouting her name up the chimney.

2

FIRST SCHOOLDAYS

★

When I think of school I smell carbolic soap. I see the caretaker by the wall of one room ringing the bell. I deposit my weekly fourpence on the master's desk. I go round, as a privilege, filling the scores of inkpots from a tin with a long thin spout. I join in the one-verse hymn before and after lessons. I see large light bare rooms with a map or two, and boys in long parallel desks facing a master; for we were soon separated from the girls. We repeated aloud 'Witney on the Windrush manufactures Blankets'. We learned the names of the tributaries of the Thames for ever and ever. What I most enjoyed was doing maps of Great Britain and Ireland, inking in the coast lines with red, and marking the mountain ranges with thin parallel strokes arranged herringbone fashion. I never tired of the indentations of the western coasts, especially of Scotland. The line of the Hebrides I think I actually loved. One of the masters, named Jones, was little, with dark prominent eyes, round plump red face and quick steps and fiery temper;

another, named Spragg, was a tall fairer bony man, who had a deep resonant voice; and I think that once when the two quarrelled the tall one lifted the little one into the air. There was a third named Wigley, a mild man, a chewer of his moustache, who struck me as feeble even before Spragg got the better of him in a tussle. The head master was short, square-shouldered, lean, pallid, bearded, took long rapid strides with head low and projecting, flat high overhanging forehead, deep-set eyes, always on the verge of anger, a harsh barking voice, a general expression of dark solitary determination. He appeared unexpectedly from time to time in the several classrooms which I passed through in the course of three or four years. Sometimes he went by me in the street, his hands in his black overcoat pockets, an umbrella under his arm, overtaking everybody, with rapid sidelong dark glances.

I remember crawling in and bursting out, but very little about school itself. We were huddled close together in great lofty rooms with big windows and big maps and on Mondays a smell of carbolic soap. Addition, subtraction, multiplication, parsing, were easy to me, and I did them pretty well. Sometimes things were tediously easy to me, sometimes I took a pleasure in overcoming what looked hard and of course in earning praise, reward, a superior position. I rather liked wearing the numbered ticket on examination days, and took pride in having the numbers neatly printed in black ink with a 4 rather than a 4 and so on, as I did in saying, when questioned, that my father was an 'Officer' in the Civil Service. Discipline was strict. I think I must have been usually fully employed, save for glances at the clock. At any rate I know more about what I did before and after than in school. The one moment in school at this time which I cannot forget is when I found myself being lifted from a grating where I had fallen, having been hit hard in the stomach by a boy on my way from the classroom to the main exit. In the hard asphalt playground we played rounders and egg-cap and games with tops, marbles and cherry-stones. Going home, we spun our tops or two of us helped ourselves along by bowling hoops or by playing a progressive game with a marble or a stone each, called Buckalong. We used to exchange things and ratify the deed by touching the iron with which our heels were shod, saying 'touch cold iron can't change back'. We used to make fun of a solitary boy, pro-bably of a better class than ourselves, who used to live in the same street and walked about with a snake round his wrist. We called him 'Soppy', prepared to run away. But he never retaliated or took any notice of us. My friends were chiefly boys of our street; if other boys harassed us we used to say 'My father's a policeman' to frighten them. But only one grievance remains in my mind, that an older boy, not of my acquaintance, once lured me to drink urine by offering it to me in a bottle as ginger-beer. Some time later on a Sunday I pointed out this boy standing with others by the Three Island Pond, and my father clouted his head.

School was not an affliction, but church or chapel or Sunday school was. At an early age I did not go regularly, nor I think did my parents. They were sober reverent people without a creed, though their disbelief in Hell and the Devil almost amounted to a creed. My father and I made merry over the Devil and the folly of believing in him as we supposed many did. He used to try different chapels or different preachers, sometimes taking me with him, more especially when he had become an almost weekly attendant at a Unitarian Chapel. Here from the prickly silence of two hundred or three hundred people I gradually came to feel a mild poison steadily creeping into me on all sides. I never made a friend of any of the boys who attended there. A deathly solemnity filled the chapel. After the service couples walked to and fro or gathered into knots on the pavement outside. The deathly solemnity was strong enough to cling about the people even there in the sunlight: some of them it accompanied to their one o'clock roast beef or mutton. But at first the Sunday-school was my particular allowance. I liked singing and liked the melodies of 'Jerusalem the Golden' and 'Fair waved the golden corn', and I liked going with all the rest for the annual treat somewhere in Surrey, where I could run about in a wood, become fond of another girl or two (I remember one with a very deep but I think also husky voice), eat bread and butter, watercress and slices of cake and drink tea. The confinement in the schoolroom was not quite a positive ill. It was regular, it was inevitable, and until later on there was usually nothing in particular of which it deprived me except liberty. But Sunday was a bad day and this was the worst part of it. That deathly solemnity, whether we respected it or not, was equally thick in the schoolroom. I became accustomed to making a sort of drug of boredom. I did not rebel, but taking this poison became fairly oblivious to the good or evil that befell Jesus Christ, or Servetus, or myself. Moreover, I did positively loathe with continuous loathing the trailing with one or more of my brothers along the Sunday streets, in our stiff Sunday clothes and our Sunday hats. I hated these clothes and hats and I felt also that they made me ridiculous in the eyes of others. If the hat was blown off by the wind it was some relief: and I could then stamp on the thing and put it down to the wind and mud. What wonder that I made no friends under this Upastree. The majority of the children came from homes poorer or less refined than mine, and with the exception of one or two girls whom I thought pretty I looked down on them though ever so slightly. The few boys whose parents knew ours, if they never visited one another, never became our friends. Some suspiciousness existed between us which our best clothing did not permit us to destroy. Chapel and Sunday-school were to me cruel ceremonious punishments for the freedom of Monday to Saturday. I have still a profound quiet detestation of Sunday in whatever part of England or Wales it overtakes me, but most of all in London. I think I began learning to hate crowds and societies, and grown-up people, and black clothes, and silk hats and neatly folded umbrellas and shining walking-sticks, and everything that seemed a circling part of that deathly solemnity as I was not. Nevertheless, I may have looked decidedly a part of it with my shy bored silence, my fear of disagreement or quarrel in public, and my thin long narrow face that always shrank and chilled and stiffened into solemnity under the gaze of grown-up people, strangers, and numbers. There was, however, always one good thing about Sunday, and that was the biscuits, two large oval ones or one of these and two small round ones, which I found on a bedside chair upon awaking. The crumbs of these biscuits among the sheets became a nuisance; for we got up later on Sundays than weekdays.

The best of life was passed out of the house and out of school. I remember going out for the first time after scarlet fever. Perhaps because the spirit of many days had been stored up within me untouched, I felt that I was very strong and could do anything. I started to run; the eagerness of the spirit was overmuch; I stumbled and fell down.

One Christmas morning I woke up and felt a long lean smooth straight cold thing with straps at my bedside. It had a handle, and pulling that with one hand I brought out what I discovered to be a sword, while in the other hand was a scabbard. The daylight came upon me still unsheathing and sheathing the sword, trying hard for the hundredth time to put it back the wrong way. As soon as I could I fastened the belt round my waist so that the sword hung on the right instead of the left side and went out alone. The streets were empty. I was proud though without spectators. Once or twice the weapon caught between my legs. I marched up the street, crossed the road separating it from the Common and turned to the left between the elm-trees of Bolingbroke Grove, having the road upon my left, the Common upon my right. At the top of one of the streets parallel to ours, but at that time divided from it by that big private meadow with the pond and elm-trees, I stopped and looked down. For there lived Mabel Looms, a schoolfellow whom I adored. She had had a Christmas card from me that morning. The street was empty. I walked backwards and forwards along the Grove past the top of the street, waiting, sufficiently proud not to be overcome by long disappointment. How many times since have I waited thus for somebody, with a dog's patience. There began to be others in the streets. At last Mabel came up towards the Common, in the company of some elders. Without a sign I continued walking backwards and forwards. They turned to their left at the top, away from our street. I turned in the opposite direction homeward, pleased with my swinging sword and believing that the passers-by admired it. At home they knew well where I had been. My attachment to Mabel lasted for several years and more than once after it had been broken I attempted to renew it. She was a perfect loving friend. I thought her beautiful. Her hair was light brown, her face round rather than a long face. She had elder sisters—one named Agnes—whom I did not always like; and a brother named Arthur to whom I was indifferent; and a freckled slighter cousin, with a name something like Catherine Haythorn, whom I liked equally for her own and for Mabel's sake.

Girls practically never joined in our games: even bowling our iron hoops beside their wooden ones was rare. Those girls who did play much with boys were scandalously talked about, but they were older than I was, and I neither knew nor know anything positive against them. I only have an idea that I had seen one of them—a deep-voiced dark-skinned good-looking girl who walked with long strides and a slight stoop—coming from among thick bushes with a boy or two boys. This caused laughter and was afterwards mentioned with hints and jeers which I do not think I understood: I became faintly curious and expectant; the veil over the sex thickened.

The Common and the streets leading up to it were the scene of our principal game. It was played chiefly on Saturday, our whole holiday. We assembled, for example, at the top of the road in the well-trodden garden of a doctor who had a rowdy son; each bringing a weapon or several weapons, wooden swords and pikes, or daggers, shields, pistols, bows, arrows, and with horns and trumpets, and perhaps some bread and cheese and an apple or orange. There sides were chosen. One side went out to seek a fort, in some one's garden or among the gorse bushes. Ten minutes later the other set forth, often in two divisions. Sometimes stealth was the rule of expedition; we advanced whispering and in some order. Sometimes everyone was shouting for his own plans and against another's. At other times the methods alternated: the stealth would become wearisome, we began to chatter and disagree; or the riot of anarchy would suddenly strike us as wrong, everyone said 'hush', and for some minutes we modelled ourselves on Sioux, Mohicans, or Hurons, crouching, pausing, trying to hush the sound of our breathing. We forgot everything in this Indian ideal. Nevertheless, the enemy had to be found. Nor were they loth. Some one was sure to show himself and wave defiance, or to leap out on us, supposing we passed by. If seen at a distance they might change the stronghold and there would be a chase. If they were content to stand a storm, the second army would gather all its numbers together and, with yells and counter-yells, batter and push them out or be battered and pushed out itself. The struggle was one of character, not weapons. The side possessing the fiercest and most stubborn boys won. The winners would then in turn fortify themselves and sustain an attack; and so it went on, until a mealtime, or nightfall, or rain, or a serious quarrel, finished the war.

At long intervals fiercer battles were waged. The boys of a neighbouring school of the grammar-school standard looked down upon the Board-school boys, or 'Boardy Blags' (i.e. blackguards). The Board-school boys resented this. The feud was usually hardly in so much as a smouldering condition, and so far as I know must have been all but forgotten. Then suddenly it would flame out. A loose army of Board-school boys several score strong moved along the Grove at the edge of the Common towards the enemy's school. The army was continually being swelled from the side streets. With all the smaller or more timid boys hanging on its fringes, more angry than warlike, more curious than angry, the numbers were considerable. Stones were the long-distance weapons. But rarely, I think, did both sides muster a fairly equal army at the same time. When they came in sight of one another they began to throw stones. They halted, odd stones were thrown here and there, the hangers-on disappeared. I doubt if both sides ever advanced and clashed in hand-to-hand conflict. Usually after some challenging shouts, some wavering and dissension, the victors knew themselves and set up a shout and moved forward confidently. The smaller army broke and fled down the streets; the larger broke and pursued. Here and there a group kept together and set upon any solitary enemy it could discover. I, who was too small to be in the army, was content to hang on the outer outskirts, pick up the news, and occasionally insult one of the enemy if I remembered that he was one.

As a relaxation we hung about in corners smoking cigarettes of rolled brown paper. Making these, lighting them, puffing them, coughing, relighting them, asking one another if they were alight, and silently enjoying the act and the seclusion, filled hours.

Our sense of discipline was slight and transient. It was not encouraged by doing lessons, a few ridiculous exercises under the eye of an unsleeping master, and playing mostly individualist games in the playground. Being in a little mob increased our boldness and also our ease and safety. According to our tempers, I think we hoped that the others would either shelter us or support us in doing signal deeds. As member of the army, any one of us could most likely insult a passing outsider with impunity: if, however, there had been any swift retaliation the victim of it would often have been left to suffer alone.

Therefore the armies did not always wait for a formal order of disbandment. The Common, for example, offered many temptations to more irregular games and aimless rovings. For it was an uneven piece of never cultivated gravelly land. Several ponds of irregular shape and size, varying with the rainfall, had been hollowed out, perhaps by old gravel diggings. It was marshy in other places. Hawthorn and gorse clustered tall and dense in great and in little thickets. Tall elms and poplars stood about irregularly. And the level spaces suitable for cricket, football and tennis were not many. With this variety the Common, even though the railway ran through it parallel to Bolingbroke Grove and only two or three hundred yards away from it, was large enough to provide us with many surprises and discoveries for years. We could spend a day on it without thinking it small or having to retrace our steps. We wandered about it with or without our hoops. For any kind of hiding and hunting game the thickets were excellent. We played the other games in the open spaces. The ponds were for paddling in. One of them, a shallow irregular one, weedy and rushy-margined, lying then in some broken ground between the Three Island and the railway, was full of effets and frogs. Bigger boys would torture the frogs, by cutting, skinning or crushing them alive. The sharp penknives sank through the skin and the soft bone into the wood of the seat which was the operating table. This seat and the earth under and about it would be strewn with fragments, pale bellies slit up, and complete frogs seeming to be munching their own insides. At that time I could not have done it myself, but my horror lacked pity and turned into a kind of half-shrinking, half-gloating curiosity. I fished for sticklebacks and gudgeon in the long pond on the far side of the railway, which owed its name of 'Backaruffs' or 'Pack of Roughs', so I always thought, to the poor ill-dressed boys who used to swarm to it from Battersea on Saturdays and bank holidays. I fished with a worm either tied on the cotton line or impaled on a bent pin, and put my stickleback or my rare lovely spotted gudgeon in a glass jam-jar. Once at least I did as I had seen others do, hauling a heavy fruit basket out into the pond and dragging it in full of weed and mud and the little 'blood worms' that breed in mud, and sticklebacks, even a red-throated one, but never a gudgeon. The gudgeon was so attractive, partly for its looks, perhaps chiefly for its comparative size, that many times I willingly paid a halfpenny for one and let it be believed that I had caught it. Even when dead it was hard to part with, so smooth and pure was it. I liked even its smell, yet never dreamed of eating it. There were carp, too, in this pond and in the roundish Box Pond that lay half-way between the top of our street and the railway. By the longer pond I once saw a carp many times as big as a gudgeon in the possession of a rough: he had torn its head off to make it fit his jar. Much larger ones were talked about, caught in the Box Pond by the elder brothers of one boy. I saw them fishing there once or twice without a motion of the float in the motionless water. Once I tried there myself all alone. My expectations were huge: that I failed completely only increased my respect for the sacred pond. Bigger boys used to fish in the Penn Ponds at Richmond Park and allowed me to buy from them a perch of four or five inches long, which looked magnificent with its dark bars, standing almost on its head in my little round bowl. There in spite of worms and breadcrumbs it shortly afterwards died. I was pained at coming down in the morning and finding such a magnificent, uncommon and costly creature dead. Nor did I ever like the perch's stiff hard prickly corpse, faded in death, and looking much smaller out of the bowl than inside.

The streets were a playground almost equal to the Common. The labyrinth of them, all running at right angles and parallel to one another, with some *culs de sac,* could be mastered but indefinitely extended; every month or two I should think I added a street or two to my knowledge. Alone or with others I bowled my hoop up and down them either in purposeless pleasure or on some errand for my mother. Best of all errands was to the blacksmith's to have a broken hoop mended. The smithy was a primeval forest cave that broke a line of ordinary shops. The bellows snored, the sparks spouted up, and the pallid, gaunt, bare-armed man made the anvil ring its double or its single song. When it was very cold I ran along with hands in pockets striking sparks out of the rough kerbstone with my ironshod heel. At night we often played games of hide and seek with lanterns. We picked up sides, fixed the boundaries which were not to be exceeded, and laid down rules against hiding in our own houses. One side went out to hide, to be followed in a few minutes by most of the other side, except one or two who were left behind to guard the home, which the other side had to reach without being touched. Setting out with bull's-eye shining and a good companion, and exposing the others behind laurel bushes and catching them after a chase; or ourselves being the quarry and eluding capture for the whole evening whether with constant obedience to rules or not—these were great joys. If the game became monotonous we rang people's bells and ran away, or we went into shops and asked for sweets with ridiculous names just invented by ourselves.

On a Saturday sometimes I would go to Lambeth, two miles away, to take a message or a parcel for my mother, riding back by tram, or walking in order to spend the fare on sweets. I remember once, too, walking to Chelsea and back with an elder boy. As we went along the far side of the Thames he explained to me why it was women could plunge from greater heights into water than men. The Battersea side of the river was strewn with prodigious broken architecture very impressive to me and seeming of unknown giant antiquity.

When I was eight or nine, the boundaries of my

domain were stretched by several miles all at once. I walked to Wimbledon Common. Of the first visit I have no recollection. But I can distinguish two later visits: one because I discovered the joy of throwing stones over into the unknown depths of a great garden and hearing the glass-house break; another because I limped all the way back with a low shoe gone wrong. I did not go alone, but as one of several hangers-on to older boys and girls. We fished here and there with hopes of better things than came out of the Wandsworth Common ponds. We met strange boys there who occasionally possessed or talked about enviable fish. The three-mile walk was, however, good in itself, whether we went by Wandsworth, Earlsfield, or Wimbledon. We always recognized the old landmarks with pleasure and a kind of surprise. There would be a cage of pigeons or rabbits or guinea-pigs to look at outside a cornchandler's, or an old man with some trait of surliness or quaintness whom we hoped to see again, or a chestnut-tree where we had to stop to throw up at the 'conkers', or a shop where we had once bought a specially good halfpenny cake. Other shops and houses had an altogether indescribable charm. Then All-farthing Lane was worth going down for its name's sake. We invented explanations and repeated those of our parents. At the top dwelt an old woman in what looked a one-room hut who presumably knew and had something to do with the origin of the queer name.

But above all, whichever way we took, the Wandel had to be crossed. Going by Wimbledon we had to cross the bridge by the copper mill. You might stop to look down at the fish or along at the fishermen, or to carve your name on the parapet. In Wandsworth there were two bridges, fishermen hanging over the less frequented one who were never seen catching anything but never exhausted our curiosity. But best of all was the middle way through Earlsfield, crossing the Wandel at the paper mills. The smell of the mills wafted over a mile and a half on certain still evenings gave me a quiet sort of poetic delight. Hereby the water ran over a steep artificial slant, swift, glittering, and sounding; and sometimes we stayed here and caught minnows instead of going on to Wimbledon. It was the first place where I saw and realized the beauty of bright running water. We paddled with our stockings in our shoes and our shoes tied together and slung over our shoulders. We talked and laughed and shouted and splashed the water. I cannot remember cold or rain or any clouds there.

Perhaps we went away for a part of each summer holiday. If we did, I have forgotten. We went several times to stop with my father's mother at Swindon, and once at least to Brighton on a Sunday. At Brighton the shops were shut. It seemed very much like London. The close smell of meat steam in a restaurant where we had dinner will not altogether vanish. I went out in the *Skylark* and was sick.

3

HOLIDAYS

★

Swindon was a thousand times better. It was delicious
to pass Wantage, Challow, Uffington, Shrivenham, to
see the 75th, 76th mile marks by the railwayside, to
slow down at last to the cry of 'Swindon' and see my
grandmother, my uncle or my aunt waiting. My aunt
was an attendant in the refreshment bar, and sometimes
gave me a cake or sandwich to eat amid the smell of
spirits, or took me to the private apartments, talking in a
high bright voice and showing me round to various
other neat women in black with high bright voices and
nothing but smiles and laughs. My uncle was a fitter in
the Great Western Railway works and knew everybody. He was tall, easy-going, and had a pipe in his
mouth and very likely a dog at his heels. I was proud to
be with him as he nodded to the one-legged signalman
and the man with a white apron and a long hammer for
tapping the wheels of all the carriages.

The look of the town pleased me altogether. I could

think no ill of houses built entirely of stone instead of
brick, especially as they seemed to exist chiefly to serve
as avenues by which I happily approached to my
grandmother's. It was for me a blessed place. The stone-
work, the flowers in the gardens, the Wiltshire accent,
the rain if it was raining, the sun if it was shining, the
absence of school and schoolmaster and of most ordinary forms of compulsion—everything was paradisal.
No room ever was as cosy as my grandmother's kitchen. Its open range was always bright. There was a
pair of bellows frequently in use. A brass turnspit hung
from under the mantelpiece. The radiant steel trivet
was excellent in itself but often bore a load of girdle
cakes or buttered toast or more substantial things. An
old brown earthenware teapot stood eternally upon the
hob. Tea-caddies, brass candlesticks, clay pipes and
vases full of spills, stood on the mantelpiece. On its
walls hung coloured engravings entitled 'Spring' and
'Summer' and painted in England some time before
the Fall, and photographs of me and Mr. Gladstone's
Cabinets and Mr. Gladstone, of Belle Bitton, and of an
uncle who had died long before I was born. There were
chairs and there was an old mahogany table piano at
one side. The smell of 'Westward Ho' tobacco hung
about the room. My uncle got us chatting instantly.
He seemed grown up, yet a boy, by the way he laughed,
whistled and sang a bit of a gay tune. At supper, with
our bread and cheese, or cold bacon, or hot faggots, or

chitterlings, and pickles, he would now and then give us a little tumbler, or 'tot', of ale.

My grandmother being all important, omnipotent, omnipresent if not omniscient, she stood out less. She marketed, cooked, cleaned, did everything. She made pies with pastry a full inch thick, and many different undulant fruit tarts on plates. Above all, she made doughy cakes, of dough, allspice and many raisins, which were as much better than other cakes as Swindon was better than other towns, and always as much better than other so-called doughy cakes. She knew, too, where to get butter which taught me how divine a thing butter can be made. On the other hand, she was a Conservative and a churchwoman. Without her, these holidays would have been impossible, and she gave me countless pleasures. But if I loved her it was largely because of these things, not instinctively or because she loved me. She was marvellously kind and necessary but we were never close together; and, when there was any quarrel, contempt mingled with my hate of her inheritance from semi-rural Wales of George the Fourth's time. She was bigoted, worldly, crafty, narrow-minded, and ungenerous, as I very early began to feel. She read her Bible and sang hymns to herself, some-times in Welsh. She also sang Welsh songs that were not hymns, in particular one that an old beggar used to sing at Tredegar when she was a girl, something about a son whom the mother was begging not to be married.

When she wanted to warn me against going fishing some miles off with a strange man she hinted that he might be Jack the Ripper.

She first took me to church. Clad in those uncomfortable clothes, I walked beside her, who looked more uncomfortable in her layers of black. I felt that everyone enjoyed being stiff, solemn, black, except myself. On entering the church she bent forward to pray, dragging me down with her to blur my sight for a similar period. I rose with an added awkwardness in gazing at the grim emotionless multitudes of hats, bonnets, and bare heads. It was an inexplicable conspiracy for an hour's self-torture. The service was a dreary discomfort in which the hymns were green isles. When all was over, we crept with a shuffle, a pause, a shuffle, a pause, out to the tombstones and the astonishing fresh light. I was introduced to other women and discussed. I was always being told how like my mother I was and how tall for my age. My grandmother took me to several old Welshwomen, and they all said, 'He's a regular ——.' They used to remark how well my father was doing, my grandfather who had long been dead having only been a fitter. To hide something from me, they spoke in Welsh. Sometimes I was more elaborately shown off. Behind a shop smelling of bacon, butter and acid sweets, I stood up before a stout woman smelling a little less strongly of the same, to recite 'The Charge of the Light Brigade'. My reward was a penny or a screw of sweets. The only visit of this kind which I enjoyed was to a farmhouse a mile away, though I can only recall the walk, the various gates, the best parlour with a Bible in the window between the lace curtains, and the glass of warm milk. Between her and my uncle who kept the house going I saw much bickering. Spending most of his evenings out at club or public-house, he neglected the garden and I dare say other things. I dimly knew that he was usually courting a farmer's daughter somewhere a few miles out, not always the same one. Sometimes when I was walking with him the girl appeared and joined us and at twilight I returned alone.

The little ivy-covered house, therefore, though I enjoyed the meals and evenings there, was above all a convenient centre for games and rambles. In my earlier visits the rambles of any length were on a Sunday with my uncle. He and I and usually my next brother who was two years younger would set out after a late break-fast. The Club was the first stop. It seemed to be full of grown men in a good temper and very much like schoolboys over their ale, their pipes of shag or 'West-ward Ho', their *Reynolds News*. My uncle would tell them a little about us. They chaffed us. The men talked or whispered. Then before we were really impa-tient my uncle drained his glass and we got on to the canal-side and out of the town, not without greetings or a word or two from men lounging in their back-gardens over their vegetables, their fowls and pigeons. We kept to the canal for a mile or two, and sometimes another man joined us. The roach played in the deep green streams among the reeds, many of them bigger than any fish we had ever caught, here and there a monster. Better still my uncle would discover a long thin jack close inshore, as if anchored. If it did not shoot out with a kick and a swirl of water my uncle probably aimed at it with a stone. One great jack excited us by leaping again and again out of the water, at times so near the bank that we made sure he was ours. But the chief Sunday sport was with water rats. We were fascinated as men yelled encouragements, threats, advice, or praises, and a terrier swam down a rat in spite of its divings. When no dog was handy a rat surprised in mid-stream was a good mark for a stone, a snake's head a more difficult one. The moorhens in the reeds had no more mercy from them, but more often than not escaped. A dead dog was a good deal better than nothing. Not that we were unhappy without something for a mark. We threw flat stones to make ducks and drakes along the sunny water, or sheltering from rain under one of the low stone bridges plunged heavy stones with all our might down into the black depth.

Alongside the canal were many narrow copses of oak with underwood of ash and willow, the resorts of lovers and gamblers. The pleasantest thing I ever did in

them at that time was to peel rings off the bark of a
willow stick, in imitation of a carter's brass-ringed
whip. My uncle taught us. He could also fashion a
whistle by slipping the bark whole off a section of
willow, but I never could. Or he made a 'cat' or 'catty'
by tapering both ends of a round stick six inches long.
Hit at one end by a downward blow from a longer
stick the cat rose spinning up into the air and had then
to be slashed horizontally as far as possible. My uncle
could play tipcat better than any boy. In these copses or
in the hedges or roadside trees, as we went along, he
pointed out the nests.

And then at one o'clock after another visit to the
Club, home to a dinner of lamb, green peas, and mint-
sauce, followed by rhubarb tart and custard.

Perhaps it was a little later that I first went out fishing
with my uncle. He had not the patience of a fisherman.
But there was nothing he did not know: the very winch
that he used was made in the factory surreptitiously.
He caught roach, and before long I followed him. Even
better than this was the sport of seeing him confound
the water bailiff who asked for his licence. What with
gay lies, chaff and threats, the man had to go. We
feared nothing at my uncle's side.

These, however, were special week-end delights, for
Saturday afternoons or Sundays. The rest of the week
was spent mainly in the streets, on the canal-side adjacent, and in the nearer meadows. I liked seeing the

thousands of men going by on pavement and roadway for ten minutes before work started and after it ended at the factory. The variety of staid men and jaunty men, old men and boys, tall and stocky men, the frowners and the smilers, fascinated me with endless indolent inarticulate half-conjectures; and suddenly out of the multitude my uncle—or for a moment once or twice a man extremely like him. Straight out of that mysterious pageant, the one positively and entirely living one, he used to come into the house, into the kitchen, into his chair and begin to eat.

The slower thinner weekly procession to market was the other great sight. Curious wizened old men with old hats, enormously stout women with shawls and black bonnets, smiling rosy ones with feathers, drove by. Their little carts were laden with eggs, butter, fowls, rabbits, and vegetables, from Lydiard and Shaw and Parton and Wootten Bassett. One or two always stopped at our gate, and the woman came to the door with a broad flat basket of eggs or butter under a cloth, and, very rarely, some mushrooms. She said, 'Good morning. How are you this morning? Got your little grandson here again. Nice weather we're having. Mustn't grumble. Yes, the butter's one-and-two now. . . .' While my grandmother went for her purse I stood at the open door and looked at the shrewd cheerful woman or at her dog who had come for a moment from under the cart. She with her cheerful and shrewd slow way was as strange and attractive as any poet's or romancer's woman became afterwards, as far away from my world. I never knew her name, nor did she use ours.

I very soon knew a score of boys living near. I could tell them about London and share with them the young carrots stolen from my grandmother's garden. I got some credit with them by telling them that at home we got our coal a ton at a time; for they were all sons of fitters or even labourers at the factory, earning smaller salaries than my father. They in turn taught me their speech and their games. The best game was an evening one, called Urkey. One boy who was Urkey stood still by a tin can while the others hid. When a shout told that they had found a hiding he went in search of them. His object was to see one and run home to the can, crying 'I Urkey Johnny Williams'. If the one thus singled out, or any other, could get to the can first and kick it away, the game began all over again. Otherwise the one successfully Urkied had to take his place at the can. We used to have eggs boiled brown in coffee grounds at Easter, and to wear an oak-spray on May 29, 'Oak Apple Day'. In August we went together to the Fête in the Park and had a bag of cake, and tickets for roundabouts.

But my strongest and most often considered memory of this period was my second visit to Wales at the age of nine. It is associated with an incident which preceded and almost frustrated it. One evening after tea I went up on to Wandsworth Common with some bigger boys and sat on the seat by the Box Pond. A cigar was produced, lit and given to me to smoke. A few minutes afterwards I was crawling down the road by giddily clinging to the railings of garden after garden. I slunk into the house neglecting my mother's question 'What's the matter?' but soon answering it by deeds not words. My father said that I should not go to Wales. Nevertheless, I went. I remember the names of the stations, 'Risca', 'Cross Keys'... I walked through a park among great trees that stood at stately distances from one another: there were long-horned shaggy cattle about. I saw the river Ebbw racing over stones, and mountain ash trees on rough rising ground. I saw chimneys and smoke and ruins and whitewashed walls. I stopped at Abertillery with friends and met Welsh people who spoke no English. Above all I remember a house alone on a hill with a parrot and a dark girl named Rachel, pretty and dirty, who was down on her knees scrubbing the kitchen hearth. I made friends with the boy and the girl of the house in Abertillery and played with them among rolls of stuff in a dark shop. With my mother I drove out along a road among trees and above running water to Pontypool. I went to Aberbeg. . . . That is all the stuff of an abiding memory. These things joined forces with the street in Caerleon, the river and the Round Table, and also with phrases and images from *The Adventures of the Knights of the Round Table,* and a curious illusion of a knight with a shield kneeling at the foot of a pillar in the photograph at home of Tintern Abbey.

When I returned to London and school and a question was asked about a Welsh town beginning, the teacher hinted, with Aber, I frantically raised my hand muttering Abertillery, Abertillery, sorely distressed at being unnoticed, at being positively rebuked with Aberdare, which I had never heard of. But a nucleus had been formed, to which I gradually added fact and legend, the legend, e.g., I know not how true, that an ancestor, a sea-captain, riding home from Neath with money killed a man who set upon him to rob him.

At about this time I went to stay at my great-uncle's house at Limpley Stoke: it may, in fact, have been part of the same holiday which took me to Wales. The deep husky voice out of my uncle's beard, the goat in the garden who playfully butted the old man and drove me down the steps of the area, a story of a pet monkey who burst and died from overeating, and a vision of pale quarries, are the absurd total of my recollection. After the visit my uncle sent me a French Dilectus with the hope that I should soon master 'the French genders'.

I was now comparatively good at lessons, enjoyed excelling, only once played truant and did not enjoy it, was hardly ever caned, and earned a leather-bound gilt-edged New Testament as a prize. And at home I read many books of travel, natural history and fiction. As birthday or Christmas presents I received *The Compleat Angler*; *The Marvels of the Polar World*, about ice, snow, Esquimaux and seals, and other books containing picturesque descriptions of torrid or frozen lands; *Dick's Holidays and what he did with them*, an adult's chronicle of a boy's country holiday, with insidious information on every page; Hans Andersen, Grimm, Holme Leigh's *Fairy Tales*, *The Swiss Family Robinson*, *Westward Ho!* . . . Thus I grew to think of places where jaguars lay in wait for men upon overhanging branches, and of times when houses were made of barley sugar and witches cooked children and ate them. I was still well content to remain, except during these readings, a citizen's son of London in the 'eighties of the nineteenth century, but a citizen with a sometimes fantastically light grasp of facts, as when I slipped a letter addressed to my father in one part of the country inside a newspaper for my mother in another part. Part of the pleasure of a book was still, I think, the strangeness of words as well as things. Thus I was arrested by the quaintness of Izaak Walton's spelling, as in 'pearch' for perch, of his archaic names, such as 'luce' for pike, of unfamiliar personal names like those of the travellers Speke and Grant, as well as by the nasty horror of Africans eating fat torn from a live human body in Sir Samuel Baker's book. These things were no less and no more remote than the fairy tales. I did not often feel that they were part of my world of newspapers, a comfortable home and a clockwork school. But several houses became associated with certain wonders out of books, either by accident or because at some point they resembled places in the books. The gravelly shore of the Long Pond on Wandsworth Common was confused in my mind with the sea sand where Robinson Crusoe saw the cannibals' footprints. In return, there were people and houses without associations possessing qualities in common with the people and houses in wonderful books, and I cannot decide whether my life owed more to my books or my books more to my life. I slipped from one world into the other as easily as from room to room. I do not know how much I may have dwelt on the story in later years, but Grimm's *Hansel and Grethel*, the children going out into the wood to be lost, dropping a trail of stones behind them and finding their way back, but failing to do so when they used breadcrumbs which the birds ate, came to be to my mind one of the great stories of the world.

4

BOOKS AND SCHOOL FRIENDS

*

For the most part I remember rather the joy of having and reading books than particular passages. I remember the eager walks over Wandsworth Common to borrow volume after volume of the Waverley novels, but of *Waverley*, *Heart of Midlothian*, *Peveril of the Peak* and *The Talisman*, not a rack is left. Of *The Last of the Mohicans* and *The Pathfinder* rather more is left. They gave me an idea of a noble savage. The Pathfinder himself towers in memory as grandly as Milton's Satan but more dimly. The name of the girl Cora has folded itself up in my mind like a gentle snake. . . . I read some of Scott's poems in the same year. They made deeper impressions than the novels. I was continually repeating with a throb:

> *With Chester charge and Lancashire,*

or

> *Charge, Chester, charge! On Stanley on*
> *Were the last words of Marmion.*

The duel between FitzJames and Roderick Dhu was

the greatest thing of all. The next best was Roderick Dhu's whistle that caused armed warriors suddenly to rise up out of the mountain bracken. I could scarcely bear the excitement of describing these scenes to another boy as we walked along Bolingbroke Grove. My voice was thick and broken with the effort of 'And, Saxon, I am Roderick Dhu'. The excitement caused a not entirely unpleasant aching tenderness in a certain part, just as open praise did and still does. Of course when I found a family of Rodericks in Swindon I linked them to the poem.

The only poems which I remember having read aloud to me at an early age were Longfellow's. My father used to read or recite *The Children's Hour* very often. The pathos, or his sense of it, touched me, and I received faint but delicious images of 'grave Alice' and 'laughing Allegra' and 'Edith with golden hair'. I could also enjoy impressions in the minor key. The only one of the many songs we sang at school which I can recall was in the minor key. It was a kind of dirge for a North American Indian. I can still hum the melody, but I remember no more of the words than 'Far far away in the depths of the wild wood'. These were several times repeated. The rhyme to 'wild wood' was I believe 'childhood'. I used to sing this to myself, and have periodically returned to it ever since. I liked also 'Lucy Gray', the one poem which I remember to have learnt at the Board-school: but I never could understand 'and snapped a faggot band'. I do not think I had any tangible sadness to which the song gave utterance. There was for me at that time no sadness, e.g., in the destruction of the orchard of the great house near by, and the portioning of its park-like meadow into streets. Anybody could enter now. We pillaged artichokes. Some boys took sackfuls of the soil and I helped one to drag his down the street; out of the wounds thus worn in it, it was bleeding dark mould on the pavement.

My books did not hamper my games, nor in any way alter them except that I could not wear sword and shield hereafter without FitzJames haunting and inspiring me. I played as much as ever and walked to Wimbledon more and more. I could also enjoy kinds of fighting where it was impossible to think of poetry. For example, I had a long tussle with a rough after a quarrel during fishing, and was only beaten by the intervention of a third party armed with an old kettle. It was fun, too, to battle at a distance with stones, dodging and casting at the same instant. In one of these combats I got a deep scalp wound made ever memorable by my aunt fainting at the blood.

While we were at this house my mother presented me with four brothers at intervals of two years, but, as I have no recollection of them during that period beyond the fact that on certain dim occasions in our street or at Swindon one or other was present, I say nothing about them. Being thus seven in family we moved to a large house in one of the roads parallel to the old one. The great long low windowless van that we stamped about in—the bread and cheese eaten anyhow in the confusion—the odd jobs of fetching and carrying—these were pleasures. I am not at all sure now whether I made one of the journeys on the tail of the cart. And yet I am perfectly sure that the name of the elder boy who shared these pleasures was —— and that my mother said he was a good boy and had been very useful.

On the first few days after the move I went several times most of the way down from school to the old house before realizing my mistake. Whether I had regrets for it or not, it began almost at once to have a dreamy charm too faint to be describable. It was a visible piece of the past, a skeleton, a hollow shell that did without us. Of course the new house had also a charm. Its size allowed an empty room for us to play in, and a box-room. Perhaps it was not until a little later that the box-room became attractive, because it was dark and because in it was a wooden box containing inexhaustible treasures. These were chiefly old books, old magazines, old photographs of unknown people. Many and many a time I took them all out, sometimes in search of something I had noticed among them before and then not troubled about, sometimes in more uncertainty but equal eagerness, at other times with no object save testing the inexhaustible surprises of the box. At intervals of a year or less I must have taken everything out and put it back again, with moments of hastiness when things were moved in armfuls, fully a dozen times. I think I could do it at least once yet. . . . My slender undefined expectations connect the search with that lost book of my earlier childhood about the key of knowledge. But I forbear to amplify this. One of the discoveries I made was of *Pickwick Papers*. Sitting in the dust with dusty eyes I read about sticklebacks in the Hampstead Ponds. I could not get on much farther. Too many of the people had ridiculous names. The book had nothing in common with the Waverley novels or the *Compleat Angler* or Sir Samuel Baker's travels. At about this time I began to keep my own books on a shelf of their own and to paste numbers inside them as I had seen done with library books: to raise the numbers to a respectable size I took my two next brothers into partnership and we lent them out to one another with formality. The sum of our united ingenuities would at no time have been very great.

However, I had my own way. It was usually easy for me to get it. While I was still at the Board-school I was conscious of possessing some power over my physical superiors, though the use of it was unconscious. I cannot say how much it was exerted, if it was at all, by means of wheedling, begging, cringing, or perhaps putting others into the position of feeling brutal or awkward if they refused me.

My later days at the Board-school were pleasant
enough. My class sat in the same room and was taken by
the same master as a special small class of the oldest boys
in the school. They used to read accounts of the
Massacre of Glencoe and produce essays on what they
remembered. I made friends with one or two of them,
laughed at their jokes and catch-phrases, and was
expected to enjoy the picture of the gravid uterus of a
rabbit in a book which one of them showed me.

Towards the end of these days I spent the greater
part of a summer term in a Board-school in Swindon
where the head master was a friend of my father's. I
became a Wiltshire boy in accent. I made friends and
sweethearts too, and at the Fête in August spent all the
day and evening with a girl on each side of me—I do
not think I had ever before or since so much pride and
confidence. To one of the girls, a dark sturdy beauty
named Laura, I was more or less faithful for several
years. Though she knew and did nothing that I valued,
to have a girl by me on a walk pleased me intensely.
I suppose the love of having my own way guided me
surely for the most part towards girls who were not
flirts. I liked also elder girls. Some of the most blissful
hours I ever spent were in country walks with a buxom
Welsh cousin named Florence, who was probably eight
or nine years my senior. She was staying at my grandmother's one summer when I was, and she and I used
to walk along the quiet road, or over meadows, to

Shaw or Lydiard. I thought her beautiful, her rosy face, her voice, herself beautiful. To me she was all sweetness and kindness. We used to go into a farmhouse door or into the milking shed and get milk and perhaps eat a lardy cake. I remember her taking out her purse. Everything about her was somehow sweet and perfect. I suppose I had a sort of happy unfettered adoration for her without knowing it. I never saw her after that summer.

I exchanged the Board-school when I was ten for a private school. Here there were fifty or sixty boys of from ten to seventeen years of age, perhaps half of them boarders. They were the sons of tradesmen, professional men, moderately well-to-do clerks, and men of small independent means. Only one of them had I known before. He preceded me by a term from the Board-school and at once asserted his superiority by making a fool of me. In the small gravel playground there was a swing consisting of a long board suspended at either end by a pair of chains. A boy at each end could work it up to what seemed to me a terrible height, the prime feat being to jump off backwards from your position just as the board began to swing forward. I took my first ride with this old schoolfellow. The bell for lessons rang while we were well up, and he dropped off, leaving me helplessly to wait and watch the school assemble, and pointing me out with malice as well as grins when I at last took my place. The schoolroom was a large single hall adjacent to the large old brick house where the boarders lived with the head master. The three classes under the head and two assistants all occupied the same room, but faced different ways. In the fourth quarter of the room stood the boarders' more substantial desks, where they kept silkworms and white mice. The boarders predominated in other ways. Their familiar life together had given them a style and subject matter of their own. Knowing the masters privately they treated them with open ease and half-concealed amusement. They were pretty faithfully imitated by the day boys. But the head master was of stone. He wore a black gown. So long as he was in the room no sound was to be heard beyond a dismal foot shuffling, a pen dropping, a boy asking a question, a master answering or explaining, the head dictating or clearing his throat. While he was out the hubbub was so general that the assistants could hardly single out a particular one to punish, for if it had a ringleader it was some spirited bright popular boy whom it would be unpleasant and ruinous to punish.

I continued to accumulate information in history and geography, to do harder and harder sums, to copy models of handwriting. I learnt a few Latin declensions and conjugations. With the rest of the school I sat listening to Mr. —— talking physiology as if the body were a newly discovered machine and we were angels. Just before the holidays like everyone else I wrote a letter to my dear parents telling them what had been done during the term, when the holidays began and how long they were to last. But I learnt also how to keep silkworms alive, and added to the boarders' pocket-money by buying as many as I could. I had a penny or twopence a week.

One of the masters, a black-haired snub-nosed kindly energetic freshman, was fond of me. He chaffed me about the freckles I got in the summer holidays; he gave me the *Lamplighter* and numbers of *Horner's Penny Stories*; he came round to see my father and offered to take me to the baths and teach me to swim. I had no particular liking for him or gratitude for his liking for me, and when I left the school I left all but the first of his letters to me unanswered and so tired his attention.

I only knew one boarder at all well. He was a Welsh boy from Flint several years older than myself, and wanting to do something to please him, I gave him the leather-bound New Testament which I had received as a prize at the Board-school. I cannot recall that boarders and day boys had any united or organized games except paper-chases.

A paper-chase made one of the Saturdays at this school a great and notable day for me. For I then discovered a piece of country, as it seemed to me, exactly like the real country at Swindon and quite unlike the commonland at Wimbledon. Here were private but not inaccessible copses, hedges with oaks in them, and wandering paths, rough lanes, scant cottages. I got left behind and lost the rest of the school except one older boy. We had bread and cheese at the 'George Inn'. That day I ran, walked and crawled six or seven miles out and the same distance back. For a year it may be I left this piece of country unrevisited.

I made several friends among the day boys. One who had a deep voice and must have been much older used to take me out to share his adventures on a double 'sociable' tricycle; and he gave me white rats. But I had most to do with a boy only a year or two older than myself, named Jonathan, who introduced me to some of his father's workshops, and particularly the carpenter's shop. Adjoining this shop were roomy houses for pigeons of several kinds, Belgian hares, rabbits, guinea-pigs, and white rats. Fine afternoons, therefore, had now scarce any advantages over wet ones. Making additions to the cages, cleaning them out, feeding the birds and animals, handling them, selling or exchanging them, talking about them, set the hours rolling lazily, swiftly. In a day or two I had learnt all, alas! that I ever did about the use of saw, hammer, screwdriver, and brace. That is to say I was now a quick unscrupulous maker of cages of all sizes. I fitted doors to them, fronts of split wood and wire-netting, roofs of tarred felt laid upon laths. I spent all the shorter sections of my spare time in making, altering, and mending cages for pigeons, rabbits and white mice.

I retained few of my old school friends. One of them, though he too had moved and in the opposite direction, made several attempts to keep up our friendship. He was a very swift runner and always walked in the middle of the road wearing sandshoes. The short period of separation made me shy when he came to the door on a Saturday afternoon, so that I was almost inclined to deny that I knew him. He must have felt this and at length altogether ceased to come. Before long I was sorry for this.

I must have begun keeping pets soon after entering the new school. Through them, or rather through the pigeons, I got to know other fanciers, men and boys, in the neighbourhood. For example, a pigeon house hung on the wall of a house in the street at right angles to ours and visible a hundred yards away from the back garden where I kept my pets. I used to see the owner, a much older boy called Henry, leaning out of the window to attend to his pigeons or to set them at liberty for a flight. They ascended half a mile high and remained circling for a great time, or if they did not and tried to perch they were driven up again with loud clappings. The boy's whistle to his pigeons, a peculiar shrill anxious one, and a mild luring one, I acquired as soon as possible. Still I felt that the boy looked down on me. My birds never flew much higher than the topmost chimneypots, and they used to get lost or caught by cats. One day I was sure that a pigeon of mine had entered his cage and I went round to ask for it. Thus we became acquainted. He began by denying the fact with a mixture of indignation and chaff, and I think he made a small charge before restoring the bird. But I supposing this was the custom or admiring his superior age, skill, and aplomb, was far from complaining. I accepted his patronage gladly. He used to come round for me in the evening with a whistle instead of a knock —not like either of the pigeon calls, but very expressive. He would begin with pairs of notes imperious in tone, and repeated if necessary several times more and more loudly. Then he waited, sauntering backwards and forwards outside. If I did not come out he changed to a more questioning call which had in it a despairing quality or one meant to raise despair in me. It gave me a last chance. Often he had a bird to show me for admiration or for sale. I found it hard ever to refuse anything he praised to me. In my case to acquire a new pigeon was a delight. So in I used to go, if success was at all possible, to tell my father and mother about this supreme opportunity, in short to ask for a shilling or one-and-six. Not too seldom I succeeded. At times I possessed a dozen of different breeds—athletic homers, heavy wattled antique-looking dragons, dainty almond tumblers, feminine owls. For a few days I rejoiced in a pair of red-ruffed Jacobins sent me from Wales, deli-cate pretty birds; but they never flew beyond the roof and seldom higher than the fence, where a cat caught first one, then the other. This was one of the few sorrows of pigeon-keeping. The pleasures were innumerable. Chief of all was to set the birds free, watch them to the roof, clap till they flew round and round, draw them down by whistling and scattering seed. The mere purchasing of seed out of my pocket-money was a pleasure, especially as I was always experimenting with my own fancifully proportioned mixtures of dari, barley, maize, tares, and peas. Even the four useless eggs laid by a devoted couple of hens were not thrown away on me: I discovered that no young ever came from them, and thereafter I diligently blew every one and treasured them. The great excitement was tempting a stray bird down with the rest into the pigeon house. Only once did I have a stray safely trapped and housed. She was for me a bird of mark, with the name of the Columbusian Society on her wings; I kept her proudly with infinite expectations of her offspring. I was disappointed. For her one pair of fertile eggs I could not leave patiently to hatch. As soon as the young began to make a stir in them I answered them by chipping the shell with a pin; they were pricked and died unborn.

The rabbits were less interesting. But they were possessions. I learnt to handle them in the right manner. It was something to bury one from time to time. Also the business of rabbit-keeping took me to new country. One of our servants had a brother-in-law in Battersea who was a fancier, and I used to go down there to see his animals, and occasionally to buy one. One of the shops in his neighbourhood sold bran or pollard more cheaply. Such were my triumphs. And I remember that once when coming home from a visit to this man I found in my overcoat pocket a sum of money amounting to about a couple of shillings. Probably it was the change from some purchase for my mother which I had forgotten to hand over. It happened a second time. I mention this only for the sake of pointing out that after the first surprise at each find I had a feeling of good fortune, mysterious indeed but not puzzling. I believe that I really thought the money had entered my pocket by some unique, magic accident.

My companions were now boys exclusively. I had no sisters; my girl cousins I saw but two or three times in all my childhood; none of my friends had sisters of their own age; my father and mother had but a few close acquaintances, who rarely came to the house and hardly ever brought their children, boys or girls, with them. Mabel and I had forsaken one another. If we met we smiled without words, without stopping. Then there were the servants. Usually one general servant shared the work of the house with my mother, everything except the washing. That was done by a woman who came over from Lambeth every week on Mondays. Her great red arms and her clean rapid ways awed me, her glass of beer and plate of bread and cheese in the middle of the morning awed and delighted me.

Her rule lasted for many years; the servants rarely stayed more than a year or two. Their names, Eliza, Emily, Jane, Martha, call up individual but indefinite images of the bodies and natures of those girls: Eliza, grey-eyed, round-faced, bustling, laughing; religious Emily, cross-eyed, mild, severe; clever Jane, white, hazel-eyed, pretty but with a large nose and a tendency to a cold; Martha, Irish, black-haired, always talking or singing her song of

> *The press-gang came for William*
> *When he was all alone,*

but safe and sound, and much missed when she went to Australia. Then there were two sisters, Alice and Clara, who were with us together, and had conspicuous powers as actresses and managers. They were always dressing up themselves or us, to surprise my father, who had no wish to be surprised. Alice, the elder, a tall dark girl, had the supreme gift of being able to step out from the attic window on to the gutter and up on to the roof, and move freely there or look down on us in the garden. These sisters regarded themselves as not exactly servants. That they knew an aged German count whom we used to see about in the streets gave them a sort of glory. Our quiet stiff home could not contain these two very long: even Alice without Clara proved impossible. For a time we tried mother's helps instead of servants. We called them 'Miss' Brown and so on. One was a prettyish small thing who once hid herself under my bed and emerged while I was undressing: it made me indignant at first as I always was if taken unawares, but a little vain afterwards because I thought she liked me. The most exciting was a girl from Hampshire, a rather handsome, tall, bony, and pale girl, a farmer's daughter who had left home after some quarrel. I think she said her father was a gentleman farmer. She talked a lot about horses. At supper she did practically all the talking, and I remember that my father did not much want to be amused when she was telling of the lovers who would get lost in her father's copses on fine evenings. She was a merry creature. She and a pretty friend who came to see her, an actress with soft dark hair and a romantic name, wanted to romp with us and be familiar. But I drew off, suspiciously, feeling that I did not understand them, wishing not to give myself away. I left them alone with my younger brothers, drawing enigmatical figures on paper and asking riddles and laughing both openly and to themselves. If I could not hold my own I would retreat and not be victimized. Miss —— also did not stay long. I was sorry when she was gone. Nearly all these women I liked in some way. For one thing, they were very patient and kind, while several of them, I can see now, I admired and enjoyed admiring for their sweet looks or language or presence. The only woman I had anything to do with regularly was my mother, and except at meals and bedtime I did not see much even of my mother. Occasionally we played cards or draughts together in the evenings. My mother played the piano a little; my father sang 'Bonny Mary of Argyle' to her accompaniment. No doubt often I went to London with them. For example, I was taken to a pantomime, where the mannish donkey and the clown wreathed in sausages seemed to my memory worth retaining. London made no impression: I simply recall sitting inside a bus and studying the list of fares at the inner end. I suppose I had gradually in my own populous and busy neighbourhood become accustomed to something like all that could be seen or heard in London except the river. Even a visit when I was thirteen with only a lesser boy for company left me nothing to recall it by except my pride at making my way to a big shop in Cheapside unaided. I only knew enough to make a dim picture of squalor, rags and blood, when I heard the newspaper boys hoarsely breaking the silence of the cold foggy night with shouts of 'Horrible murder in Whitechapel. Another Ripper Murder. Horrible murder.'

Of course I continued, more and more often, to accompany my parents to the Unitarian chapel on Sunday. For a time I was a regular attendant because I sang in the choir. The sound of 'How lovely are the messengers' was pleasant to me, but it was a curious sensation altogether remote from my games and walks and pigeon-keeping. It was an oasis, the mirage of an oasis, in the chapel desert. Sitting between my father and my mother, I watched now the sad solemn gentle preacher against a background of Faith, Hope, and Charity, now the feathers in the stout lady's hat just in front of us, now the momentarily visible exquisite profile smooth soft cool glowing skin and perfect scarlet lips of her daughter, the bald head of her husband, and now fleetingly the serried multitudes, the spectacled women, the old men, the pale young men, all in suspended animation. Though some of these seemed to me absurd I had never a glimmering of the courage needed to laugh at them. Faith, Hope, and Charity were words which I could perhaps just dissociate from their vulgar uses, but as I knew of no other use the process left them words pure and simple. Perhaps my weariness in chapel was mingled with something which specialists would label as religious. I only know that where people were sad and solemn I was overcome, half-suffocated by the sadness and solemnity. What was read and preached was to me airy nothing. I knew of no virtues except truthfulness, obedience, self-sacrifice, total abstinence from alcoholic drinks. Because it was more comfortable than disobedience as a rule I was obedient. I habitually told the truth when I had nothing which I thought could easily be gained by lying. I stole biscuits and sweets from my mother's cupboard and was tearfully penitent when found out. I never wanted to drink ale except when my uncle poured it out for me in a tot. As for self-sacrifice it was mostly incredible. But I liked to please my mother and keep undisturbed the love that was between us. I sometimes did little unexpected kind things out of my tenderness for her, and was always glad to be the one to take up tea for her if she was unwell, and so on, or to help her with the housework when she was left servantless. But with her as with everyone I was deceitful and had dread of being caught doing what I ought not to do. It was a great and frequent dread. For I felt that most things a boy liked doing annoyed some elder or another; that to annoy an elder was the essence of wrong. My solution was to try not to annoy at the same time that I was doing almost as I liked. Deceit and dread increased rapidly. My mother never attempted to add to the religion of the chapel. On the contrary she roused my indignation at the two conspicuously Christian aunts who had made her childhood in that dark house at Newport miserable. If she or I had taken more trouble I might have been convinced that all religious people were cruel hypocrites. My grandmother was the only influence on the other side. She persuaded me that I should be really good if I knelt down night and morning by my bed and 'said my prayers', and for a short time I did so. It was 'Our Father' which I repeated, though it was and has ever remained Greek to me. Once only I tried hard to mean something in prayer. There was to be a treat in the country next day, and as

I was going downstairs I turned in to my mother's dark room and, throwing myself down beside the bed with a violence intended to thwart hesitation, doubt, and ridicule, I begged 'God' to make it a fine day to-morrow. The day was fine, but I never prayed again. I used to tell my father and mother of this half in jest. I suppose there was religion at my second school. It has been forgotten along with all but the names of the *Lamplighter* and *Horner's Penny Stories*.

Not even yet can I recall anything distinctly of my brothers beyond the fact of an inconstant feud with the eldest of them. Black-haired and dark-eyed like my father, he was shorter for his age, more athletic and acrobatic than I, and shared none of my tastes or hobbies. He was the favourite of my Swindon uncle. Whenever our differences culminated we began by each abusing the other for his darkness or fairness. My brother shouted 'pale face', though I had in fact more colour than he ever had; what I called him I do not know. Then we came to blows. I could overcome his strength, but not his spirit. This feud was at times exceedingly bitter, and in one quarrel I was wounded on the head by a clothes prop. At other times it took a less violent form. If he admired one hero, I admired his enemy. On the wall of our bedroom facing us as we lay in bed hung a picture of two little girls, one slightly fairer and littler than the other. We laid claim to these girls as sweethearts. I of course chose the fair one; my brother of course chose the dark one, as he called her because she was the less fair. Our hostility had very deep roots. A fright that I once unintentionally gave my brother by rising up unexpectedly draped in a green tablecloth may have had something to do with it; and I remember that when he awoke screaming and sweating at night sometimes nobody was less likely to quiet him than I; he screamed all the more at sight of me. We saw little of one another except on Sundays and on holidays, since he and one or two of our younger brothers still went to the Board-school.

5

SCHOOL GAMES AND EARLY READING

*

I did not stay long at the second school. The head master moved into the country and his successor not attracting my father, I was sent to a day school about two miles away in Battersea. This meant that I had my dinner at school, thus spending eight or nine hours a day at a stretch in greenless streets. The playground was asphalt; again there were no organized games, but a dozen groups playing leap frog, fly the garter, or tops, or chasing one another, or simply messing about. 'Fly the garter'—if that is its right name—was a grand game to see played by a dozen of the biggest boys. I forget how it came about, but by degrees at length there were four or five boys bent double, forming a continuous line of backs. Each grasped the one in front of him and the first of them had his head, protected by his hands, against the playground wall. From half-way across the playground a big boy ran at a gallop, his ironshod heels pounding the asphalt, towards this line of boys who could see him approaching between their legs. Reaching the line and putting his hands upon the first back to help him leap he leaped forward into the air. A brilliant leaper would use only one hand for the take off: the other gave a sonorous smack on the right place in passing. With legs outspread he flew along the line of backs, and alighted upon the fourth or fifth of them. The lighter his weight, the more fortunate was the steed thus accidentally mounted: the heavier, the greater was the chance that both together crashed to the ground. Then, I think, the leaper added another to the line of backs and set the next leaper an impossible task. The last stayer had a good double row of admirers, silent during the run and the leap, uproarious at the alighting. We smaller boys climbed or tried to climb any upright or horizontal post and rails about the school, on the scaffolding, for example, during some repairs. Tops, chiefly peg tops, we played endlessly. We tried to destroy our opponent's top by casting our own at it and impaling it with the peg. Or we 'chipped' brass buttons or other tops into and out of a ring, by taking up our own top on to the hand while spinning, causing it to sway upon a fixed centre hollowed in the palm, and then casting it at the object with all the rotatory force thus gained. Or we strove against one another at hurling our tops out of the string a long distance, yet so that they should be spinning when they came to a standstill. The best spinners always threw their tops with the pegs pointing away from the ground instead

of towards it, which I could never achieve nor understand. Girls did it my way. Cricket and football we had
to organize between ourselves. Clapham Common
was our ground. Mustering perhaps as many as eleven
on paper we assumed a title as the —— Cricket Club;
we elected officers and committee; we bought a few
necessities by subscription; we practised with considerable intervals of fooling and quarrelling; we even
played a match or two with similar sides. Only on
occasional inspired moments did we labour as if ours
were the same game as was played by Abel, Bonnor,
Spofforth, Lohmann, Quaife, S. M. J. Woods, Gunn,
W. W. Read, Sharp, A. P. Wickham. I remember the
strolling home, casting a stump now and then into the
turf, or pausing to play 'French cricket' or 'tip and
run', better than I do the games. I much preferred football. Later on we joined a football club and played
matches with some regularity. Sometimes when the
sodden ball was like lead it was but a sad pleasure, and
not that if in punting one kicked the ball full in one's
own face; but as a rule the full game, or any sort of
game, or just kicking about till it was dark, was all I
wanted.

In the class rooms history, geography, grammar,
arithmetic, algebra, freehand-drawing, handwriting,
Latin, French, chemistry, or the avoiding of the same,
took up about five hours a day for five days a week.
The one charm of the place was the temporary youth,

a different one each week, who came over from a neighbouring training college to help the permanent master of each class. These students we looked upon as prey. In a few minutes the corporate brain of the class knew their victim thoroughly in so far as he concerned them, knew whether he need be obeyed, whether he could be both disobeyed and cheeked, whether he could also be mocked for some peculiarity of manner or accent. Funniest of all was a Frenchman who said 'What do they call you?' instead of 'What is your name?' The permanent masters were a strict sardonic one with ginger hair, a mild incalculable black-haired one with a ridiculously mild voice, and an altogether humorous one with bulging eyes and an amused unastonishable look who managed the top form with a smile. Then there was the head master, grey-bearded, spectacled, squat, and bandy-legged, but rapid. I remember him coming in once when the funniest boy in the class was amusing us all, the master being absent. He did not see the head entering the door behind him. He had a broad smile on his face when that devil from behind struck him hard on ear and cheek with his open palm, without a word. We who saw the blow coming were hardly more abashed and upset than Jack was. Our own master, the sardonic one, often caned Jack to his face. It was an unemotional ceremony. The master liked Jack but had to do it. Jack didn't mind at all, and held out his hand smiling, with only the slightest twitch of his cheerful face at each blow. Jack was a strong, easy-going, kind-hearted dunce. With him and various lean and fat, diligent and idle, and intermediate boys I did my lessons. I could learn anything easily and was seldom lower than fourth in the class, more often than not first, and had usually on one side of me a silent good boy. I who was never good at languages, least of all at Latin, sometimes knew more Latin than the master. The pleasure of being top, and nothing else, except the interest of my father, made me do such homework as I did in the evenings. We learnt Byron's *Prisoner of Chillon*. But I was in a period of prose which the place encouraged. I rattled off the lines I had committed to memory. The task endowed me only with the idea that it was possible for a man's hair to grow white in a single night from sudden fear. I remember the electric battery, the smell of the acids in the chemistry room, and the treacly look of sulphur melted, and shame of my only caning. It was but one stroke, for I was a sort of 'good boy', being shy, restrained, secretive, and never a leader, and with an expression quite super-ficially and accidentally resembling that of the virtu-ous. I passed some examination in chemistry but, as with other things, cared nothing for it, except for doing as well as most at it. For a while I played with magnets and amber, and rubbed the cat's fur in the dark. My father made me attend evening lectures for a time on sound, light, and heat—with no effect.

The midday hours when I had dinner at school, played in the playground or wandered about Battersea or visited boys' homes, and saw their pigeons, were a relief from no great servitude or labour. How I enjoyed the strongly spiced unusual soups and the sausages—and the sweets bought instead of food—and the pennies saved up and at last spent on a new pigeon. Then I had to pretend that I had won the pigeon in a raffle. Once or twice this was believed. I was found out because one day when I wanted to tell my parents that I had sixpence I bent over the front garden fence while my mother was gardening, and pretended to pick up the sixpence. Probably I was already suspected. My mother disbelieved the story. I confessed. My father spoke to me angrily. As I hated anger and blame, I became wretched. The result was that very soon indeed afterwards my father came with a very sad but kind face in to the room where I sat alone and told me he was sure I should not do that sort of thing again. His shaking hands with me made me feel half hero, half saint. Naturally I did not do quite that sort of thing again. But the pleasure of coming home with a new pigeon was irresistible. The purchase excited me. Sometimes I took a fancy to a particular bird. Perhaps more often I had to have some bird—almost any bird at once. The shilling was in my pocket. I could not possibly go home in this condition. Then it was a pleasure to hold the legs between the two forefingers, the thumb and shorter fingers almost meeting over the body. You might have thought the bird was a divinely beautiful, immortal, or miraculous bird, had you known how the acquiring and the first possessing it thrilled me through and made me forget weather, time, meals, father and mother and native land. Every step towards the boy's garden or the shop—a crowded fancier's or a corn-chandler's with a couple of cages only in the doorway—gave me again the pleasure of anticipation and the pain of delay together.

I had no love to give Byron's poetry, but, in the intervals of pigeon-keeping, I read avidly. On wet days and dark winter evenings I bolted scores of books by Mayne Reid. Fenimore Cooper was now much too dilatory. Henty was often beside the mark. Better even than Mayne Reid were some of the anonymous mixers of blood and thunder. I always retained at least an affectation of scorn for 'Deadwood Dick' stories in particular, but not for the class to which they belonged. I varied them, if it was a variation, with a never-ending serial entitled *Jack Harkaway's Schooldays* and more improving things of the same kidney in the *Boys' Own Paper*. *The Headless Horseman*, *The Scalp Hunters*, *The Boy Hunters of Kentucky*, *The Secret of Adam's Peak*, are now but words to me, 'Open Sesame' powerless to open more than a slit in the door behind which Indians, cowboys, and Mexican greasers mounted on fiery mustangs, armed with beautiful big guns, bows and arrows, revolvers and bowie knives and lassoes, hunt, fight, and round up cattle night and day for ever and ever. While I read the books I polished up the silver falcon crest shield, which all of us wore on our caps, with mercury.

Could it have been now—it was certainly not much later—that I began to want to have back my *Fairy Know-a-bit*? It had been lent to some one in Lambeth, and through my vague recollections of it, mingled perhaps with a desire for what had departed, especially as it had been my own, it acquired a fantastic value, as that book about 'The Key of Knowledge' had done; for several years I was always remembering it, pestering my father and mother to try to recover it.

6

PLAYFELLOWS AND SWINDON
EXPERIENCES

*

I made a few friends at this school, rather among
those who lived in our suburban neighbourhood than
among Battersea boys. One boy I used to go home with
to a public-house where we ate scones out of a glass-
covered dish: but when I went home with other Battersea boys it was to see the pigeons and rabbits only; I
was admitted to the garden by a side door and never
entered the house. My aunt was shocked at my pro-
posal to go to tea with a boy whose father kept a public-
house, even a very large one. On the whole they were
a coarse rough lot, worse than the Board-school boys,
or such was my opinion soon after I had left. Of my
closer acquaintances only one lived very near us. We
used to walk to school together almost daily. At this
distance of time I recall but a single virtue that he
possessed, that of perpetually laughing and scoffing,
turning things and words round so that they could be
laughed or scoffed at. He was puny and skinny, and his
face was screwed up with quick Cockney malice and

amusement. He had several sisters very much like him, always pattering and grinning. The family was a cheerful one, excellent at Christmas parties, just what our family was not: game was linked on to game and meal to meal with the utmost ease and jollity. I believe there were skeletons in the cupboard. Years afterwards my particular friend, to pay for racing and other pleasures, embezzled a large sum of money from his employers, and went first to prison and thence to a colony.

My other school friends lived farther away. I can scarcely recall more than their names and the streets they lived in. Two of them, brothers, reappear in my memory not at home but at Eastbourne, where it happened both our families were spending a summer holiday. Our lodgings were small and uncomfortable and indoors we were always squabbling or annoyed our father. Out of doors all was well. We loafed about listening to black minstrels who sang the songs of the day. We whistled the tunes till we sickened one another. We threw pebbles about. We ate as much nougat as we could afford. Every day we heard an old man with a rascally jaunty leer singing:

> *So, boys, keep away from the girls I say*
> *And give them plenty of room.*

I think it was only against matrimony. We rarely bathed, because we could not afford bathing machines every day and we could not swim and had not incitements to learn. The most strenuous thing we did was to walk up to the top of Beachy Head and then race the mile or more down into the town. The elder of the two brothers was by far the best runner. But as great as any of the joys of Eastbourne were the joys of looking forward and starting, and of returning and looking backward. How early I began to dislike the crowd and the conventions of the seaside it is impossible to say. Certain it is that the crowd on the beach and the constraint in our narrow lodgings had such an effect that I can recall practically no enjoyment in these earlier visits.

I try to guess why it was that I liked Charlie ——, a dark-haired, tawny-skinned boy, whose family moved away to Norwich, or some such place, in the middle of our acquaintance. I can hear a common friend saying to me once, 'You'll miss old Charlie ——, won't you', but I cannot recover anything about the boy. And there are some dimmer, and others who are just faces with a certain expression which from time to time I recognize on the platforms at Victoria, Waterloo, and Clapham Junction.

Though I may have liked Eastbourne better than I think, I liked Swindon infinitely better than Eastbourne. Probably we were only two or three weeks by the sea, and then my next brother and I went to Swindon to finish out the holidays. For some good reason I preferred the sons of Swindon mechanics and labourers to

PLAYFELLOWS AND SWINDON EXPERIENCES

the sons of Battersea tradesmen and clerks. I had forsaken the girls. With the boys I fished, played and
rambled as before. When I was thirteen or thereabouts
I was first introduced to a slaughterhouse. It backed on
to the canal and had a disused door at that side with a
broken panel imperfectly covered from within by a
piece of sacking. Through this we peered, often to no
purpose beyond sniffing the smell of blood and stale-
ness, more rarely to see a carcass being cut up or the
floor being washed out, three or four times to see a
cow killed, or a calf, still jerking from the beam overhead, being flayed. The novelty drew me, and over-
powered the horror and uncertain expectation which
made my heart beat furiously and my lips go dry. A
sort of broken-down half loafer, half drover, led in the
cow. A rope round her neck was put through a hole in
the doorpost and pulled tightly so that her head was
low. The man held on to the rope-end with all his
might. The tall pale butcher came along, shoved her a
little sideways to get her perfectly into position, and
brought down the pointed knob of the poleaxe smartly
upon her forehead. The rope was slackened, she fell
heavily. The man thrust a cane into the opening in her
forehead, 'to stir the brains', said my fellow watcher.
The butcher cut her throat and the blood rattled into a
bucket, while the man stood, with one foot on the
ground clear of her gesticulating legs, and one upon
her flank, working it up and down to help the blood

out. . . . I always looked on with dread equal to my hope that there would be something to see. The silence alone made it endurable: the shrieking of a pig I never could have endured. The only physical pain I could myself inflict with pleasure was upon fish. My usual bait for jack was a small living roach. By means of a tiny needle the line was threaded under about two inches of the fish's skin, so that the big double hook lay close against its side and was not easily torn away by the act of casting the bait out to a distance of ten or twenty yards. Thus armed, the roach swam about to the best of its ability until it was seized by a jack or became so feeble as to be unattractive and useless. Now in order to damage the bait as little as possible I always used the utmost care to prick the skin only and not the fish in attaching the hook; when it was done for, either I threw it into the water to die slowly, or I destroyed it. And there were several ways of destroying a little fish. For example, I could stamp it violently out of existence. Or I could break its head off. Gradually I found myself mildly enjoying the act of driving my thumb-nail through the neck or into the back in several places. The body quivered violently; but no sound was made, nor did the eyes express anything. If the root of the tail was squeezed hard between two finger-nails the quivering went on for a long time. Several times I forced the bladder out of the body. But these were isolated brief pleasures. I did nothing else of the sort. I never inten-

tionally tortured an animal, though I did protract the
drowning of a cat by putting it into a copper that had
not been quite filled: as I sat on the lid I sang street
tunes very loudly to hide the sounds within and to keep
up my courage. I hated having to kill a wounded
pigeon. Nevertheless I did it, with a beating heart.
When I killed my first snake—it was in reality a blind-
worm—I stabbed it so frenziedly that I was lucky not
to hurt myself; the frenzy being due partly to suppressed fear, partly to the novelty. As to fish, I very
soon began to pride myself on killing what I caught
instead of throwing it into the hedge behind, as the
factory men usually did, there to die slowly. Pressing
the under jaw of the jack against a stone I bent his long
body up and over until his neck was broken and his
back met his upper jaw. With a smaller fish I inserted
the two first fingers into the gills and forced back the
head until it was loose. I think that care and pride in
doing this neatly and swiftly obliterated any mere
pleasure in pain, though it was, I think, accompanied
by a slight suffocation and beating of the heart and
clouding of the brain.

There was a new game which I never cared about
even on my first and last evening with its inventor.
Known by the name of foxing, it meant following up
lovers in our meadows and lurking behind hedges to
watch them. Our leader had a spy-glass of some kind
and seemed to think it worth his while. He apparently

knew far more about the ways of girls than I had any
chance of knowing or guessing. To me they were
attractive but remote, forbidden, and, even so, inferior
to boys and somehow incompatible with them. The
ordinary Swindon games never had time to lose their
flavour. The speech of the boys, the humming mellow-
ness of it, the rolling r's, the strange idioms and words,
remained a half-conscious delight. One day one boy
said to another named Bacon who was losing his
temper: 'Simmer down, rasher', and I was continually
recalling and tasting the phrase and the accent and the
boy's look. These boys were regarded by my elders as
below me. They were never invited to the house and,
if they called, my grandmother affected a very comical
look of ignorance as to who they were and what they
wanted. Efforts were made to lure me away from them,
up to the schoolmaster's house, where there were a boy
and a girl of about my own age. They were all very
well but tainted in my fancy with the dreary virtue of
elders, so that I could never treat them quite seriously
as playmates. The atmosphere of the house was awful.
The fact that the father was a head master was enough.
It seemed inhuman that a head master should also be a
parent, should concentrate upon two helpless children
for hours together. Man and wife were entirely kind.
But I remember his kind voice. I supposed it was a
pure sham. And then the cake there! was it a regularly
recurring accident or was it choice that brought on to

the table at teatime what had been, or might have become, but was not, a cake? It was *in crumbs* and *steaming hot*. Once inside the mouth doubtless it was much the same as a true cake, but the revolted eyes always condemned the thing. Perhaps nothing in that house could have been right. For example, the pictures of hunted and dying stags by Landseer on the walls of one room were simply among the instruments of torture which we endured there, for about two hours, once or twice a year, for our parents' sake. But fishing was now the chief pleasure; the chief glory to come home with roach even no more than six inches long strung through their gills on a thorn stick with a crook. Whatever fish I brought home I as often as not scaled, gutted and fried myself, unless they were big enough to be worth my grandmother's serious attention. So long as it was not cold only the necessity of being in to a meal brought me away from the canal-side. Roach were good enough. Tench were the height of my ambition. When a fish kept biting gently without being hooked, and especially if the float dipped slantwise, I began to hope for a tench. This hope was better than catching roach. Time after time I threw out my line softly to this one spot until it was too dark to see the float. After a series of such evenings I caught my first tench. It was at the edge of the town, not in fact beyond the first bridge, through which nothing but fields were to be seen, but at a disused landing stage.

The water here was much disturbed by ducks. But the position had this advantage—that I had behind me a street or a back-garden where I could run and hide if the water bailiff or 'cut fellow' appeared. For I still fished without a licence.

And now, when I no longer needed his help at fishing, my uncle packed a box, had a man in to paint his name on it in large white letters, and when it had stood in the passage for a day or two, departed with it for South Africa. Home can have had little charm for him. He was tired of the same job, the nagging, one year after another; better pay and a new life lured him away. With a jaunty laugh deprecating my grandmother's tears and blessings and my aunt's fierce distress, with a sixpenny bit each for my brother and me, off he went, walking beside the man who wheeled his box to the station, a woman in a cap with her hands under her apron watching him from half the doorways in the street, he once or twice waving. It was said that there were some girls who would have been sorry to see him going.

At home now my mother was nursing her sixth and last boy. I had known very well for some time that a baby was to come. I had been anxious for my mother, walking beside her with care lest she should trip at the kerbstone or over a skipping rope. She never said a word about what was approaching, though I dare say she knew that I knew. Then one night I heard a baby's

crying. A little afterwards my father came upstairs, I
think to get some sleep in my room. Finding me awake
he spoke to me; and presently I said something about
'the baby', by which he learnt that I knew. It was the
end of July. In a few days we were at Swindon out of
the way.

After Wiltshire, I believe, a month or two had to
elapse before we condescended again to Wimbledon.
But Merton, at length rediscovered, was in some ways
equal to Wiltshire. It was our very own. Henry, the
pigeon-keeper, had a hand in the rediscovery. He used
to talk about Cannon Hill, about an inn called the
'George', and so on, with more facts that convinced me
this was the land I had slipped into on the day of the
paper-chase. So finding my way back again I began an
exploration of a couple of square miles of country
which had never been completed. I learned to know it
so well that Henry used to put it down to me when he
found a rare nest robbed there. When I say rare, I mean
anything more important than a thrush's or blackbird's
nest. I was flattered when he said to some one: 'Mr.
Bloody Thomas has been there.' This must have been
later. I had only just become a collector.

There were caterpillars on lime and poplar, sluggish
mousy moths in the grass tufts, of our own suburban
commons. To cherish the caterpillars and kill the moths
with the fumes of crushed laurel leaves added something more to the zest of life. But as yet I had hardly

taken my first bird's egg, and for a year or two yet the chief merit of winter was that it provided materials for skating, sliding and snowballing. Not that I was a good skater. I was even quite a bad slider, unable to avoid turning slowly round on a long slide and so ending with my face towards the start. Sledging suited me far better. When the snow was hard and not too deep I speedily laid a few boards on a pair of runners; and in an hour or two after the plan was made I was being pulled or pulling another over the snow to the tune of as many bells as could be had. It was a refinement to shoe the runners with strips of zinc, which, however, wore out in a few days. This was glorious in the sun. But I think perhaps it was somehow better at night in the thick fog. People went about with lanterns and you could get lost, or if not you could pretend to, and stay out late. It was good also to belong to a search party and, perhaps, in spite of a lantern, turn out to be lost yourself or back at your starting place. Clapham Common on those foggy nights was in many ways like desert undiscovered country, yet perfectly harmless.

Even the way home from school held its adventures. There was, for instance, a fight with a schoolfellow who gave me once for all the felicity of holding him round the neck with one arm while I punched his face with the other. More memorable still was the solitary adventure of ringing, not for the first time, the bell of a big house and being run down by the coachman. As he was the son of our greengrocer, an agile middle-aged respectable woman with long curls, I expected him to behave leniently. But he shut me up in a dark outhouse for two hours. I took my revenge. The place contained sacks of oats for the horses, and into these I put a number of steel pens, having first broken them so as to make two sharp stiff points. These, I firmly hoped, would ultimately destroy the horses belonging to my tormentor's master. The hope gave me not only consolation, but a feeling of glory and power and evil as I at last hurried home to tea.

7

ANOTHER NEW SCHOOL

*

When I was about twelve I entered my fourth school as free scholar. The scholarship examination is a lively memory. All the competitors, about twice as many as there were places to be filled, were from my own school. The humming, ha-ing head master hovered about us, yet failed to see that one of us was cheating by very freely using a book. He was not a boy whom I should otherwise have feared, and in my eagerness to win I over-rode the customary objection to telling tales and, with a friend, I gave an account of the matter to the head. Both of us informers were elected to scholarships.

The boys at the new school resembled those at the private school. They were superficially more refined than those I had just parted from; their speech was better; their code of honour more strict; and there was an *esprit de corps* amongst them. The elder boys conducted themselves in a dignified manner, which I admired, apart from their skill at games or at the performances of *The School for Scandal* and other plays at the end of the winter term. Cricket and football were organized. Two or three elevens played a succession of matches with neighbouring schools; and the practice was keen and regular. The very fights were decorous. A ring was made: the enemies fought decently, silently, and, to my judgement, with great skill. The games were linked to the school work by the drill. Our drill-master was a florid pompous old sergeant of impressive erectness and chest measurement. With a great voice and a little cane he compelled us to execute compli-cated marchings and stationary wavings of poles and dumb-bells. When one of the indoor masters joined him as a spectator the sergeant bent towards him, smiling from time to time with ineffably respectful superiority.

The head master was a serious high-minded incap-able martinet with the boys, a meek husband to a stout, possibly imperious wife. This mistress of the head master was continually bursting into the school assemblies or the class-rooms to complain or to ask for an explanation of some breach of manners. A boy wearing the school cap had not doffed it to her in the street. The workmen about the place had complained of the bad language used by the boys. Her daughter had seen boys behaving rudely to one another. An unindustrious noise had been heard coming from a cer-tain master's class-room when he was known to be out.

She shrieked; she panted; she introduced tears into her voice; she appealed to us as Englishmen, sons of gentlemen, scholars of 'our school'. The head master or master bowed his head, gravely endeavouring to translate her tirade in a style at once moderate and pleasing to her; the boys assumed the frightful solemnity of those who dread to laugh. I remember her once present at an election of officers for the Second Eleven football club. A friend and I were rivals for one office, and after politely voting for one another, we were announced equal. The dear lady now raised her voice to give the casting vote to a young master who, she was certain, would not go wrong. I expect I need not say that I was not elected.

The head master had the fiercely sad attitude towards idleness and vice. He would have had us love virtue, yet could not make us love him. Praise of the classics in spite of their commercial uselessness was often on his lips, among boys who seldom got above hate of Caesar and Virgil. Though we all believed that he was a model of virtue he inspired us always with either fear or amusement. Many were the boys he caned in his study, which was near enough to give a certain class-room an envied distinction as an auditorium. He had a rapid, nasal, slightly Irving-ish speech, which was extraordinarily funny when he was trying to show the stages by which the Latin form of a word had passed into the French; funniest of all when he was mingling ordinary words (about leading the horse to the water but not being able to make him drink) with hums and ha's at the annual prize-giving. He laughed with discomfort. His bearing was phenomenally erect, his square face bald except for a moustache that did not hide his thin lips.

The under-masters came and went, except one. He was a small clean-shaven, bluish-white-faced man, demurely grave in expression, whose breath had a sort of stale dryness that was not quite malodorous. He earned respect and obedience without fear from nearly all his class, by being a just, quiet, serious man, even of speech and kindly. Boys could not put him out or take him off his guard. His small exquisite legible hand-writing must have been formed by annotating text-books with a constant desire not to disgrace the printed page, and by admiration for Greek script. With slow wrinkling his stiff face relaxed now and then into a feminine tender smile. After a time I found myself frequently addressing him as 'Father', so naturally did he touch the gentle docile side of me. The one time I ever cried in school was when he blamed me with a severity that seemed to hurt him. He awarded me prizes for essays on the Sicilian Expedition and on Imperial Federation, which I had taken pains with and was proud of. I had a grandiloquent turn. But the master had no insight or no time to exercise it. He had only a momentary power over me, not an influence. Neither a goal nor a love of work could he give me. When I saw him approaching with quick short steps and 'downcast eyes demure' in his soft hat and cape, I laughed inwardly.

Through him I became accustomed to the first book of the *Aeneid*, to Shakespeare's *Richard II* and *Henry IV* and *V*. To me they remained prose rendered obscure and tedious, in the one case by foreign language, and in the other by archaisms, inversions and other unfamiliar and as yet impotent forms. Often they were worse than obscure. The passages that stuck fast in the ruts which they wore in our brains were bandied about for their comicality. 'All became silent', 'The strawberry grows beneath the nettle', 'By thinking on the frosty Caucasus', 'Tennis balls, my liege', and other phrases had to be uttered with a grin and received with a grin. Possibly the master cared nothing for poetry: or he may have despaired of communicating to us anything but a dead knowledge of words. If I remember rightly, the music of Virgil's hexameters never at that time fell on my ears, whether or not I was capable of knowing it for music. The snake attacking Laocoon and his children was the one vivid thing contributed by those months. Shakespeare meant rather more. He helped me to a faint apprehension of certain human heights and depths, as in Henry V's ardour and Richard II's dejection; the energy in 'Cry Havoc and let slip the dogs of war' wakened in me the elements of acting and adventure. Blank verse I regarded as a form of prose, licen-

tious in construction and divided wantonly into lines as
if it were poetry.

My father probably went over the plays with me
when I was doing my home-work, but his taste was for
directly elevating philanthropic and progressive literature. Or was it only with a view to inspiring a love of
virtue that he read 'Abou Ben Adhem' and how he
'loved his fellow men'? I learnt to recite it myself with
a lofty histrionic thrill. Its real effect was equal to that of
the gilt 'Faith', 'Hope' and 'Charity' in the Unitarian
Chapel. These words and Shakespeare's plays and
Leigh Hunt's poem did help me to feel that there was
something for men besides eating and drinking and
getting a living or having it got for you.

But at this period 'good', so far as it concerned the
world and not me personally, meant chiefly if not
solely Liberalism. Through my father's enthusiastic
political talk I learnt that Mr. Gladstone was a glorious,
great and good man, greater than Robert Abel. Any
Liberal candidate who ventured upon our constituency
was, though in a lesser degree, glorious, great and good.
I used to distribute handbills of political meetings in the
cause, sang a Liberal parody of the 'Men of Harlech', and
followed the elections as keenly as I did cricket scores.
Conservatives I thought were an inferior race, partly
because they were wicked, partly because they were
stupid. There ought never to be any Conservatives; and
as time went on they would become fewer and fewer

and at last all would be well. Until then Liberals had to fight to rescue the downtrodden in Ireland, in London slums and elsewhere; and the Conservatives, indifferent to pain and suffering, ambitious to drink beer with no interruptions except from war, had to be attacked. I used to go with my father to the Washington Music-hall on Sunday evenings and hear John Burns, Keir Hardie, and the Socialists. Once there I saw Michael Davitt standing by an iron pillar, dark, straight, and austere with his armless sleeve dangling. I think I knew that he had then just come out of prison, and this pro-bably helped him to a place in my mind with the Path-finder and Milton's Satan. John Burns was another glorious, great and good man. I honestly admired his look and voice and was proud to shake hands with him and also to have my middle stump bowled clean out of the ground by him once on Clapham Common. On the contrary, what a ridiculous creature was our Con-servative member on his horse, just a rich gentleman who had once been an athlete but could not make a speech as my father could; and his coachman was fre-quently drunk or half-drunk or not sober or had been drinking or looked like it.

Poetry was nothing to me compared with Home Rule. Or rather Home Rule took the place of Poetry, and was really an equivalent in so far as it lifted me to vaguely magnificent ideas of good and evil. It was on the same level as the signing of Magna Charta, the

Dissolution of the Monasteries, the beheading of Charles I and dethronement of James II, which to me were splendid Liberal events of the past. Some kind of sense of this splendour gave part of the thrill to my voice when I recited before an adult audience at the chapel:

> Ring out the old, ring in the new.
> Ring out the false, ring in the true.
> The year is dying, let him die.

I was sufficiently stirred by the Home Rule election to declare myself Liberal at school in a form which I think was three-quarters Conservative.

My enthusiasm pleased my father. It must have atoned for my peculiarities and for my bad language among my schoolfellows. This vice was reported to my mother by Henry, who had teased and tormented me one day on the Common and drawn from my lips every filthy word I could muster. I denied the fact passionately and when I saw that my mother did not believe me I gave way and passionately repented. Home life was very largely grumbling, deceiving and repenting, driving my father to anger or sorrow and then being miserable consequently. I stayed out late, or I was unwilling to go to chapel, or I told lies, or I talked nonsense at the Sunday dinner-table. It was almost the only meal as a rule which the whole family had together. There was plenty to eat of the best things known to my mother, such as boiled mutton and caper-sauce, with carrots and turnips, followed by apple tart and custard. Nor did my father despise these things. But he wanted us to talk about the sermon. For I think very often he himself only went to the evening service. We had hated hearing the sermon and now had to improvise an essay on it. It was so loathsome that I could never seriously attempt the task, even to avert the Sunday dinner anger, which became almost a regular thing. Either I showed my loathing too openly or I caught one of my brothers' eyes and one or another and then both tittered. My father reprimanded us by calling us 'donkeys'. I made an effort, but his anger and my shame only made me duller than ever. Probably I broke down in the middle of a sentence with, 'Oh, I don't know.' Then came a lecture from my father, or just a few words of abuse, and then all remained silent for a time. Some days my father, relenting, would choose what he thought a lighter pleasanter subject; everyone would be absurdly eager to keep it going, and my father absurdly pleased with trifles. On other days one of my smaller brothers would let out a titter; another did the same; I felt and looked enormously sad, perhaps too sad. Then one would be sent out of the room, to be followed presently at my mother's request by his plateful of dinner.

We had very few visitors, none to turn us inside out. Once a lady and a daughter, remote cousins or friends of friends, came, and the girl left me with a yearning heart for some days and a curiosity for years like my curiosity about the lost childish books. Christmas was eagerly waited for, but the day itself meant chiefly watching for the postman, disappointment, chapel, a heavy dinner and crackers, some squabbling comparison of our presents, tea ... supper ... I think I had always an eager haste to unveil the mystery, always a fluttering look of wonder which always sank dead like an extinguished torch into disgust with the imperfect thing. If it had only been something better or different. It mattered not how many or good were my presents: they fell below an indefinite imagined standard. If they were simply below last year's it was worse. The disappointment is vivid yet of the Christmas day when the postman arrived at last, hours late, and brought me only a long narrow box of crackers. We children gave no presents to one another or to our parents: we were content to send out a few picture cards paid for by our parents, to people who would send us cards. The faculty for ceremony and festival was not in any of us.

Our boy friends seldom came to the house. Nor were we very anxious that they should, knowing that we should be constrained by the presence of father or mother. For we had one way at home, another abroad. But at the new school I made several friends. There were the boys I sat next to in class, and the other members of the football team. One of these named George lived a hundred yards away from us. Every morning he came whistling past the house for me to join him on the way to school, and he was fairly often in the house. He had a Grecian nose which he had learnt to be proud of, and carried himself carefully, partly because he valued his appearance, partly because a London Scottish volunteer of superb appearance was courting his sister. This Scot was his hero: he never tired of telling me the man's measurements and how you could strike him as hard as you liked on the chest. Politeness to women, seemliness of speech and behaviour, were among his daily ideals. Being more skilful than I and keen to excel, he took a patronizing but genuine interest in my football play, and blamed my slackness. In politics he was a thoroughgoing Conservative. Our intercourse was long, regular, always superficial. He was cold and hard and never came out into the country with me or kept pets. I think we always talked about games and school affairs. At least I know that though we continued to be close neighbours I hardly ever even spoke to him six months after I had left the school, and a few years later was miserably uncomfortable at meeting him and having unavoidably to stop and exchange words.

I was far more intimate with a boy of something like my own nature. As a girl he would have been beautiful, with his plump dimpled cheeks, delicate rosy skin, Cupid lips, perfect features, fine light brown hair, soft grey eyes, smiling timorous expression, head slightly bent. But he had thin legs; he was easily frightened; he played games slackly and awkwardly. We sat together at school. He was always drawing, chiefly faces in profile. I remember his sleek tender way of touching the paper. Pointing out the faults, he drew me. I admired his face as I did my mother's, and envied them both, and became intensely conscious of my appearance. I used to look at myself in a glass, with eyes for the faults, the coarse nose, the weak chin, the underlip too much behind the upper, the ear without a lobe; always retaining a sort of belief that the faults were not the whole. This boy and I, presuming on our position at or near the top of the class, laughed endlessly in class during lessons, which caused us often to be reprimanded or separated. He lived two miles from us and was never at the house.

I remember other boys with whom my whole intercourse seems to have been exchanging endless jokes, playing football together, and in summer eating ices together bought at the Italian stall outside the school. One boy I remember through one incident only. We were being examined in the *De Bello Gallico*, and he was shamelessly using his copy of the text. I told him to shut it up and when he refused I loaded my pen and discharged the ink over his shoulder on to the book. Then, because his sister was engaged to the master, he had the effrontery to go and complain, thus compelling me to give him away. Another boy I can still see playing back with me in the football field. He was a sturdy energetic boy with a Roman nose in a freckled red laughing face. Probably he was a year or two older than I, and knew boys and young men older than himself, and the lore he had learned from them used to impress me. One story he told was of a Spanish girl who bit her lover's chest, one of a man being set upon among the Welsh hills by factory girls and shamefully handled. Others were of the same class. These things he spoke of, as it appeared to me, without indecency. I thought him chivalrous and frank and manly. In fact I had a great respect for him, and after I had left the school I used to wish we could meet again. Several older boys with physical prowess and masterful confident bearing won my admiration.

Other boys I see at some one cardinal moment. One was the idiot of the school, a pale fat round-featured being who talked through his nose and could be persuaded to sit upon a round stone like a hen upon an egg till he was called off. Another, a short square-shouldered boy, lean, pale and square-jawed, with almost waxen hair, screamed like a wild beast on having a window shut hard on his fingers. A third was a leering dark fattish boy whose time went to girls instead of games. His nickname among his admirers and affected despisers was Sally. According to rumour, founded chiefly on his own boastful shameless narratives, his conquests were many and complete. And for a time he stirred me to imitate him. I singled out the most notorious of his alleged paramours, a pale slender black-haired girl several years older than myself, with small features and round dark eyes and a light name that seemed perfectly appropriate, and for some days or weeks pursued her. By day I walked after her at a distance without ever catching her up; I managed to meet her face to face without daring to speak. By night I would say as much as good evening and silently walk alongside her and perhaps her tittering younger sister. My desire was to be with her, to be intimate with her in some unknown degree. In truth, I think I wished to be loved by her. I should have liked to kiss her. I ceased to believe what I had heard Sally tell about her. For many nights I hung outside her house watching the blinds for her shadow and the door for herself, slipping away to a distance if she appeared and only showing myself reluctantly. On this starvation diet of neither encouragement nor rude words my affection died utterly away. The girl herself was but a chance object, or chosen because I had begun by imagining she would meet me half-way. Even while I was after her I was thinking also of another girl, a friend of hers, actually the Mabel of my childhood. Perhaps she had forgotten me; she certainly allowed no rights to the old attachment. Though she smiled to me once from between two others, she passed on. The dark girl speaking of her had said something which made me conceive a faint hope, but we were never to be friends again, and since then I seem never to have seen her. There was a very faintly mysterious sentiment in my thought of her which made me shy of being friendly, as I had a chance of becoming on the football field, with one of her brothers. For a year afterwards I paid little attention to girls. Sally became a distant acquaintance.

The boys who came up with me from the old school remained friendly. The most friendly of all left for a Yorkshire town before the first year was out. Another used to walk with me occasionally in the bird-nesting season. Being from Battersea he could regale me with slang terms of abuse, such as 'Blinking potherb'. His father, a Liberal, had taught him a poor opinion of the ancients. The Greeks in his opinion must have been poor runners to have dropped dead in their races. I, however, respected the Greeks, believing where I could not prove.

I had not many friends among the cleverer foot-ballers and cricketers. I think I still preferred chases and fighting games such as I played years before. There were now more violent affrays. The fighters were armed with singlesticks but no masks, and they gave and took good blows before their forts among the gorse bushes were lost and gained. Thus in one of them I and another boy had a long serious duel, until I had my upper lip split and a front tooth or, as I thought at the time, all my teeth, knocked out, thus suffering a slight disfigurement which added to the sorrows of the mirror. My one satisfaction after the incident was the doctor's compliment when I bore the stitching up without noise. Very few of my tears and glooms at that age were caused by physical pain, unless it was toothache. When I lost my teeth at the dentist's it was with ostentatious fortitude, encouraged by my father's praises. Both at football and cricket I was good only on rare occasions. There were days when I could shoot a goal from corner and do almost anything I wanted to. There was one day at least when bowling a boy out with my first ball after school gave me a happy irresistible feeling, so that with dangerously fast balls I took several wickets running. And somehow, I suppose through quiet exercise of my will to prevail, I was usually after a time elected to some office in the second eleven. As vice-captain I went up to London with another boy to buy a set of goal-posts in Cheapside. As I said before, my pride in conducting the expedition is all I can remember of what I know was an adventure.

I was not better than anyone else at running, jumping, or swimming. In the sports I entered only for the walking and the swimming race. As I never learnt to dive I had to jump in, and arrived last in the swimming race. But I fancied myself at walking; and John and George had spread reports about my performances and I started at scratch with a dozen boys in front of me. All of them were behind in a quarter of a mile or so, except one, and him I was just passing. His five yards, start had all along seemed to me unfair. However, he was done with; so was the boy who notoriously ran. But their footsteps and their panting sounded close behind, I had enjoyed catching up and walking through the others. Still more I hated being pursued. Soon after George began to run beside me, and when I was within a hundred yards of the tape, I began to believe that the running boy was gaining on me. I could not stand it. Turning off the track I threw myself down on the grass on the pretext that I had a stitch. A master came up and looked at me, saying they had expected me to win. I was wretched. The only worse thing possible was to have been beaten. But nobody else thought so. My father blamed me for cowardice, and for years after used to say to me at intervals on various occasions: 'Ah well, it's no use, I suppose. It's just that mile race over again.' 'Half-mile,' said I: it was the only answer. Secretly I was as well pleased with the tragic singularity as I could have been with victory. Moreover, I always firmly believed that no boy could beat me in fair walking without a crowd.

8

BUTTERFLIES, MOTHS AND PIGEONS

*

I was soon all but indifferent to games. When I entered the school I was an entomologist who had specimens of the yellow underwing and the magpie and the common white butterfly. It may have been a year later that I met a boy who made me ashamed of this ignorance, and helped to set me on another path out of doors. Hearing that he had a collection of moths and butterflies and was selling his duplicates and charging one penny for a swallow-tail, I ordered one. I expected the majestic swallow-tail butterfly. What came was the almost untailed mediocre moth. I handed over the penny without a murmur, for fear of betraying my ignorance. I do not know how we became intimate in spite of this. John was a handsome fair boy, delicate complexioned, dimpled at cheek and chin, of regular large features, strong but not a cricketer or footballer, and for that reason an object of some slight degree of contempt from me and far more from George. George, in fact, mistaking for girlishness

John's delicate skin and better manners, warned me against him. For a time I hesitated between the two. Or it is more truthful to say that I receded slowly from George to John? Henceforward I merely had George for company to school: with John I spent many evenings and most of my half-holidays. I was more at his house than he at ours. His was larger and we were perfectly free there: also I had some shame of our slightly inferior social position or what I believed to be such, for his speech seemed to me more refined, his manner was freer and more generous than mine, his elder brother was at a great public school, and wore a silk hat on Sundays, he had more money to spend, several of his relatives lived in great big houses. Indoors and here and there in Surrey I rapidly learnt the names and seasons of most common moths and butterflies. I learnt to catch and kill and display them in the orthodox manner. To acquire all the tools of the trade I begged from my father and mother and bartered with everyone. The little round pill boxes made of thin wooden chips, of three or four different sizes one within the other, delighted me as a novelty: so did the neat corklined boxes that closed so softly and tightly . . . and everything else in turn. I was in a terrible hurry to be abreast with John. To spend and to get were the things. An ancient glass case of moths and decoratively mingled butterflies in a second-hand shop seemed the most desirable thing in the world—till I had paid for it and opened it and saw that all the specimens were only so much coloured dust, and faded at that. What I could not catch at once I must buy from John or from a wonderful 'naturalist' at a shop. At intervals too I made my own necessaries, fitting a lining of cork into boxes and covering it with white paper, and so on, too hastily to do it well, yet learning or educating some degree of lightness and skilfulness with the fingers.

In the summer evenings we searched gardens and shrubberies for moths and caterpillars. On Wednesday and Saturday afternoons now we used to go to Wimbledon Common. Or if we had a whole holiday we took a train to Barnes station and walked through Richmond Park over Ham Common to One Tree or Teddington lock, to fish in the Thames. For I was very soon far from being a stern-spirited collector out of doors. I might go out with nothing in view except butterflies, but the moving to and fro among quiet places in the warm weather was the substantial part of the pleasure. Fishing after a time was more to my taste. The infinite possibilities of a river containing pike, barbel and trout fascinated me; I liked the silence; failure never bored me, but on the contrary the last minutes of fading light were intensely exciting. I think I was usually the most impatient of conversation or other interruption, the last to give way under steady lack of incident. When we did give way we used to try casting our lines to the farthest possible distance, or we

kept pretending to have bites and struck ferociously so
that our lines flew up high into the air, or we used
ridiculous baits, until at last our tackles became entangled, or one lost his temper, sulkily packed up and
went off alone, to wait, however, at no long distance.
We had no great success in the Thames. The most
alluring thing that ever happened to me there was
hooking a fish of inestimable size which got away with
my hook in its mouth. But the walk there and back
was never tiring. On the outward journey I think
expectation would have carried me through nothing
but streets: the long turf stretches of Richmond Park
broken by ponds and copses and islanded by great
single trees and clusters were pure additional delight as
we talked of the chances of sport or weather or whistled
the current popular songs. The little rustic cottages at
Ham Common beyond, and the very old man sitting
outside one of them were always a welcome sight. The
broad green-edged river and the swans were enough to
fill my eyes for six or seven hours on end, with an
interval for bread, cheese, apples and ginger beer. The
men towing pleasure boats and brushing down the
riverside grass and bushes with their ropes were the
only nuisance. Going home we filled our creels and
pockets, in the season, with horse chestnuts from way-
side trees. As I remember having half a dozen different
companions on these expeditions I believe that others
found it more dull.

John and I talked endlessly about our sport and about the implements, of which we got, with every obtainable penny, far more than it was necessary or even possible to use, and about the extraordinary catches recorded in the fishing books and newspapers. Politics we tried not to touch because John was a staunch Conservative. He was, however, less firm as a churchman and I experienced some of my first (and last) pride of argument in impugning the immortality and even the existence of the soul. At this moment I know the place where I proved it impossible that man should have a soul unless the animals had one also, or rather that if he had one he had acquired it on the upward course of evolution. Having read Darwin's *Descent of Man* I was sure that men were but animals advanced by exceptional stages from a common level with other animals. At what moment then, said I to John, had the soul entered man? We were walking with great strides along Northcote Road in the gaslight, carrying bags of seed for our pigeons. I thought myself a discoverer and was much elated at being unanswerable except out of the Bible, a work of men, in some ways ignorant men. Yet as I was not interested in the soul except out of dislike for religious people who talked about it, I did not inquire further. This intellectual level was not one which we frequented. Personal talk was, of course, our staple, discussing the abilities and pretensions of other boys, laughing over such follies as that of the boy who assured us that he knew 'a nest of Red Admiral butter-flies' at Wimbledon—this picturesque technical slip we continually brought up for ridicule. We were not inventive boys. At most perhaps for the sake of vivid-ness or glory we would relate an experience we had heard of and claim it for our own. I remember pre-tending to have seen a naked girl in a copse near Swindon. Of my grandmother's cottage I used to speak as if it were in the same rank as the houses of John's uncles and aunts. I was guilty of no single great untruth or calculated misrepresentation, but I spoke of the ivy on the cottage walls with a desire that it should be understood to be a considerable mass and expanse, and of leaning out of my bedroom window to reach a nest as if there were a respectable number of other windows, instead of only three altogether. My comparatively wealthy distant relations were not omitted from the picture which I was creating. If my cousins at the Herefordshire vicarage had a donkey or a pony to ride, I took the liberty of referring to their horses and stables. And, of course, when I heard that my uncle had taken part in the fighting against Lobengula and the Mata-bele, I magnified the splendour which I really con-ceived: I had always been careful to speak of him as an engineer not as a fitter. It was easy for me to slip into a course of lying. Thus I once suffered from constipation and my mother knew of it; but for a day or two after-wards I asserted, when asked, that I was still suffering.

I did not, however, dream of throwing up the companions whom I did not want to introduce John to. For example, I always went out if possible to Henry's whistle. Other boys who had met me with him had referred scornfully to Henry. Jonathan had asked me, 'Who was that low-bred fellow you were with?' But then Jonathan had very subtle rules of gentility. Once he met me while I was at my third school and he also had left the school we had attended together, and on hearing where I now went he remarked, 'Oh, that is quite a cad's school.' I liked to feel the equals of these squeamish boys without looking down except in temporarily affected contempt on their inferiors. So I used to enjoy going about with Henry to look at the pigeon shops in Wandsworth, Battersea and Clapham, occasionally to visit the back-garden lofts of working men in the same neighbourhoods. He had me in tow and I think I remained for the most part silent in the background unless I had a bird to buy. These long rambles among crowds of working people under the gaslight, in all sorts of weathers, were a great pleasure and were interrupted by a greater one when we stood and looked at pigeons in an atmosphere of shag smoke, grain and birds. At one time I paid a good many visits to the lofts of a tradesman in our neighbourhood, a tall gross pale-faced dark man with a truculent geniality. He was said to ill-treat the small wife who did most of the shop work and to be going under an assumed name for some bad reason. John would never have endured him: if he had to deal with men below him he preferred game-keepers and such like who had to be tipped and knew their place. But the man kept scores of long-distance homing pigeons. Their high circlings visible from our back garden, and their rushing lower flight between the chimney-pots, were sublime to me. It was a great day therefore when I went round to him to get the pair of young black chequers which I had been awaiting for many days. I was to have them, so I understood, for two-and-six the pair. When I already had them in my hands I learnt that they were two-and-six each. This was beyond my means, nor did I want to have one of them at such a price. So he took them back into his hands at the door. Then while I was still lingering he put the head of one bird in his mouth, as I imagined in fun, or to slip a grain into its beak. His teeth closed on the slender neck tighter and tighter, the wings flapped and quivered, and when he opened his jaws the bird was dead. I was speechless, on the edge of tears. He looked down at me with a half-pitying grin, remarking that I was 'still soft-hearted'. My tenderness turned to hatred for the man, yet I could not speak. I dared not show my feeling. With only a meek resentfulness I even accepted his gift of the surviving bird. It became the prize of my pigeon house, always distinguished as 'the young homer'. The man I never did more than nod to again.

It was Henry, too, who introduced me to much better company, a family with half a dozen boys who let him keep his main store of pigeons in their back garden. An unlocked side door admitted the most distant connections of the Joneses or of their friends to the back garden. It was practically never without some of the boys and their friends or hangers-on, their dogs, their pigeons or Henry's. The house itself was scarcely more sacred. The boys' rooms, and dark library lined with books and littered with magazines and newspapers, were freely invaded. The elder boys, who went neither to school nor to work, were always indoors or in the garden when they were not training for athletic sports. The younger boys were licensed truants, getting to bed or to breakfast at all hours. The father, an unemployed mysterious professional man with a long coat and a cigar, looked on dubiously cheerful, reigning rather than ruling, but treated with respectful familiarity. Mrs. Jones, sadly tolerant, was busy chiefly indoors. The chief attraction for me was the family collection of birds' eggs from the moorland and seashore of Wales. The curlew, the henharrier, the buzzard, belonged to a past which to me was romantic. For the present they had to be contented with the fields and copses of Merton for a hunting ground. I was free to go in and out of the house and garden, a very humble follower and admirer of their free idle ways. One of them taught me to ride a bicycle. Sometimes one joined me in a walk to Merton. For a wet or an unoccupied afternoon I had the garden and the roomy pigeon house, only a few minutes' walk from home, as an easy resource. But John never went there with me, nor did any of my other school friends. I was not intimate with any of the boys. In fact John was my one constant friend. We had become essential to one another. We quarrelled and differed, of course, but one quarrel only lasted in my memory and that because John sent me a note next morning at school, saying: 'I was a cad. Will you make it up?' I kept the paper for years afterwards.

I did not make friends easily, perhaps because I was exacting. I wanted someone who would be ever ready for an afternoon and evening of walking or talking, and I think I wanted to have the upper hand and to have it easily. With me, to think of a walk to Merton or a tour among the shops in Battersea meant to do it immediately, and I could usually get John to accompany me. So we were separated hardly at all except in the holidays.

I remember the summer holiday when I was fourteen. My two next brothers and I spent two or three weeks with four boys and a girl whom my mother's sister was looking after during their parents' absence in India. We took the train journey alone, enjoying most the change at Templecombe and the wait which we spent in hunting butterflies near the station. It was at

Burnham in Somerset that we stayed. The eldest boy was entering Sandhurst, the next two were at the public school which he had just left. They were comparatively wealthy people and their ways were different from ours or even John's family. My aunt was careful to instruct us in the use of fish knives. The boys' slang delighted and impressed me. But I made no friends among them. My next brother, a franker, more athletic boy, was the favourite, and was often mildly in league with them against me. The eldest boy despised me. He made me conscious of being shy, timid and sneaking; and, if I was naturally that, I must have been far more so among people whom I could not be free with, partly at least because I was so anxious not to show my more awkward manners and all that they betokened. Nevertheless I had many pleasures there. I began to learn to swim in the sea. I chased the clouded yellow butterflies which I now saw for the first time, among the sandhills. I fished with the others out in the mud flats at a river mouth, above all in a big pond inland, a long pond, with a margin downtrodden by bathers and others at one end, but a steeper bushy bank overshadowed by trees in places at the other. Here I caught eels and perch, and one day pulled to the very edge, and then lost, the biggest perch I had ever seen. After this excitement I should have been content to spend all my days beside this pond. But the other boys drew me with them half unwillingly on other expeditions, inland, or along the

shore, or in boats. When we quitted the pond at evening we had sport out of a big deserted house by throwing stones at the surviving window-panes.

My next brother stayed on a week or so after I left
these people for Swindon. There I was delighted to find
the clouded yellow butterflies as plentiful as by the sea.
I gave more time to butterflies in those weeks because
I had now made friends with a Swindon boy who was
very little of a fisherman. We chased the butterflies; we
jumped the narrow brooks; we trespassed hither and
thither with a St. Bernard puppy who drew after us all
the cattle in the fields and provoked the farmer; we sat
talking in the crown of a pollard willow. Fred was
something of an athlete and we ran and jumped in
friendly rivalry in the fields. I could beat him only at
walking. I never met the boy of anything like my own
age whom I could not beat at walking. So I stamped
the dust furiously from one milestone to another
towards Wootton Bassett in the hope of some day
covering the mile in less than seven minutes. Also as I
now had an old bicycle with me, we raced on bicycles.
The great feats of the big boys at his school were always
on my companion's lips. But in spite of all this, I made
a poor show when next I had a chance of using my fists.
Two of Fred's schoolfellows were now pursuing the
dark bushy-haired girl whom I used to walk about
with. In fact, I am not sure that pursuit was necessary.
However it was, I jeered at her, and one of them was

keen for a quarrel. One day as I stood fishing alone, with Fred somewhere in the field behind, hidden by the canal-side hedge, this boy came up beside me. He took off his coat, rolled up his sleeves, put himself in attitudes of offence and defence, clenched his fist close to my face, taunted me, did everything but strike me. He was a smaller boy than I, active, stout and ruddy, and at that time as fiery as I was cold. I do not think I was afraid of him, but I certainly was not ready to fight. I wanted to fish; I was in the wrong; Fred in the background, at least as much his friend as mine, added to my discomfort. During the whole scene I do not think I took my eyes off my float or ceased to hold out my rod horizontally. In the end my enemy left me to enjoy my shame. Fred came up from behind the hedge, and I made my explanations. The fact is that, not having been prepared for a quarrel, I could not get free enough from thought about the whole affair and the circumstances of the moment to fight. Thenceforward I never fought, never once pitted my strength, skill and courage seriously against an opponent. I boxed very little, I toyed with singlesticks and foils, only once or twice did I wrestle with John until I fell on him or under him.

9

A LASTING ACQUAINTANCE: RICHARD JEFFERIES

★

When Fred was not free I had some very different company. One acquaintance I had made at Swindon was a stout coarse lad of fifteen or sixteen who had been in prison and had plenty of spare time. His name also was Fred. He would do almost anything to please me, from fishing with me all day, to killing a neighbour's cat for me to skin. Moreover, he always behaved to me with the utmost decency, faith and honesty. I only surmised that he was not a saint. The report that he had been in prison was against him; and there was another thing. Sometimes a big half-witted tousled girl and a young sister used to pass us on the canal-side, and one day I and Fred, who knew them, rambled about with them in the gorse, I looking for late linnets' nests, Fred frequently importuning the elder girl but with no success.

But a more entertaining and lasting acquaintance was an old man whom I called Dad, in the Wiltshire style, almost from the first day. I remember him first as a stiff straight man, broad-shouldered and bushy bearded, holding his rod out and watching his float very intently. Suddenly up went the rod and a little roach flew high over his head into the hedge behind. 'Daddy bin and caught one!' shouted the boy with me. We laughed and the old man laughed too. As every day he fished not far from me and Fred or whoever was my companion, we began to chat. We used to sit and eat our dinner together. He being toothless had to chew prodigiously, his nose and his beard almost meeting at each bite, to get through his brown bread and watercress. The bread he brought with him, the watercress he gathered from the brooks. His eating grimace amused me, his gravity, the simplicity of the meal, and his thanks to God for it impressed me. At that time he lived with his wife under the roof of a son who was in the factory. The rod and half a loaf helped him to fill up his time with obvious satisfaction, and what he caught he kept, however small. Very soon I sought him out and got him to walk with me when I was tired of fishing. I shared my doughy cake with him, or if we had a meal at a village shop I paid for the tea and bread and butter and egg and lardy cake. He knew the names of most birds and could imitate their cries: his imitations of the jackdaw calling his name, and of the young rook crying and swallowing a worm at the same time, were wonderful. The flowers, too, he knew, both the common pretty flowers and those whose virtues he had read of in Culpeper's

Herbal. With dried and powdered dock root and with extracts of leaves, flowers or bark, he composed dark medicinal-looking draughts. His ointment made of lard scented with elder flower was delicious. Then he had a way with country people. He spoke to everyone. All the old men to him were 'Dad' and the old women 'Granny' and the younger men 'young man'. He would stop by a stonebreaker to say, 'How many ups and downs o' that to a pound of mutton, young man?' The pity was that he was too poor to get friendly with keepers. If we were caught trespassing he was no good. Out we had to go, the old man muttering, 'We beant poaching', and the keeper retorting, 'Looks very much like it wi' they thick sticks.' He was a much better hand with the labourers and especially the women with whom he had an ineffably grave knowing manner: many times they gave us tea and an egg which the fowl had just laid in the cupboard; and the son would tell us perhaps where there was a magpie's nest. The only man he seemed to feel himself above was the yellow half-bred gypsy youth, the 'diddikai', who used to slouch by us sometimes. Dad had done some poaching in his younger days. Odd-job man under a wood-ward, militiaman, and latterly outdoor assistant to grocers, he had not had time to become very respectable. So he was the first man old enough to be my grandfather with whom I was on thoroughly good easy terms. He did not hide anything or invent a moral code for my benefit. He would say of the round-shouldered sour man living alone in the sham-Gothic house with the orchard, 'It's the women has put old Dicky's back up', and leave me to make what I could of it. Or he shook his head solemnly as he saw the once decent middle-aged gaffer from the works going up the canal-side with an obvious loose woman and later on emerging from the ash copse. It merely amused me. Sex was alluring and amusing, whenever it was revealed, because the whole grown-up world for the benefit of the young was endeavouring to keep up the appearance of doing without sex. Thus Dad's extraordinary free-dom was equally amusing and alluring. At first I sup-posed him to be a wicked old man until I came to believe that all men were radically like him but most of them inferior in honesty. He was not in the least un-seemly or obtrusive, but grave and roused very rarely to his Shakespearian laughter and the words, 'Well, well, what a thing it is!' Nor did he ever use foul language. What is more, he spoke what he thought, whether his sons, or anyone else such as myself, were there, which was very new to me. I had always had an idea that either parents were not of the same weak flesh as children or that they were religiously obliged to con-ceal the same: John who had seen his father's nakedness had committed a sort of sin. These three sons of Dad's treated him as an equal, but in misfortune. I got to know them also. The middle one with whom he lived used to fish in the evenings in a more business-like way. He could not, however, resist a shot with a catapult at any rat swimming across at a convenient distance. Once he drove a large bullet clean through a rat, and of course I had to have a catapult of the same strength. The eldest son was a bald old Indian soldier often out of a job. The youngest was a rambling character. I sometimes saw him as brown as a berry from harvesting, his large blue eyes glittering, his fair hair bleached like hay. As they were all friendly I had rather, if I had to be indoors, be with them than with my grandmother.

John meantime had covered himself with glory by catching a jack of eight pounds somewhere in Kent. Nevertheless we did not break our custom of not fishing in autumn or winter. Whenever I was not bound to play in a football match I spent my half-holidays with John, walking, to Merton or Wimbledon, or taking the train to South Croydon and exploring southwards and eastwards. We had no single definite object now that no eggs were to be found. Talking, and looking at the earth and the sky, we just walked about until it was dark. Students we were not: nothing was pursued to the uttermost. We merely became accustomed to the general life of the common birds and animals, and to the appearances of trees and clouds and everything upon the surface that showed itself to the naked eye. Some rare thrush or robin we might stop to listen to; or we might watch a wren threading a bush or a tit on a birch-spray, or look at a mossy greenfinch's nest or climb up with some sort of unfounded hope to a big nest which had escaped us in spring; but for the most part we were moving and usually fast. When it froze we were content with what we saw as we stalked up and down the rough ice of Beverley Brook. Only at night did we join the throng of skaters pure and simple. If the weather was bad and we were not together and no school work had to be done, I read books of travel, sport and natural history. I remember those of Waterton, Thomas Edward, Buckland, Wallace, Charles Kingsley, but above all Richard Jefferies. If I say little of Jefferies it is because not a year passed thereafter without many copious draughts of him and I cannot pretend to distinguish amongst them. But very soon afterwards I was writing out in each one of his books and elsewhere—as in a cousin's album—when I had the opportunity, those last words of *The Amateur Poacher*: 'Let us get out of these indoor narrow modern days, whose twelve hours somehow have become shortened, into the sunlight and the pure wind. A something that the ancients thought divine can be found and felt there still.' They were a gospel, an incantation. What I liked in the books was the free open-air life, the spice of illegality and daring, roguish characters—the opportunities so far exceeding my own, the gun, the great pond, the country home, the apparently endless leisure —the glorious moments that one could always recapture by opening the *Poacher*—and the tinge of sadness here and there as in the picture of the old moucher perishing in his sleep by the lime kiln, and the heron flying over in the morning indifferent. Obviously Jefferies had lived a very different boyhood from ours, yet one which we longed for and supposed ourselves fit for. He had never had to wear his best clothes for twelve or fourteen hours on Sunday. Enforced attendances at church and Sunday school could not have been known to him. The crowd parading in their Sunday-best clothes along the walks of the Commons was impossible in that southern county.

I had begun to write accounts of my walks in an approach as near as possible to the style of Jefferies. They had grown out of the school essay on holidays which I was able to take some pains over, as, for example, in arrangement and in making a dignified conclusion, with a Latin quotation. After the last summer holiday I won a botany book as a prize at the Sunday school with one essay of this kind. The minister encouraged me in my outdoor tastes with much kindness and the best of his ability. He even persuaded the editor of a children's paper to print my descriptions of country walks. But like all other grown-up people he inspired me with discomfort, strangeness, a desire to escape. I could never answer him naturally. I unconsciously affected a suitable solemnity and what I imagined to be an adult way of looking at things. My face was very easily robbed of all expression by fear of any kind, and this expressionless expression bore a resemblance to pathetic gravity, though out of fear and a dislike of inflicting visible pain I always seemed to agree and obey: then ran out into the dark street and round a corner to laugh with John or Jimmy. However, I think the minister had something to do with the essays I wrote and the natural history notes I kept day by day besides the almost daily entries in a general diary.

No book read at school was to me ever anything like as delightful as *The Amateur Poacher*. Of schoolwork I did only what, in order to avoid much trouble with masters and parents, I had to do. I did not like not being able to answer a question, particularly if another boy could. Therefore I learnt nothing thoroughly. I merely kept a place at the top of the form in the matter of geography, history, and English, and not far from the top altogether. Therefore, also, I did not lose my scholarship or get more than a few stern five minutes from my father and my form-master. I was praised, too, as I remember clearly, for to listen to praise gave me an aching pain between the legs. But if I made an effort, it was with half my mind, without ambition. My father wanted me to go on to a Public School and I received special lessons in Latin verse and in Greek. But Greek grammar, Herodotus and Ovid were nuisances: I attended to them only because to ignore them altogether would have brought worse nuisances. I was thinking all the time about John and Jefferies and Merton and fishing and bird-nesting. Yet I believed that I could do better at lessons if I wished, and it was one of my proud moments when I saw my name at the top of a list in Latin, with an adverse comment by the master alongside it. Excelling the rest, I had done badly.

My father made efforts to stimulate interests. He set me learning botany from books and lectures: I learnt nothing but a few names which I could not forget. He used to talk to me of books and take me to lectures. At Kelmscott House I heard Grant Allen recommending State endowment of literary genius: I saw William Morris and I was pleased and awed. But nothing I ever heard at home attracted me to literature or the arts. I saw my father reading *Wilhelm Meister* in German: it seemed to be wonderful, tedious, the sort of thing a grown-up person would do. Nor did I meet boys who cared for books that were not stories or natural history.

There were, however, several hundred books at home, and among them volumes of Shakespeare, Chaucer, Spenser, Shelley, Keats, Byron, Tennyson, and Browning. From the Tennyson, which was a gilt-edged selection belonging to my mother, I had had to learn parts of *In Memoriam* for recitation, as my next brother had done *The Captain: A Legend of the Navy*. Exactly when and why I began to read some of the other poems with pleasure, I cannot say, but it was when I was about fifteen. I know that I read the *May Queen* over and over again. I enjoyed the beauty of spring mixed with the sadness of early death. I liked the soft sadness as I had liked the severer sadness of

> *The ploughman homeward plods his weary way*
> *And leaves the world to darkness and to me.*

I liked saying the saddest lines aloud with appropriate solemnity. I liked the name Effie. So on Sunday when Jimmy and I walked out in our best clothes I took Tennyson with me. The fact that there might be a girl there whom I wanted to know did not enable me to stand much of the Sunday crowd, and very soon I turned aside and began to read Tennyson, sometimes aloud. Jimmy scoffed impatiently. Neither the verses nor my indulgence in them pleased or interested him at all. It was long before I learnt to escape from Sunday by going into the country. Chapel and Sunday school broke the heart of the day. At most I got away sometimes to Wimbledon, or, starting very early, walked to Kingston and back in time for morning service. As John was equally enslaved, I still sometimes strolled out with Jimmy, fortified by Tennyson.

I am almost certain that the reading of poetry was connected with my liking for a girl named Blanche. At any rate I was delighted to find in *King John* the lines

> *If lusty love should go in quest of beauty,*
> *Where should he find it fairer than in Blanch?*

She was a tall thin freckled girl of about my own age with good rather large features, dark hair and grey eyes, and an austere expression. Always in her company for the Sunday parade, or ordinary walk, were two fair-haired sisters, her cousins, one distinctly younger, one older than she was. John and I admired them. We sought every opportunity of meeting them and taking off our hats to them and getting smiles from them. Though they usually approached us with suppressed smiles and were certainly not exceptionally inaccessible we were slow to get on speaking terms with them. When we did we had no idea what to say; nor had they. If one of us said something about the weather and got an answer it was enough. If silence lasted long they were certain to giggle. Dread of being met by their parents or friends of our own added still more to the awkwardness of these short meetings, though when we did all run into Blanche's mother she had nothing but smiles for us. She was a red-faced woman whom we regarded as in every way inferior to our own mothers: in fact the girls themselves were a shade below what we desired, though we never confessed it or that any greater bliss was possible than in being accepted by them as sweethearts. I hardly imagined that I should ever kiss Blanche: to hear her deep voice, to receive her grave smiles, often would have been enough. And so concentrated was I upon her that I treated contemptuously a pretty lusty full-lipped red-cheeked girl who sometimes waylaid me and sometimes sent messages by a young sister. I was more tempted by the prostitutes, coarse, middle-aged, ill-dressed, who addressed me as 'darling' and used to walk up and down out of darkness to the light of a lamp and back again, in the less frequented Common pathways. But I was too timid and too ignorant.

10

PUBLIC SCHOOL: FIRST IMPRESSIONS

*

With Blanche I never got beyond buying her roses and lilies of the valley, and once an expensive prayer-book. That was when I had already gone on to a Public School. I had failed to win a scholarship; only in English did I make any show at all: and I entered a form consisting of a few boys who had won or were going to compete for history scholarships at Oxford or Cambridge. All were older by two or three years than myself. I had never before met boys like them. They not only read many books and saw many plays, and held strong opinions about them, but they argued about persons and events and movements in English and foreign literature. When Maupassant died they discussed his merits as a story-writer. When one of them, in answer to a question, got out of me the state-ment—which was not true—that we had Meredith's books at home, he smiled with delight and said some-thing to the effect that a house containing Meredith's work was blessed. I continued to read chiefly Jefferies and the naturalists, whom these boys knew nothing of. 'What are you reading, Thomas?' asked one of the boys who already wore a scholar's gown. '*The Game-keeper at Home*,' said I. 'The gamekeeper's place is the woods,' said he. And I kept silence, not venturing to remark that the woods were his home.

The whole school impressed and alarmed me. The head master, a thick old grey-bearded heavy-lidded gruff-voiced man with creased florid face and creased black clothes, impressed and alarmed me. I should have done anything he told me, but he never told me to do anything except, 'Speak up. I'm an old man.' Once or twice he glanced at my Greek as I sat with a very few other boys in the great hall. I knew nothing; I was humbled but hardly stirred to effort. The hundreds of boys also humbled me. Many of them wore men's clothes, carried their books in bags like clerks', and seemed to me grimly earnest and thinking only of work and success. Many others looked well off, spoke in more refined voices than I was used to. I came alone in the morning, and in the afternoon I went home alone, often in a railway carriage containing three or four schoolfellows, but alone, in a state of discomfort which would I imagined have been multiplied if they had taken any notice of me, which they never once did, in spite of my morbid looking out for signs that they noticed my discomfort. During the middle of the day I was alone: I stood alone watching Rugby football or practice for the sports. For most of the boys in my form went home to lunch; the rest also disappeared. If I had lunch at school I sat alone and was spoken to only once. Opposite me sat several much older boys whose serious faces and eager voices in argument fascinated me, so that I could not but stare, until one day one of them, a pale black-haired youth with strong lean scowling features, asked me why the devil I couldn't mind my own business. Perhaps it was to avoid this school meal that I took to having lunch out, or, rather, buying a few buns to eat in the class room while I read Jefferies. The reasons why I did not play games are that I was never asked to and was shy, and that I was unaccustomed to Rugby football. When I was not reading or watching games I walked along the far side of the river watching the gulls and swans, sometimes in such wretchedness that I wanted to drown myself. My formmaster, seeing me reading when he came in long before afternoon school was to begin, asked me what I did with myself, did I ever skate or take any decent exercise. He was abrupt and looked contemptuous. I muttered something about skating and country walks. My wrists and hands and arms were always decorated with scratches during the bird-nesting season, but of course he knew nothing of that. Nor had he seen the words which I had written, perhaps not quite without ostentation, in the worst possible Latin on the flyleaf of my algebra book: 'I love birds more than books.' Seen by a clever boy who sat next to me in the mathematical class, these words caused a contemptuous smile in him and in me one of sickly shame for the badness of the Latin. I felt unimportant, isolated, out of place, and only not despised because I was utterly unnoticed; but afterwards I developed some sort of pride in the great names connected with the school in past centuries, and also in its present successes at the universities, on the football field and elsewhere. Naturally then I felt extraordinarily unimportant. I had now a faint ambition, both definite and indefinite, to do something in connection with learning or literature. My father wished me to try for a history scholarship and I occasionally read as hard as it was possible to do without any interest in history beyond the attempt to memorize facts. I suppose there never were duller books than Bright's *England*, Kitchin's *France*, Lodge's *Europe*, anybody's *Political Economy* (Marshall), and I had no idea of history beyond assimilating these. When I was persuaded to propose something at the debating society which included my class and a few of our friends, my opponent began by congratulating me on my 'admirable summary of Bright'. It had simply not occurred to me that there was anything to do but summarize Bright. I never had any grounds for differing from the historian I had last read. The other boys either had enormous appetites for books of many kinds, or they had native wit. I seemed to have nothing.

The one thing I may have had a native taste for was composition. I had feelings which I could not have explained as to forms of expression; I had at the back of my mind sometimes what seemed to me a right phrase and I groped for it. Writing was not a mere nuisance. Whether I had any ability I have no ground for saying. I must usually have been aping forms I had observed in books and newspapers. That I had begun to euphemize I know, because I said in an essay on holidays that some people waited for the twelfth of August, instead of saying that they went grouse-shooting. Running his pencil through this decidedly, my form-master substituted the natural and direct phrase. I saw the fault and blushed for it. With or without the help of English I began to be near the top of the form as soon as the two scholars had gone up to Oxford.

Apart, however, from the personal influence in the direction of scrupulousness on the part of a master who dropped a beautiful bryony in the middle of discussing the *Bacchae* with disgust because a boy said the plant was an American, I was hardly doing more than acquiring unrelated information, and forming the habit of reading what did not interest me. I read the Greek Testament slowly and the *Bacchae* more slowly, and large quantities of history and historical geography rapidly. Some books were less dull than others, but still everything at school was an aimless task performed to the letter only. It cost me many night hours, all the more because I was reading of one thing and thinking of another, and had therefore again and again to go back to a point where I had begun, merely to see the print without understanding.

I made no close friends at the new school. The elder boys either took no notice of me or soon got tired of trying to get something out of me. They alarmed me, and since I did not want to give myself away, and words came darkly and with difficulty when I was disturbed, I said almost nothing: what I did say I often felt to be obscure or false, but for fear of worse I did not correct it. I admired them for their free abundant conversation, their easy manners, their scrupulous nail-cutting during conversation, the material of their clothes, which were so different from my black or blue or grey ready-made clothes. When we were left to ourselves for a time, two of them would begin saying their parts for amateur theatricals; three or four would chat; the one bookworm looked up something in a lexicon wherewith to convict the master; and I would look out of the window at the white clouds, the dark trees, the green grass and the black rooks canting on it, and the pigeons flying up with sticks for their nests, and perhaps made a note of the alternation or mingling of snow, hail, rain and sunshine in late February. Only one boy in the class did I ever visit, though with one or two I had a shy friendly feeling. This one was a boy who lived in a big house with a billiard room. His father had his boots pulled off and his slippers put on by a beautiful youth. I sat at dinner there between a pretty sister and an old aunt who tried hard to get me to talk about my walks and about my printed descriptions of them. For these I had mentioned to several boys, concealing the name of the paper where they appeared, because I was ashamed of it, and at least once when one was making guesses, admitted that I had contributed to a well-known Liberal evening paper—which I had not done. This evening visit was an agony to me. Shyness made me terribly severe and reticent and gave me an appearance of great calm which was perhaps useful to me and was certainly annoying to others. I never went again. The boy made an effort to meet me more than half-way by joining me in Richmond Park to fish, though he was no fisherman. When he arrived I had had a very glorious quarter of an hour. I was the only person fishing there and was trying to land a jack of some size without a landing net, when a girls' school came by. In my excitement I very brusquely asked one of the girls to bring me my net, which had been out of my reach, which she without consulting the mistress rapidly and very sweetly did, thereby doubling the pleasure and glory of my catch. The fish was over four pounds in weight. The girl—whom I scarcely looked at —was beautiful. It was still early morning. After that I remember the boy coming and being very helpful and obedient in what he did not understand. Above all I remember coming home with my bag on my shoulder and some inches of the fish's excess sticking out of one corner. My strides were huge. Before opening the gate I smiled proudly in at our windows as I passed. The fish was stuffed, not with sawdust, but with good chicken stuffing, for Sunday's dinner. As for Johnson, I remember that in the summer after I had left he sent me a letter with a ticket for the school sports, and that I did not go, nor thanked him until some months later, when I pretended that the letter had been mislaid and unopened until that very day. I never saw Johnson again.

On going to the Public School I had without thinking of it dropped all connection with my old school. I never went once again inside its gates. For I was shy and the boys I knew there had been accidental acquaintances with the exception of John. George, though he continued to live close by us, became a mere nodder. At most we stopped and exchanged a few casual questions and answers about our schools, the masters, and so on. The other boys I practically never again set eyes on: if I did I very carefully avoided meeting them, for fear of the discomfort of uselessly disturbing for a moment the sleeping past. I feared also the mere coming face to face with anyone who was not an intimate. People in shops, distant relatives, all older and assured men and women, alarmed me. If I had to speak to them I unconsciously assumed a slow stiff manner and speech that probably did sometimes conceal my intense uneasiness. For those I liked I would have done anything, though what I did was little beyond waiting up and down for John or Henry, outside their houses, or outside some house where they had to call, often for hours and hours, dully but uncomplainingly destroying time, half stupefying myself with recurring thoughts and repeated efforts to stifle them. I was not on friendly terms with more than a very few. Occasionally I saw Jimmy, who had been with me at my last school but one, and lived only a few doors away. For a time he was eager to possess many eggs. Also he was willing to join me now and then on a long walk. It was with him that I set out at daybreak for Ashtead on the first Good Friday after I went to the Public School and soon after my sixteenth birthday. Easter was early, yet pushing through thorny copses we found thrushes' eggs in hedges and shrubberies not many miles along our road, and climbed amid clouds of wood powder to an empty pigeon's nest. Not for anything else did we stop, three times perhaps in the fourteen or fifteen miles before dinner. Ewell and Epsom could not stay us. The day was clear, bright, mild—not too mild. I think we spent the afternoon in the woods and returned by train. Jimmy soon gave up such things. He had begun to smoke and to work at a bank. The last time he came with me to Merton was a November afternoon. We started too late. As we looked over the flat fields and line of poplars beyond Morden station the light was already going. Jimmy lit a pipe: our spirits flagged. Suddenly the idea came to Jimmy of the coffee tavern a mile back. He proposed to return. I leapt at the idea so eagerly that he sniggered his snigger as violently as possible. So we returned, running, to eat pastry and drink hot coffee. At long intervals I had Henry or one of the Joneses for company. Of these walks I only know that I crossed new commons and went down new deep chalk lanes in Kent and Surrey, and that once during the greater part of a walk to Curlsdon and back, which was well over twenty miles, my boot was chafing my heel. Periodically for ten years the heel reminded me of that walk by being unable to endure a shoe on it.

My whole holiday on Saturday I spent usually with John, and sometimes Sundays, for it was now increasingly painful to me to sit in chapel, on account of my shyness and the waste of time. Out of doors we fished or walked. Indoors we looked at our collections or skinned a squirrel a gamekeeper in Kent had sent to John—once we had a woodcock—more often it was a rat or a starling. As there was no obvious opportunity for playing games, I never seriously played football or cricket again. At most John and I would join his younger brother in kicking a ball about at nightfall. But some evenings, and for several series of early mornings, we used to put on vests and shirts and run a mile or two. Though we desired to be strong and fit

PUBLIC SCHOOL: FIRST IMPRESSIONS

this is all we ever did deliberately with that end in view. The result was no more than that we could always trot two or three miles or run a mile at a fair pace without discomfort. I at least often went jaded to school from overdoing it before breakfast. John was beautifully made all over, with clear ruddy skin, and could run, jump, climb, swim, and feared neither men nor tree-tops. My body was nothing to be proud or careful of. I was tall for my age, large-footed, skinny everywhere, and as John had pointed out, pigeon chested. I could not jump high or far, or run better than the average boy. I was no climber. On tall trees even where there was plenty of foothold I was very nervous, though not in the least dizzy; and I could not swarm at all. Anything troublesome to climb had to be tackled by John. When we got climbing irons I paid my share but never ventured a yard upon them. That I had quick sight and hearing, and could walk fast and far, was nothing to boast of. How I should have liked physical prowess! How ashamed I was of my chest! What efforts I made to clear away any risk of being called knock-kneed. On the other hand my health was good, except that I sometimes had headaches and in the summer bleeding of the nose. I hardly remember lying in bed during the day since I was ten. I had few coughs, colds or fevers and never anything worth calling influenza. So that one feverish home-coming when I was thirteen was memorable, for as I lay on my bed in the broad daylight I had a not unpleasant half-dream, seeing myself going far up an infinitely long pillared corridor. It may have been soon after this that I began to have a trivial but strange experience which has been repeated once or twice a year ever since. It happens mostly when I am lying down in bed waiting for sleep, and only on nights when I sleep well. I close my eyes and I find myself very dimly seeing expand before me a vague immense space enclosed with invisible boundaries. Yet it can hardly be called seeing. All is grey, dull, formless, and I am aware chiefly by some other means than sight of vast unshapely towering masses of a colourless subject which I feel to be soft. Through these things and the space I grope slowly. They tend to fade away, but I can recover them by an effort perhaps half a dozen times, and do so because it is somehow pleasant or alluring. Then I usually sleep. During the experience I am well awake and am remembering that it is a repetition, wondering what it means and if anything new will occur, and taking care not to disturb the process.

DIARY

1 January — 8 April 1917

★

JANUARY

1. Shooting with 15 pounders and then 6″ howitzers. All week at Lydd, I being f/c [fire control officer] or observer daily, with map work for the next day at night. Thorburn away. Beautiful clear bright weather always, but sometimes cold.

5. Left Lydd on mobilization leave. Night at Rusham Road with Father and Mother.

6. Julian to breakfast. With Mother to stores. Lunch with Eleanor and tea with Joan and Bertie [Farjeon]. Home with Bronwen (returning from Chiswick). All well.

7. Walks with Helen and children. Fine day.

8. Eleanor came and stayed night. Wrote cheques for next 6 months.

9. Eleanor left. Helen and I walked in forest.

10. Dentist's. Lunch with Jones and Harry [Hooton]. Tea with Ivy Ransome and then Ingpen and Davies. Saw V. H. Collins. Home.

11. Said goodbye to Helen, Mervyn and Baba. Bronwen to Rusham Road. Lunched with Mrs Freeman: afterwards saw [E. S. P.] Haynes and McCabe. Tea with Jesse [Berridge] and T. Clayton and met Lipchitz. Supper at Rusham Road with all my brothers.

12. A letter from Helen. Goodbye to Bronwen, Mother and Father. Lunch with Mary [Valon, Helen's sister] and Margaret [Mary Valon's daughter]. Saw Irene [MacArthur]. To Lydd

and found only Horton[1] and Grier; Thorburn gone on to Codford. Letters from Helen and [G.R.] Blanco White; to Helen, Mother, Mrs de la Mare, Frost, [Vivian Locke] Ellis, [C.] Hodson, Eleanor, and John Freeman.

13. Nothing to do but test compass which never gives same results. Walk and tea with Flawn. Cold drizzle. Horton and the battery left early for Codford. Even wrote verses.[2] Early to bed.

14. A Sunday and no letters as I am supposed to be at Codford. Letters to Helen and Blanco White. A bright cold day. Walked with Flawn through Old Romney and Ivychurch. Flawn to tea with me. Packing.

15. Up 6. Packing. Left Lydd at 9 with Q.M.S. [Quartermaster Sergeant] and Grier and 3 men. Light snow and red sun. 4 hours to spare in London but could only see T. Clayton and D. [A. Duncan] Williams: could not find J. Freeman. Then to Codford in the dark, writing to Helen and beginning 'A Sentimental Journey'. Arrived too late for dinner.

16. Letters from Helen, Eleanor, Mervyn, [Edward] Garnett, [John W.] Haines, Mrs Ellis. Took route march to Wigtye, Stockton, Sherrington, and had great luck in short cuts and bye-roads over river. A frosty clear day: men singing 'Dixie', 'There's a long long trail of winding [sic] to the land of my dreams', and 'We're here because we're here' to the tune of 'Auld Lang Syne'. Only Smith and I and Capt. Fenner left of the 6 officers. Afternoon walked with Smith to Chitterne and had tea there. Evening dined together and talked about practical education—pronunciation of 'girl', 'soot' and 'historian'—and about rhymes to eye.

17. Light snow in night; hard frost. Men on fatigues or drawing overseas clothes etc. Office full of boots, blankets, pails, axes, shovels, dixies, stretchers etc. Route march to Tytherington, Heytesbury and Knook. Afternoon walked over Downs by

---

[1] A fellow officer. Others mentioned in the Diary are Berrington, Cassells, Fenner, Flawn, Lushington, Rubin, Smith, Thornburn, and Witchall.

[2] See 'Last Poem'.

Stockton Wood to Chilmark with Smith: tea at the inn and
Smith played ragtime etc. A cloudy clear frosty day. Back over
the downs on a dark night, but only went astray 200 yards.
Letter from Helen, Mother and John Freeman. Letters to
Helen, Mother, Haines, Eleanor.

18. Letters from Helen, Hodson, Mrs de la Mare, Father. Letters
to Helen, Irene, Father. To Warminster to the bank. Still frosty.
Afternoon lectured on map-reading. Orderly officer for camp
from 6 p.m. Indoors all evening, talking to Smith about marching songs etc.

19. Letters from Mother, Helen, Miss Coltman, [W. H.]
Hudson. Letters to Mother, Helen, M. Freeman, Lady New-
bolt, Oscar [Thomas, Edward's fourth brother]. Morning
orderly officer—latrines etc.—lectured on maps—paid Battery.
Afternoon learnt to ride motor cycle. Mild and drizzly. Guns
are due to arrive. A cake from Mother. Shakespeare's Sonnets
from Helen. Capt. Fenner talks of having to take sick leave.

20. Letter from J. Freeman. Letters to Garnett, [James] Guthrie,
Harry, Coltman. Mild snowy. Arranging stores. Guns arriving.
Smith to Bath. So I had to see to unloading and parking the
guns till dark. No use walking after dark. The roads are pitch
dark and crowded with men going to cinemas, darkness worse
from blaze of motor lamps and electric light in camps nearby.
Long queues waiting outside cinema at 5.30. Tested battery
compass. Talk with Fenner about martens in Ireland, badgers,
plovers, barrows etc.

21. No church parade for me. 9.30–1.20 walked over Stockton
Down, the Bake, and under Grovely Wood to Barford St
Martin, Burcombe, and to lunch at Netherhampton House
with Newbolts. Freezing drizzle—freezes on ground, white
grass and icy roads. 2 families of vagrants in green road roasting
a corpse of something by slow wood fire. Beautiful Downs,
with one or two isolated thatched barns, ivied ash trees, and
derelict threshing machine. Old milestones lichened as with
battered gold and silver nails. Back by train at 5. Tea alone.
Guns in line out on parade square. Smith back. Letter from
Helen, Ingpen, Eleanor, Hudson. Letter to Helen, Ingpen.
Talk with Fenner after dinner about fishing—river and sea.

22. Set the men branding and sorting stores. Left at 10.30 for Gloster to see Haines. Still frosty and dull. Gloster at 2.50. Sat till 12.15 gossiping about Frost, de la Mare, and the army, marching songs etc. Haines gave me Frost's 'Mountain Interval'.

23. With Mrs Haines and Robin most of morning. 3.30 left Gloster via Mangotsfield and Bath for Codford. Read 'Mountain Interval'. Horton, Rubin and Thorburn back. Fenner merry; he is probably to go on sick leave. He and Rubin returned late and had a noisy parting from 2 others. Thorburn had a screaming nightmare.

24. All men on fatigues. A short walk with Thorburn to test compasses. Letters from Helen, Father, Mother, Harry. Letters to Helen, Father, Mother, M. Freeman. Parcel of medicines etc. from Helen, cigars from Harry. Walked in afternoon with Thorburn to Chilmark for tea, and back over frosty Downs with new moon and all stars. But my ankles chafed by new boots lame me.

25. Resting my sore ankles. Dial sights tested and stores arranged for packing tomorrow. Guns leave on 27th and Battery on 29th. Fenner is to go to hospital and Horton to take charge. Very cold with East wind. Letters from Oscar, letters to Oscar, Helen, Mother, Mrs de la Mare, Frost, John Freeman, Mrs M. Freeman, Harry, Eleanor. Capt. Lushington is to be our new o/c [Officer Commanding 244 Battery (Acting Major Lushington)] and to take us out.

26. Letters from Helen, Eleanor, letters to Helen, Mervyn. Loading lorries and attaching guns to 4-wheel drives—standing out in dusty icy East wind doing nothing but getting cold and dirty. I sleep badly too. Also I have taken charge of mess and mess accounts. Thorburn is on my nerves—he had a nightmare lately—asking 'Can you tell me how much 55 lbs. is?'—the weight of officers' luggage. I feel useless. Am still in slacks and shoes on account of bad ankles. Thorburn and I dining alone, the others with Capt. Lushington in the village—our mess kit being packed. Can't even walk far enough to get warm. Thorburn goes tomorrow with guns. Dined with him and then talked about philosophy and poetry, and Yes and Perhaps, and

DIARY

the lyric and the Bible. I have a cold. The frost is worse tonight.

27. A clear windy frost dawn, the sun like a bright coin between the knuckles of opposite hills seen from sidelong. A fox. A little office work. Telegram to say Baba was at Ransome's, so I walked over Downs by Chicklade Bottom and the Fonthills to Hatch, and blistered both feet badly. House full of ice and big fires. Sat up with Ivy till 12 and slept till 8. Another fine bright frosty day on the

28th. Wrote to Bronwen, Helen, Ivy, Eleanor. Letters from Bronwen, Helen, Mother, Eleanor. Slept late. Rested my feet, talking to the children or Ivy cooking with Kitty Gurd. Hired a bicycle to save walking. Such a beautiful ride after joining the Mere and Amesbury Road at Fonthill Bishop—hedgeless roads over long sloping downs with woods and sprinkled thorns, carved with old tracks which junipers line—an owl and many rabbits—a clear pale sky and but a faint sunset—a long twilight lasting till 6. We are to move at 6.30 a.m. tomorrow. Horton and Smith and I dined together laughing at imbecile jests and at Smith's own laughing. Had to change in order to send home my soiled things. Letters. Mess accounts and cheques to tradesmen.

29. Up at 5. Very cold. Off at 6.30, men marching in frosty dark to station singing 'Pack up your troubles in your old kitbag'. The rotten song in the still dark brought one tear. No food or tea—Freezing carriage. Southampton at 9.30 and there had to wait till dusk, walking up and down, watching ice-scattered water, gulls and dark wood beyond, or London Scottish playing improvised Rugger, or men dancing to concertina, in a great shed between railway and water. Smith and I got off for lunch after Horton and Capt. Lushington returned from theirs. Letter to Helen from 'South Western Hotel', where sea-captains were talking of the 'Black Adder' and of 'The Black Ball Line' that used to go to Australia. Hung about till dark—the seagulls as light failed nearly all floated instead of flying—then sailed at 7. Thorburn turned up. Now I'm in 2nd officer's cabin with Capt. and Horton, the men outside laughing and joking and saying fucking. Q.W.R.s [Queen's Westminster Rifles] and Scottish and a Field Battery and 236 S.B.

DIARY

[Siege Battery], also on 'The Mona Queen'. Remember the
entirely serious and decorous writing in urinal whitewash—
name, address, unit, and date of sailing. A tumbling crossing,
but rested.

30. Arrived Havre 4 a.m. Light of stars and windows of tall
pale houses and electric arcs on quay. March through bales of
cotton in sun to camp. The snow first emptying its castor of
finest white. Tents. Mess full of subalterns censoring letters.
Breakfast at 9.45 a.m. on arrival. Afternoon in Havre, which
Thorburn likes because it is French. Mess unendurably hot and
stuffy, tent unendurably cold till I got into my blankets. Slept
well in fug. Snow at night.

31. Had to shift our lines in snow. 12 to a tent with 2 blankets
each. Ankles bad. Nearly all water frozen in taps and basins.
Mess crowded—some standing. Censoring letters about the
crossing and the children and ailments etc. at home. Had to
make a speech explaining that men need not be shy about
writing familiar letters home. At 'Nouvel Hotel', Havre, while
we had tea, waitress kissing a Capt. and arranging for another
visit. 4f. for 2 teas. Battery had to be specially warned against
venereal in Havre. Read Sonnets in evening: to bed at 9 to
escape hot stuffy room. Officers coming and going. Some faces
you just see, drinking once and never again. More fine snow
like sago.

FEBRUARY

1. Freezing and overcast. Hospital train goes through camp
(wounded men say we have advanced at N. Chapelle). Battery
on route march. I arrange to eat midday ration in tent to save
lunch in Mess (2f.50). Guns and stores not here yet. Other
officers mostly in Havre but my ankle prevents me. Down in
lorry to Ordnance Store for field boots. Snow. Route march,
but not for me. I write and censor letters. No fire in the mess till
3 p.m. Guns are coming today. Detachments reorganized.—
Mess fills up.—Cockney rankers with two stars come in and
drink standing and talk of Singapore and Pekin and duration
officers look up. Some rapacious and sneering, some gentle.
Read Sonnets.

DIARY

2. A still colder night and my new boots hurt my ankles like the old. Tried to get shoes from Ordnance in vain—rode past quays and stores of hay, grain, cotton etc.—cattle—German prisoners—French sentries hooded with long loose cloaks and long rifles and curved bayonets. Afternoon into Havre to look for low shoes—but all too tight: bought low soft boots. Tea in teashop with Thorburn. In a hole over value of English shillings. Bought a good root stick with leather sling for 2f.50. Hard clear night again. All other officers out. Argument with Thorburn about morals, shame, whether poets must go through not only 'sin' but 'repentance'—Dante, Shakespeare. Cold supper in our cold tent—iron ration and cheese and marmalade.

3. Not quite so cold. Overhauling guns and rearranging stores on roadside by camp. A pleasant change, but not very much for me to do. Shall the guns be George, Andrew, Patrick, David? Again on the guns in afternoon. 236 Battery leave tonight: most of the officers are in Havre ignorant. All 244 except Smith dined and wined at the Normandie for 10fr. The view is that it could possibly be better placed. Back to Rest Camp 9.30— great stark ships black with level flecked snow below and big engines and troops arriving.

4. Cold and bright again. Took the section sliding, then work on guns. At 11 came warning to move at 5.30. Packing, Censoring. New servant—Taylor. Asked if he had done anything of the kind before, said 'I've a wife and family and I know what comforts are.' Started at 4.45 for station with guns—held up 1½ hours by train across road—2 hours at station doing nothing, 1½ hours entraining guns—platform all cotton bales and men singing 'The nightingales are singing in the pale moonlight'. ('There's a long long trail awinding'.) Sgt Major did practically all the work.—The long waiting before train starts—men quite silent after first comic cries of 'All tickets' and imitating cattle (35 men in each cattle truck: we have a compartment to 2 officers). As we start at 11 suddenly the silent men all yell 'Hurray' but are silent before we are clear of long desolate platform of cotton and trampled snow and electric light.

5. At 7 a.m. after many stops and starts we were close under partly wooded chalk hills, among railway trucks, and near a

village with here and there an upper storey quite open like a loft. Snow. Gradually flatter and poplars regular as telegraph poles, orchards, level crossings, children. Buchy at 10 a.m.— Y.M.C.A.—Leave train. Nearly lost train. Fine snowfall. Furzy cuttings. Mistletoe in field, poplars by Alaincourt. Amiens at 2 and train left a score of men behind for a time. Pale sky and crimson sun at sunset. Doullens at 8. Guns all the time. Night with Thorburn at Resthouse. Thorburn had been very worried on journey—by things like tunnels while shaving etc.—then by dirty stories after tea. A restless night.

6. Still very cold. Men had only just drawn rations at 10 when parade was. Much ice on road and pavement. Hanging about in cafés or cold Resthouse. Fine dusty cold day. 2.50 fr. breakfast; 6 fr. lunch. Horton's amusing jaunty talk full of old army proverbs and metaphors and 'I mean to say'. Letter to Helen. No letters received since Codford. Suddenly at 7.30 we have to shift to Mendicourt without guns—I go on in lorry and choose billets—all in half-ruined barns—barns and farms here are a quad, entered through high arch and self-complete. We got an elephant sergeants' mess to sleep in. Bitter cold, this being highest in Northern France. Roads ice and frozen snow. Farmyards all frozen. Kaffirs digging.

7. Bright cold. Horton's way of suddenly saying 'I will arise and go to my Father and say "Form Fours".' Indoors mostly, talking silly, arranging mess funds etc.—I being secretary— cooking our dinner. Battery on short route march. We are to move up very soon. A very merry evening.

8. Weather as before. Physical drill, a hasty Welsh Rabbit with honey, and then off in lorries through Alaincourt, Barly, Fosseux, to Berneville—men billet in huge barn of a big uneven farmyard surrounded by spread arched stone barns and buildings with old pump at one side, kitchen at upper end. We forage. Enemy plane like pale moth beautiful among shrapnel bursts. A fine ride over high open snowy country with some woods. Rigging up table in mess and borrowing crockery. The battery is to split for the present: Rubin has taken guns to Saulty. We are for Dainville. A scramble dinner of half cold stuff, mostly standing. Taylor makes a table and says 'Very

good, Sir' and 'It's the same for all. You gentlemen have to put
up with same as us.' Bed early. Rubin returns late. Heavy
firing at night. Restless.

9. Bright bitter cold. Rubin and Smith move off to join 146.
Heavy firing near. Afternoon marched through Warlus to
Dainville, billets on Arras road, with shell holes behind. Bitter
cold. Tea with 146. Beds in the mess for night. (Remember
Berneville courtyard, with ruined pigeon house by well and
church behind and what was manor house.) Graveyard for 3
'Mort pour la patrie' below our billet. A wonderful night of
all the stars and low full moon. Officers of trench mortar
battery detained here dine with us on bully, cheese and white
wine.

10. Slept warm. Making latrines. With Debenham of 146 to
see O.P.s [Observation Posts] and what was visible from them
—through Achicourt and over railway towards Beurains. One
dead man under railway bridge. Maison brulé[e] dangerous.
Map, field glass and compass over snowy broken land with
posts and wires and dead trees. No infantry visible in our lines
or Germans, except those we passed in trenches—Somersets and
Cornwalls. Cloudy night and light wind but no thaw yet.

11. Milder and misty first—sun warm at noon. Maps in morning. Afternoon with digging party at our position by Faubourg
d'Amiens at southern edge of Arras in an orchard. After tea
paid the battery for first time in France. Tested compass bear-
ings by map. Cold. Rubin influenza. Thorburn to Arras. No
letters yet. Censoring as usual. Gramophone playing 'Wait till
I am as old as father' and 'Where does daddy go when he goes
out?'. 9 p.m. Great cannonade thudding and flashing quite con-
tinuously away South in Ancre.

12. Disappointed in not going again on trench Reconnaissance.
Maps in morning. Working party at gun position in afternoons.
Got a chill and was very weary. Thorburn and Rubin have
colds. Evening as usual censoring men's letters. Half battery
moves to Faubourg d'Amiens—Thorburn there too, thank
God. Smith back from Saulty—no news of our letters or
lorries. Not much firing near us today, but 146 lost a man
killed and one wounded. Gramophone plays the rotten things

DIARY

and then Gounod's 'Ave Maria' and 'Dormez-vous' which makes us rather silent after smut.

13. Awoke tired and cold though it is thawing and cloudy with a breeze. No work this morning, but I pore over map and think how I may enjoy doing it when this is all over, which is not a good feeling, I suspect. Taylor says (as he makes my bed and as usual asks if he does it right): 'I am not proud, but I likes to be comfortable. I have been domesticated since I joined the Army.' Nothing to do all morning, afternoon at our position—hare, partridges and wild duck in field S.E. of guns. I feel the cold—the morning sun turns to a damp thaw wind. Letters home to Father, Mother and Eleanor. Some grass showing green through melting snow. Thorburn worries because he can't laugh at silly low talk. Evening censoring letters and reading Sonnets; others writing—when I began to talk to Rubin, the Captain said 'You get on with your Sonnets' and then all was silent. Awful fug.

14. A bad night but feeling better. All day with Horton, and then Horton and Smith, examining O.P.s above Agny and Wailly, and then between Achicourt and Beaurains. Fine sunny day—snow melting. Black-headed buntings talk, rooks caw, lovely white puffs of shrapnel round planes high up. Right Section does aeroplane shoot in afternoon. Dead campion umbels, and grass rustling on my helmet through trenches. Pretty little copse in deep hollow high up between Ficheux and Dainville, where guns look over to Berneville and Warlus.

15. With Captain observing for a B.T. [Battery Training] shoot on Ficheux Mill and edge of Blairville Wood. Fine sun but cold in trench. With working party in afternoon. Letters arrived at 6. We sorted them and then spent an hour silently reading. 750 letters for men; 17 for me—from Helen, the children, Father, Mother, Eleanor, Freeman, Mrs Freeman, Guthrie, Vernon and Haines. Evening, reading and writing letters. A quiet evening indoors and out. Taylor says as he mends the fire, 'Well, we have to put up with many discomforts. We are all alike, Sir, all human.' A still starry night with only machine guns and rifles. Slept badly again, and then suddenly with no notice got up from breakfast on the . . .

16th to do fire control on aeroplane shoot (only 10 rounds, observation being bad). Dull day. Left Thorburn on guns at 11.30. Bad temper. Afternoon up to O.P., but too hazy to observe. A mad Captain with several men driving partridges over the open and whistling and crying 'Mark over.' Kestrels in pairs. Four or five planes hovering and wheeling as kestrels used to over Mutton and Ludcombe. Women hanging clothes to dry on barbed entanglement across the road. Rain at last at 4.15. This morning the old Frenchman living in this ruin burst into our room while we were dressing to complain of our dirt and depredation, and when Rubin was rude in English, said he was a Frenchman and had been an officer. Nobody felt the slightest sympathy with his ravings, more than with the old white horse who works a mill walking up and up treadmill.

17. A dull muddy day. No observation, no shooting. On guns all day and in dugout, writing up our fighting book. Another letter from home. Could only just see A.P. [(First) Aid Post]. Kit arrived late last night. I slept badly, coughing. Very mild and the roads chalk and water, Grandes Graves 2.50 a bottle. Thorburn asks where he shall put the letters he has censored—decides on the crowded table—then I have to tell him the mantelpiece is the obvious place.

18. Another dull day down in 146 Dugout. Afternoon to Arras—Town Hall like Carreg Cennin. Beautiful small white square empty. Top storey of high house ruined cloth armchair and a garment across it left after shell arrived. Car to Mendicourt and back by light of star shells. Shopping at Bellevue B.E.F. canteen. Returned to find I am to go as Orderly Officer to Group 35 H.A. [Heavy Artillery] in Arras tomorrow.

19. To Arras and began showing sectors and arcs on 1/10000 maps. Field Cashier's; waiting in long queue of officers to cash cheques etc. Learning office work. Place Victor Hugo white houses and shutters and sharpened fuller and dome in middle. Beautiful. In class it was like Bath—retired people, schools, priests. Gardens, courtyards, open spaces with trees. I still funk the telephone and did not use it once today. Sentries challenge in street and answer 'Sussex' etc.

20. Rain. To Fosseux in the car for cash and gas helmets. Rain

and mud and troops and Hun prisoners and turbaned Indians at a barn door holding a sheep by a rope round its neck, all still and silent. Afternoon through Fosseux again with Col. Witchall to Mendicourt in rain and mud and back in darkness along main Arras Road—could usually only see 2 or 3 of the roadside trees except when we ran into the blaze of 18-pounder battery by roadside. Blast of 18-pounders near the billet blows mortar from ruins against our window linen. Called at 244 for letters—none. C/O [Commanding Officer (Colonel Witchall)] and Berrington and Cassells as before sat up till 12.30 and I could not get my bed before

21. Clearer and no rain. Checking inventory of new billet in fine modern house at corner of Rue de l'Abbé Hallain and Boulevard Vauban. Big vacant house, red brick and shutters, oak floors, panelling and pictured ceilings and mirrors—a few beds, chairs and tables left. A small backyard with a few trees and grass. We supplant Cameronians. One ruined house has still an engraved 1850 portrait hanging on wall high up, without glass broken. Rubin brought in letters from Helen and Eleanor. Hung on at old billet till telephone connection was made at new. It being very cold, we got to bed at 11.30.

22. Cold and wet. Fuel damp. Office work and maps. Court of Inquiry on gassing of 4 men. Am I to stay on here and do nothing but have cold feet and ask Cassells What is to be done? No thrushes yet, but a chaffinch says 'Chink' in the chestnut in our garden. Pipits sing up at Dainville, where I have come to see 244, but they are all out—they came in, all but O/C, and we had tea, and Rubin drove me back. Letter from Father. Evening in Mess with Wallace as guest. Cold and still: no artillery all day. At night I quite thought someone was knocking excitedly at one of the doors, when it was really machine guns. Troops going out to trenches singing and whistling 'It's nice to get up in the morning' or a thing with part of 'The Minstrel Boy' tune in it.

23. Chaffinch sang once. Another dull cold day. Inspected stables, checked inventory of new billet for men in Rue Jeanne d'Arc, went with Colonel round 244, 141 and 234 positions and O.P. in Achicourt. Afternoon maps. Partridges twanging in

fields. Flooded fields by stream between the 2 sides of Achicourt. Ruined churches, churchyard and railway. Sordid ruin of Estaminet with carpenter's shop over it in Rue Jeanne d'Arc— wet, mortar, litter, almanacs, bottles, broken glass, damp beds, dirty paper, knife, crucifix, statuette, old chairs. Our cat moves with the Group wherever it goes, but inspects new house inside and out, windows, fireplace etc. Paid the Pool gunners (scrapings from several batteries doing odd jobs here). 2 owls in garden at 6. The shelling must have slaughtered many jackdaws but has made home for many more. Finished Frost's 'Mountain Interval'. Wrote to Frost. A quiet still evening. Rubin brought over letters from Helen and Oscar.

24. Why do Huns not retaliate on Arras guns? Some day this will be one of the hottest places this side of Hell, if it is this side. Nothing to do here today. Clearer, but still dull and cold with more breeze. Gas Alert off. Wrote to Father. Lushington calls and goes out with Colonel W—. Dined with 244 and Major Berrington and Capt. Angus—a dull long meal with maraschino chocolates at end. Benedictine, whisky and coffee, after soup, hors d'oeuvres, tinned turkey, roast mutton, Christmas pudding, apricots and cream. Gramophone but no fun. Walked back to Arras in dark with Thorburn, challenged by *only 2 sentries* who were content with 'Friend' though they could not see a yard among the ruins. Owls on Dainville Road. Machine guns and hanging lights above No Man's Land. Cassells and Colonel alone up when I returned at 11. New moon— *last* as I walked from Hatch to Codford.

25. A dull morning turns sunny and warm. Chaffinches and partridges, moles working on surface. Beautiful 18th century citadel with church ruined in middle of green barrack square. Huge bastions with sycamores in moat and tangled grass. Walked over citadel to new position with Colonel. Talked to Horton in our orchard. Wrote to Oscar. Artillery lively in the clear sunny noon. I got hot and spring-languid walking up at 4.30 to 244. Gramophone here played 'Anitra's Dance', 'Death of Troll' etc. and 'Allanwater'. Does a mole ever get hit by a shell?

26. A clear morning. 8.15–9.30 a.m. incessant field-gun firing—

raid—German prisoners back at 10.15. Sunshine in white ruins and white squares with Scots standing about. A few shells arrive in Arras, but nobody looked as if anything were happening. While our guns were firing we could not hear one another speak. Afternoon to Achicourt to see if a gun position was visible to Huns. Shells and machine gun bullets came over. An 18-pounder on a fire point fired when I was 3 yards off (in front). Fitting aeroplane photos together. Paid out. A sunny day but cold in this house. Wrote to G. Bottomley. Gramophone. Talk with Berrington and Colonel.

27. Fine but chilly. 2 English planes fell, one on fire, as I walked up to 244 in afternoon: machine gun bullets cut telephone wire close by. Letters from Helen and Irene. Nothing to do but go and see about a billet of 244's collared by another Battery. Tea at 244 after seeing 2 of our planes down, one on fire with both burnt to death after alighting. Letters from Helen, Irene and Eleanor.

28. 244 to go into position. Out identifying gun positions. Up to 244 to pack for a change of billet. Tea with Rubin, Thorburn, Lushington and Horton. Letter from Helen, parcel from Mother. Shelling town at night. Walk out to Dainville by citadel and marsh—moorhens in clear chalk stream by incinerator, blackbirds too, but no song except hedge-sparrow. Evening, ruin with Colonel and Cassells.

MARCH

1. Sunny and breezy. Wrote to Helen, Mother, Eleanor and Ellis. Indoors all morning doing nothing. Mostly a quiet morning. Out with Berrington round the marsh towards 244 who were doing their 1st shoot. Enemy planes over. 2 rounds across 244 position on to Doullens Road. Great deal of anti-aircraft shells singing by. Sat down on hill above 244 and watched German lines. At Beaurains ghastly trees and ruins above Achicourt church tower. A bullet passes. Quite warm to sit down for quarter hour. Evening in mess. Colonel talks of the General (Poole) who was for 'Fire, fire, fire! Loose her off! Deliver the goods! Annoy the Hun' with artillery. Shelling heavy from about 5 a.m. I only dressed because I thought it

DIARY

would be better to have my clothes on. In any case I had to be up at 6 to go to Achicourt. A very misty still morning: could see nothing from bedroom except the trees and the stone dog— our artillery really made most of the noise, and I being just wakened and also inexperienced mistook it.

2. Up at 5.30 and went out to Achicourt Château to see 141's gun into its forward position. A misty frosty morning luckily and no plane could observe. Afternoon to Faubourg Ronville, its whistling deserted ruined streets, deserted roadway, pavement with single files of men. Cellars as dugouts, trenches behind and across road. Dead dry calf in stable. Rubble, rubbish, filth and old plush chair. Perfect view of No Man's Land winding level at foot of Hun slope, and Beaurains above to one side and woods just behind crest on other side (M.B.110) [a map reference (?Bench Mark)]. With Horton and Lushington to see 3 O.P.s there:—Letters from Helen, Mother, Eleanor and J. Freeman.

3.[3] No post. Morning dull spent in office. But afternoon with Colonel to Achicourt to see O.P.s and then to new battery positions. A chilly day not good for observing. Court of Inquiry on a man burnt with petrol—Lushington presiding and afterwards I went back with him to 244's new billet and saw my new quarters to be. Wrote to Mother and Helen.

4. Cold but bright clear and breezy. Nothing to do all morning but trace a map and its contours. Colonel and I went down to 244 before lunch to see the shell holes of last night and this morning. Hun planes over. More shells came in the afternoon. The fire is warm but the room cold. Tea with Lushington and Thorburn. Shelling at 5.30—I don't like it. I wonder where I shall be hit as in bed I wonder if it is better to be on the window or outer side of room or on the chimney on inner side, whether better to be upstairs where you may fall or on the ground floor where you may be worse crushed. Birthday parcels from home.

5. Out early to see a raid by VI Corps [the main Army Command Group in this area], but snow hid most but singing of Field shells and snuffling of 6".—Ronville's desolate streets. To

[3] Thomas's thirty-ninth birthday.

244's orchard which has had numerous 4.2 shells over, meant for the road. Wrote to Helen, Mervyn and Bronwen. Afternoon indoors paying etc. After tea to 244 to dine, not very happy with Lushington, Horton and Smith. They have the wind up because of the shells (which may have been meant for the road behind). Letters from de la Mare, Helen, Bronwen and de la Mare. A beautiful clear moonlit night after a beautiful high blue day with combed white clouds.

6. Bright and clear early and all day and warm at 1. Walked over to 244's position with Colonel and then up to 234 beyond Dainville station, and listened to larks and watched aeroplane fights. 2 planes down, one in flames, a Hun. Sometimes 10 of our planes together very high. Shells into Arras in afternoon.

7. A cold raw dull day with nothing to do except walk round to 244 to get a pair of socks. The wind made a noise in the house and trees and a dozen black crumpled sycamore leaves dance round and round on terrace. Wrote to Pearce and Irene. Rather a cold and depressed, solitary.

8. Snow blizzard—fine snow and fierce wind—to Achicourt O.P. but suddenly a blue sky and soft white cloud through the last of the snow—with Colonel and Berrington. Returned to hear that the Group has to leave this billet. I liked the walk. Indoors afternoon fitting together aeroplane trench photographs. Letters from Helen, Eleanor, Oscar and Frost (saying he had got an American publisher for my verses). A still quiet night up to 11 with just one round fired to show we have not left Arras. Up till 1 for a despatch from Corps. Colonel snotted interpreter.

9. Snow and very cold indoors doing nothing but look at a sandbag O.P. My last day at the Group. Weir of 2/1 Lowland takes my place. I return to 244—Lushington, Horton and Rubin. I am fed up with sitting on my arse doing nothing that anybody couldn't do better. Wrote to de la Mare, Frost and Eleanor.

10. Up at 5.45 for a raid, but nothing doing. A misty mild morning clearing slightly to a white sky. 10 rounds gunfire C.-B. [?Command Battery]. Snowdrops at foot of peartrees by

DIARY

Decanville Railway. R.F.C. [Royal (?) Flying Corps] wireless man reading 'Hiawatha'. 3 shoots of 10 rounds gunfire suddenly at N.F. targets [no fixed targets] unobserved. Men mending a caved-in dugout in the dark. Parcel from Janet Hooton.

11. Out at 8.30 to Ronville O.P. and studied the ground from Beaurains N. Larks singing over No Man's Land—trench mortars. We were bombarding their front line: they were shooting at Arras. R.F.A. [Royal Field Artillery] officer with me who was quite concerned till he spotted a certain familiar Hun sentry in front line. A clear, cloudy day, mild and breezy. 8th shell carrying into Arras. Later Ronville heavily shelled and we retired to dugout. At 6.15 all quiet and heard blackbirds chinking. Scene peaceful, desolate like Dunwich moors except sprinkling of white chalk on the rough brown ground. Lines broken and linesmen out from 2.30 to 7 p.m. A little rain in the night . . .,

12. . . . then a beautiful moist clear limpid early morning till the Raid at 7 and the retaliation on Ronville at 7.30–8.45 with 77 cm. 25 to the minute. Then back through 6 ins. of chalk mud in trenches along battered Ronville Street. Rooks in tall trees on N. side of Arras—they and their nests and the trees black against the soft clouded sky. W. wind and mild but no rain yet (11 a.m.). Letters, mess accounts, maps. Afternoon at maps and with Horton at battery. Evening of partridges calling and pipsqueaks coming over behind.

13. Blackbird trying to sing early in dull marsh. A dull cold day. One N.F. shoot at nightfall. I was in position all day. Letters from Eleanor, Mother and Ellis: wrote to Bronwen, Mother and Eleanor.

14. Ronville O.P. Looking out towards No Man's Land what I thought first was a piece of burnt paper or something turned out to be a bat shaken at last by shells from one of the last sheds in Ronville. A dull cold morning, with some shelling of Arras and St Sauveur and just 3 for us. Talking to Birt and Randall about Glostershire and Wiltshire, particularly Painswick and Marlborough. A still evening—blackbirds singing far off—a

spatter of our machine guns—the spit of one enemy bullet—a little rain—no wind—only far-off artillery.

15. Huns strafe I sector at 5.30. We reply and they retaliate on Arras and Ronville. Only tired 77s reach O.P. A sunny breezy morning. Tried to climb Arras chimney to observe, but funked. 4 shells nearly got me while I was going and coming. A rotten day. No letters for 5 days.

16. Larks and great tits. Ploughing field next to orchard in mist—horses and man go right up to crest in view of Hun at Beaurains. Cold and dull. Letters to Helen and Janet. In the battery for the day. Fired 100 rounds from 12–1.30. Sun shining but misty still. Letter from Bronwen. The first thrush I have heard in France sang as I returned to Mess at 6 p.m. Parcel from Mother—my old Artist boots. Wrote to Hodson. A horrible night of bombardment, and the only time I slept I dreamt I was at home and couldn't stay to tea . . .

17. . . . Then most glorious bright high clear morning. But even Horton, disturbed by 60-pounders behind his dugout, came in to breakfast saying: 'I am not going to stay in this — army; on the day peace is declared I am out of it like a — rabbit.' A beautiful day, sunny with pale cloudless sky and W. wind, but cold in O.P. Clear nightfall with curled, cinereous cloud and then a cloudless night with pale stains in sky over where Bosh is burning a village or something. Quiet till 3 : then a Hun raid and our artillery over us to meet it: their shells into St Sauveur, Ronville and Arras. Sound of fan in underground cave.

18. Beautiful clear cloudless morning and no firing between daybreak and 8. Drew another panorama at 7. Linnets and chaffinches sing in waste trenched ground with trees and water tanks between us and Arras. Magpies over No Man's Land in pairs. The old green (grey) track crossing No Man's Land— once a country way to Arras. The water green and clear (like Silent Pool) of the Moat of the Citadel with skeletons of whole trees lying there. Afternoon washing and reading letters from Helen and Eleanor. I did 2 shoots. News came that we are in Beaurains and near Mercatel. Letters to Helen and Eleanor. The pigeons are about in the streets of this Faubourg more than ever

and I could hear a lark till the Archies drowned it. Fired 600 rounds and got tired eyes and ears. Then early to bed and up at 4 to go to O.P. on

19. Nothing to do all day at Ronville but look at quiet No Man's Land and trenches with engineers beginning to straighten road up. Back to sleep at billet, but preferred to return to O.P. as I've to go to the front trench O.P. at 4 on the

20th. Stiff deep mud all the way up and shelled as we started. Telegraph Hill as quiet as if only rabbits lived there. I took revolver and left this diary behind in case. For it is very exposed and only a few Cornwalls and M.G.C. [Machine Gun Corps] about. But Hun shelled chiefly over our heads into Beaurains all night—like starlings returning 20 or 30 a minute. Horrible flap of 5·9 a little along the trench. Rain and mud and I've to stay till I am relieved tomorrow. Had not brought warm clothes or enough food and had no shelter, nor had telephonists. Shelled all night. But the M.G.C. boy gave me tea. I've no bed. I leant against wall of trench. I got up and looked over. I stamped up and down. I tried to see patrol out. Very light—the only sign of Hun on Telegraph Hill, though 2 appeared and were sniped at. A terribly long night and cold. Not relieved till 8. Telephonists out repairing line since 4 on the morning of the

21st. At last 260 relieved us. Great pleasure to be going back to sleep and rest. No Man's Land like Goodwood Racecourse with engineers swarming over it and making a road between shell holes full of blood-stained water and beer bottles among barbed wire. Larks singing as they did when we went up in dark and were shelled. Now I hardly felt as if a shell could hurt, though several were thrown about near working parties. Found letters from Helen, Eleanor and Julian. Had lunch, went to bed at 2 intending to get up to tea, but slept till 6.30 on the . . .

22nd. (Beautiful was Arras yesterday coming down from Beaurains and seeing Town Hall ruin white in sun like a thick smoke beginning to curl. Sprinkle of snow today in sun.) A cold bright day with snow early. We fired twice. I on duty at Battery. Letters to Helen and home and Gordon and Deacon. Partridges twanging in open fields. Not much shooting to do.

DIARY

Several windy snow showers half-hail and then sun. Talk with Thorburn about his fate if he loses his commission. Gramophone plays Ambrose Thomas's 'Mignon' gavotte (by Raymond Jeremy's Philharmonic Quartette), 'D'ye ken John Peel', Chopin's 'Berceuse', Tchaikovsky's 'Fantasia Italiana'.

23. Frosty clear. Ploughs going up over crest towards Beaurains. Rubin back from F.O.P. [Forward Observation Post (in No Man's Land)] believes in God and tackles me about atheism—thinks marvellous escapes are ordained. But I say so are the marvellous escapes of certain telegraph posts, houses, etc. Sunny and cold—motored to Avesnes and Fosseux to buy luxuries and get letters. Crowded bad roads through beautiful hedgeless rolling chalk country with rows of trees, some along roads following curving ridges—villages on crests with church spires and trees. Troops, children holding hands, and dark-skinned women, mud-walled ruined barns. Parcels from Mother and Helen, letters from Mother and J. Freeman.

24. Out early to Beaurains. The chill clear air pains my skin while it delights my mind—both walking and in car. Only tombstones recognizable in Beaurains and that little conical summer house among trees. Sat all day in copse in old chalk pit between Agny and Achicourt which is perhaps to be our new position. Warm in the sun, but no thrushes in all those ash, hazel and dogwood. Parcels from Mrs Freeman and Eleanor. Letters to Helen, Mrs Freeman and Mother.

25. Up at 5 and to O.P. beyond Beaurains with Thorburn and stood all day in trench behind hedge till head ached with staring at Wancourt and Neuville-Vitasse and the ground between and beyond. A cold but sunny day. Many R.F.A. and infantry used the O.P. We were discovered and the O.P. 20 yards away had a shell on to it, and we had several over our shoulders. Larks singing. Drawing panoramas. Left Thorburn there at 6 p.m. tired enough. Letters from Bronwen, [R. C.] Trevelyan and Guthrie.

26. Preparing reports and panoramas for 35 H.A.G. [Heavy Artillery Group]. Rainy and dull. Letter to Bronwen. Packing up for move to the chalk pit. Up late in emptied billet waiting for A.S.C. [Army Service Corps] lorries to come up. Off at

last on foot to the Achicourt billet at 1, in white cordite flashes in dark roads.

27. Rain and sleet and sun, getting guns camouflaged, stealing a Decanville truck, laying out nightlines. Letters from Hodson, Eleanor and Sgt Pellissier. Still that aching below the nape of my neck since my last O.P. day. Sat till 11 writing letters. As I was falling asleep great blasts shook the house and windows, whether from our own firing or enemy bursts near, I could not tell in my drowse, but I did not doubt my heart thumped so that if they had come closer together it might have stopped. Rubin and Smith dead tired after being up all the night before. Letters to Helen and Eleanor.

28. Frosty and clear and some blackbirds singing at Agny Château in the quiet of exhausted battery, everyone just having breakfast at 9.30: all very still and clear: but these mornings always very misleading and disappearing so that one might almost think afterwards they were illusive. Planes humming. In high white cloud aeroplanes leave tracks curving like rough wheel tracks in snow—I had a dream this morning that I have forgot but Mother was in distress. All day loading shells from old position—sat doing nothing till I got damned philosophical and sad. Thorburn dreamt 2 nights ago that a maid was counting forks and spoons and he asked her 'Must an officer be present'. Letter to Helen. Tired still.

29. Wet again. Getting refuge trenches dug for detachments. Marking crests on map. How beautiful, like a great crystal sparkling and spangling, the light reflected from some glass which is visible at certain places and times through a hole in cathedral wall, ruined cathedral.

30. Bright early, then rain. New zero line, planting pickets. Arranging for material for new O.P. dugout—old one fell in yesterday. Clear and bright and still from 6 p.m. on. Air full of planes and sound of whistles against Hun planes. Blackbirds singing and then chuckling as they go to roost. Two shells falling near Agny Château scatter them. Letters from Helen and Mother and parcels from Mother and Eleanor. Too late to bed and had no sleep at all, for the firing, chiefly 60-pounders of our own. Shakespeare's plays for 10 minutes before sleep.

31. Up at 5 worn out and wretched. 5·9s flopping on Achicourt
while I dressed. Up to Beaurains. There is a chalk-stone cellar
with a dripping Bosh dugout far under and by the last layer of
stones is the lilac bush, rather short. Nearby a graveyard for the
'tapferer franzos soldat' with crosses and Hun names. Blackbirds in the clear cold bright morning early in black Beaurains.
Sparrows in the elder of the hedge I observe through—a
cherry tree just this side of hedge makes projection in trench
with its roots. Beautiful clear evening everything dark and soft
round Neuville-Vitasse, after the rainbow there and the last
shower. Night in lilac-bush cellar of stone like Berryfield.
Letter to Helen. Machine gun bullets snaking along—hissing
like little wormy serpents.

APRIL

1. Among the ragged and craggy gables of Beaurains—a beautiful serene clear morning with larks at 5.15 and blackbirds at 6
till it snowed or rained at 8. All day sat writing letters to Helen,
Father and Mother by the fire and censoring men's letters etc,
an idle day—I could not sleep till I went to bed at 10. Letters
from Helen, Baba and Deacon. A fine bright day with showers.

2. Letter to H. K. Vernon. Another frosty clear windy morning. Some sun and I enjoyed filling sandbags for dugout we
are to have in battery for the battle. But snow later after we
had fired 100 rounds blind. Snow half melting as it falls makes
fearful slush. I up at battery alone till 9.30 p.m. Writing to
Helen and Frost. Rubin and Smith sang duets from 'Bing Boys'
till 11.

3. Snow just frozen—strong S.E. wind. Feet wet by 8.15 a.m.
Letters from Gordon and Freeman. The eve. Letters to Gordon,
Freeman, Helen. A fine day later, filling sandbags. MAC-
BETH.

4. Up at 4.30. Blackbirds sing at battery at 5.45—shooting at
6.30. A cloudy fresh morning. But showery cold muddy and
slippery later. 600 rounds. Nothing in return yet. Tired by
9.15 p.m. Moved to dugout in position. Letter from Helen.
Artillery makes air flap all night long.

5. A dull morning turns misty with rain. Some 4·2s coming over at 10. Air flapping all night as with great sails in strong gusty wind (with artillery)—thick misty windless air. Sods on f/c's dugout begin to be fledged with fine green feathers of yarrow. Sun and wind drying the mud. Firing all day, practising barrage etc. Beautiful pale hazy moonlight and the sag and flap of air. Letters to Mother and Helen. HAMLET.

6. A lazy morning, being a half day: warm and breezy, with sun and cloud but turned wet. Billets shelled by 4·2: 60-pounders hit. In car with Horton to Fosseux and Avesnes and met infantry with yellow patches behind marching soaked up to line—band and pipes at Wanquetin to greet them, playing 'They wind up the Watch on the Rhine' (as Horton calls it). After the shelling Horton remarks: 'The Bosh is a damned good man, isn't he, a damned smart man, you must admit.' Roads worse than ever—no crust left on side roads. Letters from Helen, Mervyn, Mother, Eleanor.

7. Up at 6 to O.P. A cold bright day of continuous shelling N.-Vitasse and Telegraph Hill. Infantry all over the place in open preparing Prussian Way with boards for wounded. Hardly any shells into Beaurains. Larks, partridges, hedge-sparrows, magpies by O.P. A great burst in red brick building in N.-Vitasse stood up like a birch tree or a fountain. Back at 7.30 in peace. Then at 8.30 a continuous roar of artillery.

8. A bright warm Easter day but Achicourt shelled at 12.39 and then at 2.15 so that we all retired to cellar. I had to go over to battery at 3 for a practice barrage, skirting the danger zone, but we were twice interrupted. A 5·9 fell 2 yards from me as I stood by the f/c post. One burst down the back of the office and a piece of dust scratched my neck. No firing from 2–4. Rubin left for a course.

★   ★   ★

DIARY

On the last pages of the diary are these notes:

The light of the new moon and every star

And no more singing for the bird . . .

I never understood quite what was meant by God.

The morning chill and clear hurts my skin while it delights my mind.

Neuville in early morning with its flat straight crest with trees and houses—the beauty of this silent empty scene of no inhabitants and hid troops, but don't know why I could have cried and didn't.

Loose inside the diary, strangely creased by shell-blast like the diary, are a photograph of Helen and an army pass to Loughton/Lydd dated 3.12.16. Also a slip of paper with addresses of S. N. Jones of Newport, H. K. Vernon of Oxford, J. N. Benson of Upper Tooting, Lewis John of Upminster, his brother Julian Thomas in Tooting. On the reverse of this in pencil is written:

Where any turn may lead to Heaven

Or any corner may hide Hell

Roads shining like river up hill after rain.[4]

[4] Cf. 'Roads', fourth and seventh stanzas.

ThunderPoint Publishing Limited

First Published in Great Britain in 2013 by
ThunderPoint Publishing Limited
Summit House
4-5 Mitchell Street
Edinburgh
Scotland EH6 7BD

ISBN: 978-0957568921

www.thunderpoint.co.uk

This book is dedicated with love
to Daniel and Siobhan,
my beautiful, amazing, children.

2012; when Elizabeth met Mary

I stopped in my tracks, realising instantly that she was the Virgin Mary.

It was obvious it was her; the outfit gave her away, yet there was something unfamiliar about her. She wasn't smiling or radiating a heavenly glow, not in the way you would expect. There was an air of arrogance I wouldn't have anticipated, would refuse to believe if I wasn't witnessing it for myself. Her stance was cocky; leaning against the door her back was straight, her right foot tapping impatiently, the wooden sole of her sandal penetrating the floor with the intensity of an axe. The tone was more Miss Jean Brodie than gentle Virgin.

And yet she was radiant. It took everything I had not to spill adoringly into her arms, entwining myself in skinny, angular limbs. I stood for a moment, remembering. There was a time I'd prayed, relentlessly and religiously, for exactly this, the chance to meet Mary, to bring to life the cheap statue perched ominously on the table beside my bed. I pulled my shoulders back in satisfaction, content that the incoherent ramblings of a seven year old girl had been worth it: the statue had ears. Then the recognition slapped me hard, my cheeks burning fiercely when it occurred to me that she really had been listening, watching, judging. I swallowed quickly, recalling a childhood without innocence.

And then I allowed myself to remember the moment we'd met once before, the night they said I should forget because it was all in my overactive (insane. . .) imagination. Maybe they were right, maybe it was, and maybe this moment was too. I didn't know. I didn't know anything anymore. I resisted touching her, just in case there was nothing there.

I needed time to think so I stopped the clock, not forever, just long enough to steal some of the scene. I blinked softly, my surroundings misty, clouded by the place I climbed to when a moment demanded my withdrawal. I used the sanctuary as a platform from which I could study her face, the features of an apparition, this inopportune visitation from the Virgin Mary, the Mother of God. Swallowing softly I searched for inner strength, trying to stay tough, focused. But it wasn't easy. She was younger than I had always remembered, beautiful in the way the word was really meant to be used. And tall; I could trace the definition of her legs beneath the long white dress that pinched her neck and gently hugged her breasts and hips, her soft brown skin finally visible where it smothered the small round bone of her skinny ankle. The crisp cotton dress was in contrast to the blue robe, rolling in gentle waves from her shoulders, crashing to the floor like an overture.

Just as the statues and the paintings depicted her hair was long, dark tresses that shone like polished pavements on a rainy day. Her eyes were a piercing blue, her cheek bones high and pronounced, barely-there pink lips full and pouting. Her teeth were straight and white, bar one interloper, a lopsided incisor that sat cheekily out of line. It was a cutting edge that flattered rather than flawed. Her tongue was also sharp.

'Right Elizabeth, you can stop right there cos this is as far as you're going wae this stupid idea of yours. You'll be killing naebody the day, the next day or any other flippin day, so you can just catch yourself on an' forget it.'

She was talking, her sweet Virginal mouth giving me lip in a broad Glaswegian twang. I smiled, inspired and driven, filling my lungs with chilled air. I drew my right hand to my mouth and pressed the dandelion clock against my lips. I released my breath and blew, my lips pursed tightly, my tongue channelling the air directly to the tiny fibres. It was going to take more than a vision to stop me now. The head of the flower shattered, a flock of angels breaking free, faltering for a few moments before fluttering into the air beside me. I tipped an imaginary hat, wishing them well on their travels.

The clock had called time and his was well and truly up. The bastard was about to die. Not even the Virgin Mary, whether she was here or she wasn't, was going to get in the way of that.

1989; when Elizabeth met Bananarama Girl

It was more of a demand than a question, the moment she spoke to me for the first time.

'Have you got a light hen? I'm totally gaspin.'

It was a pronouncement that would change so much and yet whilst I could hear her I was choosing to ignore her existence. The words were falling from the sky, emerging from somewhere above me. I shivered a little, my senses heightened, my bloody nose imagining shit from a seagull sliding with menace through my tousled hair.

I heard her talking to me, asking the question in her gravel voice, the second time she said it the syllables grating in the small of her throat with that little bit more menace. But I didn't budge, preferring to stare at the floor. I had been engrossed, submerged in brown carpet tiles, thick coarse squares of trampled horse hair which for the moment were the be-all and end-all. I knew what I was doing was stupid, I was waiting on her calling me a fanny, but I couldn't help it, all I wanted was to be able to spend whatever time I could not having to deal with myself or the world that I was living in.

I was sitting on the row of seats nearest the door, my bum at an angle, my feet poised to run in its direction. If – when – I had to. There was no-one sitting beside me, the other girls preferring to huddle together at the back, the low whispers of their incessant chatter rumbling along the floor and tickling my feet with loneliness. I was an outsider, even in a unit for homeless women. I was a target, and even now, here in this place that was supposed to lend itself to sanctuary, I was it. The one folk would bear down on with derision.

There was nothing else for me to do but clench my teeth and try to focus on discounting her scratchy voice, but a shadow stole into my line of vision. Reluctantly I responded to the shape that emerged in front of me, its irritating presence knocking me to my senses, kicking me back into the nothingness of my existence.

As soon as my lashes flickered I realised that I hadn't blinked for ages. A dull ache hit me between the eyes and I screwed them shut, the harsh motion tugging at the rest of my features. My nose and forehead wrinkled, the taut furrows pulling my lips forward so they pursed in a kiss. I opened my eyes slowly, taking a sharp breath, waiting for the irritating black dots that had invaded my eyes to disperse and return my sight to normal. I blinked again, my swollen cheek searing with pain as I puckered my eyelids, pushing them wider than I could bear, the thin skin stretching, my eyeballs bulging like ugly little beasties.

For the voice my movement was an invitation to speak again.

'I'm not looking for hassle hen, just a wee light for ma fag.'

Raising my head I glanced towards the source of the sarcastic comment allowing my lips to tease open, a simple gesture confirming I'd heard. Far more polite than *I fuckin heard you the first time* which was what I was tempted to say but never ever would, because it wasn't the make of me. I wasn't the type of person to stand up and make myself heard.

The voice belonged to *her*. She was the same age, or maybe a year or two older than me. But she wasn't like me, she was streetwise; I could tell by her stance, her neck pressing forwards, her head held high and self-assured as if she ruled the world.

She was standing directly in front of me, her legs slightly apart, a fag dangling from the side of her mouth, the filter stained on one side, dark purple lipstick usurping the pale brown paper. Her hair was dark, long unkempt tresses scrunched in chaotic perfection. I scanned it from crown to tip, wondering how she managed to get it to look like that. It was like the singer's hair in Bananarama.

A leather bike jacket drowned her upper body, bulky

shoulders collapsing into sleeves so long they smothered the knuckles on both hands. It was tattered, torn in places, tiny scratches of another life before finding Bananarama Girl. There was something cool about it though, like an old person's face, the ingrained wrinkles proving that sometimes life was there for the taking.

I looked at her, instantly wanting her. The realisation overwhelmed me in a single heartbeat. She was everything I needed to be. I arched in her direction, my body gravitating toward her pale white skin like a cartoon magnet, an invisible force pushing me to where I had to be. In my excitement the air became trapped in my throat and I coughed, my fingers urgently grasping my neck, trying to free me, to make sure that she wasn't taken away from me in a tragic asthmatic attack. Gradually my breath returned but I still gasped, my knees shaking, my heart beating unnaturally, its rhythm unsettled by the uncertainty of it all.

The feelings weren't entirely sexual, not then, not at that moment. In that very instant, in that defining second right there and then, I wanted to be her, to be the person who stood as bold and tall as she did. I flicked my own long hair across my shoulder, imagining its limp split ends were strong and scrunched like hers. My spine straightened in response to my illusory confidence.

Bananarama Girl was wearing black leggings and white slip on pumps, tattered at the front, the tips black and grazed yet still screaming *pretty shoes*. As soon as I saw them I recoiled, pushing my own feet under the seat, my battered Adidas Kick trainers shamed into submission.

I watched her carefully, my fingers tingling at the way she peeled the cigarette slowly from her plump lip and rolled it between the first two fingers of her right hand. I sniggered when she turned to the security guard at the door and sneered '*what the fuck are you looking at?*' and then my mouth tried to mimic hers as she tickled the tiny space between her front teeth, flicking her rich red tongue across her lips. My attempt to copy her stuttered awkwardly, my own tongue unfamiliar with such a confident route, like a little girl toddling uncertainly in her mother's high heeled shoes. And yet I found the strength to talk to her.

'I've got matches in my bag but you're not allowed to smoke in here.'

Fuck. I heard the words as they spilled from my foolish lips, couldn't believe it was my mouth they were gushing from. I sounded like the school grass, *you cannae dae that cos you'll get intae trouble*. I tore at the edges of my tongue with my molars, chastising my stupidity. I swallowed hard, hoping she would see that I wasn't myself, that I was fuckin stupid with exhaustion. I could feel Bananarama Girl staring, sizing me up. I avoided eye contact.

'I . . . didn't mean that to sound like that, I just mean . . .'

She interrupted before I could finish, cutting off my feeble attempt to inject a personality. My chin fell to my chest, waiting, knowing she had the opportunity to bite, to tear at my insecurities before spitting me out in disgust. But she didn't. Bananarama Girl laughed and I raised my head and watched as she danced in front of me, spinning round, pulling one foot around the other, her body twisting, twirling like a lion trying to locate its favoured position, writhing around in a slow deliberate circle. Her arms outstretched in search of balance she settled on the spot she had rejected only moments before, raising her toes like a big cat gnawing in satisfaction.

I stopped feeling sorry for myself and laughed, the movement discharging fresh blood from my lip, the warm syrup trickling down my chin and along the underside of my jaw. The laughter sank deeply and it surged to my stomach, a violent reminder of the heavy ache that was tearing ferociously at my insides, but it didn't matter, it was reassuring, comforting to know that not everything inside was dead.

Her routine complete, Bananarama Girl bowed gracefully, tipping forwards like a little ballerina in a music box, crossing her feet in a pas de deux, the hair around her face lifting gently in the slipstream her spin had created. She was everything to me already.

'It's cool, ah hear you hen, the Gestapo's watching. The least we can dae is give them something worth gawking at.'

She turned to the security man, snaking her eyes, blowing him a sarcastic kiss. Glaring, he stepped forward. Changing his mind he leaned against the wall, drawing one leg behind him, resting a dirty black boot on the woodchip wallpaper, perfecting his *I couldnae give a fuck about you* stance. Bananarama Girl shrugged her shoulders, grabbing a strand of hair from her face and scrunching it with her fist. The movement revealed a purple bruise on her forehead, a crescent shaped slice of the distant moon.

I stole a glance at her eyes, and the urge to take her in my arms and hold her close was so strong I had to sit on my hands. In that instant I could see that she was an addict, her pale blue irises screaming the secret, unashamedly revealing that her pupils were swathed in heroin. A tenner bag was enough to stride the floor with a confidence forgotten about in the cold storm of withdrawal. I rolled my eyes, realising we shared a pathetic streak. Maybe without the dragon she was as weak as me.

'Can you give me a wee shot oav your matches then hen?'

Her voice was urgent, irritated, my matches the most important thing in the world. I furrowed my eyebrows, questioning her fractiousness.

'I'm no meaning to nag you hen, ah just cannae go another second without a smoke, this fuckin place would drive you nuts. And don't get your knickers in a twist, I'm gaunae go outside tae smoke it.'

She was smiling, pointing a skinny finger in the direction of my groin. I watched her closely as she scanned the room, tutting, her thoughts in another place as she held out her hand impatiently. Her toes were tapping out her irritation, the vibration reaching the soles of my feet, energy that I lapped up, the rhythm of Bananarama Girl gyrating into my tibia and beyond. Nervously I fumbled in my bag, suddenly craving the nicotine rush as much as she did. I passed the box, the contents rattling as they slid from my hand to hers. I tried to concentrate on the sound, wondering if I was listening to a shared moment.

'Fancy wan?'

I shook my head.

'No thanks. My wee girl is playing over there; this isn't somewhere I'd like to leave her on her own.'

I grinned childishly at Collette, waving reassuringly, reminding her that I wasn't far away. Bananarama Girl turned her head, pulling a funny face in my wee one's direction, identifying Collette as mine amongst the four kids congregating in a filthy corner. A faded 'children's play area' sign and a few broken toys and books with their pages torn and worn had secured their interaction.

Collette smiled back at my new friend. She looked exactly like me, a once upon a time version, a tiny mirror of better times. I watched her quietly until Bananarama Girl distracted me, her lips just shy of touching my face, her hot breath as thick as soup, her voice strained, the syllables crackling as if she was walking over gravel.

'The weans could dae without any of this shit. We can handle it tae a certain extent but wance they know what's going on, you need tae . . . well, you're daein it hen, you need tae get yourself tae fuck away from it all.'

She raised her arm towards me, drawing it back and letting it fall across her stomach without making contact. I swallowed quietly, disappointed her burgundy nails hadn't come closer. In a split second I imagined her arms caressing me in the warmth of a hug, her fingers tearing at the layers of protection. And then just as quickly the desire was gone.

'Do us a wee favour hen and gies a nudge if the wifie at the desk shouts me.'

My response to say sure was without connection; my thoughts were with Collette, wondering if today would fuck her up, inflict long-lasting psychological damage on her impressionable young mind. Yet I didn't need to focus on such things, not now I had a diversion. Bananarama Girl was

on her way to the door, clutching the fag and matches, a
lifebelt, her incessant humming interrupting the dynamics of
the room.

Homeless and heartless

I coughed, trying to clear the smog in my veins but it was a half-hearted attempt. There was too much pain. The woman at the desk shouted a name and I pushed my aching bones into the back of the chair, hoping that this time it would be me.

'Mrs Shaw.'

My shoulders curled when I realised it wasn't and I sighed, wiping dried blood from my lips with the index finger of my right hand. I rubbed the hard substance between my finger and thumb, slowly, feeling it crumble and fall like little stained snowflakes to the floor. I watched the desk and a voice bellowed from behind it.

'MRS SHAW . . .'

Fuck it *was* me.

I pushed myself on to my feet, ignoring the impostor that had attached itself to my hip, a numb lump of a leg that had lost all sense of life during the wait. I stumbled across the floor, my gait as pathetic as me, my jaw slurping as I tried to contain the attack of pins and needles that arrived alongside the feeling in my leg. The woman behind the desk was waiting impatiently, hitting her pen methodically off the desk, the continual dull thud like a death march. I slumped painfully into the seat in front of her, signalling to Collette to join me.

'What's the matter Mrs Shaw, did you forget who you are?'

No smile, no friendly introduction, just a sarcastic tone, a couldnae care less attitude. I stared at her blankly, my head spinning, my woolly brain not sharp enough to challenge her, demand that she empathise, woman to woman. I didn't respond quickly enough. She nodded towards the direction I'd come from.

'You didn't recognise your name when I was calling it. Are you sure you are Mrs Shaw . . . ?'

Her mood was impatient and disinterested; conversation for conversation's sake, but it did sink in. I got the jist of what it was she was twittering on about and I tried to explain.

'Oh yes that, no, it's no that, it's . . .'

I was stumbling, stammering like an eejit. I'd lost my ability to converse, everything too much of an effort.

'Yes?'

A bored stare executed the curt retort from across the desk. She was an older woman, in her late twenties with round cheeks and pale blue eyes smothered in matching eye shadow and mascara. Her poise was stiff, her chin resting on her hand, a diamond engagement ring and a gold band eating her finger.

'I didn't realise you were talking to me. I forgot . . .'

She stared, vacantly. Thinking I was nothing. But I fumbled deep inside, locating a tiny slither of sense to give back to her.

' . . . I'm not that long married, I've not got used to that name yet but it doesn't actually matter, I'm not going to be using it anymore. I'm going back to my maiden name.'

It was a revelation and I raised my voice, excited that I'd made a decision about my future, that I'd taken control.

'Can you change that and put me down as Miss Reilly?'

As quickly as I'd decided it I changed my mind again.

'No, Ms Reilly.'

I leaned over the desk, encouraging her to take a pen and cancel out the other life. I mouthed it quietly, following her hand, a crab scuttling across the page, red words on pale white paper.

Ms Reilly.

Even that didn't sound like someone I was familiar with. I pulled my chair towards the desk, pushing my body against the table until my stomach rubbed along its harsh edge. It grated painfully and I struggled with a watery mouth before composing myself. I focused. If I kept looking at my name on the paper maybe it would help me remember something about myself that I didn't have to forget.

'Fine *Ms* Reilly, you can call yourself whatever you like as long as you understand that if we re-house you this time it will be the last time. Now . . .'

She pulled out a file and I followed it closely. The cardboard cover flopped open and I watched as her fingertips engaged in an intensely personal moment, my secrets revealed, my fucked up life flapping in the wind like a line of wet washing. Hauling my elbows onto the surface of the desk I covered my face. I didn't need to hear that I'd fucked up again. Same place, same story. I raised my head when a soft fingertip brushed against my wrist.

'I'm sorry love, I'm not meaning to be harsh, I'm only trying to do my job. You've been homeless twice already, once when you were pregnant and then again, what, about a year ago? It's some going for someone your age, wouldn't you agree?'

'Yes.'

I coughed softly. I wasn't in any position to deny it. Mum and dad had kicked me out when they found out I was pregnant. I didn't know where else to go so I phoned the social worker they'd made my case worker when I got out of the hospital after my treatment. I was sixteen then and she sent me here without the hope of a helping hand. I phoned Patrick from the coin box outside to tell him where I was and he came in and stole me away, a knight in shining armour. No bird of his, he said, was going to live like scum.

The second time I had been homeless Patrick kicked me and Collette out of the car at the door, *get to fuck and don't come back*, he'd said. I didn't even wait long enough to be sent to a temporary home. I cuddled Collette in the sling on my chest and went back to Patrick, limping along the road, the pain in my body searing. It was my fault and I told him I understood that when I begged him to let me stay. Third time lucky.

'What age are you anyway, twenty, twenty one?'

She smiled, ever so slightly, as she flicked the pages on my file. I saved her the trouble of looking.

'Nineteen.'

It sounded ridiculous; I could hardly believe it myself. But it was true and I repeated it so we could both hear what a fuckin mess I was in.

'I'm nineteen, I'll be twenty in a couple of days though.'

She dropped her chin. My eyes involuntarily latched onto hers, her pupils spilling a shred of pity as she remembered her own teenage life.

'Look love, you need to be sure, *really* sure, that you're going to stay away from him this time. You're running out of lifelines.'

Her voice was kinder and I hated it, the softness would make me cry if I let it soak into my soul and I couldn't do that, not any more. I had to be strong for Collette. But she was right, I had run out of lifelines. My body was aching, everything hurt, even my teeth. I curled my tongue around my mouth, checking for the hundredth time that they were all still there.

'Don't worry, we'll sort you out with somewhere to stay but before we send you up to the homeless unit I think you should get down to the hospital. That cheek looks broken for a start.'

I raised my hand to my face, not too close as contact was unbearable. But the woman was right enough. He'd smashed it tae smithereens.

Lifesaver

Bananarama Girl wandered back into the waiting room and threw the box of matches towards me. The Swan Vestas fell like maracas onto my crotch, the closest I'd come to hearing sweet music in a long while. I picked them up, drawing the rough edge of the box towards my nose. The smell of burning sulphur drifted towards my lungs and I inhaled it sharply, smiling as Bananarama Girl coughed a message to me.

'Thanks . . . a lot . . . . you're a life . . . . . . saver so . . . . . . y'are.'

I waited until she caught her breath then smiled, a drip of excitement trickling down my throat like the sweetest honey. We were sharing a moment. It was completely irrelevant that the only thing that had struck us together was a box of matches and the lack of anywhere else to go.

'Do you mind leaving us alone? We're actually in the middle of a meeting here.'

The woman behind the desk looked at Bananarama Girl in disgust, her hand flapping in derision, shooing her away as though she were an intrusive bee. Ignoring her I shook the matches, holding them up for adoration like an altar boy ringing the bell during the High Prayer.

'Thanks for returning these, anytime you need them just let me know, I'm always happy to help.'

Bananarama Girl winked, the action manly yet endearing as she beamed sarcastically at the homeless officer. She glared back, her stance cold and rigid as if her vertebrae were rooted in the slats of her chair. In contrast I resembled a stray dog; my buckled body slumped on the desk, my legs splayed uncomfortably beneath me.

Bananarama Girl hollered, 'Did she call me then?'

I laughed, my neck straining skywards as if I was about to bark.

'No, she called me and given the fact that I didn't know who I bloody well was there was fuck all chance of me speaking up on your behalf.'

She screwed the features on her face, their chaotic collusion meaning confusion.

'Ha, sorry, I should explain. I haven't got a clue who you are, I don't know your name from Adam. How was I supposed to know if she shouted you?'

I hauled myself up on to my elbows, uncurling my palms, revealing my lack of information.

'Sorry hen, my heid's mince the day, I never thought tae tell you who I am. To be honest naebody usually wants to know. I'm Sadie. Ma name's Sadie MacLean.'

I raised a hand to reciprocate with my own information but I was interrupted by a haughty tone.

'That's great but would you mind sitting down and letting me continue my discussion with Elizabeth. I'm actually trying my best to help her here.'

The voice was as unyielding as her stance, a command more than a comment and Sadie and I giggled childishly. Collette drew me back to reality, clambering like a kitten on to my knee and grabbing my face. The gesture was gentle, a little girl's affection towards her mother, but her fingertip was like a sharpened claw. I drew breath to conceal a squeal, the action enough to suppress an onset of tears, the fierce pain a stark reminder of the terror of the earlier hours of the morning. My recall passed unnoticed.

'Look, do you want help or not?'

I pulled my aching body from the chair, her lack of compassion driving me to my feet. Collette swished down my legs, her journey not as fun as the slide at the play park. A hand clambered onto my shoulder, gently pushing me onto the chair. I had no pride to fight and I fell willingly.

'I'm sorry, that didn't sound right. I know you need help.

Now what are you going to do about seeing a doctor? Your face is a mess love . . .'

She spoke slowly, her eyes spotlights examining my face, her mouth spilling open as her heavy words fell to the floor.

'You must be in agony.'

She said it as if she understood the pain but I could tell by her rosy cheeks that she didn't have a clue. She had *seen* hurt, she was mildly intrigued by it, but she had never ever experienced it. I didn't resent her for that, just myself for being such a failure.

I loosely covered the left side of my face with my right hand. What little heat I had in my fingers was still enough to radiate towards my face, heightening the pain. I knew how bad it was even though I hadn't looked in a mirror. I didn't need to; I had heard the bone crack, a banger exploding in the long run up to Guy Fawkes. With my eyes closed I could see him, in slow motion, his head cascading towards mine. I must have hoped the wind would change direction because I didn't move, I didn't peel away from the inevitable onslaught.

It stopped time, just for a moment, him completely still, a statue looking right through me, shock I think, followed by reality, the boot in the stomach that left me on my back, unable to get up, never ever able to fight back. I caressed my good cheek, reminding myself that there was something to save.

'I'm not going to the hospital, they'll just hassle me to go to the police and I can't cope with that just now. I just need to get Collette out of this place.'

I couldn't face the consequences, the furious reaction if I grassed him up. Hiding was the only option. I shook my head, slowly, hoping the language was powerful enough to let her know that I wasn't going to change my mind. She wasn't listening.

'It's your decision, but do you not think it might be a good idea to let the courts deal with him? There's a good chance he could do it to someone else. Let's face it, he's been violent towards you on more than one occasion. Which poor girl will be next on his hit list?'

'What are you, a fuckin psychiatrist? You don't know anything about me or him so why don't you just stop analysing me and tell me where me and my daughter are going to sleep tonight. Is that too much to ask or do I need to sing or do a wee turn for you before you decide if you can help me or not?'

My outburst simmering I sank back in the chair, the base of my spine rubbing harshly against the cold plastic. I dipped my chin on to my chest, curious that *I'm sorry* was all I could manage when Patrick was kicking fuck out of me. *I'm sorry* was my mantra, it shaped my prayers as a child and bounced off the psychiatrist's wall throughout the duration of our weekly Wednesday afternoon sessions.

I'm so sorry, you must really hate me for wasting your time, my little teenage voice would squawk at him weekly.

I kept it sweet and innocent and yet all the while I was wishing I had the balls to kick him in the teeth, ram my boot into those condescending lips that asked the same questions over and over again. He had no idea, no fuckin idea whatsoever who I was or what I was thinking and I wasn't prepared to change that. No matter what he threatened. It was easier to take the pills and shut the fuck up. If there was one thing I was good at in life it was doing as I was told.

'I'm going to let that go, you're obviously upset.' She was at it again, pontificating, judging, but I'd calmed, resigning myself to the fact that she could walk all over me if she so desired.

'We'll send you up to the homeless unit. You and your daughter can sleep there for the night and then you'll be placed in longer term temporary accommodation tomorrow.'

Thanks was all I could muster, I was too tired to say I was sorry. A first.

'You know, you should at least think about contacting the police, they'll be able to impose some sort of court order to keep your husband away from you.'

Another one who didn't have a clue.

'Forget it, it doesn't matter, I just want somewhere Collette and I can be safe. When can I go to this place?'

She rolled her eyes, tutting her displeasure between her teeth and her lips.

'The minibus will take you over but I'm not sure when it will be here, you'll just have to wait. Could be a couple of hours I'm afraid. Why don't you take a rest from this place, go and get something to eat and come back in half an hour or so? I'll have a better idea of what time the transport is going out then.'

My pockets were empty, there would be nothing to eat. I walked away from her searching for respite in the form of the beautiful Sadie. But she wasn't there. Bananarama Girl had fucked off and with me in the vicinity who could blame her?

The Princesses' Castle

In another life the security man must have been a cattle drover. He clapped his hands loudly, the audio crackling sinisterly as it raced to the edges of the cold room.

'Right *lay-dees*, time youz were on your way, the mini bus is outside and it's no gaunae hang about so you better shift it.'

Collette threw her slight frame towards my chest, fumbling with my underarm so she could climb under my clothing and into my skin. I wondered if she knew that the sound echoed her father's thick fingers every single malicious time they thrashed violently across my face.

A slap's not as hard as a punch, but it does its job all the same, stopping you dead in your tracks, the shock providing a diversion as you wait, a crack-crack-crack that sounds like lightning then rolls in with the intensity of thunder.

I eased Collette on to my knee, peeling her like an orange from under my jacket, hushing her silently, lying to her and to myself, come on my gorgeous baby girl, it's okay, we're going somewhere warm, a special place where we can be safe. Kissing the top of her head I ran my finger down the side of her face, soothing her, an action that had always worked, ever since she pushed herself kicking and screaming into the world five weeks ahead of time. It was as if she knew already that I could only survive with her love. Turning her face towards mine I smiled. Even when life was hopeless I could always manage a smile for my beautiful little lady. Her mouth fell open, loosely, the tension shooting for the stars as she placed her trust in what I was going to say next. I used my fingers to collect pockets of tears from her eyes and pulled her closer, teasing the wrinkles in her black woolly tights, imprints of tiny sand worms circling squidgy knees.

I leaned forward fingering the zip of her red boots, rolling the hard metal clip between my finger and my thumb. I smiled, adoring them, rich red leather with black stitching and crimson zips that motored up the inside like a reversing car, one set of shiny teeth skidding tightly against the other. I buffed the round toes with the sleeve of my jacket, preparing us for a fresh start. I lifted Collette from my knee, one hand bearing her featherweight frame and the other pulling her denim skirt down as far as it would go, protecting her dignity whilst I checked to see if she was dry. Trauma can make you pee your pants; I knew that better than anyone.

I pulled her back on my lap, whhhhhhhhheeeeeeeeeeee, bouncing her up in the air with my knees, swallowing the pain from the bruises pulsating from deep between my legs as she laughed sweetly, the contagious squeal attracting the attention of the woman opposite who smiled but never really engaged, lacking the energy to care the way she once might have.

She was older than the rest of us and the cynic may have said she should have known better, had enough about her to be able to avoid life's crap. Her teenage children were painfully quiet, one on each side, keeping her upright yet not quite steady. I made eye contact and then quickly diverted my gaze. But it was too late. Impulsively my memory snapped an image of her tired face and rolled it towards the front of my mind. It swished like a winter wave, cold and grey yet so engaging you couldn't help but stay with it.

I felt an overwhelming need to distance myself from a wee broken woman who had had enough but would still take more. She got up, answering the security man's call and as she walked she dragged her feet, teeny weenie steps that weren't strong enough to take her in the direction that she needed to go. She was going to go back to him; it was just a matter of time. I searched for pity. It was there in abundance but selfishly I clung on to it. If I gave it to her I would have no energy left to save myself. I was never going to go back. I was going to stay away for ever and ever amen.

I grasped Collette around the waist, clinging to her with

all my might, my right hand winning the race to meet my left and form a magic circle so tightly around her that nothing could penetrate the thing I called 'us'. I drew her in close, my lips pursing loudly at the base of her neck, her shoulders wriggling as laughter peppered her shallow breathing, a lasting remnant of the tears that had flowed so frequently since we left. I prepared to speak, concentrating on making my delivery strong and steady.

'There's nothing to be scared of baby girl. We're going to stay in a big massive house with loads and loads of rooms and the very best one is going to be for us.'

I looked towards the floor. The Penthouse at the Hilton was a million miles from the place we were about to call *home*.

'Jis slike a cassle mummy?'

Collette slid off my legs and turned around, her words slurring as she pulled the cuff of her sleeve across her soggy face. I sought some comfort in her eyes, big and green and gullible, tumbling into them head first.

'Yes baby girl, it'll be our special castle.'

She jumped high in the air, squealing as she skipped in the direction of the door, hopping to her adventure. I watched her closely, envying her energy, her zest for a life that was heading to God knows where.

'I'm a Prinsiss with a cassle . . . I'm a Prinsiss with a cassle . . .'

She waved to me, attempting a curtsey. I giggled and then shouted out as she tripped, one leg buckling under the other. Engulfed with panic my instinct was to run to her, to be with her but almost instantly I was smiling, giggling at the raucous laughter that was channelling its way through the tight bouncing curls suffocating her pale face. She flung her head back in a motion that said, *don't worry mummy, I'm absolutely fine.*

Relaxed, I began to ease myself off the seat, taking care not to move too quickly, concentrating on stopping the pain from mapping its journey on my swollen face. The hand encroached from behind, unexpectedly, strong fingers curling around my upper arm just as another hand pressed its urgent fingers on my lower back, pushing pushing pushing. I gasped, struggling to collect another breath, not wanting to take another breath, knowing that it was him, that Patrick had come to take me back. I didn't turn round, I didn't need to see his grin, the *ha ha up yours* message that said game's a bogey, you're coming home with me. I pushed my weight purposefully on to the chair and readied myself to say sorry.

'Fuck sake hen, you're a ton weight for such a wee skinny thing are you no?'

My teeth tingled with the shock. I snatched a tear with a trembling hand and deposited it on the leg of my jeans. Sadie was smiling, one side of her mouth turning upwards as if she'd been snapped mid-chew.

'Any chance you can put a wee bit of effort in here an' all hen? I might be built like a house but I'm not as strong as wan.'

She moved alongside me, both arms outstretched, her fingers snapping, the music designed to urge me to my feet. She winked; the action was still crude, still manly, but totally in keeping with her and everything I wanted from her.

I uncurled my fingers and accepted her help, reaching my hand out to another girl for the first time since Jenny. *Beautiful, beautiful Jenny.* It was a mammoth step, a momentous occasion, an action of trust, a compulsion to move on. Sadie grasped my hands tightly, her palms coarse, her skin chaffed and raw, but her strength formidable. I felt the energy immediately, the most tentative of touches, but the surge came and I shivered, shaking as Sadie filtered through my body, her existence the be all and end all, her entry into my body spiritual and as it rolled downwards, gently sexual in its message. She pulled and I pushed and Collette laughed and sang see saw Marjorie daw, *Jenny* shall have a new master until the cattle drover interrupted, shuffling towards us with his bow legged walk, snarling, move it you lot you'd think you wanted tae miss the bus.

His tone was dark, uncaring. We were the scum of the

earth. The pains intensified, a furnace smouldering inside my chest, the poker still hacking at one side of my face. I urged Collette to hurry towards the door but she bounced up and down in front of me, 'hand out for the bus mummy?'

Her right arm was outstretched as if she was preparing to make the sign of the cross. I exhaled sarcastically. So far praying had achieved nothing. Mary, the Virgin, the mother of God's children, was nowhere to be seen. I hunched my shoulders, the pain ripping across my back, spiralling sinisterly from my lungs to my stomach, in turn lunging ferociously into my painful groin, bruised and battered from thunderous kicks delivered by a burgundy doc martin boot.

'It's all right honey you don't need to put your hand out for this bus. This is a very important bus, it's only very special people that get a wee shot on it.'

I could feel Sadie's eyes, knew that she was watching me closely, listening to my contrived explanation. She brushed past me, stroking my back gently as she passed in front, not once looking at me, the whole time gazing at Collette. Sadie knelt down in front of her, her movement as graceful as a swan, her legs folding onto the floor in absolute silence. She tugged at the zip of Collette's yellow jacket, tucking her inside it, making her safe, her large round eyes peering through her curls like Orville the duck.

'Your mammy's right hen, you're a very lucky wee girl tae be going on such a great adventure. It's very exciting, I wish I wiz coming wae you an' all.'

Collette smiled, pursing her lips as if she might quack and flap her wings in excitement. Sadie tucked the loose strands of hair behind her ears.

'Can come too?'

Collette croaked the words, quietly but enthusiastically, glancing at me, then Sadie, then back to me again, please please please written all over her face.

'I'll ask my mummy if you can come too.'

My brow furrowed, wondering why Sadie was only wishing

she was coming with us. I felt a wave of panic wondering what life would be like without her. So much, so soon. Sadie stood up, her gaze fixed, answering my question before I had the chance to ask it.

'Like ah said, I'd love to but ah can't so that's that.'

She shrugged her shoulders offering no explanation.

'What are you talking about? The bus is outside.' I pointed towards the door. 'Come on the now, the driver's not going to leave without us, no matter what that wee prick says.'

I sneered in the direction of the security guard, daring him to fuck this up for me.

'Na, it's not that hen.'

A flash of pain flickered across her eyes so quickly I had to convince myself that I'd actually seen it.

'I'm no allowed tae come, it's only lassies with weans that are allowed tae go up to the unit you're going tae.'

She fumbled inside her pocket and like a magician pulled out a Kit Kat and handed it to Collette.

'So you don't have any kids?'

I took a tiny step back, faltering, my surprise affecting my balance. I would have bet on her being a mother. I could feel it, understand it in the way she watched Collette.

'But . . . I thought . . . I assumed you had a child. I . . . thought one of the kids playing with Collette was yours. I'm really sorry Sadie, I just thought . . .'

'Aye, you're right hen, I dae.' She nodded, throwing weight to her sentence. 'I've got a kid so I have, a wee lassie called Laura. She's nearly four, no much older than wee Collette here.' She smiled at Collette, teasing her finger through a tight curl in her hair, Collette oblivious from her chocolate heaven.

'So where is she then?'

I could feel my features pulling together to make a face, my confusion as discreet as a Doctor Whites.

'Look, not that it's any of your business she's staying wae my ma the now, all right?'

She glared at me, reaffirming that it wasn't supposed to be a question.

'Ah'm gaunae pick her up once I've sorted my head out and got us fixed up wae a wee council house of our own somewhere.'

She held her hands together tightly, white imprints sweeping across the backs of her hands. I didn't have time to agree or disagree; Collette was pulling me, demanding my attention.

'Mummy, mummy, we can't get this bus.'

I waited for the punch line, but I should have known better, I should have interpreted the tugging as the beginning of something else. The hand was pulling, urgency grappling for flesh, tiny fingers tearing at my jeans.

'What's the matter baby girl? We don't need money for this bus, I already told you it's a special bus for a special journey.'

Collette sighed, a big deep breath that made her shoulders rise to her ears and then fall sharply and dramatically.

'But mummy you're being silly, daddy's not here yet and he's special too.'

I wanted to fall over, stop the bus, take the battery from the clock, tell time to go and take a good fuck to itself then take a big fuckin noose and tie it tightly around my neck. I looked around, searching for support from Sadie but she was falling into her drug induced world where everything was shiny and far far better than mine.

She was on her knees.

'Collette hen, gaunae give me that wee bit of silver paper off your sweetie hen, I need it for after.'

Glory be to the Father

Barefoot and bare-chested Alan Findlay stood over the
bathroom sink, his skinny hips devoured by pale grey boxer
shorts that draped his puny thighs, the waistband sitting just
below two sharp dimples on his lower back. He was clenching
the cheeks of his buttocks together tightly. The action was
part in reaction to the cold, part in apprehension, but mainly
because of the intense pain that was burning the rim of his
arse.

Continuing to clench his cheeks he considered filling a
basin with cold water to sit in to sooth his burning flesh, the
residue from the fire-like substance that had been trumpeting
from his weary bowels all night like an Orange Walk in July.
He turned on the cold tap and quickly changed his mind, the
chill of the water enough to deter his finger, never mind his
balls which would have to endure a place in the freezing water
alongside his chaffed bum hole. He drew breath and jostled
his weight from one foot to the other, the cold linoleum of
the bathroom floor beginning to seep into his thick feet, solid
blocks of bluish skin that nursed sickly yellow nails,
protruding veins and bunions.

He leaned forward and bending his right knee up towards
his chest he caressed his right foot, briskly warming the sole
with the palm of his skinny hand. The action put him off
balance and he grasped the sink to avoid falling over,
accidentally kicking the wall in the process.

'Fuckin stupid prick.'

He hollered angrily at his image in the mirror and then
punched the wall. A dull thud coughed back at him and the
impact broke the skin on two of his knuckles. Not a sturdy
man by any manner of means Alan reacted to the pain,
screaming as if someone had just twisted a spear into his groin.

'Ayyyyyyyyyyaaaaaaaaaaaaaaaaaahhhhhhhhhhhhhhh.'

Petrified at the noise and the onslaught of an imminent danger his body jolted in fear. He sat on the edge of the bath for a few moments, nursing his hand, scratching his balls and feeling sorry for himself. He was in a mess but none of it was his fault, it never was. Once again, Alan Findlay was about to argue that he was a victim of circumstance.

Buoyed by his conviction he got back to the business of getting ready and swirled a syrupy mix of toothpaste and water around his mouth, puckering his lips whilst he examined his lopsided chin in the oval looking glass, the mirror peppered with white stains, residue from something long forgotten.

After a few seconds he spat the mixture into the sink and then drawing from deep inside his throat he spat again, watching the yellow green substance flop onto the ceramic of the sink, slide for a second, and then stop firmly in its tracks as if someone had rammed on the brakes. He leaned in closer, his pelvic bone rubbing against the cold basin whilst he examined the disgusting blob with some satisfaction. Standing straight he turned on the tap, centring the flow of water onto the contents of his nose and throat.

Standing in silence he watched the gunk put up a pathetic defence before breaking up and swirling down the plug hole. Having lost interest he reached for his chin again, contemplating a shave and then deciding that his excuses would be more convincing from the thinning face of a broken man. Hopping slowly and methodically from foot to foot he pulled the corners of his lips towards the floor and turned his palms towards the sky in his *it wiznae me* stance. Searching for the picture of innocence he glared into the mirror, feigning tears, but he didn't have to struggle too much; they were beneath the surface bubbling away. Underneath his gallus exterior Alan Findlay was shitting himself.

He hadn't slept. Initially it was the anger that had kept him awake and then latterly it was the fear, apprehension that the Boss wouldn't have the time to listen to him crawl his way out of the shit. His fear was substantial and had been growing in intensity, a deep terror grating inside his ribs in a series of relentless electric shocks that had become as regular as his bowels. His breathing was laboured and painful, his sense of panic compelling him to do anything to get out of the mess he was in.

He was also sober, the comforting rush of his last bag of heroin a distant memory, a recollection of a time before the permanent knell of death had gathered around his neck and knotted itself like a hangman's rope. He was desperate for a hit but the fear of the meeting kept the serrated edge off the withdrawals. It did nothing though to dull the constant pain in his legs and the cold and hot sweats that were descending with regularity. He consoled himself with a scenario he envisaged ahead, the Boss sympathising with his predicament before offering him a wee bag or two to keep him going until he got the business back up and running.

He rubbed his face with a damp towel and retched as a smell similar to that of a wet dog drifted up his nose. Disgusted, he threw the heavy lump into the empty bath and glanced at his watch. There was still an hour and a half to go to the meeting, a vast improvement on the twelve hours which had kick started the long countdown the night before. As soon as she left he knew the shit was going to hit the fan.

He tapped his watch, drumming the index finger of his left hand off the glass as he continued to outline the routine in his head: his appeal to the Boss that it wasn't his fault. After a few seconds he stood still, at a loss as what to do next. A chill fell on his shoulders and trickled down his back reminding him that it might be a good idea to get dressed. First things first though he took a piss, holding his dick in his left hand, his right hand palm to the wall, his arm outstretched, the side of the building holding him in an upright position. His bladder emptied but there was nothing satisfying about the process. It was slow and painful, the stinking orange liquid dripping without rhythm or purpose. He stood for a few seconds shaking the residue from the tip and glaring at the limp dick he held in his hand.

He wandered through to the bedroom and scanning an untidy pile of clothes he pondered over what to wear. He lifted several items then discarded them scathingly on the floor beneath him, wondering how his corpse might look when it was cold and pale and saturated in his own blood. Losing sight of his plea for clemency his bowels gurgled in terror, a situation not helped by the scene that was replaying in his head, the image of shitting himself on impact.

In the end he settled on a pair of black underpants. If the inevitable happened then at least they would contain a bit more than boxers, carefully assessing that with shorts there was always the danger of leakage. He found and then ironed clean denims, climbing into them whilst they were still warm, the heat temporarily comforting as he trawled through drawers, cursing Sarah for not putting anything where he could find it. Thoughts of her refuelled his anger and he pushed his fear to the side, imagining punching her repeatedly in the face, one thundering blow for every thousand pounds that was missing.

He opened the veranda door and ventured outside. He negotiated his way past the broken baby walker and collapsed cot, but he couldn't find a path past the Barbie doll so he kicked it violently, pausing to follow its severed head as it launched into the air. It finally collapsed on top of a black plastic bag, its contents nothing Alan could remember. Still furious he clung to the veranda railing tightly, his arms spread wide and his knuckles turning white, his fingers tensely curled around the cold grey metal.

Exhaling a violent roar he thrust the top half of his body over the edge as if he was flying, his pelvis pushing against the iron mesh, diamond shaped patterns engraining his knees and thighs. It was a mild October morning but seventeen floors up the wind was considerable and for a split second he wished it would topple him over the edge, discarding him like a leaf filtering from the weary autumn branches of a lime tree.

Succumbing to the cold and the ticking clock he forced himself back inside and continued to dress, settling for a plain black t-shirt over which he threw his Levi's denim jacket, lifting the collar Elvis style before folding the cuffs back across his wrists, giving his hands the freedom to move and react if they had to.

Best described as a ned, Alan was attractive in an uncultured kind of way, although in recent months he had lost weight and the jeans that once hung like a sexy skin around his curvy ass now sagged and fell, the spare material leaving nothing desirable to the imagination. His hair was thin and wispy, the days long since gone when he preened and gelled and studied his reflection for ages before reaching satisfaction. His face was a weird conundrum; proportionately it was fine, two eyes situated on either side of the nose as they should be, yet he was a shade off properly handsome, sunken cheeks and a red runny nose new elements that added a pathetic aura to a reflection that once held the ability to demand a double take. He did, however, continue to possess a gallus smile and a silver tongue that his girlfriend had found irresistible and nauseatingly plausible as time went by.

Sarah was fifteen when they met, misguided and mischievous, searching for a little something in her life that would lift it from the drudgery of demanding parents and an inability to concentrate at school despite her dreams of grandeur. He was standing at the corner of the school road when she saw him for the first time, drawing heavily on a cigarette, one Doc Marten boot thrust on the wall behind him, his leg cocked as if he was holding the weight of the world on the sole of his foot. His hair was dirty blonde, spiky on top and falling long and fine around his ears and down his neck like Paul Weller. A mod parka lay at his feet as obediently as a dog, the painted target on the back of the coat an open invitation screaming *come and get me* Sarah later said.

They kissed that afternoon, at the flag pole in the local park, after picking magic mushrooms and swallowing them whole with a bottle of Gordon's Gin nicked from Alan's mum's kitchen cupboard. Within two months of that impassioned date on the grassy slopes they were expecting a baby. And two months after the difficult birth of their daughter Laura, Alan's girlfriend, the mother of his child, was hooked on the drugs he supplied to all those that had the money to endure them.

Alan scowled as thoughts of Sarah entered his head and he got rid of them by trying to focus on his own situation. By the time he was ready to leave for the meeting he was feeling a lot more confident. He was a dab hand at getting out of trouble; he knew the lines, he was an expert at the apologetic delivery. He knew he could promise the earth with conviction; Sarah fell for it each and every time. At the heart of this was his own assessment that he was entirely innocent of any wrong doing. Sarah fuckin MacLean was a bitch from hell and deserved to be punished and if he played his cards right he'd be just the one to deliver the blow.

That bravado had faded somewhat by the time he reached the venue for the rendezvous. After pulling away from the door many times, with his jacket on and then off, with his hands deep inside his pockets and then folded across his chest, it occurred to him that he might be dead meat. He took deep breaths, smoothing his hair in a reflection in the window next to the meeting point. Concentrating on his pale face, a shadow of its former self, he caught a glimpse of a sign in the window.

MONEY PROBLEMS?
WE CAN HELP NO MATTER
HOW LARGE OR SMALL

Alan sighed, muttering under his breath that nothing could get him out of this one except a miracle or the return of the prodigal girlfriend.

'Stupid fuckin cow ah could kill you . . . !' Alan called out in rage, forming a fist with his left hand, thumping the window with his other, his despair unnerving an old woman who was walking by with her dog, the little creature as grey and tired as she was. Despite the fact that he was known as a selfish prick he apologised to the old woman, the fear in her eyes reminding him of the look he had often seen on his mother's face when his dad was due back from the pub and he had been ordered to stay in his room no matter what he heard. Nothing more than an innocent child he would stay there, like a rat in a trap, because it was only a matter of time before his dad came in and reminded him exactly who was in charge. It was a pointless exercise; as if he would ever forget.

'Sorry hen, ah didnae mean to startle you there ah'm just having a bad day know what ah mean?'

The old woman scoffed, shaking her head as if she knew everything that the world had to offer.

'Bad day? Wait till you get tae my age son you'll wish you'd never been born.'

She shuffled past him mumbling to the dog. Her words grated painfully inside his stomach and he toyed with hollering after her that there wasn't much chance of him getting to her age, but he reined his hysteria in even though he was more nervous than he had ever been. Yet when he finally plucked up the courage to go in to his meeting he tried to disguise it, flirting with the girl behind the glass window in the taxi office.

'Awright doll, ah'm here to see the Boss, would you let him know that Alan's arrived? And by the way, ah don't suppose you're free the night are you, though it would be a miracle if a cracker like you hadnae been snapped up already.'

His knees bouncing he tapped his right foot repeatedly off the ground and winked, genuinely believing he looked cool and composed. His nerves, though, were pulling both eyes shut making him look as if he was caught in a dust cloud. She ignored him, hard as nails and unimpressed by his sallow cheeks and prickly face. Alan caught her gawking at the tramlines on his arm and cursed his decision to opt for jacket off. He was freezing and instead of looking tough he appeared strung out and desperate. He flicked his denim jacket from around his waist and pulled his arms through the sleeves, instantly feeling the warmth and fearing it would cause him to faint. He couldn't win.

Susan, the telephonist behind the desk, hadn't needed an introduction. She'd been waiting for Alan, and she'd been told to make him sweat. The Boss had phoned and spoken to her directly. The one to one contact with him had her travelling a million miles down the road, propelling towards a future together, fast forwarding to the day she was bending her legs and lowering her arse so she could slot into the passenger seat of his Mercedes convertible as his new bride.

Umberto Donati, the Boss, had fucked her once, at the back of the taxi office during her break. She was leaning against the wall having a fag when he followed her outside and dragged her under the yellow stair-light, to take a closer look at her pretty face, he said. Desperate to feel him inside her she was already pulling her skirt up when he kissed her, and even keener to respond when he whispered in her ear that he liked to fuck a girl that took her own knickers off. As it was they never came quite off, they came to a halt just above her knees whilst Umberto fucked her energetically, her arse bristling off the pebble dash wall with enough vigour to draw blood. For Susan, it was a pain well worth enduring. She longed to be his girl.

When she was ready to deal with Alan she sauntered over to the window, her pink patent stiletto heels click click clicking on the beige lino. Her legs were long and chunky, black fishnet tights emphasising the bulges that buckled around her knees and thick ankles. Undeterred she wore a short red skirt, its hem taken up further than the manufacturer had designed, its cloth covering her arse tightly as she tottered uncomfortably, taking short strides to avoid bursting the fragile seams. The skirt was teamed with a black and silver boob tube and huge breasts that spilled out of the top whistling a big hello to the world. Her make-up was bold, her lips full and red, eye liner thick and black.

She gave the impression of a girl in the dancing on a Saturday night, on the pull, looking for a man to devour. Yet she was a one man woman, only interested in the Boss. That one shag, as quick and furious as it was, was taken as a sign. It allowed her to cling to the hope of it happening again and again and again. And to Susan's credit there was a chance her resilience would pay off. There was as much chance of it happening as not happening. Umberto wasn't fussy. Fucking didn't take a lot of thinking. If he got a hard-on, he fucked. Susan knew his methods because he'd told her, licking her ear as he described exactly how he expected a girl to behave. So Susan dressed every day with the specific intention of pumping blood into Umberto's prick to win the prize of having it settle deep inside her.

Out to maintain standards and enhance her reputation with the Boss, Susan sent Alan packing without as much as a smile, ordering him to wait by the seats beside the fruit machine at the back wall. He duly obeyed, recognising that now wasn't the time for bravado. As he wandered towards the three seats lined together at the back of the waiting room he paused briefly to look at the notice board on the wood panel wall, not really reading anything that was pinned on it, the action another attempt to appear calm and focused, his knowledge that there was a security camera watching his every move encouraging him to act cool.

Whistling, he turned and sat on the middle bucket seat, sinking harshly on to the cold plastic, crossing and then uncrossing his legs, tapping his fingers on his thigh as if he was playing the piano. Moments later he was back on his feet, one hand deep in his pocket looking for change, the other pressing the buttons randomly on the fruit machine. He threw some change into the slot and the coins trundled into the gaping mouth, the machine swallowing them hungrily. The discerning user would have taken the hint from the sound, a warning that it had recently paid out. But Alan wasn't thinking, he was just trying to pass the time, trying to keep alive as long as he could, using the moments to run through his sob story in his head. The money supply was soon dud, the flashing lights more of a tease than an answer. He turned to Susan and shouted at her through the small glass partition, tapping the glass as he spoke.

'Ah don't suppose you could lend me a few quid to play the puggy could you hen, ah've got a feeling it's about to pay out.'

Susan's reply was simple, a *fuck off loser* delivered with the thrusting of two fingers in the air. Two hours later she opened the window for the last time, gazing up and down, taking a final look at what Umberto Donati had called a dead man walking.

'Black Capri, get in it and do whatever the driver tells you tae dae.'

The window slammed shut before he had a chance to acknowledge her and he made his way outside, his bowels loosening and churning as he tugged at the silver handle on the door. The windows were dark, tinted glass that would hide everything, the music loud, drowning out anything that shouldn't be heard. He tried to relax, humming along to the Fun Boy Three track that was blasting into his ears as he folded his legs to climb inside. He shut the door and nervously turned around to face his maker.

Your wish is my command

I could hear her shouting after me, hoi, wait the now will you, ah've got something I want tae tell you, but I just ignored Sadie, turning my back and letting her words wash down its surface as I closed the door behind me.

The bravado was an act. I turned around when I could stand it no longer, craving another glimpse of her as I stepped onto the bus, lifting Collette theatrically through the sliding door, my wwwweeeeeeeeeeeeeeeeeee disguising the pain of the red and purple petals that stained my swollen wrists. They might have looked pretty if they hadn't been tattooed by Patrick's fingers. I peered over my left shoulder, my eyes living the pain for a moment, a second that would allow me to see if she was there.

She was. Watching, leaning against the door with lips that didn't open, lips that didn't shout that we should come back, yell that she had been waiting for me her entire fuckin life. I could still feel the intensity, even when I got on the bus, even when I looked behind for the hundredth time wishing that the moment hadn't passed. I thought of her, imagined her huddling pathetically in the corner of a toilet, her Kit Kat wrapper weighed down with smack, those same lips curling around a rolled up note as she chased the dragon, collapsing when she caught it, the roar consuming her body in the kind of warmth that said there there now, stop your tossing and turning.

I wiped the condensation from the window slowly and deliberately with my knuckle, realising that the swiftness of Sadie's actions had blown me away, her coming and going taking me equally by surprise. I placed my lips close to the glass and breathed heavily, mist spreading onto the surface like cold air on a winter's night. I traced her name, the moisture disappearing under the weight of letters that were hanging heavily in my heart. Collette was standing on the seat, her feet lodged between my parted legs, the deep maroon fabric sour with the putrid scent of piss and tobacco. Oblivious, she commanded the moment, her body long and tall yet still not dominant enough to challenge the void between her and the roof. She swayed with the bus, the heat and her movement causing a sickness to rise from deep within my stomach, teasing me, racing to the back of my throat before falling sharply. After an eternity the engine stopped. I edged to my feet, carefully, curling my head towards my chest, my chin grating off the zip of my jacket. I bent my knees, losing a few more inches from my height to help me clamber outside.

The building sat on a dark grey skyline, bellowing aggressively. It was vast, its width smothered in rich red brick, thick steel grates castrating the windows, the metal winking at the sun which suddenly emerged from under the clouds. I fell to the end of the queue, considering making a run for it, but a woman with a baby in a sling cornered me, her left eye so swollen there was just enough space to squeeze a penny in a piggy bank lid. She didn't grab me, but her words broke my fall, suspending me in mid-air as I toyed whether to stay or go.

'Awright hen?'

I nodded, sheltering the low autumn sun from my eyes with my left hand, trying to keep walking. She brushed her hand against my forearm.

'How dae you know Sadie? I saw you talking tae her back at the housing office.'

Hearing her say Sadie was like being thrown a lifeline. I cleared my throat, quickly and deliberately.

'I don't really know her to be honest, she's just some lassie I started talking to whilst we were waiting. If I didn't do something to pass the time in there I'd have ended up brain dead.'

Sweat was dripping down my spine, slipping slowly into

the crack of my arse. I clenched my bum cheeks, trying to break free from the discomfort.

'Aye, I know whit you mean, fuckin nightmare int it?'

I grasped Collette by the hand.

'Yeah, it was, I just hope it gets better for us from now on.'

We stood in silence, the uncomfortable moment finally interrupted by my desire to know more about Bananarama Girl.

'So how do you know Sadie then, is she a friend of yours?'

The woman nodded, then shook her head as if the question was too difficult.

'Aye, well, ah wouldnae say she was a pal, she was here wae her wee lassie the last time I was in here. We hung about thegether for a few days and that, but ah lost touch with her when we got re-housed. The stupid cow went straight back to her man after the first night on her own. Didnae take much, all he had to do was wave a bag of smack in front of her face.'

I ignored her, refusing to listen to negative talk about Sadie. My own thoughts were complicated enough. I walked away, taking a final look at the outside world, scanning the vicinity for signs of Patrick, listening for his song, *ah'm gaunae get you, break your neck and kill you.* I could hear the curdled laugh that was synonymous with the first punch but I calmed my breathing, convincing myself that it was just a misguided reminiscence; an album of horror photographs, sequentially imprinted inside my head. It was a gaffe, a case of mistaken identity. The pictures belonged to another life. For the moment, we were safe.

Somebody's knocking at the door . . .

I followed the leader, the climb upstairs making me weary. I stood quietly on the landing, watching the housing officer as she placed a long, bronze key in a tall, maroon door, the silver letterbox chattering softly against her jacket as she pushed her way inside. I panicked, remembering the Wednesday afternoon sessions with a shrink who stole the air that we shared between himself and the door, the smirk that accompanied his face when I told him repeatedly about the Virgin visiting me as a child.

I turned to run, but Collette grasped my hand and I followed, without enthusiasm, knowing the kind of intolerable darkness that would be waiting to welcome us inside. An explanation of where everything was, what to do and how to behave quickly followed, the words hitting me on the face like I was being thumped with bouncy balls. She left us standing there, the mouth of the door gaping open, the key now thrust into my hand. I swallowed, noisily, the dryness in my throat gathering in the stairwell and chuckling at me from the floor above. I closed the heavy door behind us, shutting one world out from another as I tentatively pushed my way inside.

Yet the place was lovely. A thick purple carpet fortified the hall, its rich tone warm and inviting. I slipped one foot from my shoe, my sock embracing its softness. I swiped my fingers along the bright yellow wallpaper, its texture as buoyant as it appeared. It was soft and spongy with big bold patterns swimming like sea creatures from top to bottom.

The living room had a red carpet with masses of thick black swirls sweeping across the floor like scoops of blackcurrant ice-cream and there was a separate bedroom, with two single beds, a claret red duvet cover and two matching pillows on each one. Black ash bedside cabinets separated the beds and I glanced at one wishing I had a book to place on its strong edge. I sat on the thick duvet, allowing my lips to curl into a smile.

The front door burst into life, taking another form when the letterbox hammered off the shiny seal with a cchhhhhapppppppppp cchhhhhapppppppppp ccchapppp. Instinctively Collette ran towards the door shouting for her daddy.

She was too small to open the latch but I grasped her hand anyway and pulled her with me on to the floor, our fragile bodies hiding beneath the handle, frightened to move in case he peered through the letterbox. I urged Collette to be quiet, raising a finger silently across my lips before resting it on hers, my fear forcing it on her face too harshly, her reaction eyes that swelled in instant tears. Then the creaking gave it away, let me know that the letterbox was lifting, that the outside world was about to filter into our protective universe. I braced myself for the stench of his poisoned breath.

'Coooooeeeeee ladies, ah forgot to give you your breakfast things.'

I climbed slowly to my feet, drawing the latch towards the floor. My face said it all.

'Sorry hen, I didnae mean to give you and your wee lassie a fright there. Nobody can get in here, I can promise you that. You're totally safe.'

She reached towards me, placing her hand gently on my shoulder before rubbing it reassuringly.

'Right, like I said ah've got a five-star breakfast for you. Follow me intae the kitchen and I'll show you what excitement awaits.'

Collette was eyeing the bag inquisitively bouncing on her tip-toes to find a way to see inside.

'Aye, and no peeping hen, you'll find out soon enough if you hurry up.'

Dutifully we followed, Collette skipping, three tiny steps to our one, her stocking feet gliding above the carpet as she raced to keep up. The woman, Clare as the badge on her lapel read, pulled several contents from deep within a rustling plastic bag. My stomach flipped in hunger when she lined two square sausages, two slices of bacon, two potato scones and two eggs on separate plates and placed them in the fridge ready to sizzle and crisp alongside the breaking dawn of a new day. She reached back into the bag, producing a pint of milk, holding it high like a rabbit from a hat before popping it noisily on the tray inside the door. She forced the door closed with a brash nudge from a bare elbow and it groaned softly. She pulled her arm from the door to her waist, the pale freckled skin of bruise free hands reaching inside her black trousers, the plastic bag changing from lifeline to a roll of nothingness as she curled it beneath her long thin fingers inside her pocket. My stomach rumbled loudly, cueing Collette's declaration of hunger. Clare responded instantly, her jovial tone both uplifting and exhausting.

'You know a lot of the lassies don't bother waiting till the morning and they just eat the breakfast at night. I try and bring them up a wee bite of cereal so I could do the same for you, if you like?'

She pressed the palm of her hand on my shoulder and moved away from me, her body brushing along the kitchen wall, a sssssssshhhhhhhh noise from the Starship Enterprise following her sudden movement. The front door closed gently behind her and I stood for a few minutes in silence.

'Right my little adventurer, how about we have a wee picnic in the living room? I'll cook, but first things first we'll need to build a camp to shelter in.' Collette grasped my hand, excitedly drawing me away from the kitchen so we could begin our game. Her touch was light, gentle, but the pain hit me all the same, my ribs gnawing like toothache when I moved. I smiled anyway, suggesting that we race so she could edge in front of me for long enough to stifle a cry.

But she would never have heard me over the chap chap chapping, the letter box once again clanging loudly, metal kissing metal, both sets of lips passionately embracing the other before being ripped and then thrown apart.

It took a second to register that it was Sadie, her tall figure pushing past me so she could squeeze into the hall without anyone catching a glimpse. Bananarama Girl was back. I prayed it was a good thing.

Just another day at the office

Alan Findlay recognised the driver of the black Capri and it wasn't who he had been expecting. Relief saw him shoot his arm onto the driver's shoulder, his body clambering forward in an un-cool embrace.

'Ya dancer, whit are you doing here?'

'Fuck off eejit. Paw me like that again and ah'll cut your fuckin hands off.'

Paddy's response was cold and decisive, his reaction doing everything it needed to live up to his reputation as a man who didn't mess about. He was a total bastard but his evil deeds didn't even come close to emulating the sick tendencies of the Boss. Realising that his immediate fate lay in the hands of Paddy rather than Umberto, Alan threw his back against the seat of the car, rubbing his hands on his jeans, the sweat now feeling cold and clammy as his heart rate began to fall to something closer to normal.

'Ah man, ah'm sorry, ah don't know what the fuck happened there. Ah wiz just surprised to see you Paddy me ole mucker. What are you daein here anyway?'

Alan fiddled with the volume control on the stereo, bravado giving him ownership of his surroundings. Paddy pushed Alan's hands away, glaring into his face incredulously.

'Are you on another fuckin planet? I've been told to sort out this fuckin mess or you take a wee swim in the Clyde wae a pair of concrete slippers oan.'

Alan thrust his hands behind his ears, his bowels releasing a long burst of gas. Paddy turned and thumped him on the shoulder in response.

'Fuck sake you smelly bastard this is a new fuckin motor. Dae that again and you can deal wae Umberto yourself.'

'Sorry man, ma fuckin stomach's churning ah've been shitting myself aw day wondering whit the Boss is gaunae do. Ah half expected to be deid by now I really did.'

'Aye, an' you fuckin would be if it wiznae for me. Ah tellt him that you were probably just wasted and you'd forgotten where you stashed the money. Now, where the fuck is it cos we're gaunae go and get it the now and then give it back tae the Boss and hopefully that will be the end of it cos if it's no mate you had better pick out an outfit for your burial because the funeral march is gaunae be the next track you hear.'

Alan shrugged his shoulders then threw his arms in the air, conducting his next bit of speech.

'Paddy man, ah've not got the money. That fuckin bitch Sarah's nabbed it and she's done a runner.'

Paddy pushed the middle pedal through the floor, smoke trundling from the front wheels as it screeched to a halt in the middle of the road. A line of traffic tooted in unison behind the Capri and Paddy reeled down the window to fling an aggressive 'V' sign in the air. Back in his seat he lowered his voice, speaking slowly and deliberately. He faced the steering wheel instead of Alan.

'Alan, you better be fuckin at it mate, I've no stuck my neck out to end up wae a bullet in ma throat. Ah brought you in man, ah tellt the Boss we could trust you. Don't make me look like a fuckin fanny. I'm warning you.'

He delivered the final few words face to face, leaning forward at the same time so he could direct the warning right into Alan's eyes.

'Paddy, ah wish ah wiz but she's lost it. She locked me in the fuckin living room and then fucked off wae the money just as ah was heading out tae do the delivery for the boss. Ah've phoned everywan looking for her. Naebody has a clue where's she fucked off to.'

'Bullshit.'

Paddy pushed the car into action, pulling away at speed, honking the horn at a woman with a pram about to cross at the green man.

'You're a fuckin prick Findlay. If you'd looked properly you would have found her. Fuck sake have you no got any common sense? Where does Sarah's ma stay? She'll know where she is.'

He thumped the wheel violently. Alan looked at the leather casing understanding that it could have been him feeling the force of Paddy's fists.

'Dae you think ah havenae tried that already mate? Ah've phoned her twice. When I rang last night mrs fuck-face said she hadnae heard a word from Sarah and didnae want tae either and then when I called again this morning she said she still diznae have a clue where she's gone.'

'Fuck sake Alan, are you stupid? Of course she knows, mothers have got witch's powers, they always know shit about you that they shouldn't. And besides, it's not exactly gaunae be difficult to find her, she's a fuckin junkie, she'll turn up at somebody's door trying to blag a bit of gear.'

'Aye Paddy, she's a junkie, but she's a junkie wae twenty grand, she's got enough cash to keep her in smack for fuckin ever.'

Paddy roared, the raw bellow crashing off the windows. Alan knew him well enough to realise that he was angry at his own stupidity which probably meant things were just about to get worse.

'You're one fuckin stupid prick dae you know that?'

Despite Alan's fear he was fascinated by the change in Paddy's handsome features. His face was distorting, his neck wrinkling like a tortoise, his narrow eyes blackening and bulging in rage. Alan chose to listen carefully though; with Paddy in a mood like this it paid dividends to pay attention.

'You're a fuckin dick Findlay, if ah end up in the shit because of you ah swear tae God ah'll fuckin shoot you myself.'

Alan knew he meant it and in response his face paled to grey. He wrung his hands together, but the wrong doing stayed inside his dry skin.

'Ah'm sorry man, ah didnae mean any of this shit tae happen, ah didnae think the daft cow would steal Umberto's money.'

Paddy was suddenly calmer, a plan of action releasing the pressure on the veins on his temples that were beating like a kid with a new Christmas drum.

'No, you don't fuckin think dae you? Now where does the wee boot's mother stay, ah want a wee quiet word in her ear.'

Alan held his breath, suddenly scared he would blurt out something in Sarah's defence that would result in his imminent destruction. He had an idea what was coming, but he also knew he didn't have the bottle to try and prevent it.

Salt 'n' vinegar

Sadie folded herself onto the chair, her long skinny legs buckling under her torso, her spine curved and her elbows bent and cemented on the chunky arm of the seat, one hand resting lazily under her chin, the fingers of the other entwined loosely around her wrist. She was quiet, stoned, her face telling the story in far more detail than she could. I filled my lungs sharply, trying to concentrate on something other than the erratic thumping of my heart, fear and excitement thrashing it around my chest in equal measures.

My eyes traced her outline and I fought against the reaction of my body, begging it to be still. I tucked my thumb tightly in the palm of my hand, encouraging the wriggling object not to betray me as it itched to use its nail to measure Sadie in all her chaotic proportion, my fingers wandering back to art class and a sudden desire to capture the moment as I saw it, and as I would one day hope to remember it. I closed my eyes tightly, watching my hand work the smoky charcoal across thick white paper, etching, scribbling, pushing and pulling its way back and forward across the page until it was finished, the drawing complete and as stunning as the vision that had entered my boring, frightening, excruciatingly painful life.

My senses heightened I was aware of something else, a strong scent that was filtering towards my nose. I located the white plastic bag lying snugly on Sadie's calves, spread over hard muscles that I imagined betrayed a childhood of Irish dance. I smiled, shyly, curious that we might share another trait, another element of our past. My fingers dropped below the hollow at the back of my knee and as I rubbed the muscle at the back of my leg I stole a magical dance, my elbow locked against Sadie's, our fingers clenching tightly, our wrists embracing as we told the story of the claddagh ring.

The bag interrupted the dance. Its bulk was hiding something as equally tempting. The curved white handles were talking to me, *come and get me*, flirting with me from a position outwith my reach. Sadie ignored the intense aroma, the world she had disappeared into providing more than enough of whatever it was that she got whilst she was in there. The fragrance drifted towards me in cartoon fashion, a chain of meandering smoke that twisted and twirled as it trundled towards my receptive nose. I swallowed hard, the pain pulsating through my body no longer due to the bruises and fractured bones. It was now deeper in my stomach, rising sharply to my throat, making me nauseous and excited all at the same time. I sat opposite her. In silence. Watching.

Collette was in the room, somewhere in the background. I could pick up her outline in my peripheral vision. I was sketching again, my mind encouraging me to focus on everything, to remember it all, leaving nothing to chance as I noted every little detail, mapped it all with the greatest attention. She was building an imaginary camp fire outside her imaginary tent in her own little world. She was talking to herself, her tone sharp and assertive as she placed dolls and teddy bears around the picnic rug that only existed in her head. I stole a glance, turning away from Sadie briefly, my eyes resting on Collette propping up a cushion, calling it a good little girl who had to sit nice for her mummy. I toyed with moving, meandering across the floor and drawing her close to my chest but the moment was too intense, too painful, too fuckin real. I didn't want to focus on the fact that we had nothing.

We'd left everything behind, all Collette's toys, our clothes, our lives. And my treasure chest, a mesh shopping bag with big metal handles that contained remnants of my jumbled life. My diary was in there, the one my mum and dad had given to the psychiatrist, the one they said let them see that I was mad. I didn't have any fuckin idea why the Virgin Mary had visited me as a wee kid and then bailed out as soon as I actually needed her. I just knew that she had been there, and Jenny knew that she had, she knew everything. She believed me and

48

most importantly, I had believed her.

Collette was oblivious to my stare, she was engrossed in her childish world and Sadie was somewhere else, submerged in whatever fables were unravelling inside her complicated head. And still the bag lay across her legs, and still my stomach tugged harshly, pushing high inside my body, strangling my ribcage, consuming my oesophagus with a grip so tight I felt my body buckle and tense. I pulled my hands towards my ribs, massaging the pale skin clamped tightly against my bones. Then my heart flipped. My muse was finally alive to my presence.

'You . . . awright . . . hen?'

Sadie was stirring, filtering back to the real world, mumbled words escaping from her mouth amidst a deep slow yawn. She met my gaze head on, one eye taking a few seconds to lazily catch up with the other. I stifled a yawn sharply, pissed off and yet excited that everything about Sadie was seemingly contagious.

'Oh, *it's* alive then, I thought you'd passed away into oblivion.'

She smiled, rubbing her eyes slowly, being careful not to wipe away the thick calm that was shrouding her. She blinked repeatedly, finding some capacity to engage in conversation, emerging back to my world. I should have warned her not to bother, screamed that she was better off out of it but I listened and yearned, hoping to quietly consume every precious moment we had. I knew already it was just about moments. Mary had left, the precious little Virgin skulking away from my bedside and leaving me to it. And Jenny, she left too, but it wasn't her fault, she had to go.

'Aye sorry hen, I'm a wee bit wasted but I can now offer you my undivided attention.'

'That's very generous of you.'

I was trying to be serious, but a slight curl of the lip did little to hide my intrigue and delight that she was there. I turned to make sure that Collette was out of earshot.

'So, are you going to tell me what the fuck is going on here?'

I slid from the settee to the floor, constant movement the only thing that helped ease the pain, even though the slightest movement intensified the agony that was my battered body.

'Aye, of course I am. That mob fae the housing shoved me in some dump up the west end and ah figured I might have more fun spending the evening wae you.'

She smiled but the sentiment was distant, melancholic. I watched her for a second, the gallus buzz that had zipped around her exterior earlier now firmly resigned. She looked lonely.

'Sadie, this is totally weird, I don't even know you. If somebody finds you here I'm fucked, they'll kick me out and God knows where I'll end up after that. I'm not sure if I'm up tae dealing with something else that's mental right now.'

She rose to her feet and then slipped down onto the carpet, her back to the chair, her left leg aligned with mine, her foot gently pressing on my hip, her own thigh catching the sharp edge of my Adidas Kick that had only moments before led her in a merry dance across the floor. She sighed, lifting the plastic bag and pulling it onto her lap, the movement releasing more of the smell, the strong waft from the bag making me swoon, making my tongue roll towards my lips, saliva collecting in its centre. Collette smelled it too and stumbled towards us.

'I'm hungry mummy.'

Her cherubic face folded; her features were withdrawn and tired, the weight of my life pressing down on her shoulders. I rose towards her, grasping her tiny head in my hands, pulling her face upwards so I could smother her cheeks in tender kisses.

'It's okay baby, I'm going to go and make us something now, maybe Sadie will help build your campsite whilst I go and do the cooking.'

Collette sniggered, a cheeky grin embracing the breadth

of her face. She had just turned three years old but she was aware that engaging an adult in pretence was much more satisfying than sharing playtime with a gullible child.

'Oh shit ah nearly forgot. Never mind cooking anything hen.'

The bag was finally opening, the scent stifling the air.

'Anyone fancy a nice big bag oav chips an' a wee buttered roll?'

I joined Collette in an excited cry of *me me me*. I was so hungry. I couldn't remember the last time I had taken the trouble to eat. Fear has a habit of suppressing your appetite but suddenly it was alive and I was starving, ravenous, hugely excited about the prospect of chips, hot and steamy, doused in lashings of crumbly salt and sharp vinegar. Sadie laughed too, enjoying being the one, the messenger of good news, the person who for a moment at least could make everything feel all right.

We ate without speaking, sitting on Collette's makeshift campsite in the middle of the room, newspaper on our laps, the only noise the slurping of our lips as we sucked the salt and vinegar from our greasy fingers. Collette climbed onto my knee for a second, her salty lips banging mine with a slippery kiss. We smiled and returned to the soggy chip bags, our hands reaching from the paper to our mouths in unison, a rhythmic beat as we shovelled the taste onto our tongues, the food thundering down to our empty stomachs, swelling our insides with a warm contentment. Sadie watched us quietly, eating slowly without passion, her silent lips stocking a slow burning fire.

The Beginning

Collette fell asleep right away, her slender frame hardly visible under the thickness of the duvet. I kissed her goodnight and sat on the edge of the bed, watching her eyelids flicker, her imagination still speaking incessantly as she slipped to somewhere different. Her curls smothered her cheeks and I pushed their softness behind her ear, my fingers lingering for a moment on the soft skin of a face in full bloom. I drew the curtains, pushing the bright moon away from the room, but its silver lips gently kissed the windowsill and eased inside, the white light protective and commanding. I resisted the urge to open the drape and peer beyond the moon, wondering if the people I'd once loved were shining brightly from the brilliance of the night constellations.

In the living room Sadie was mirroring my thinking, her lanky frame pressed against the curtains as she stared out of the window. My eyes resisted the lure of those tempestuous stars, falling from her soft curves to the bottle of wine that had appeared on the table. I bunched my hands on my hips, my own place giving me the temporary assertiveness I had often longed for as I eagerly urged her to share the fruit and give me a drink.

'Aye hen, crack it open will you, there's a corkscrew in my bag.'

She turned half of her body towards me, the other portion still in front of the window, examining the outside world for clues. I reached for Sadie's bag and fumbled inside without looking, not wishing to know anything that wasn't mine for the taking. The corkscrew jabbed me and I pulled away from the dagger sharply, drawing my finger towards my mouth where I sucked the pin prick of blood. My wrists ached and I struggled with the bottle, but Sadie took it from my hands and opened it effortlessly, the plonk plonk plonk sweet music as it slid from the bottle to the cups. She wandered back to the window, keeping edge, for the both of us I hoped.

'Ah can feel you looking at me Elizabeth, but don't panic there's nothing out there, ah'm just looking for a distraction, something to stop me being a fanny and heading straight back tae Alan.'

She dropped her head in her hands and a low roar funnelled through her unbrushed hair, the long strands pushing the audio this way and that, the captured air finally escaping when she pulled her head back, her tall thin neck stretching high into the soft line of her round jaw. The snarl fell to the floor and she grasped her hair in her hands, scrunching it tightly at the back of her head, the skin on her forehead stretching thinly in response.

'Ah'm a stupid cow, I can't believe ah'm thinking of going back tae that prick and any of his shite.'

She stared through the glass, looking at something I couldn't quite see, clenching her weakness in the palms of her hands, rounded fists white with tension. My heart was pounding, I'd been there, made the same mistake many times before. I couldn't do it again. *Be strong Sadie, don't take us into that way of thinking, we can't walk backwards into the darkness of the night* . . . 'Have you spoken to him?' I kept my tone low, trying not to sound incredulous, opinionated. I was in no position to judge.

'Na', she snorted, the word rolling noisily down her nose. 'But he'll be looking for me, he needs me tae get him out of some real major shit. He'll no be long in finding me if I hang about at the hostel and then ah'll go back and life will carry oan being wan big fuck up wae the two of us spending our days wasted out of our stupid little heads.'

'Aye, but how will he be able to find you? I thought th' places were supposed to be secure. Are we not safe .

I glanced in the direction of the door, pullir across my chest, wrapping myself within.

'Fuckin hell Elizabeth, stop panicking, you're totally fine.' She turned towards me, rolling her eyes. 'Look, Alan's got a bit of a mental business partner, he asks a few questions, dishes out some really heavy shit an' then he could find a fuckin needle in a haystack if he wanted tae. He's just like that, he diznae gie up.'

She shrugged her shoulders, acceptant of the approach, her fingers uncurling in an acknowledgement that being found was simply a matter of time.

'But . . .'

I stopped myself, remembering to think before I opened my big fat gob, trying to ensure that my words were helpful, not judgemental.

'So what sort of business is he in, are you okay to talk about it?'

Sadie dropped the edge of the curtain from her hand and it peeled away from her. I watched as it fluttered gently, floating like a first communicant's mantilla in a chilly December wind. She paced across the room, ignoring me. The air in the room was tight, what little there was was crushing my chest, stealing a march on my lungs.

'What's going on with your man and this other guy, Sadie? You look fuckin terrified.'

My intonation was soft, almost a whisper, my neck pushing back as I raised my head to follow her movements across the floor. Finally she slumped on the soft sofa beside me, her voice raised, laced with an exaggerated laugh that revealed even more still.

'I'll tell you whit's going on. All oav a sudden Alan will be thinking about me more than he has done his whole fuckin life. And it'll no be in a good way but it fuckin serves him right, ah'm fed up wae him just walking all over me as if ah don't exist. Ah've told him a million times ah want tae get out of this shitty life and dae something proper for the wean but he's even stopped promising that he'll try. All he cares about is making sure he gets things right for his fuckin boss.'

I gave her a second, readjusting my feet so I could lean over to the table, grabbing the two cups, handing Sadie one before taking a long slow drink, the sharp taste of the bonanza bottle of cheap wine burning the back of my throat. I waited on her to do the same.

'Did he hit you?'

The question set her alight.

'Did he hit me? Fuckin right he did but I'll tell you this for nothing, that prick'll no be hitting me again that's for sure.'

For a split second I wished I hadn't asked the question, suddenly scared of what the answer was, of what I might be dealing with. She was fractious, her shoulders bobbling as she tried to control her breathing. She had let it out but looked like she wished she could take it all back.

'Jesus Sadie, what the fuck have you done?'

I lifted my heavy body from the seat, creating distance, clambering for more wine.

'Fuckin hell hark at you, ah'm not a flippin leper, you don't need to run for the bloody hills, ah'm not some fuckin mad psycho you know.'

I lowered myself on to the edge of the coffee table, my heart beating faster when it was too late to question if it could take my weight. I held my breath until I was sure it was safe.

'Bloody hell Sadie, don't be daft, of course I know you're not a psycho.'

But I didn't, I didn't know what she was capable of, I didn't even want to know what she had done. And anyway, what was a pyscho? Me, they once said. Idiots that they were, amusing themselves with their questions and sniggers as they came to stare at my empty face in that cold, sad roc

'Let's be sure of something, I'm not going to you're your own person.'

It wasn't true. I was judging, assuming th though I had no indication of what that migh' even look at her. She dropped her hand onto r contact, clawing back the distance that my psychotic mind was creating.

'Look, it's not as bad as you think. Ah didnae know what else to do. I said the last time ah came back that ah was giving him six months to jack it all in. Six months and then we'd get away, get off the junk and dae things right for Laura. But he's no interested Elizabeth, he's got no intentions of changing.

'Ah'm fuckin stuck with this shitty life. Sometimes I think ah deserve everything I get. Ah shouldnae have allowed myself tae get into all this crap in the first place. He didnae force me. And now ah've taken it too far and it's totally out of his hands.'

The hardness was gone and I grasped the hand resting on my leg. Her fingers were cold and thin, her skin tough and chaffed but they responded with warmth.

'Sadie . . .' I raised my other hand to her face wiping the now steady flow of tears, moving my fingers from cheek to cheek, '. . . I'm no expert but I know you can't blame yourself; not all the time, very occasionally, despite the laws of average and the rules of the big wide world, it's the big asshole whiter than white man that's in the wrong.' I smiled but her face remained the same, distant. 'Look, talk to me, tell me what you need to do, it might help you see it differently.'

I lifted her chin, my thumb and forefinger raising her face towards mine, a mix of mascara and tears covering my hand in a sodden grey liquid smoke. She drew back, pulling a rolled up piece of toilet paper from under her sleeve. She swatted her face, the left side and then the right, slowly and methodically as if she was thinking of her delivery, trying to work out how to tell me what she'd done. She threw her shoulders back and pressed her long spine against the couch, the movement silent, deliberate. A finger made its way inside her mouth and she chewed it silently, adding another and then another before dropping her hand to her thigh where she wiped it softly, the saliva from her mouth disappearing into the folds of her leggings. Suddenly she jumped up, pushing me out of the way, wine slopping over the edges of our cups. 'There's a very good chance that he's gaunae want to fuckin kill me. And if he doesn't there will be others that will. Ah'm fucked Elizabeth, ah don't even know if going back the now is gaunae sort it.'

She hugged her arms across her chest, drumming her fingers on the tips of her shoulders, the lines of her face suggesting she was imagining the pain of death. I stood still, taking a moment to examine her twisted torso, to query her hen toes, her slender feet discussing the drama amongst themselves. Her hips were unruly too, the sharp bones sculptured into her sides were sloped at an angle at odds with her knock knees, her body topsy turvy and yet all the while beautiful. I was trying to get it all straight in my head but it hurt, the whole story was just a muddle. I let it blur, deciding that kissing her would be a far more pleasant experience. In my head I leaned towards her and placed my left hand on the side of her head, my fingers slipping gently towards the softness of her face, my lips brushing the fullness of hers. But I didn't dare.

'Jesus Sadie. I thought when you came in you were saying that you'd done something to him, that you'd bloody maimed him or something because you said he'd never be able to hit you again.'

'Aye, I said he wouldn't hit me again because ah need tae get out, ah need to get as far as fuck away from here as possible. Ah need to, ah've no choice cos if I stay he'll find me and if he doesn't kill me one of his flippin cronies will. Like ah said, unfortunately my man doesn't mix with the best of company.'

She pushed back down on to the sofa, asking me to toss her bag over. When I placed it on her knee she held it up in front of her like a chalice.

'Did you notice anything in ma bag when you were looking for the corkscrew?'

I shook my head, hauling my hair away from my face. She pushed her hand in and then threw something at the table. A plastic bag fell with a dense thud, an empty cup collapsing on its side.

'What the fuck is that Sadie?'

My voice croaked, my mind racing, imagining that cold gun metal was teasing the density of the table.

'Have a look.'

'Why, what for? It's yours, you look.'

'I know whit it is, you don't so on you go, you might be surprised, it's no gaunae bite you.'

With some hesitancy I finally lifted the bag, feeling it, weighing it up, realising that it was heavy but kind of soft. I dropped it quickly, thinking I felt it squelch, imagining Alan's balls on a platter.

'Jesus, you're a total fanny. Gies it here will you?'

I stepped back from the table. Sadie pounced on the bag, pulling it open and throwing the contents towards me. It was money, tons and tons of money. The notes didn't glide gently to the ground, it was harsh, like an onslaught of locusts, wings thrashing ferociously, the hum penetrating my eardrums. The swathes of paper fell heavily, bunches tightly wrapped in elastic bands thumping to the ground, one catching the side of my damaged face and pushing me onto my knees and on to the floor. Hundreds, maybe thousands of pounds, consuming my tender senses, smothering me in a temporary indulgence from God. I raised my eyes, just to check. The loose notes floated, origami dragons, teasing the air. I turned away, swallowing hard when the dragons in my line of sight changed shape, my childish eyes seeing the broken angels of a dandelion clock, tiny wings closing in and falling to the ground as the white seraphs called time.

Sadie ignored my discomfort, gently pulling me so my back was on the carpet. She draped her thin arms around me, bathing my orange hair in brown and blue and pink and green. A fifty pound note was resting on my chest, balancing precariously on my breasts like a flamingo. I blew softly and it took to the air, faltering for a moment before falling on the ice-cream floor, its identity immediately submerged in the swirling pile of more. I rolled onto my side, crisp notes crackling like the first frost of winter.

'Sadie . . . ?'

She rolled towards me in response, our eyes meeting in the middle of a mattress of stolen money. My eyes recoiled at the intensity of her look, my lids closing tightly shut. It couldn't happen, not after Jenny. It could never be right with anyone but Jenny. I opened my eyes, my breathing sharp.

'Aye, I know. This is pretty fuckin mental.'

Sadie released her free hand from under the folds of my floundering hair, her movement sending a pile of money into the air. We watched in unison as if saying a fond farewell to a pair of doves. Sadie's other hand was resting on her head, her elbow holding her weight, her fingers unconsciously scratching her scalp.

'Well, it seemed like a good idea at the time.'

Her arm slipped from its anchor and she rolled over, her body collapsing onto mine. I caught her willingly, my fingers uncurling and finding a home on the strong curve of her shoulders. I laughed, even though I knew my look had lingered for just a second too long.

'Hoi, steady on, I'm not ready to be crushed to death thanks very much.'

She weighed nothing, little more than Collette, but her hip bones were protruding through her leggings and catching my bruised stomach unawares; it hurt with an intensity I'd experienced often before. The tears that followed flowed softly but without permission.

'Sorry hen, ah'm an idiot, I can see how much pain your wee broken body is in.'

She sat up and I dutifully followed, self-consciously pushing away the tears. 'You okay now?' I nodded but we both knew it was about as far from the truth as a happy marriage.

'Ah suppose you'll be wanting tae know what I'm doing with all this money?'

She did it again, threw a bunch in the air, watching the five pound note win the race as it trundled to the ground first, collapsing on to the carpet in a state of exhaustion.

'I wouldn't mind, just as a matter of interest . . .'

'Okay, but sit up on a comfy seat will you, you look in bloody agony there. That prick oav a husband of yours deserves tae have his balls ripped off.' I hauled myself on to the sofa laughing as Sadie declared in a Jackanory voice that she would begin. We sniggered like schoolgirls, despite everything. We didn't know each other and yet here we were, warm, attentive, focused.

'Okay, so it started out like any other day with me and Alan having a hit, but it wasn't the same it was different. It wiz tae be our last. He promised me Elizabeth, said he was right behind me an' we'd gie up together. Six months and then that wiz it. Well yesterday was the last day oav the six months wasn't it? Ah've been tae the counsellors and that, they were all set up tae help us. There's a residential place you can go tae down south where they help you get through the withdrawals. It was aw sorted, my ma had taken the wean and we were gaunae get her back and move tae Wales or somewhere like that tae start again away fae aw the mad folk we know. We're supposed tae be going to the clinic today. But that's not gaunnae happen is it?'

I nodded as if I understood what it really meant to her.

'So, there I was talking shite, making plans and he just breaks the news as if it didnae matter at all.'

'What news?'

'The news that he was nipping out tae meet the boss wae the money for the last lot of gear and that he was taking another batch so he'd need tae keep working for another few months yet. So I jumped up and pulled the bolt across the living room door so I could grab a few things and get out of there before he persuaded me tae stay. Ah certainly didnae mean for the rest of it tae happen.'

'How, what did happen?'

'Well, Alan heard me locking the door so he starts kicking it and thumping it, shouting at the top of his voice that he's gaunae kill me and ah get a fright and fall against the hall cupboard and bang ma head aff the shelf. Next thing that poly bag full of his dirty drug money lands oan ma forehead and ah'm running down the main road like Benny Hill.'

I didn't know whether to laugh or cry, couldn't work out if she'd been right or wrong.

'Fuckin hell Sadie, this is just crazy stuff. I'm sorry, I must sound like some sort of stupid snob but I've never been involved in any of this kind of stuff. Patrick is a bastard but he doesn't do drugs, thankfully.' I scanned the room again, reminding myself that he was a bastard and that I needed to stay focused and committed to escaping. 'But I'm confused, if you've had all this money on you all the time why did you go to the homeless place? Couldn't you have just fucked off somewhere far away?'

'Good question, you've obviously been paying attention. Ach, ah said to myself if he comes and looks for me at the homeless place ah'll go back and give him his money an' another chance. But, guess what, no fuckin sign. The stupid prick wiznae even smart enough tae dae that. Anyway, he's fucked. We both are. The money's tae pay for the gear; Alan gets a load on tic and then pays for it when he gets the next batch. There's about twenty grand there and he's a fuckin dead man if he doesn't turn up with it but ah just wanted him tae stop. Ah didnae really want tae steal it.'

'Fuck sake Sadie, you're going to have to give it back, jeez, what about Laura? This is serious, they'll no be after Alan, it'll be you they want, you're the one that nicked the cash. Oh my God, do you think these people will try and kill you?' And me. A thunderbolt crashed into my chest, the realisation that I had touched the dirty money too. They would be after me.

'Look Elizabeth, calm down, there's no reason for you to panic, he diznae know you fae Adam.'

Sadie was hanging on to my arm, pulling me away from the door when all I wanted to do was peel Collette from the bed covers and run. Her whisper felt harsh and dirty, her hot vinegary breath staining my lips.

'Fuckin let go of me before I break your face.'

I meant it; I would have throttled her if I needed to. Nothing was standing between me and my baby, not anymore. She did nothing to release her grasp and I tore my fingers across her forearm, ripping my nails deeply into her flesh, feeling the cold red blood spill from her pale white skin. Even that didn't stop me. The harder she gripped my arm the firmer my fingers tore into her milky flesh. But suddenly I was on my knees, a sudden crack across my face a firework exploding into my broken cheek. It yanked the life from me, a film of black the only thing I could see as I plummeted to the floor, my senses disintegrating as I tumbled head first into the swirling darkness. I did nothing until the light flickered back to the surface revealing a horrified Sadie, her face partially covered by a hand clasped tightly over her mouth. I launched myself up and grabbed her legs, tucking my arms around the back of her knees and pulling her down to the floor, her head crashing off the ground, her throat croaking a cry of pain and bewilderment and then a plea, 'for fuck sake ya maniac have we no been through enough oav this pish already . . .'

I released my grip, watching my fingers uncurl, the tension evaporating in a cloud of shame and a sense of despair. I leaned towards the bedroom door listening for Collette's frightened cry but the silence that filled the hall was lingering in her room too. She was safe, the chaos leaving her be. Sadie shrugged her shoulders as she raised her torso from the floor and sat upright leaning her back against the hall wall.

'Fuckin hell hen, this is no meant tae be part oav the script. Ah'm sorry I slapped you, ah just panicked, ah cannae stand that feeling when somebody's clinging on to me it totally freaks me out. But I shouldn't have hit you Elizabeth, I know that an' I'm sorry I really really am.'

She stretched her arm out, holding it nervously in front of my face. I pushed it down by her side, annoyance at my actions overriding the original sense of anger.

'Forget it Sadie, let's just fuckin pretend it never happened. We're both good at pretending that, right?'

She offered her hand again and this time I accepted it, avoiding glancing at the tramlines, the series of raw cuts my fingernails had tattooed into her arm. We sat still, our breathing loud and rhythmic, its music melancholy, a traditional song of sorrow.

'Look, I know this is a pure cheek but can I stay here tonight, just for a few hours tae get my head down? Ah'm gaunae get away from Glesga the morra, ah'm heading to Ireland, I know a wee place, a wee island in the middle of nowhere that I can get myself settled into and then bring Laura over. It's not as if Alan's ever gaunae even think of looking for me there. And ah know ah shouldnae have taken the money but ah need it if ah'm gaunae get out of this shitty life and start again. Ah'll just end up going back. Fuck's sake Alan had his chance and he's made his choice, he doesnae want a different life he wants that fuckin life. Ah want something different for me and Laura ah really dae.'

I inhaled deeply, welcoming an opportunity to discuss escaping.

'How are you getting there?'

'There's a bus, it runs from the Citizen's Theatre down at the Gorbals and takes you right on to the ferry and then up the coast.'

'A bus? But you're quite minted m'lady.' I laughed, exaggerating my vowels, the words swooping off a silver spoon. 'Would air not be a more convenient method of travel for madam?'

'Oh for fuck sake Miss Marbles in her bloody mouth, I don't know about that. Ah've never been on a plane, I honestly don't fancy being in a big metal tin that could fall nose first out of the air. Besides, I need to watch what I do with the money, I want to make sure ah get a nice place for me and Laura to stay until ah can get a job and that.'

I flicked her hair behind her ear, lost for a moment in her

vulnerability, even though she was embarking on a heroic journey. I wished I was as brave.

'Tell you what though, you and Collette you could come wae me. I've got enough money to get us both started in a new life and the weans would love it. You could get away from that nut job Patrick once and for all . . .'

Like I said, I'm not as brave, one step at a time for little old me. Once upon a time I thought the world would let me do anything but they knocked that out of me, one by one. Even Mary, the little Virgin with the big eyes and big smile. She still wasn't where I needed her to be.

'Don't be mental, I'm not going anywhere. We'll make what we can from wherever they put us tomorrow and then I don't need to worry about anything else. Patrick's not going to have a clue where we are, I'll make sure of that.'

'Ah don't want tae burst your bubble or anything like that hen but can you be *sure* about that, the council's duty bound to put you in similar housing to what you were in before. What are you gaunae do if you end up in the next block of flats to him? I think he might notice you somehow.'

I sighed, refusing to hear it, I just needed to take it one step at a time. It's funny, I used to laugh when the psychiatrist - let's call him "Piggy", but only because that's what I called him then - said, *let's just build things day by day, step by step*. I thought it was he that was mental, not me. Maybe I was, maybe I am.

'Come on, let's go to bed, you can stay if you want to stay but I need you to leave before Collette wakes up in the morning. She's been through enough upset and I don't want to confuse her any more than needs be.'

Sadie grinned, drawing her arm to the side of her head and pulling an *aye aye captain* salute with her right hand.

'Nae bother, you're the boss. I'll go and get my head down on the couch.'

I grabbed her arm. She didn't need to do that. I wanted to feel her next to me. Flesh next to flesh, fear next to fear, life next to life.

Some mother's do have them

Alan's eyes were fixed on the red front door. He was in the car, waiting, the tension spilling from his nose. He didn't bother looking for a hankie. With a childlike innocence he dragged his index finger under his dripping nostrils and wiped it on his jeans. The slurp was followed by a sniff and then a violent splutter, a hollow bark that bellowed from his throat as if he had woken up from a deep sleep to find a hand wrapped tightly around his neck. His breathing was laboured, heavy rasps rolling within the confined space, their incessant waves sickening him to the stomach. The noise heightened his anxiety, which was already a complicated mix of heroin withdrawal and fear, a panic that was rising from deep inside that said Paddy's approach with Sarah's mum wouldn't be the same as his own.

Paddy had been with her for several minutes, in her face, his right foot wedged between Mrs MacLean and the door. From the passenger seat Alan could only just make out her profile but he could see enough of her face to know that she was worried; her thin neck was pushing her head back, her brain forcing as much distance as possible between her and the intruder that was invading her quiet life. Alan cleared his throat and reached for the handle of the door but he didn't go so far as actually opening it. Paddy had said stay and he did as he was told. Like an obedient dog. Although Alan wasn't looking to please; he was avoiding the violence that would occur if he disobeyed an order.

He forced his attentions towards the foot that was setting the scene; the door stopper that said Paddy was in control of the situation. Alan clocked Paddy's Tukka boots. They were short, layers of burgundy suede collecting in ripples of bright colour at his ankle, the toe emerging in a long point that looked out of context with the natural shape of a human foot.

The boots, Alan thought, were decidedly feminine. Alan couldn't really get his head around the New Romantic thing; blokes in frilly shirts and girly boots didn't appeal to his *a man's a man when he's in his jeans and leather jacket* wardrobe. And yet in that moment Alan was consumed by jealousy. He was wise enough to know that even if he had actually liked the stupid purple boots he could never have worn them; he would have been slagged senseless, shot down in flames for looking like a prick. A cool dude he wasn't.

He pulled the sun visor down and glanced in the mirror but his tired features put him off and he quickly slammed it shut, cursing the day he had fired the first hit into his veins. He had been desperate to impress, to be one of the gang. The rest was history, the exact same as every other hard luck junkie tale. It was a trap.

Stroking his sallow cheeks he glanced back towards the house, a simmering anger failing to ignite into anything of substance in his stomach. Paddy was lunging forward, his snarling teeth bearing down on the milky features of a petrified face. A man walked by, shoulders broad, waist narrow, a staffie dog obediently clipped to heel. Alan pushed forward in his seat, straining to see if he would steer left and challenge Paddy's dominance on the doorstep but he simply nodded, a Glasgow salute, and moved on, his dog's hackles rising in tune with Paddy's snarl.

Alan shrunk into the leather, his body coiling into its thickness like a snake. He knew it wasn't going to end well. Paddy could get away with anything. Paddy, the guy who brought him into the fold, the geezer who gave him his first hit and trusted him to sell the gear on Umberto's behalf with the promise of a few extra quid, free junk and a 'friendship' that meant he was one of the boys. It didn't matter then that he was the pathetic outsider, or that he was the butt of everyone's jokes.

It was Paddy's reputation as Umberto Donati's sidekick that afforded him the right to wear whatever he liked. He had status, he was Umberto's right hand man. One word against him and the Boss, Alan was quietly informed, would put a fuckin bullet through your head. From the safety of the car Alan eyed Paddy's little trendy boots and skin tight jeans. He guffawed, a snort of satisfaction emerging as he decided that Paddy's skinny pins were just like a wee lassie's. Alan curled his fingers around his calf, tensing the muscle, measuring it against the lean shape that filled Paddy's trousers. For a moment he comforted himself, trying to light that fire in his belly that would give him the upper hand. And yet he knew otherwise, his mind quickly recalling the night he watched Paddy and Umberto play-fighting in the back garden. It was the one and only occasion he had been allowed into their secret haven but the visit told him everything he needed to know. He pushed his feet to the floor remembering Paddy's strength, the rock hard muscles that rippled in the late evening sunlight as they rolled violently and yet seductively around the garden lawn. It was a surreal experience, with all the weirdness of Alan Bates and Oliver Reed wrestling naked in *Women in Love*.

Alan's face sizzled as he remembered how he'd grasped his own groin, embarrassment consuming him as his cock, uninvited, grew in his shorts, his prick bursting into action and shouting *hoi, I wouldn't mind a juicy wee piece of that*. He would have died, keeled over in utter shame if anyone had noticed the rock hard bulge in his 501s but he also knew that if needs must there were moments when he would have taken it tight up the arse just to keep his head above water.

Over at the house Mrs MacLean had turned her body away from Paddy and Alan could see more of her face. It was pale and tired, thin lines tracking across her forehead and down the sides of her mouth. Alan lowered his jaw in a vain attempt to disassociate himself with the situation. He swallowed hard, his conscience recognising Sarah's frame in the shadow of her mother on the doorstep. The way she moved stirred his insides, just like Sarah, defiantly and yet with an endearing vulnerability. In his imagination Mrs MacLean's eyes bore into him from a distance and he cowered, avoiding their penetrating gaze. The intensity had long since dulled but Sarah had bright blue eyes when he first met her, colour that hypnotised like the night sky. Her mother's hair was thick and dark. It bounced when she turned her head, a twist of curls spiralling from her temple and landing on her forehead as she turned to face Paddy. Sarah's hair did that once upon a time.

Alan curled his fingers into a fist, torn between wanting to kick Sarah's head in and holding her, having a laugh like they used to, a long time ago before the most important thing in his life became the junk. Smack was even more important than his daughter, Laura. If he was honest he would admit that he didn't give her a second thought, not really, yet when he was wasted he would imagine family life in Technicolor, a 1950s movie where everything was just right. It was sentimental bullshit. There was no place for that kind of weak love in the life of a bone-fide hard man. The business came first. Paddy had made sure Alan was aware of that, and of the consequences if he fucked up.

In the early days, when his conscience still yearned for a relationship that wasn't built on the foundations of fear, Alan wanted Sarah to meet Paddy. He thought it would help her understand that it was his way or the highway but Paddy told him in no uncertain terms to take a good fuck to himself. If he wasn't such a daft little prick, Paddy had explained, he would know that the less people in the background knew about him the better chance they had of continuing to wreak havoc. In the end Alan thought it was the right decision. Paddy was a powerful character. Sarah, he reckoned, would probably have wanted him as much as he did.

The intense conversation at the front door continued. Alan wondered what the fuck Paddy had found to speak about for so long. He'd spoken to her for less than two minutes. *Is Sarah here? Do you no know where she is? Gaunae tell her I need to speak tae her urgently?* End of story. She wasn't in so there was no point in dragging out the uncomfortable moment. Sarah's ma hated him, hated everything he had made her daughter become and her penetrating anger bore deeply into his skull. And yet Alan didn't really mind her, she had pissed him off a hundred times but he got the jist of it. If his wee lassie grew up and brought a prick like him to the door he would want to stick a knife in him.

Alan craned his neck, peering through the window like a meerkat. How long until the scene moved on to something more manageable for his conscience? A group of kids ran past the car, screeching menacingly. One boy was holding something high in the sky, pushing his arm into the clouds, hosting a trophy of sorts. He couldn't make out what it was but the others jumped on tiptoes, giggling, trying to rub their hands on the big kid's triumph. They turned around and faced the road behind the car, taunting, a unified cry of something disruptive filling the urban air. Alan looked in the wing mirror, seeing nothing, and then finally the tormented shadow of a smaller kid, his skinny frame hopping along at a distance, a white stocking sole revealing that the trophy was his shoe. As he drew closer Alan could see a mirror of his former self, the tears in the boy's eyes the same accompaniment to his own weakness, those long summer nights when his dad, then the local gang, kicked fuck out of him just because they could.

He rubbed his eyes and turned back towards the safety of the house. It was perfect timing, his movement coinciding with the raising of another trophy. This time the bile rose in Alan's throat as he watched Paddy's forehead come crashing down on Mrs MacLean's face, Paddy's heavy head hammering pale white skin. Alan watched the explosion, her face collapsing like summer sand, the path of today giving way to the harsh tomorrow of a cold and unforgiving sea. He did nothing, basking on the basin of his seat as Paddy shoved her inside the house and slammed the front door. Alan gripped his throat imagining her falling to her knees behind it, pushing her back against the cold frame for support until she was able to call for help. He drew his hands across his face harshly, ridding his cheeks of the evidence of tears. Paddy couldn't know he was pathetic too.

Alan had been at this scene many times before, watching his father bear down on his mother with his fists, and then when he had tired of her and his fists he'd beat Alan with the nearest object that came to hand. It was no excuse but he did the same. Like father like son, he hit Sarah. The first time it happened they were both strung out, the smack delivery was late and Sarah was fraught, not for drugs, but for money for nappies. Trivial crap when everything he had worked for was on the line. Just for a change he'd messed up, trying to do the *right* thing. He'd picked up the gear from Paddy but he'd been talked into a wee crafty side deal to cut the smack that would double his money. Like everything Alan tried to be clever with the grand scheme went decidedly tits up and he almost lost all Umberto's money. Sarah questioned his stupidity and he lashed out, slapping her across the face. The control made him feel good, reminded him that he didn't always have to be the kid on the other end of the punch.

'What the fuck's wrong with you? You better not be freaking out sunshine cos your fuckin life's oan the line remember?'

Paddy jumped inside the car and turned the engine on. Alan said nothing, listening instead to the indicator clunking intensely like an old grandfather clock. The lavish cuffs of Paddy's white frilled shirt were speckled with dots of red, the new patterns varying in shape and intensity, a couple of isolated bloody blotches having travelled as far as his elbow. Alan squirmed in his seat and watched as Paddy caressed the steering wheel, his long brown fingers emerging from under the cloth of his cuffs as his hands ran round the circumference. Alan counted as Paddy swung around the wheel, the big hand and little hand of his fingers ticking past the three, the six and the nine before stopping at 12 o'clock. Alarm bells started to ring in Alan's head.

'You've probably already guessed this mate but the auld biddy diznae have a fuckin clue where Sarah is but don't you worry, if she hears from her I can guarantee you that ah'll be the first person tae know.'

Alan said nothing.

Mary

Elizabeth was praying.

She had watched Sadie, observing every frame of every second until she finally stopped thrashing and moaning and fell asleep, her thin arms closing in on her chest, her long legs curling at the knees and pressing into Elizabeth's, the soft skin pushing firmly into the gaping hole in her heart. Elizabeth's breathing was taut and shallow. She was biding her time until it was safe. She had to be sure no-one was watching. They did that at the hospital, continually observing, waiting for the moment her actions would confirm their declaration of madness. She had learned to disguise it, pretend that they were right and that Mary had only existed in her far-reaching imagination.

She prayed and she waited. And exactly like they said, nothing happened. No-one came and so she pushed herself into the past, channelling energy from the time when she did come. In her memory the mother of God arrived from nowhere, and yet so obviously from somewhere, before leaving with equal haste, her sad eyes confirming for Elizabeth that she had been there for the taking. Elizabeth remembered every thread of the fabric she wore, every strand of the polished hair that shaped her cheeks and dressed the paleness of her face. That was the only evidence she needed.

She prised herself away from the softness of Sadie, the warmth disappearing into the night as she emerged from the covers and pushed her back against the coldness of the wall. The room was dark and yet the moon still teased, its light penetrating the curtains and lapping gently inside, soft waves caressing Collette's small frame on the opposite bed.

Elizabeth lifted the medal from her throat and held it in her fingertips. She began with the usual angered plea, her lips cursing the Virgin Mary for abandoning her to the narrow minds of the unbelievers. She pinched the cold metal in her fingertips, conducting her anger into her bitten nails, her right hand coiling her long red hair into a bun, her wrist drawing the fingers towards her shoulder, her hair tensing and tugging her pinking scalp.

At first her prayer was more of a monologue. A resumé of the events of the last few days, an urgent plea for guidance, a sign that the path she was taking was the one that would lead to somewhere more forgiving. And then she fell into the pattern of a lifetime, the repetition of the Virgin's song, the Hail Marys that helped her drown out monsters of the day and night. Like always, she repeated the prayer two hundred and ninety eight times, one rendition for every time it had happened.

On your marks, get set, go...

Alan watched Paddy as he stood at the oak counter, taking control, flirting with the barmaid as she pulled the pints. She smiled seductively, curling her hair behind her ear as she puffed out her chest, pushing up her breasts in the kind of come and get me movement he reckoned Paddy was altogether familiar with. She was attractive, not the sort of girl to turn heads but that wasn't the type of thing to stop Paddy, he just did it for the craic, to see the look on a lassie's face when he pulled out and walked out in a seamless move, dropping the used condom on the floor as he strolled casually through the door. Alan had heard him boasting about it, saying he had learned the art from the master, Umberto. Taking a leaf from Paddy's book he gazed seductively at the girl behind the bar. He received a sneer and a mouthed *what the fuck are you looking at?* for his trouble.

Paddy put one pint in front of Alan and raised the other to his lips, winking at the barmaid at the same time. Embarrassed, Alan looked away, searching for small talk, anything to make it up to Paddy. He had spent the night at Alan's, torturing both him and his conscience, his disappointment at his ineptitude consumed by his anger, his fists finding different ways to share that powerful message.

'Dae you fancy going tae the game tonight, I know a bloke that can get tickets, decent seats in the Main Stand. We're playing Hearts, should be a good game.'

Alan drew back sharply when Paddy slammed his pint down on to the table. The contents spilled from the glass, white froth splashing onto Alan's hand. He pulled it back quickly, shaking it furiously as if he'd been scalded with hot oil. His face singed red, embarrassed that he'd somehow managed to fuck up again. Paddy roared, leaning over the table to bellow into his face, stealing Alan's breath, taking that for himself as well.

'Are you still oan another fuckin planet? After everything ah've tellt you? Listen dickhead ah don't care if Celtic were playing Rangers the day tae lift the League title. We're no going anywhere until we find that fuckin bitch Sarah and get the Boss his money back.'

Alan lowered his head sheepishly, chasing his thoughts for something to say that wouldn't offend Paddy. There was nothing there. His legs began to shake like a wet dog and he pushed the weight of his arms onto his thighs so Paddy wouldn't notice.

'Aye, that's right just fuckin sit there like a dummy man and ah'll dae aw the fuckin worrying for both of us. Ah've got a good mind tae just tell Umberto that it was you that robbed him, that would have you up and running eh?'

He spat the words out, saliva dripping down his chin. He drew his hand across his face then wiped his fingers on Alan, pressing each nail heavily into his forearm. It was the wake-up call he needed.

'Why don't you Paddy man, why don't you just fuckin tell him? It would save you a lot oav hassle. Let's just get it over and done wae the now eh?'

Alan felt himself fall backwards, the ceiling rolling into his line of vision. Several fingers were squeezing his throat and he tried hard not to panic, to give in and let Paddy have his moment, but he couldn't. Strength arose from within and he heard Paddy yell *ya fuckin wee bastard* as his Doc Marten boot connected with Paddy's balls. Despite the chaos he sniggered, knowing that a Tukka boot would never have achieved the same impact. Paddy swooped backwards, his frame jostling across the room, his limbs soaring as if he'd been caught up in Dorothy's tornado. Alan's satisfaction was short lived, reality kicking him in the teeth when he saw a barman prising Paddy from the floor, his embrace tighter than anyone should dare.

Alan clambered to his feet and flung a fist, his knuckles

encountering fresh air but as ever Paddy was two steps ahead, the barman swallowing hard as the cold metal of the knife pushed into the small of the perfect 'v' at the base of his thick neck.

'Now you fuckin listen dickhead.'

Paddy was spitting, saliva spraying all over the barman's face.

'You don't fuckin mess wae me or ma mate dae you hear me?'

He pressed the knife into his throat, a droplet of blood spilling onto the blade.

'Dae you hear me?'

The barman mumbled, words tumbling from an ashen face.

'Aye man, no problem at all, I'm sorry to have interfered. Can I get you two anything?'

'Aye, you can get to fuck out of my face. Tell you what mate you better watch your back, you have no idea who you've been messing wae the day.'

Alan was trying to stop himself shaking but his teeth were chattering in conversation. He followed pitifully when Paddy instructed him to *get a move on*. His breathing was still frantic when they got into the car, the panic still there in bucket loads. He watched silently as Paddy lit a cigarette, rolling down the window to blow the smoke into the cold air. Alan followed the smoke rings as they bounced into the evening and then disintegrated against the frost of Paddy's breath.

'You know what Al, ah think ah could do wae a wee holiday. That lucky bastard Umberto's just back fae Italy. Ah wouldnae mind a piece of that.'

Alan cleared his throat rubbing his neck to ease the bruising that he could feel pulsating deep inside his skin.

'Ah've never been on a holiday, ah wouldnae know what tae dae on one.'

'Fuck, you have led a pathetic little life haven't you Alan?

Here's what you do son, you shag and get wasted, shag and get wasted. It's fuckin mental and very enjoyable that's for sure.'

'Aye and go fishing an' walking and all that. Sarah was always going on about the holidays she had when she was a wean. She used tae go tae a wee place in the country or something like that for the summer and said it was brilliant; tell you what though, sounded more like hell the way she described it.'

Alan didn't see the fist coming; he only felt the realisation of pain when his head crashed off the window bursting his lip and nose open. He followed the blood as it spilled onto his t-shirt, flowing quickly as if it was in a desperate hurry to leave his sorry little body.

'You fuckin prick, whereabouts did she go for these holidays?'

A second fist caught him on the cheek.

'Ah don't know man, ah cannae really remember, ah wiznae that interested.'

'Well we'll just have tae go and see that fuckin mother of hers again then won't we?'

Paddy fired up the car's engine, its roar mimicking his own call to arms. He pulled out without checking the traffic, calmly offering Alan a word of advice.

'Get just one drop oav blood on the seat of my new car and ah'll fuckin kill you.'

The house that Jack built

I woke to a finger of sun filtering lazily through the curtains and dancing on my nose. The colours in the room were vibrant, like a picture postcard of a crisp autumn day, red and yellow and orange swallowing everything. I wondered if I would be able to see my breath scramble towards the ceiling in a foggy haze. I exhaled harshly but all that escaped was my imagination.

I could feel the warmth of a body next to me, not touching but lodged against the wall. I raised my head slightly, trying to check if Collette was still asleep in the other bed, forcing myself to remember that Sadie most definitely had to go. The two single beds sat almost side by side. They were separated by the bedside cabinets, like the units in hotels and hospitals housing the Bible and whatever the previous occupant had left behind.

Patrick and I had stayed in a hotel, once upon a time. They called it a hotel but it was a hostel full of desperate people, just like us. Idiots who'd run away to London with nothing other than an aptitude for self-destruction. I closed my eyes remembering the room, the thick air heavy with stale cooking and burnt chip oil. The walls were brown, dark chocolate wallpaper making it dark even when the curtains were pulled sharply apart from the window and the daylight was trying to chisel a path to reach inside. The mattress was cold and damp, fumes of urine stretching into your nose in waves that crushed the resolve to keep whatever bit of sustenance you had managed to steal inside your stomach.

I scratched my neck, my fingers itching at the impinging memory of coarse blue blankets that entrenched you in the unfamiliar smells of previous inhabitants. Patrick and I weren't the only guests: cockroaches, the size of your thumb with thick stodgy legs, clanked across the floor in suits of armour. I envied their protection, even when I was emptying the beasts from the big old pots in the communal kitchen, scooping them out into the dank back yard before cooking our cheap packet pasta. We stayed in the hotel for what felt like a lifetime, living in each other's pockets, breathing the same stinking air. I pretended that none of it mattered, not even when Patrick was on top of me, punching my face repeatedly because - well, just because.

I cracked my head off the little bedside table once. I fell over, too stupid to master the art of walking sensibly with one foot in front of the other. My head burst open with the impact and I watched the blood ooze down the side of my face, staring into a cracked mirror from the other side of the room. There was something beautiful about that moment, watching myself unfold, my very being stutter and crumble and then pull itself together despite the sharp, nasty pain.

The duvet on Collette's bed was ruffled, rising in the middle like a little mountain, Vesuvius about to launch forth and create havoc with the world. I leaned forward quietly, the pain all still there, my face searing in agony, the day disappearing into night having done nothing to heal the mush that was cemented on my bone. I whispered to Sadie that she should get up but she didn't stir. I stifled a moan and raised my head from the pillow, stretching to check that I hadn't wakened Collette. But she wasn't there. Panic pushed strength into my wrists and I used them to claw at the duvet that was suffocating the space between me and wherever my baby had disappeared to.

'For fuck sake Sadie, wake up, *where's Collette?*'

I pushed her firmly, pulling the covers from her sleeping frame. It took me a second to see it was Collette that was snuggling beside me. She stared at me in horror, her startled features like stone. I hugged her tightly as she burst into tears. Sadie had already gone, her wings fleeing the nest somewhere in the darkness of the night. I swallowed hard, knowing that there was no reason to be disappointed. She had done exactly what I had asked.

Still at odds with the strangeness of the morning Collette and I ate our breakfast quickly and joined the others, an orderly line of sullen women waiting to board a bus and battle a new tomorrow. We didn't speak to one another on the journey, our experiences the same and yet different, our unity the single thing that stood us apart. The route was coloured by that same uncomfortable indifference, the bus trundling in and out of one dilapidated housing scheme after another, our stone faces carved from the sorrowful understanding of knowing exactly where we'd ended up. Collette and I were last, our journey coming to an end in a world I didn't recognise but felt familiar with all the same.

I helped Collette off the bus, my own steps tentative, the air of my new surroundings smothering my swollen cheek. A housing officer called Yvonne was pointing me in the direction of a guy sitting on the bonnet of a car on the opposite side of the narrow street. Red sandstone flats were pressing into the skyline, hapless foliage stretching into a forest of unfamiliarity. I hollered at her, shouting to make my voice heard over the spluttering diesel engine.

'Are you sure this is the right place?'

'It sure is love; home sweet home for now. Don't worry, it's as safe as houses. Umberto over there will fill you in.'

She said something else but it was snatched by the low drum of the electronic door. I clicked my heels and pushed on. The bus chugged away, leaving a cloud of thick black smoke in its wake. I guided Collette towards the man that had been identified as Umberto, his shape emerging through the haze like Jenny Aguttar's long lost father in *The Railway Children*. The memory put me at ease.

He was perched on a red sports car, his bum resting on the edge of the low bonnet, its deep polish mirroring his reflection, his shadow elongated and stretching down to the shiny radiator. His legs were long, the bulky muscles of his thighs and calves sucking in the material of his suit trousers. They were pushed out in front of him at an angle, like a children's slide, his feet acting as an emergency gate crossed tightly at the ankles. My eyes lingered on his shoes, black and white spats like those worn by gangsters in the movies, the leather thick and expensive, the point of the toe impossibly long and sharp.

I approached as quickly as my exhausted gait would allow, my gaze moving from the outline of his thigh to his shoulder, its range expansive, a broad back supporting a jacket that was obviously cut to fit. He was oblivious to my arrival, drawing deeply from a cigarette, slow exaggerated smoke rings blowing into the autumn air. He stopped to push his finger through the centre of the blue grey shapes and I watched, waiting for him to notice us slipping into sight. There was a large ring on his pinkie and as I drew closer I recognised its significance, a crucifix ring, the long body of Jesus Christ twisting around his flesh, his arms splayed widely on a golden cross. Shyly I interrupted him, introducing myself, my declaration uttered nervously and pathetically. He smiled warmly, more caring evidenced in that tiny movement than anyone else had shown in a lifetime. That kind look stole me in a second. He was going to make us safe.

He told me his name and I loved it, capturing it with my teeth and storing it on my tongue. I held his Christian name and surname silently inside my mouth, repeating it, letting it touch my lips as I released it secretively into the fresh morning air. *Umberto Donati, Umberto Donati.* Stubbing out his cigarette under the weight of his polished shoe he raised himself from the bonnet of the car. I leaned upwards, my neck straining to follow his trail. He was tall; standing well above my height, his dark face chiselled with solid good looks that had probably emerged from a long line of handsome Donatis. His hair was so black it was almost blue, the quiff at the top teased into a perfect mass, remnants of oil glinting in the autumn sunshine.

His suit was dark grey, the wool thick and warm. I resisted the urge to press the fabric between my fingers and thumb. His shirt was white and crisp, real white, not like creamy clouds or sheep, but like the robes of the Virgin Mary. I thought of her for a second and then let her go, pushing my desire for her into the distance. For the first time in a long time I didn't seek her rescue. I cuddled Collette, believing in that moment that I was enough to keep her safe.

Umberto's tie was pink, a grey stripe sauntering casually down the shaft, its tone suggestive, daring my finger to follow it, to trace it to where it fell at the buckle of his belt. I tightened the muscles between my legs, responding to the moisture that was gathering thanks to a man I had just met in the street, the man who had been sent to save me. I smiled shyly, pausing to question the time I had spent waiting for the arrival of Mary. And all the time she wasn't coming, she wasn't going to rescue me. Umberto was. I looked into his eyes, thoughts of the Virgin obliterated. Despite the pain I was flirting, pouting my lips, forgetting that my once pretty face was a nonsensical riot of the broken pieces of my pathetic existence. He didn't seem to mind, winking as he urged me to follow him to the flat.

'Very pleased tae meet you Miss Elizabeth, let's get you and your wee lassie settled intae the flat. I own both these blocks, sixteen flats in all, but ah reckon I should give the best one tae you.'

He was pointing towards the building behind me but my gaze fell on his lips, savouring his Glesga accent, the tone gentler than the Robert De Niro growl I had been expecting. He shook his head, his firm salute indicating that we should follow him and I grasped Collette by the hand so we could keep up with his energetic pace. He asked me to repeat my name, flirting *oh that's just beautiful*, as he rolled his thick purple tongue over sparkling white teeth. From nowhere I felt the energy grow inside, grasping hold of me as I imagined burying my head into his strong chest, his soft hands stroking my cheeks until he entered me gently, exploding in his desire to take care of me. Collette tore me from the image, tugging Umberto's sleeve as she asked which house was ours.

'Hey hen, your special place is that one right there. I wouldnae be giving this flat tae just anyone you know, this is my personal favourite. I only rent this wan to the prettiest girls that the council sends tae me.'

He patted her gently on the top of her head, her curls falling from her forehead and spilling into the air like a dandelion clock giving in to time. Umberto pulled a packet of Opal Fruits from his trouser pocket. He thrust them into her hands and Collette smiled and raced towards the door of the flat on the ground floor. I followed, my heart fluttering at her sudden excitement, and then my stomach flipping when I saw the flat. I turned to Umberto in disbelief. He shrugged his shoulders, his flirty smile suggesting I push beyond my hesitation.

In the last couple of years Patrick had had money. He had become a personal financier, so he said, wheeling and dealing with other people's savings, carving off the bits and pieces he could for himself. He craved that awareness, people knowing he had a bit of cash, so his ego meant we had to keep a perfect house, a clinical showpiece that stifled any attempt I had to showcase my own creativity. My own paintings were torn from their homemade frames and burned, the emptiness replaced with Patrick's obsession with Athena posters, the curve of a tennis player's ass greeting my eyeline every time I stepped into the living room. It was gross, but this was worse than that.

The mouth of the close was cracked, deep ligatures blackening the walls, veins of dampness penetrating the flaking white paint from floor to ceiling. The accompanying graffiti was unreadable, the years and the changing stories altering the narrative into a language long since forgotten. It was sprayed sporadically across the front, its main message lost to the carefully drawn 'T', its dominance stifling, the tall red letter like dripping blood, its daredevil status tattooed prominently on the cracked window. Amongst the weeds and overgrown grass lay a broken washing machine, its glass door smashed and sprayed with a thick black paint. A mattress, its yellow foam bursting like vomit from its inside straddled a broken chest of drawers, the items joined at the hip as if in anticipation of bonfire night. I struggled to compose myself, fighting tears that would punish my painful cheeks. I collected Mary's medal between my fingers and then dropped it back on to my chest, looking instead to my new saviour for assistance.

'Umberto, would you look at that fuckin window? Collette and I can't stay here, it can't be safe. Can you help us find somewhere else, please?'

I felt my knees buckle and he caught me, strong fingers prising me to my feet, my weight balancing effortlessly on the palm of a single broad hand. With his other hand he reached into the brown leather bag that was casually slung over his shoulder. The *Daaaaannnnnaaaaa* he hollered engaged Collette immediately and we both stared in wonder at the roll of black tape held in his outstretched hand.

'Sorted. Five minutes and this place will be minted. C'mon, I know you're dying to get in so hurry up.'

He winked and it triggered a panic inside that was all too familiar. I searched for somewhere to run, the bile rising in my stomach. I grasped Collette by the hand but he smothered it quickly with his, his fingers strong and encompassing. The toxins subsided, slipping back down my throat, their character changing and churning into confusion when he used his other hand to caress me softly, his fingertips running down to the small of my back, pushing the weight of his broad hand onto the crack of my arse, letting me know that he knew I was there for the taking. I imagined him thrusting inside me, hoping it would be quick and that the moment of warmth at the end of it would be long enough to be rewarding. I submitted because that was the easiest thing to do. I watched him as he placed the key in the lock, followed its journey on to the table in the hall, mapping my escape when it was over. He winked and smiled, his strong white teeth spreading across his face, his sharp cheeks protruding. He was strong. I prayed to the Virgin that it would be quick.

Collette skipped through the door first and Umberto held me back for a second, stealing my fingers into the palm of his hand, shouting that mummy would be in in a wee minute. The panic closed in, he was going to take me in front of Collette. I searched for calm. I'd long since learned that being vulnerable just made them thrust harder. He didn't speak. He pushed his tongue into my mouth, his hand cupping my breast, his fingers tearing at my nipple through my bra.

Elizabeth

Elizabeth was a fastidious child, blowing the seeds from a carefully picked dandelion each morning before she went into her babysitter's house. It was a routine she had recently been strictly adhering to, stopping in the small square garden that was on the left hand side of the narrow path to search for the day's timepiece.

The clock had to be exactly right, and that meant it could be no more than two hands high with every seed white and fluffy, strong enough to withstand the mild summer breeze yet fragile enough to break away and fly at her will. She always blew around her, at each stroke her body shifting its direction, moving slowly clockwise, the seeds sometimes falling into a sundial circle at her feet and sometimes stretching into the skyline and flying nonchalantly into the distance. Meticulous in her ritual she always began with the obligatory question:

'Whit's the time Mr Wolf?'

Then, at the end of an enthusiastic big breath in, out and blowwww she would answer herself, chanting the words rather than speaking them.

'One o'clock…' she sang as she turned, the white floss piercing the atmosphere as it launched forwards, the particles propelling forth in a cotton jet stream. After a few moments time would drag the little seeds back to earth and Elizabeth would smile as they danced their way back to nature, drifting softly to the ground like the sweeping arm of a big old grandfather clock.

Standing at her newly created one o'clock she would begin the process again, big breath in, out and blowwww before demanding: 'Whit's the time Mr Wolf?' Answering in the same, meticulous rhythm she would reply, 'two o'clock…' big breath in, out and blowwww, turning to face three o'clock and continuing the routine until the final fragment of time was freed from the shackles of the flower head. The dandelion clocks had a purpose. They were measuring the number of days she had to wait until Andrew let her into the secret garden, the bedroom opposite the living room at the end of the long, thin hall. The room held a special surprise, a surprise that would only unfold when *Mr Wolf* said the time was right.

You've got tae wait for Christmas, so you can wait for this an' all.

This particular day hadn't got off to the best of starts. Walking up Andrew's path, just as she had done every day for the previous two weeks, Elizabeth noticed that there wasn't a single dandelion clock in sight. In a panic she scurried around the green grass, being mindful to step over the daisies and buttercups, just in case she wanted to make a chain later. Standing tall above the day's jewellery was a forest of bright orange dandelion heads. Pee-the-beds were of no use in telling the time. Elizabeth stared at the dandelions. She knelt down on the grass beside the changelings, willing them to mature into pale wild cotton. She searched for help from someone she knew could do absolutely anything.

'God, gaunae please make some dandelion clocks for me, ah promise ah'll be dead good all day.'

A horn beeped loudly, its intense audio followed by an impatient voice. Both noises startled her.

'Elizabeth hurry up will you, ah'm going tae be late for my work if you don't get a move oan and get going.'

'Sorry ma, I'm just going in, ah was just going tae see whit time it was first.'

'Ah'll tell you whit time it is, it's time you were inside. Now be a good wee girl and hurry up will you. Tell Andrew ah'll be back about two o'clock the day, so you've just tae come back to the house as soon as you see that the car's back.'

Elizabeth turned and waved. She smiled at her mother, but her mood was still heavy. She didn't like anything disrupting her routine. Melancholic, she lifted and dropped the letterbox lethargically, three times in slow succession, the metal of the lid kissing the lip of the door with a drained chaaaapppppppppppppppppp chaaaapppppppppppppppppp chaaaapppppppppppppppppp that dropped to the floor like a stone.

Andrew answered quickly, looking up to wave at Elizabeth's mother, smiling as he willed his little charge over the threshold, his lips gaping to reveal a mouthful of strong yellow teeth. On any other day they would have been a ray of sunshine, yet today Elizabeth felt cold as she shuffled slowly along the hall behind him. But instead of turning left to go to the living room at the end of the hall Andrew stopped at the special room.

It's a magic wardrobe. There's a wood inside it, and it's snowing! Come and see. Normally when Elizabeth asked to go in he'd rub the top of her head, smiling.

'You're too wee hen, you'll need tae wait till you're a bit bigger.'

'Aye, but ah'm seven, that is big, that's really big, even ma ma says ah'm a big girl now.'

'Right well we'll see, if you're a good girl we'll maybe think about it. Ah'll let you know when the time's right.'

The timing now perfect, Andrew stood in front of her, his fingertips clenched tightly around the silver handle. He laughed, beckoning Elizabeth towards him. He had a way with her, the wee girl next door who he had known since birth. When Elizabeth's mum got a part time job and Andrew nominated himself as the perfect solution for babysitting during the summer months she knew the friendly student next door was the ideal choice. Elizabeth already adored him.

'Hurry up then ah've no got all day, are ye coming inside with me or not? If you do, you might find out that ah've gone an' got a wee special present for you.'

Elizabeth responded like a jack in the box, smiling.

'Aye you're too right I am.'

And then she was finally there, beyond the door of the secret. As excited as she was nervous she drew in the air around her, shortly and sharply, her eyes darting hastily around the room. Andrew crossed the room to where she was standing. When he reached her he lifted the hand that was covering her stomach. He moved swiftly, his energy startling her. He tickled her tiny protruding belly, his fingers darting back and forwards across her ribs like a spider scurrying across the kitchen floor.

Elizabeth didn't know whether to laugh or cry.

The Buroo

Umberto threw me a twenty quid note when he was leaving. He'd see me soon, he said, pop in the next time he was dropping off another homeless lassie to one of his flats. He left me with my jeans and pants at my knees, leaning over the bathroom sink where he'd pushed me when I tried to make him stop in the hallway. He didn't touch me. It was just straight in, his cock thundering ferociously inside with such force that he had to stuff his hand over my mouth to stop me crying out.

He moaned throughout, panicking me, making me scared that Collette would know that we weren't fixing the bathroom window and she couldn't come in until it was safe. He whispered in my ear when he finished, that was fuckin magic, nice little pussy you've got for having had a kid. I didn't even turn around. I could hear him squeeze his dick back into his trousers, humming, *so* pleased with himself, giving himself credit for being fuckin irresistible. As his zip went up the money landed in the sink beside me. I did nothing. I waited till he closed the door and then hauled my trousers back up, feeling his hot spunk drip into my pants, his filth reminding me that this was exactly what life was like.

I spewed, bringing up everything I had, bile lashing violently off the ceramic like someone was ringing a big old fashioned Church bell. Collette came in a little later, wanting to know why there was blood splattered all over the living room wall. I didn't have an answer I felt able to share with her.

We walked to the buroo, Collette chirping, me in total silence. We finally found the stark reality of the social security building after an hour of aimless tossing and turning, pushed this way and that by kids laughing as they sent us in the opposite direction to the one we should have been heading. It didn't feel any better being there. It was filthy. The room was a more desperate version of the homeless office, the inhabitants wired and full of life, not beaten into submission like the women without spirit and a voice of their own.

I sussed the system and grabbed a ticket from a big red machine and waited for my number to come up. I had to glance at it twice to know for sure that it was for real. My ticket was 298. I pressed my finger along the ink, craving a *what the fuck* conversation with the Virgin Mary but there were too many people around. I'd have to wait for prayers after dark.

I looked towards the glass cubicles, they were serving ticket number 18. It would have taken about nine minutes of Mary's prayer to reach that number. It wasn't a number I particularly liked. It side-tracked me, made me remember it's what I used to be, an age that was supposed to mean something. It did, it's when I signed my life to Patrick, two years after the birth of our daughter.

I searched for the toilets, urging Collette to wait patiently for me outside the cubicle door while I clawed at the remnants of the putrid substance between my legs. She placed her red booted foot under the frame of the door so I could know she was still there. I stretched my leg and pushed the toe of my trainer forward so it kissed hers whilst I pleaded with God to leave me be, to have taken every trace of Umberto Donati with him. My instinct was telling me that I should be asking Mary, but she wouldn't be listening. I had probably scared her off.

I unlocked the door and it creaked loudly as I pushed past it, its song weary. Collette giggled and I tried to smile in retort as I stumbled towards the basin. I gazed blankly in the mirror, unfamiliar with the mysterious creature that was staring back. I searched my face in silence until a girl staggered out of the cubicle behind me. She chucked a needle and syringe on top of the bin and I toyed with grasping it, wondering if the needle was sharp enough to tear out the veins in my bruised wrists.

Collette would be better off with a new mum who didn't fuck strangers in the bathroom of a place that could never be home.

My child appeared from behind my hips and cuddled my thighs, tiny hands patting me softly, instinctively knowing that something was wrong. I looked at her in reverse, the mirror revealing a determined stalk, a head of curls round and sculptured like the clock of the dandelion. She curled her lips and smiled and I imagined the day she would blossom and break free, flying into the night. I followed her determined lead, soft fingers guiding me back to the waiting room.

After three hours they called us and I stuffed the crumpled letter the homeless officer had given me under the gap at the bottom of the glass window. A small fat man with thick black glasses read it quietly for several minutes before stamping a form and thrusting a piece of paper through to me, mumbling 'sign this' without looking in my direction. I curled my fingers around the biro pen that was tied to the counter with a piece of dirty string and thrust the letter back towards him quickly, my eyes not even stopping to scan the contents of the crisp white page.

'Right this is how it works. We give you a daily emergency payment of £3.45. You have to come here in the morning and sign the document authorising payment and then we will arrange a giro for you which you can pick up somewhere between four and four thirty. Sit down over there and we'll organise today's payment.'

We waited, and then we missed the post office. The red metal gate was bolted tightly over the front door when we finally got there. I clawed at the metal, my nails splitting, my tears falling hysterically. I folded my body shut, wilting to the edge of the wet shiny pavement. Collette copied me, sliding down onto the kerb beside me. She paddled her boots in the stream of fresh water, giggling as the splashes spilled over her toes before escaping and flowing down the metal stank. There was nowhere left to go. It was time to go home.

'Let's have a wee look in your pocket baby and I'll see if we can find a hankie to wipe my face.'

She ignored me, staring at a tin can someone had tried to squeeze down the metal stank.

'After that we'll find a phone box and give daddy a call and see if he will come and get us.'

Collette sighed and I tugged the zip on her pocket pulling out a crumpled hankie which fell heavily into my hand. There was something wrapped inside so I opened it excitedly hoping it was a bag of sweets Collette had forgotten about. I unpicked the paper churning a Hail Mary around the inside of my cheeks. Then I gasped, swallowing hard when I saw the tight roll of money.

The coach arrived at the Gorbals on time and just as we rolled away the bus stopped dead in its tracks, the driver pulling the brakes harshly. As soon as I heard the voice I knew, it was distinctive, so loud and full of presence. I peered above the row of seats to make sure. They had accused me of imagining things before. I was spotted right away, greeted with a screech that everyone on the bus heard.

'Oh my God, I thought you were already away?'

Sadie bounded down the aisle and pushed into the seat beside us in an instant.

'Na, I went tae see my mum and get the wean, figured she should be with me. We went tae the counsellor and that, sorted a few things out then me and Laura spent a wee posh night in a hotel in the town, didn't we pet?' She grinned, Laura's glossy black head shaking into the conversation, her mum pushing the strands of hair from her face to reveal large grey eyes. Sadie carried on talking, speaking quickly as her excitement took control. 'But this is mental, superb, what a bonus. Hoi Collette, c'mon here and meet my wee lassie Laura.'

Collette clambered across me and positioned herself in front of Laura, their eyes meeting, the stand-off stare reminding me of the moment Bananarama Girl and I met just a couple of days before. Sadie laughed, the loud roar coming from deep inside her stomach. I dragged myself to my feet and hugged my long lost pal, the lassie I had known for two days. She whispered in my ear as she reciprocated my hug.

'We're going to dae this Elizabeth, you an' me and the two weans. We'll get it right and say fuck off tae the lot of them. This is our time hen, you an' me against the rest of this shitty world.'

I closed my eyes and hugged her, pushing my sorry hips into hers. The fit was good. I didn't have to endure the journey alone.

Paddy's Milestone

Sadie didn't even give me time to grab my jacket, she was pulling at my sleeve, telling the kids to hurry up and get outside. I instantly regretted not lifting it, it was freezing, the initial burst of wind intense enough to take my breath away. I clambered towards Collette, anxious that the hurling gusts might lift her from her feet and thrust her weightless body over the railings. She was engrossed in what Sadie was telling her, her little arm tied tightly around Sadie's neck. The wind meant nothing to her and yet it was consuming everything. I watched it pass me by, pushing into the song of its own shadow.

Sadie was kneeling in between Collette and Laura, each of the children watching her lips intensely, following her outstretched fingers as she pointed to a massive rock in the middle of the sea. It was dark, the night sky velvet blue, bright stars twinkling like memories. The moon lifted the light, its silver sheen bearing down on the rock so we could see its serrated edge on the horizon.

Collette was saying something to me but I couldn't hear. The wind was howling and spray was swishing onto the deck like a fizzed up bottle of Irn Bru. A smile revealed her excitement, told me that her emotions were happy ones. Sadie grasped my hand and pulled me down so I was huddling beside them. Her fingers were ice cold and the hairs on my arms stood to attention despite the thick jumper.

'Dae you see it then?'

'See what?'

I teased, raising my voice to make sure they could hear me above the elements. The kids jumped up and down shouting and pointing, their faces suddenly intense and serious. Collette picked strands of hair from my lips and teeth; the wind was blowing it in all directions as if I was swimming underwater.

'See that, the alisha fraigs!'

Her face was strong and focused, her feet tip-tapping on the ground, her eyes shining with the excitement of telling me something I didn't know. I grinned. Wow, that's special I said, asking Collette if she knew what the alisha fraigs was. My words disappeared, snatched by the wind as they left my lips, thrown out to sea and captured inside a seagull's beak, its wings flapping furiously as it chased the ship, carrying on our conversation with its wild indiscriminate shrieks. Sadie pushed out her skinny arms, trying to grasp us all within her commanding span. She took flight, urging us to glide towards the heavy door to the cabin. We can look at it from inside I think she said. I leaned backwards into her slipstream, happy for it to carry me.

We sat down at the shiny table we had made our own and the girls raced to the window. I drew my jacket across my shoulders, glad of the warmth. My body was cold, from the inside out. Sadie shouted something to the girls, seemingly oblivious to the elements in her t-shirt and red jumper, pulling the bobble from her hair which she had tied loosely on top of her head like Pebbles from the Flintstones. She ran her fingers though her hair, her face lost beneath it, her fingers knotted in unruly strands. She lifted her face and released her hands, the long hanks in turn falling over her shoulders. I followed her hair as it tumbled like seaweed and berthed on her breasts. My eyes lingered on their shape, her nipples protruding through thin clothes. I swallowed the silhouette, my fingers sketching her naked image inside my head. She disrupted my thinking, barging into my subconscious.

'Aye, Columbo, ah felt the cold an' all!'

My cheeks burned.

'I'm sorry, I wasn't looking, well I was looking but I was only thinking that you were cold I wasn't, I wasn't . . .'

'Wasn't what?'

'What?'

I lowered my eyes, mortified, craving Jenny and the explosive laughter that would have followed such an awkward moment. Thoughts of her hit me hard, a tightening around my neck reminding me that I had promised there would be no-one other than her.

'You werenae what, you were saying you were looking because ah was cold no because ah wiz . . . then STOP. Were you going tae say aroused?'

Sadie pursed her lips and blew a sarcastic kiss in my direction. I dodged it as it funnelled in my direction, jumping to my feet and trying to toss the chair that was screwed to the floor out of my way. I fell over it, landing in instalments on my swollen face. The thick industrial carpet hit me like a hammer but despite the intense pain I was glad, it gave me a chance to hide from Sadie. I lay there, motionless, wishing that a giant whale would swim by and swallow me whole.

'No need to try and commit hari kari, ah wiz only messing wae you hen. You're awfy sensitive are you no?'

I peeled the hair from my face and accepted the warm hand that allowed me to clamber back to my seat. All eyes were on us, and they had been since we'd got on the ferry. I could hear the whispering, feel them wondering where our narrative was stretching to. I wish I knew too. I sat back in the seat, the pain unbearable.

'You should have gone tae the hospital when that lassie in the council was telling you tae. There's no shame in trying tae fight the pain.'

Sadie pushed a large gin and tonic in my direction and I swallowed quickly holding my breath in case the sea sickness that had just descended would persuade me to chuck it back up again. I glanced at the girls. They were on their knees, their frames small enough to allow them to fold up comfortably on the wide ledge inside the window. They were oblivious to everything other than the huge rock that was dominating the skyline in the middle of the sea.

'So what did you say that big lump of rock was called? Alisha what?'

Sadie gazed past the children to the island commanding our attention. 'Alisha nothing ye daft bugger, its Sunday name is the Ailsa Craig but plebs like me call it Paddy's Milestone.'

I smiled, the movement in my lips pushing a shard of pain into my cheek, the bone creaking, a fragile crack penetrating a floating iceberg. Collette and Laura rolled up beside us, their eager fingers picking at crisps from open packets, fresh pink lips stopping to sook from candy striped straws dipped in red and white tins. Collette coughed in her urgency to speak and soggy crisps landed on the table. A unanimous uuuggggggggggghhhhhh was followed by giggles and the remainder of Sadie's story.

'It's known as Paddy's Milestone cos it's half way between Scotland an' Ireland. But dae you want to know something ...' she lowered her voice so the kids were forced to lean in and listen. 'Hunners oav years ago, there was a huge giant called Finn McCool who used it as a bridge to walk across the sea . . . in fact, quick girls, is that him jumping over it the now . . . ?'

Laura and Collette ran to the window screaming, drawing even more attention to us. I didn't care. Sadie's story had too much significance. I knew all about Ailsa fuckin Craig. I downed the rest of my drink, the facts racing through my mind at a hundred miles an hour. The Ailsa Craig might have been known as Paddy's Milestone, but it also had another meaning. Elizabeth's Rock. Patrick and I bound together at sea, solidified as one. I searched for Mary and grasped her firmly, pushing the medal against the small of my throat. There was going to be no escaping the fucker.

Mary

Elizabeth watched the lighthouse in the distance, its rhythm ticking alongside her thinking, its stem tall and proud, the bold white head dissipating into the channels of the passing moment. Everyone else was sleeping, although the girls were mumbling under their breath, their chatter a mirror of their earlier incessant conversation. Sadie was curled on her side, her breathing deep and low, her mind entrenched in the soft melody of the drugs she had greedily consumed before bed.

Elizabeth slipped from the covers and straddled the push-out bed. She reached beyond the teasing curtains, surrounding herself in them, the fabric draping her shoulders like a cloak. She drew it to her neck, pinning it to her throat with her fingers, her hand opening to let the cloth slip in to the quiet hollow she shared with the Virgin Mary. She stayed there until her prayers were complete, her lone shadow hidden from suspecting eyes. Her duty fulfilled she carefully placed the Mary medal back under her t-shirt and tiptoed towards the bathroom. She didn't turn the light on until she was safely inside, the door a barrier between her and the rest of the world. She pulled the long cord spilling from the shaving light above the mirror, the tug loud despite her gentle touch. The room remained dark and she drew breath, waiting for Collette to stop coughing in her sleep before she attempted it again. This time her action was swift and deliberate and a soft bar of light flooded the mirror, its yellow glow casting a long shadow over the bowl of the avocado coloured basin.

Elizabeth got to work quickly, her breath hot and thick as she used it to frost the looking glass, her lips pursing and then blowing with a strength she had gathered in the aura of her evening prayer. She drew an image on the mirror, working in haste, her tongue and her teeth refuelling the same scene over and over, her lungs constantly pushing into her chest. She sketched the Virgin Mary on the misted glass, an outline of the Mary she remembered, her memory collecting the moment they called madness so she could stare at it full in the face. She took a step back and looked at her art, its gentle curves disappearing into the shadow of the passing night. She fell to her knees and prayed, adding another verse to her evening song.

Somewhere in the distance she imagined that Mary was watching, and waiting.

Homecoming Queen

'Here.'

Sadie chucked a brown paper package at me and I caught it with both hands despite it taking me by surprise. I remembered the last bag she'd thrown my way so I eyed it suspiciously, asking her what it was.

'Open it and find out for fuck's sake, it's no rocket science.'

I glanced sharply towards her, my features gathering in a frown but she was grinning, her infectious smile melting my abrasive attitude like she was dissolving a Disprin. I smiled, breathing out slowly and deeply, happy to remember that she was still with me. It was an emotion I was becoming addicted to. Every time I caught sight of her, or heard the scratchy pitch of her voice I breathed a sigh of relief because it meant we were still escaping, I was still out of reach.

I slid down off the harbour wall, inching myself to the edge before creeping to the ground slowly, being careful not to irritate my aching ribs. The task was more difficult because of the package I was holding but I grasped it tightly all the same, refusing Sadie's offer of a helping hand. I might have been pathetic but I didn't need Collette to notice how much I was struggling. Once safely on the ground I took a second to rub my backside through my jeans. My bum was numb with cold, the feeling disappearing into the crispness that had stayed since dawn. The morning air was freezing but the sky was blue and cloudless as if the Virgin had unhooked her cloak. The autumn sun was hanging low, yellow petals of light tumbling from an expansive sky, its softness teasing the frothy water playing hide and seek at the edge of the horizon.

I was tired. I hadn't been able to sleep in the bed and breakfast at the ferry terminal, its door too close to my past for comfort. We could see the port from the window, the vessel waiting in case we were tempted to go back. As the darkest hour swirled in oily puddles outside the window I prayed to the Virgin, my exhausted tone more habit than hope, 298 renditions of *Hail Mary*. And just when I thought I had finished I remembered to say another. 299. As much as I wanted to forget him, Umberto Donati had joined the party. As dawn pushed the shadow of the night behind the fading face of the moon we tumbled into a taxi, both Sadie and I breathless, the excitement of escaping making us excited and scared in equal measure.

Sadie was fractious, annoyance at my melancholy creeping into her tone as she waited for me to open the gift she had flung with ceremony into my unsuspecting arms.

'Fuck sake Elizabeth, you've been sat on your arse since we got here. Me and the kids have been up the town and done all the shopping whilst you've done bugger all, gie yourself a wee shake and start believing that we're moving on.' She was being harsh, and yet I knew she was being kind. I folded the package under my arm and raised a smile.

I had struggled to climb onto the dense harbour wall in the first place. My mission was to scan the waves for the arrival of a boat but instead I focused on the approach road to the pier, my eyes darting erratically, searching for the imminent arrival of Patrick. In my head I imagined him coming into sight, his leer apparent despite the distance. I fantasised about ending it all, feeling the pain of my body disperse as I slipped into the sea behind me. In my scene he would rush towards me, his haste because he wished it were he and not the freezing tide fulfilling the deed. I turned and glanced at the swirling water that was consuming my final moments. The waves were crashing violently on to the breakwater, each thrash creating a thunderous roar. I listened carefully but couldn't make out the notes. Ice cold spray from the waves splashed onto my face, startling my senses. I screwed my face as if I'd unexpectedly sooked on a lemon.

My lips were wet and cold but instinctively I licked them, running my tongue along the serrated lumps and bumps of the chapped surface. The salt was anathema at first but then I loved it, tasting the freedom that the sea could offer me. The waves below were building in intensity and I watched the white froth in its frenzied journey west and east, ebbs of chaos meeting in the middle and forming jagged pyramids that mirrored an army of tiny sharks.

The island, our final destination, was four miles out to sea. Its mammoth cliffs both frightened and excited me so I screwed my eyes tight to make it smaller, and arms outstretched, I caught the island rock between my finger and thumb, grasping it in my hand as the cold air whistled around my ears. Satisfied that it was within my reach I placed the tiny island back into the sea, my movement gentle, being sure I didn't disturb anything.

It was a throw of the dice. Heads or tails. Getting there was an escape, a route to freedom, but being there could be like captivity. Stupidly I allowed myself to panic, imagining Patrick finding me there, laughing as he chased me up a mountain, screeching that I shouldn't run because there was nowhere to go. Suddenly the idea of Carravindoon Island terrified me and I scanned the horizon, my eyes chasing backwards and forwards between the land and the sea, betwixt and between, terrified of what both might unfold. I searched for Patrick, comforted that he wouldn't find me and all the while terrified that he most definitely would.

'Fuckin hell Elizabeth are you waiting for a bus? Open the bloody parcel will you?'

I tore the bag open, my intrigue quelled for just a second as I struggled to remember the last time someone had bought me a gift. When I saw what it was I stuttered and stammered like a clown, *how did you know?* escaping from my broken lips as something altogether different but understood all the same. I ran my hand along the crisp paper, my fingers at once wanting to grasp a pencil and bring a page to life.

'The wean tellt me hen, I was buying the lassies colouring

books and she said that her mammy was always drawing.'

She leaned forward, edging closer.

'It's the best of stuff by the way, ah got the drawing pad in a wee art gallery up the town and the pencils and charcoal and aw that are whit the professionals use, the lassie in the place tellt me.'

I touched the back of her hand gently.

'Thanks Sadie, I really appreciate it, it means a lot.'

The moment passed when I shouted at the girls, the alarm in my voice crashing down as panic in their tiny faces when I saw them amble close to the water. Faces paling they ran towards us quickly, Collette grasping my legs tightly when she reached me. I urged her to be calm, stroking her forehead as I explained that she shouldn't wander too close to the sea. Sadie tossed the soft blonde curls on Collette's shoulder, her fingers gathering the mass of white strands in the palm of her hand.

'The wee one's hair's just gorgeous E.' She drew her other hand to join the first and Collette giggled, Sadie's fingers lingering to tickle her tiny throat, her neck so long and thin it was remarkable it held her head with such confidence. Sadie laughed too, her guffaw giving me advance notice that sarcasm was about to follow. 'Thank fuck she wiznae blessed wae your carrot top. You look like a big dandelion wae that mad orange curly hair and skinny body. A big giant pee-the-bed.'

She couldn't know, and yet somehow she could see the child in me. I swallowed hard hoping that there wasn't any of me in my child.

'This wee one here though, she's like a beautiful little dandelion clock, a wee angel ready tae break free an' change the direction oav the mad crazy world.'

I looked at Sadie closely, wondering if she knew exactly what she was saying to me. I turned to Collette, searching for hope, wanting to believe that she could fly. The tension shifted when Laura stretched her tiny arm and pointed towards the end of the pier.

'Mammy, is this where we're getting the wee boat tae the island tomorrow?'

'Tomorrow?' I asked inquisitively, 'I thought we were leaving just now?'

Collette butted in, determined to be part of the conversation. 'Ov coase timorrow mummy, we've got a big bed and the dinner hall first. C'mon, c'mon, someone might take our new stuff.'

She grabbed my hand and pulled with all her might which did nothing to actually shift me. Sadie carved a window into my silence, talking quickly, a story unfolding about meeting someone from the island in the town and knowing there wouldn't be a boat until the morning.

'I've booked us all intae the Harbour Hotel an' we've got a table for dinner in the restaurant the night. I hope you're hungry hen cos it looks bloody lovely.'

She nodded at a large hotel opposite the strand and I followed her gaze, laughing when I saw the posh location of our bed for the night.

'You're a nutcase do you know that? You're going to have none of that money left if you keep going at this rate.'

'You're telling me hen, ah'm like the cat that got the cream with this dosh.'

She linked her arm through mine to impress the notion on me that it was time to walk.

'And by the way, you've no seen the half of it, for a wee town ah've spent a bloody fortune.' She pressed forward into a long step and I followed her lead, my pace stuttering as I fumbled my way through the pain. 'Ah hope you like the new stuff ah bought you. It's a little bit musty mind; ah don't think the wee claethes shop has updated its rails since the 1950s.'

I pulled her closer, dragging her step into sync with mine.

'You're a complete header Sadie. But listen closely cos I'm definitely not going to say this again. I'm really grateful to have met you and I promise I'll pay you back for all this, I really mean it.'

'You're very welcome hen but you're also dead right, wan good turn deserves another so ah'm kind of needing to call in a wee favour if just now is convenient.'

If the truth were to be told the favour suited us both and I went to the hospital willingly. The doctor persevered through the lies of my story, listening intently as I explained how I'd tripped over the kerb and smashed my face. His eyes were warm and his accent thick, like treacle. His smile looked kind, but you could never really tell. It was exhausting, my fingers fidgeting as I fought my way through the make-believe version of my life. In the end I could see him tiring of my woe. He tutted when he examined my x-ray, drawing me towards the boxlight on the wall when he placed his hand on his chin and exhaled a long *hmmmm*.

'That was some kerb that hit you young lady, it's got you a right cropper.' He pointed to my skull, its outline staring at me abruptly. 'Look at this, see that?'

I stared intently, seeing a blur of black and white. Sadie pushed closer, peering over the doctor's shoulder.

'That there my dear is not one but two fractures. You've got a broken cheek. Like I said, that kerb did a good job on you that's for sure.'

I willed myself not to cry but the tears fell anyway, the sadness that Patrick had wanted to hurt me in this way suddenly overwhelming. It said everything there was to say about me. The piggy little psychiatrist had been right, I wasn't worth jack shit. He never actually said those exact words with his lips, but he made sure I heard them anyway, saying it over and over with his eyes. I could see it and so could Mary, if she'd been bothering to watch. I never knew with her.

He was kind, this doctor, and he urged me to shoo away my tears with his large cotton hankie while he explained what we needed to do. He spoke to Sadie, advising her to listen carefully as I felt my chin fall on to my shoulder.

'There's not a lot I can do with this here, you'll need to

get up to the hospital in the city. That's a right bad break your pal has, the plastic surgeons there will want to have a proper look at it. If I organise an ambulance for Elizabeth would you be able to sort transport for you and the girls? I'm assuming you'll want to go too. Don't worry, we'll get her fixed up, it's a bit of a mess mind, those kerbs must be stronger than they look. I just need Elizabeth's doctor's details so I can sort out the transfer of records. You got the number handy?'

Sadie nudged me, the panic in her stomach transferring to the urgent whisper she channelled in my ear. 'Fuck sake hen, don't even think about gieing him that info, you cannae risk anyone raising questions back home, it might help Patrick to find you.'

She was right, it was too risky, we were escaping, not throwing ourselves into his oncoming path. I pulled my shoulders back, the white cotton hankie floating on to the table in front of the doctor's folded fingers.

'Listen doc, I really appreciate everything you're trying to do here but we need to get over to the island sooner rather than later, my mate here has to see a sick relative and given how ill she is we can't risk delaying our trip any longer. In case, well, you know what I'm saying, she's not got much time to say her goodbyes. As soon as we're back over I'll head on up here to see you and make the arrangements to get down to the hospital.'

He raised his eyes in understanding, his furrowed forehead pushing the silver rim of his glasses from his thick grey brows. He tutted, explaining that my ribs were broken too. He strapped them up so tightly I could hardly breathe. I cried openly, my tears about pretty much everything.

'I'll give you a wee something the now to ease that hurting' he said and injected me with morphine, its magic taking effect almost immediately. In an instant I had closed my eyes and disappeared, the soft waves of comfort joining me in my continual search for Mary.

The doctor patted my arm, gently, not condescendingly, when I gave him my name (false) and my date of birth (true), his *happy birthday* message delivered with a hint of sadness. Sadie slid in between us, 'Aye, she thought ah'd forgotten it was her birthday today but ah got her a lovely wee present, didn't ah hen?' She smiled, her lips failing to disguise their melancholy. Of course she hadn't known, her gift was a total coincidence but what did it matter anyway, another year, another birthday, at least I had made it to twenty still alive. The doctor sent us on our way with his own present, painkillers and the thing I came for, sedatives for Sadie, a prescription for enough to last a fuckin lifetime. His kindness was strangely comforting.

Sadie tore the bottle open with urgency, greedily swallowing directly from it as soon as we got out of the chemist. A trickle of brown coke seeped from the corner of her mouth as she threw her head back and smacked her lips with her upturned hand.

'Thanks Elizabeth, you really don't know how much ah need these. Although ah have tae say, it took me aw my strength not to shove my arse in front of that needle when that doctor was giving you a hit. Feeling better?'

She handed me the can of coke and I just nodded my head, the irony dictating the movement. Patrick hated junk and he hated junkies even more, he was always going on about how they were the scum of the earth. If the wean ever got mixed up in anything like that he would say, *ah'll fuckin break her neck.* And here I was running away with one of the very people he despised, feeling the best I'd felt in years because I had an opiate running through my veins. Sadie pushed my hand towards my lips.

'Here hen, grab a drink. Take wan oav these as well, it'll ease the pain when the morphine runs out and it'll help you tae get a few hours kip later. We're gaunae have a busy day the morra and ah'm not gaunae be able to build the tent by myself that's for sure.'

'Tent? What fuckin tent?'

'Ah. You'll see it when we get back tae the hotel. We're gaunae need somewhere to kip when we get over to

Carravindoon.'

'Sadie, it's nearly winter, the girls can't sleep in a bloody tent. Is there not a hotel?'

'A hotel? Elizabeth there isn't even electricity over there. We can camp for a few nights until we sort something out. Don't worry, we'll be totally fine in no time at all, I promise you.'

I pushed back, my heels retracing the route I had just walked. Sadie wrenched the can of coke from my fingers, spilling it over my hand as she tugged.

'Look, forget it Elizabeth, no-one is forcing you tae come, you are allowed to make choices in ma world so why don't you just fuck off, go running back tae your scummy man if that's what you want but I'll tell you what, ah'm gaunae make a life for me and ma wean on that island, you can go and do what you fuckin like.'

She stormed off, clasping Laura's hand, marching like a soldier down the little hill in the direction of the hotel and the harbour. I hollered at her disappearing back, screaming that her reaction was childish and pathetic. I let her go, the anger chiselling into my chest as she stomped off into the distance. I turned and leaned against a shop window. I didn't fuckin need Sadie, all I needed in my life was Collette.

I had to roar, bellow at the top of my voice, the screeching hurting my chest as my confined ribs struggled to move within the tight elastic bandages. By the time the panic set in she was almost out of earshot but she heard me and tracked back. We didn't speak. There wasn't anything to say. Collette and Laura held hands and skipped down the road in front of us. Sadie handed me the pills and I shook the bottle as we walked, listening to the sense of calm the deep rattling invoked. I swallowed one of the little blue tablets gratefully, waiting patiently for the respite.

We ate in the restaurant, the kids being kids and laughing until they made themselves exhausted. Sadie got them off to bed and then dragged two chairs in front of the window. She urged me to sit, and look. The island was clearly visible, its features sharp as the light began to fade from day to night, its ascension changing the colour of the air, the scenery now tinted by a gentle purple haze. The wind had died down and the swirling tide had eased, giving everything an eloquent calm. There was a lighthouse flashing methodically in the distance, its soft white light pulsing from the south of the island, a bit of land that jutted out into the sea like a protective arm. I timed its journey. Four short bursts of light were followed by four sweeping flashes, churning without stopping, like I was blowing a dandelion clock.

'Man that island looks like heaven fae here do you no think?'

I laughed at Sadie's description, grabbing my sketch book from the bed so I could frame the scene perfectly with pencil. I scribbled intently, capturing everything.

'Those pills must be doing a better job on you than me . . . It just looks like a big rock in the middle of the sea. Fuck knows what it'll be like when we get there Sade, it's probably full of nutcases. Bloody hell, what if it's like *The Wicker Man*, have you seen that movie it's really scary?'

I swallowed some vodka, enjoying the feeling of it plummeting down my chest to my stomach. I felt pain free for the first time in a long time. I stretched over to the bedside table and took another tablet from the bottle.

'Watch it E, you're no used tae them. Take it easy.'

'I'm fine, it's not like they're the be-all and end-all. I'm just trying to ease the pain a bit, it's been a rough few days.'

Sadie leaned over and grabbed the bottle, holding it up to the light like a tabernacle.

'It's so easy to get addicted to this shit Elizabeth. They used tae call these wee harmless pills *housewives little helpers*.' She placed the bottle back on the table and stretched her toes, pushing her spine straight against the chair. 'Ah remember I used tae say that the smack wiznae any big deal, ah was happy tae take it or leave it. Ah thought I was in control of it but ah wiznae, the more I took the more I needed, still need. Ah'm determined ah'm no gaunae touch the filthy stuff again Elizabeth but ah swear there was a time ah wouldnae have thought twice about putting you through that window if I thought you were standing between me and some junk.'

I tumbled forward awkwardly, the bandages constricting my movement as I stretched over to the table and grasped the bottle. I rolled it in the palm of my hand and pushed back into my seat, a fresh wave of discomfort reminding me that I was still conscious. The pills were different from the ones I used to take, softer somehow, in that they still let me feel something, even if it was intense pain.

The first time they gave me a tablet I was in the hospital, the broad door locked at the end of the ward, the spidery glass blurring the outside from the inside. I remembered the day I woke up there, my first thought still with Jenny. I didn't want to feel back then, I just wanted Mary to come back, to tell me everything was going to be all right, that Jenny was waiting outside. Back then I gratefully swallowed whatever they gave me, drowning them out, slipping inside myself and my memories. They were all fuckers anyway.

'I'm not sure I really do understand, the only thing I've ever been addicted to is other people's orders. I just do what I'm told.'

'Well ah'll tell you what, judging by the state of your face I reckon Patrick's given out wan order too many. But listen ah'm telling you something now: ah'm gaunae do it, I'm gaunae to stay off the junk. Ah just need this shit you got from the doctor tae get me by until it aw settles down a bit. Coming off this crap isnae pleasant.'

Her arm fell to her side, the tablets jangling like a baby's rattle as the little brown bottle settled on her leg. I kept watching, turning over the page in my pad to focus on sketching her. She wore honesty well, it made her beautiful.

'Once we're on the island and this lot is tanned I'll just

need tae grin and bear it, there's not a doctor over there and the nurse diznae keep any decent gear.'

Time speaks in riddles; tick then tock, tick then tock

Paddy punched the window in the phone box and the pane escaped the red frame in one piece, the movement swift as if it had been waiting for an opportunity to make a bid for freedom. Alan watched the glass as it spiralled to the pavement below. It met the concrete path with a spectacular crash, crumbling into several pieces.

Paddy's Tukka boot kicked the remains onto the road, his rage still apparent as he pushed a surly teenager out of his way, the unheard threat as frightening to Alan as it was to the unsuspecting youth. Alan shuddered, his shoulders sinking as Paddy swept up to the car.

'I'm gaunae kick fuck out of her and then do you know what I'm gaunae dae?'

Alan shook his head, although he had a fair idea. He got the jist that Paddy couldn't wait to get his hands around Sarah's throat.

'I'm going to tear her limbs off one by one and then I'm going to cut her fuckin tits off and throw them to the dog. She's fuckin dead ah'm fuckin telling you.'

Alan cleared his throat, the repetition of their trip so far allowing him to understand that this was the part where he should enter the scene with speech.

'It'll no be long now Paddy and you can dae whit you like, the ferry leaves in a few hours and then it's just a wee drive up the coast, ah've been studying the map and ah reckon I can get us there in no time.'

Despite his pronouncement haste wasn't really on Alan's agenda. What he really wanted to say was, *I hope the motor breaks down and Sarah gets to fuck away.* Alan was an idiot, he admitted that to himself, but he wasn't a murderer. He was just full of bluster and possessed an inability to appreciate common sense. Paddy growled at him.

'Ah'm no talking about that stupid cow, she's gaunae get it don't you worry, ah'm talking about that fuckin sneaky wee bastard Elizabeth. Ah'm gaunae make her pay, she's no getting away wae taking the fuckin piss out oav me.'

The confusion was hurting Alan's head. 'What? Who the fuck's Elizabeth?'

The punch was as ferocious as the one delivered to Sarah's mum's face and it dazed him but he was with it enough to know that Paddy had leapt round to the passenger side of the car and two strong hands were gripping the collar of his jacket tightly. Paddy launched him onto a kerb at the side of the road and Alan allowed himself to fall willingly. Alan had never heard Paddy give his wife a name, she had only ever been known in conversation as the *wee shag indoors*. Once or twice he'd called her *the missus* but only if he'd been professing something about the child he called *the wean*. In that moment it struck Alan that he didn't even know if Paddy's 'wean' was a boy or a girl.

'Elizabeth is the mother oav the wean, my fuckin missus, the lassie who is married tae me and as such diznae go near another fucker in fear oav her life. Well, she did and she's gaunae have tae pay wae her life.'

He kicked a rock that had fallen from a pile of gravel deposited at the side of the road.

'Fuckin wee boot man, dae you know whit she went and did? Ah cannae fuckin believe she did this.'

Alan shook his head gently, understanding that now was a good time to stay still and quiet.

'Ah'm gaunae tell you whit she did. She fuckin shagged the boss didn't she? The fuckin higher than mighty ah-wouldnae-touch-another-soul couldnae wait tae get her knickers down when she met up wae Umberto. Ah've just had him oan the phone telling me that he'd only just realised who she was, wishes he'd made the connection at the time. Dae you know what he said to me? He fuckin said what a tidy little cunt she's got and that ah should hang oan tae her. Hang ontae her? Ah'll fuckin break her neck. Daft boot, she better no have said a thing about me tae Umberto. Fuckin cow.'

Alan kept his eyes low, recognising that mortification shouldn't be met head on.

'Ah'm sorry mate, that's fuckin crap. Ah didnae know your missus even knew Umberto. Ah thought you kept your family shit away fae work an' all that?'

'Aye a fuckin dae, ah did, but the stupid cow pissed off the other night in another one oav her *'ah'm leaving you'* outbursts when she says she'll never be back, until of course the pathetic little bitch crawls home on her hands and knees begging for another chance.'

Paddy grunted from deep inside his throat, spitting the contents onto the ground, following the trail with a match he had shaken from the box and struck alight before letting it sizzle and then fizzle out in his spittle. Alan tried to piece everything together.

'So how does she know Umberto then, did she go tae him looking for you?'

'No, but she fuckin came wae him that's for sure. The boss says she was screaming so much he had to throttle her, she was gagging for it so she wiz. Fuckin tart, as if she diznae get enough oav it fae me.' Paddy grasped his groin. 'These fuckin baws are obviously too much for the wee bitch.'

'Ah cannae believe this happened. Of aw the fuckin shithole flats in this city my fuckin wife ends up at wan of Umberto's hovels, you know those flats he rents out tae the homeless folk at the council? You must have heard him talking about them, he says the lassies the council send him are always a sure fire pump. My fuckin wife, nothing but a dirty little tramp . . . Ah swear tae fuck, wance we sort out your wee stupid bird she's fuckin next.'

Alan dusted his knees and stood up, mistakenly believing

that now was a good time to capitalise on Paddy's vulnerability.

'Listen mate, ah'm happy for you tae go and sort your own stuff out the day and ah can get a bus or something tae this ferry and go and sort things out wae Sarah.'

Paddy looked at him with the same disdainful expression his dad had used a thousand times.

'Are you fuckin mental as well as stupid? That cow Elizabeth can wait. Ah'm no fuckin losing anymore face than ah already have. We're gaunae go and get Umberto's money and then ah'm gaunae dae whit ah should have done years ago. She's gaunae pay for that whiter than white ah've had such a bad life bullshit she spouts. *Oh the doctor says it's not my fault, ah'm no well in the heid...* She's no gaunae have a heid when ah've finished wae her. Right, move ya prick, we've got a fuckin ferry tae catch.'

Alan followed. He wasn't smart enough to do anything different.

Elizabeth

Elizabeth wriggled free from Andrew, slipping from his grasp and plunging on to the carpet.

'Ah don't like it when you dae that, ma da always does it as well, it's sore.'

'So how come you're laughing then?' He knelt down and tickled her again, his thick fingers scurrying up and down her wee skinny body.

'Tteeeeeehhhhhhheeeeee, agh, stop it will ya, hhhaaaaaaa, hhhhhhaaaaaa . . . Please Andrew gaunae stoap it?'

With a brisk move she managed to squirm free, her laughter curtailed by a sudden panic, a fear that she was going to wet herself because she was laughing so much. Instinctively, she grabbed herself between her legs and rolled over on the carpet. It was a brown shag pile carpet, the kind that made kids giggle uncontrollably when they heard adults mention its name, sure that *shag* meant something to do with what adults did in bed but not quite sure what that something was.

The carpet's long fibres were warm and woolly, like a pet dog, and instead of standing up Elizabeth stayed where she was and played with it, stroking the little strands with long sweeping motions. Andrew was perched above, watching quietly. Elizabeth was thinking about her dog, Misty. She had died recently. Their lives had been entwined and she still missed her, her heart aching most vociferously at night time. Misty was cuddly and Elizabeth snuggled in, the pair often found snoring gently on top of her bed. *Ah just pure love her ma, she's like a teddy bear that works.*

The dog was Elizabeth's best friend. Her death had left a void in her life but now that the summer was here the pain was diminishing. Elizabeth's daily adventures with her new friend Andrew were becoming more vivid, her holiday a giant painting by numbers whose shapes were in transition, the greys and blacks beginning to blush with the colours of a beautiful rainbow. Every day he gave her a gift. The gifts were never extravagant, just a comic, some colouring pens, or a book but Elizabeth adored them and their connotations. They meant Andrew liked her. She had been reading Enid Blyton novels, leaning her head on Andrew's calves as he sprawled in front of the TV, Elizabeth quiet and lost in her secret adventures. Today meant another gift and Elizabeth was excited; finally it was the day of adventure she had been waiting so patiently for. The door had opened to a new chapter in her life.

Because the door had always been shut the room possessed an air of embargoed mystery. The forbidden was captivating, like *The Secret Garden* with its ambiguity concealed in the roots of a shadowy woodland. Andrew's secret room was a bit like a garden, long forgotten and overgrown, the decor favouring the browns and greens of forest foliage. If Elizabeth shut her eyes the carpet could have been a lawn, its sods unruly, yet soft and enfolding. A garden fit for the Virgin Mary.

She pulled herself up off the floor. Having waited this long to get into the room she was inquisitive. She turned around, standing with her back to Andrew. There was a window directly opposite the door and despite the fact that it was daylight the curtains were pulled together. They weren't completely drawn and a flicker of light teased its way inside the room, fingers mysteriously caressing the gap. When the rays finally breached the room they burst into life, a brilliant rustic beam, the sweeping hand of a lighthouse ticking and tocking its way across a tempestuous ocean.

But it wasn't quite right.

For the first time since Andrew had closed the door Elizabeth felt unsure. She made her way towards its frame, and the exit. It wasn't far, just six or seven steps but she approached it slowly, shuffling her feet, creeping along the surface of the shag pile that rested underneath her, toying between her desire to be both inside and outside the door. When she reached the door she raised her eyes and examined it. It had a dirty yellowy tinge, like the doors at home which were smothered in nicotine.

When Elizabeth was within touching distance, inches away from the silver handle that Andrew had clinked into a closed position, he stopped her in her tracks.

'Hey little *girrrl*', he drawled slowly, rattling his tongue around the 'r', quickening Elizabeth's breath in response. Realising her increasing anxiety he continued in a quieter, more settled tone.

'Where dae you think you're off tae? Ah was just about tae go and get your present but if you'd rather ah didnae bother . . . ?' He smiled teasingly, his voice warm yet commanding, his choice of words driven by her stance which was gradually relaxing.

'Oh well, ah'd got you something really special for the day but it diznae matter, ah can always gie it tae somebody else . . .' he continued gently. 'It's something ah just knew you were gaunae like . . .' he rattled on, teasing like a child with the upper hand, in possession of the scrap that everyone else wanted.

Elizabeth listened. What he was saying, and the way he said it, soothed her.

'Elllllliiiiiizzzzzzzzzzzaaaabbbbbbeeeeeeethhhhhhhhhhhh.'

He sang her name. It was a harmony, an orchestra. It was safe.

'Elllllliiiiiizzzzzzzzzzzaaaabbbbbbeeeeeeethhhhhhhhhhhh. Ah bet ah know whit you're thinking? Ah bet you a packet of rainbow drops that ah can tell you exactly whit you are thinking . . .'

He was still singing, but this time Elizabeth joined in, her laughter adding the backing vocals as she turned around and looked at him, flashing an innocent, trusting, smile. Of course he knew what she was thinking, he always did. He knew her better than anyone. He was her best friend, not only her best friend but her *special friend*. So special, he would say, that she would think about him for the rest of her life.

Panic over, a smiling Elizabeth climbed up on the bed to join Andrew where he sat waiting for her to return from her near expedition to the outside world. He patted his hand up and down beside him, indicating where she should sit.

'Ah wiz just going tae the toilet but ah don't need anymore.'

She positioned herself to where he directed. It was the first time she had sat on the bed and immediately it struck her how big it was, how massively catastrophic its presence was in the room. She had completely overlooked it and was now consumed by its bedspread. It was a carroty orange, exactly like the bright colour of her ginger hair. The curtains were orange too but they were a distinctively different shade, the orange scorched, like danger. They took centre stage, the curtains plummeting straight to the floor, their coned curves and shallows assembling an abundance of performances. Andrew, as presenter, reached into the wings and pulled something out from under the pillow. He teased Elizabeth, keeping it hidden behind his back.

'Right young lady. Have you been a good wee lassie? Dae you think you deserve tae get this?'

'Whit, get whit? Can ah see?'

'You'll see in a wee minute, but you have tae promise me that you'll be a good girl fae now oan and dae exactly whit ah tell you tae.'

There was no disputing Andrew was the boss. All the same Elizabeth tried to climb over him and see what was behind his back.

'Aye, of course ah will, ah'll dae whatever you say. Ah promise ah'll be as good as gold.'

'Okay then, but don't let me down, ah'm trusting you hen. Where's ma kiss?'

She lent forwards to kiss him on the cheek like she always did but he turned his face around and her lips landed on his. She pulled them away quickly, not liking the jaggy skin and bristles above his top lip. But she instantly forgot the moment, her surprise stealing the scene. It was a tracing book. Not just any tracing book but *the* best tracing book. Elizabeth smiled.

'Oh Andrew, that's so brilliant. That's the wan ah was looking at when we were at the shops. Ah love it so ah dae. It's the best present ever in the whole wide world.'

She gathered herself into a comfortable position on to the bed and elbows raised, delved into the magic of her book. Andrew got up and opened the door and Elizabeth, lost in its spell, turned her eyes briefly towards him, before allowing them to drop back quickly, returning to its rustling pages. The door opened, and then creaked, as Andrew shut it securely behind him.

She never gave the door a second thought until he came back into the room and shut it. This time he drew the little silver bolt across until it clicked into the hollow crevice on the frame. With the door locked Elizabeth stirred into an upright position on the bed. When Andrew turned round he was smirking, an enormous grin filling his face. The force of it was pushing his whiskers forward, the ginger stubble on his chin standing to attention. Elizabeth watched as the stubble got closer and closer to the bed.

'Do you know whit Andrew, ah think you look like Mister Potato Heid in wan of they adverts aff the telly.'

Take it or leave it

I reached for the pills as soon as I woke up. The pain had crept back in during the night, boring inside, the intensity worse because of the respite the drugs had afforded me. I swallowed a little blue tablet with some flat coke, the brown syrupy liquid almost causing my hung-over stomach to retch. I sat by the window, watching the early morning waves ride daringly onto the shoreline, obsessively counting the moments until the aching would begin to fade.

When it came I felt it wash over me like the sea, smothering me in new beginnings. I hugged my shoulders, wrapping my arms around my body like a shroud, running my finger along my bare arm, my skin suddenly softer to the touch. Perched on the chair I gazed at the outside world, watching without feeling, my mind finally empty of the constant rambling that had been nagging and pestering me since I'd decided I'd taken the final punch.

I grabbed my sketch pad and eased myself on to the edge of the bed. Sadie lay upon it, as quiet as a stone. I scribbled her outline on the thick paper, taking care over her hair, spraying it across the page like seaweed collecting on this shoreline. Finally she was sleeping soundly. During the night she'd thrashed about for hours, slapping her skinny limbs against the cold wall, her body unhinged and unbalanced as she struggled against the demons inside her screeching for drugs. Her emotions were as dynamic as her body, angry grunting dissolving into gentle sobs, and then an incoherent mumbling, its waves pushing and pulling her, her limbs writhing in positions that looked unnatural and frightening. I watched her quietly, ensuring my breathing continued to mirror that of sleep.

Disguising a movement as an unconscious roll I stretched

my hand over the covers, my fingers falling to rest on Sadie's tense shoulder. I closed my eyes but I could feel her turn and face me, watching, wondering if she should accept it as a moment of tenderness or reject it as interference. She lay still then pulled herself away, her thin body slipping easily from my loose grasp. She dropped onto the floor and I watched through my fingers as she curled into a tight ball, her throbbing body looking for comfort wherever she could find it. She wriggled, her skinny limbs twisting and turning as if she was on fire, her arms finally stretching out and grabbing the bottle of tablets on the bedside table.

She swallowed some hungrily, lowering her body onto the chair by the window, waiting like I just had, for the magic to come. I'd fallen asleep watching her silhouette, a silver outline from the moon casting a brilliant light upon her. I stirred as she climbed softly back to bed just as the dawn was beginning to impose its dominance on the dark, ice cold feet leaving a cool embrace on the sheet as she curled her knees up to her chest. I let my arm fall into the mane of hair and there we both slept until the pain kicked me awake.

I sketched Sadie carefully, getting the curve of her back exactly right, soft yet strong and impressionable. She looked different now that the daylight was stretching its morning arms around the room, golden rays of promise bouncing off the beige walls. The anger in Sadie's face was gone, the demons having fled to the corners of the room. The image was surprisingly angelic.

Her skin was pale, her eyelids fluttering gently over wide set eyes. Her rose red lips were slightly parted, her chest rising and falling with each calmed breath. I watched her curiously, knowing that despite everything they said I'd seen a vision like this before. I chuckled quietly, catching the soft sound before it escaped from my throat. Sadie wasn't exactly the Virgin Mary but she did look beautiful. I wondered if one day I'd crave a snapshot of the moment so I sketched quickly before reality could steal its edge.

Collette awoke with a jar, a startled cry the first sound she uttered as she struggled against the unfamiliarity of her surroundings. I smiled and pulled her into my arms, kissing her warm cheeks gently, my lips tasting the lingering essence of sleep that had crept into the air and was hanging like a damp overcoat. She began to cry, her words revealing in sobs that she'd wet the bed. I tickled her under the chin and smiled.

'No worries little darling, you can jump in the bath. You're still beautiful, even with a soggy bum.'

She threw her arms tightly around my neck and giggled, her deep chortling stirring the others. From silence we had mayhem as the Sadie I was more familiar with emerged from sleep.

'Fuck sake Elizabeth could you no have woken me up? We're gaunae miss this boat if we don't get a move on.'

She pushed the bedside clock onto its back and threw the covers to the bottom of the bed, the rage all there as she pulled clothes from her rucksack, tossing the things she didn't need into the air like an old woman on the beach throwing bread to the seagulls. Holding Collette's hand I responded, her mood filtering into my own and spoiling a contented moment.

'Aye, sorry for letting you get an extra hour of kip Sadie, for fuck sake you were thrashing about half the night. I should be the one moaning at you for keeping me awake.'

'Whit, you moaning? That wouldnae be like you now would it?'

I ignored her sarcasm, a mellow haze reminding me that my soul was enjoying a moment of respite from the mayhem. I led Collette to the bathroom and Laura skipped behind us, her presence loud and instant as if she'd just been turned on at the back. Her excitement was infectious and I spoke to the girls at pace, my words whizzing into the air as if they'd been dispelled from a tongue dipped in helium gas. Sadie was just being dramatic, I knew she was excited too. It had taken a bottle of vodka to get it out of her but before we called it a night Sadie had confessed that her father was from the island. She'd spent all her summers as a child there. She explained that it wouldn't be possible to stay with family but it didn't matter. The island had a reason to reach out to us, to welcome us into its arms. It could only mean one thing. We were going to be safe.

I placed Collette and Laura in the bath and returned to Sadie. She was in the bedroom, her eyes straining towards the island as if she was trying to see inside the windows of her childhood home. I clasped the mass of hair that draped her long thin neck and gathered it in a bun.

'Right grumpy, we've got a lot to organise, is there anything you need me to do?'

She shook her head without turning around. Her head was hot, its clammy sweat sticking to my fingers, solitude clinging to the back of her neck like a veil. I let her hair fall and swept the strands across one shoulder.

'Hey, Sadie, I know we don't know each other very well but if there's anything you need to say to me please just go ahead and say it. If we're going to make a go of it across on that island we're going to have to get to know each other a bit better.'

For a moment I thought she was going to push me away, force me backwards against the wall but instead her fingers grasped mine, her need for support rushing through my bones like a surge of electricity.

'Thanks hen, you're a pal but I'm all right, just trying tae work my way through all this shit. I've not been over tae the island for ages and let's just say ah didnae leave on the best of terms. Ah've got a few bridges to build when we get over.' She turned around, her features retracting, some sort of pain pinching the softness. 'But listen, it's a fresh start for us all and I'm going tae make sure ah sort myself out. Ah need tae for Laura, she's not going to make the same fuckin mistakes that ah did I can promise you that.'

I took a small step backwards, edging myself into Sadie's full view.

'Here, do you think I need to get changed before we head down for breakfast?'

Sadie buckled with laughter. The flannelette nightdress she had bought me was puffing up like a parachute, my crow legs dangling out from the bottom, my strapped breasts squashed against my chest like a pigeon. I was coming and going in equal measure, gravity pushing and pulling before giving up on deciding what it was trying to do with me.

'You know Sade, I've been the one bleating on about what I'm going to do if Patrick finds me which is absolutely ridiculous, there's no way on this earth he's going to have a clue where I am, even if he has bothered his arse looking for me. But are you not worried that Alan will follow you here? Presumably he knows you used to come here as a child?'

'Are you joking E? The guy's a complete fanny. Ah can one hundred percent guarantee you that he'll not gie Carravindoon a second thought. Ah doubt he even remembers me talking about it, he was always permanently wasted. Don't worry, we'll be fine, and besides when we get over tae the rock we'll have plenty of things to keep us occupied. You'll forget that Patrick ever existed.'

We sat down, moving towards the bed simultaneously, positioning ourselves side by side. The girls were giggling, water splashing loudly onto the floor in the bathroom.

'So what's your Alan like then, do you love him… did you ever love him?'

She sighed and rolled her lips, a long purr escaping into the air we shared between us. She looked at me carefully before answering.

'Good question. Do I love him? The honest answer is ah don't think so hen. Ah feel something for him, obviously ah dae, but he's too fuckin handy wae his fists. Ah know ah give as good as I get sometimes but he just goes crazy for no reason, it's as if he's always trying tae prove some kind of stupid point. Ah suppose if it wiznae for Laura and the junk ah would have left him years ago.'

I rubbed my thighs vigorously, remembering what it was like to be on the wrong end of a punch.

'I know what you mean about the violence; Patrick scares the fuckin living daylights out of me. I've lost count of the number of times I've honestly thought I was going to die. I don't know, it's hard to explain, but he makes me feel as if I deserve it. Maybe I do; once upon a time someone told me I deserved everything I was going to get in life. They've no been wrong so far.'

Sadie shook her head. 'For fuck sake Elizabeth don't be so fuckin stupid, can you no see that's what he's trying tae make you feel like? You need tae be a wee bit smarter than that. You're a lovely lassie, naebody deserves tae get the shit beaten out of them. It's no fuckin right.'

'Aye right enough Sadie, cos you're obviously in such a good position to judge aren't you?'

I exhaled sharply, my breathing trapped inside my claustrophobic chest. Sadie grasped the fingers of my right hand, pulling it from my waist and entwining it in hers. She softly settled the conjoined structure on to her bare knee.

'Hey, stop the bus, I wasn't judging you ah wiz just thinking what a bastard your man was. Ah know how difficult it is to walk away, believe you me. I wiznae criticising you ya maddie, I was feeling for you.'

A cry of *mmmuuuuuuuuuuuuuuuummmmmm* emerged from the bathroom and we both jumped to our feet.

'Me and Collette's turning into yucky prunes, we're all wrinkly.'

Sadie squeezed my hand and leapt towards the bathroom.

'Well we best get you out before someone eats you for breakfast.'

I laughed and then called after her.

'Sadie, would you mind taking the girls to breakfast? I don't think I can eat a thing, I could honestly do with a wee walk to clear my head before we go on this boat.' She mumbled *aye* and I gathered my things as quickly as I could. 'I'll just see you down there at the harbour will I? It's no as if I can help you carry anything anyway and Collette's happy with Laura. Is that okay?'

Sadie's head peered from around the frame of the bathroom door.

'For fuck's sake ah said aye, do you need me to write you a certificate an' all?'

She reached towards me, helping me pull the jumper over my head, stretching the fabric so it wouldn't make contact with my swollen face. I kissed her, my lips demanding to feel the softness of her cheek without my direction. We held a gaze, a second of something.

'Right, c'mon to fuck, if you're going for a wee walk go the now will you? Ah'm starving for brekkie and so's these weans.'

Mary

Elizabeth stood still for a moment, re-gathering the strength she needed to deliver her message. She was resting her back against the wall, the thumping of her heart resonating into the thick stone, the sound bouncing back and settling in her ears. She listened to its demanding screech, remembering the nun at the convent who had told her that every time someone whistles, Our Lady cries. She walked towards Mary, searching for evidence of tears.

Elizabeth rested beside the Virgin Mary. Neither spoke. She stood directly beside Mary, stealing the same air, her left foot pressed against hers, her right foot lodged against the wall of the alcove that circled them both. She didn't look at her, turning to face the same direction as Mary, examining her vantage point, the watchful pose she was occupying on the hill, the sea crashing below, the island of mystery sandwiched between the waves and the clouds in the distance. The silence between them was palpable.

A swallow startled the quiet, landing on the grass at the hill's formidable edge, its tiny frame lost in an autumn day it should have long since left behind. Elizabeth saluted its arrival, knowing that everything about today would be extraordinary. The little bird danced, hopping among the foliage, tiny wings stretching and folding as something and nothing caught its eye and held its watchful spell. Elizabeth's movement stirred its interest and it turned and stared, a twinkling eye holding her gaze. After a few moments the swallow stretched its wings, its polished back shining like midnight, its blackness penetrating a blue expansive sky. A gust of wind circled its feet and so it fled, pushing into the possibilities of autumn heavens, the redness of its face kissing the soft clouds mirrored on its virgin white breast.

Elizabeth sighed and let her head fall, her mane of hair slipping silently down Mary's back. She spoke quietly and deliberately. She was tired, she'd had enough. She didn't want to run anymore. 'Sadie's lovely Mary, she's going to make a good life for her and Laura. I've got no chance of doing that for Collette. I've not exactly done her any favours so far have I?' It was silence she was looking for so she was grateful when her question remained unanswered.

'I can't deal with the pain anymore, and before you make some crack about the body healing itself I don't mean this broken bones shit. I've been there enough times before to know that it gets better but nothing inside changes. You know that, I tell you that every fuckin night. I ask you to help and you don't. So maybe you don't want to. Maybe you can't, women don't really have the option to be all encompassing in life, let's face it. I don't know why I thought you might be any different.'

Elizabeth turned around to face Mary, square on, her lips inches from hers. She raised her voice, the anger making her breathless, the words bursting forth from just one lungful of air.

'What the fuck did you bother coming to me for if you weren't going to do anything to stop it? Jesus, what the fuck was the point? Nothing changed, it just got worse. You are actually worse than fuckin useless.' She pulled back, changing her tone, her stance kinder.

'I'm sorry, I'm being an arse, I know I am, and I guess you tried but just couldnae do it, couldnae persuade them that a wee lassie like me was worth saving. But what about Jenny, she did nothing . . .'

Elizabeth fell to her knees in front of Mary. The razor blade she pulled from her bag glinted in the low sun, a yellow flash of light stroking the cheek of the Virgin.

'Piggy the psychiatrist was right, ah'm no right in the head, none of this would have happened to me if I was. Collette's going to be good with Sadie and you, well if you were of any use whatsoever you'd stop me now, tell me that there's something worth saving.'

Elizabeth raised her neck, stretching her throat so she could stare at Mary, swallow the soft features that had kept her struggle going until now. She said nothing and Elizabeth closed her eyes, willing the strength from the soil beneath her feet to traverse her limbs to bravery. It was them and not she that would have to cut the tie between her and Collette.

Mary lunged forward, her weight crashing towards Elizabeth from above, her blue cloak collapsing into the grass, the sky swallowing earth. Elizabeth rolled backwards, the heel of her trainer gripping the cliff's precarious edge. Mary tumbled onto the spot that Elizabeth had coveted, her frame consuming the silver blade. Elizabeth hurdled the Virgin's full size statue and fled the grotto, her lungs fuelled by Mary's prayer. She was well on her way to 299 by the time she got the harbour.

The long road home

Sadie was standing on the pier, puffing furiously on a cigarette, the hot red tip burning right down to her fingertips before she shooed it away like a wasp. She jumped onto the harbour wall, her hand shielding her eyes, a captain's lookout as she strained out to sea, searching for the boat that would take her back, a sweet sorrow that was sending salty tears to her cheeks. Her cackling cry reached me through the swirling air, the breeze sending it this way and that before it finally arrived.

'Fuckin hell you took your time, ah was beginning to think you'd done a runner.' I wrinkled my lips, *as if* doing its best to deliver a huffy, insincere message. Sadie turned her attentions back to sea unconcerned by my blatant lie.

'Ah'll tell you what though, ah cannae believe he's taken the boat out in that, it's a bit choppy out in the channel. You'll need tae make sure you put those waterproofs on or you'll get soaked.'

I stared at her nonchalantly wondering why we couldn't just sit in the bar on the ferry like we did before. I reached into my bag and released a pill from the bottle of tablets, stopping for a moment to think before deciding to make it two. I swallowed them without a drink, enjoying the bitter taste as they lodged in my throat, the chemicals melting into my flesh and sinking into my veins. It was all part of the experience. I rubbed the outside of my throat with my finger, cursing the rubbish crap that Piggy the psycho doctor had given me, drugs that had numbed me and sunk me for so many years. At least Patrick put a stop to all of that, he wasn't having any wife of his seeing a shrink and taking happy pills. He said he would be the provider of everything I would ever need. Or something like that anyway.

The wind was picking up and it had found a place at my feet, whipping up against the cold harbour wall before smashing off my face, swirling more intently as it crashed against my cheek. The pain was searing, I was alive and had feeling but fuckin hell it was sore. Sadie had bought me a scarf and I pulled it around my head wrapping its length around my face as tightly as the pain would allow. The waiting was making me impatient, my impatience allowing the severity of my injuries to find a voice and steal their fifteen minutes of fame. I looked out to sea wondering if Sadie's fabled ferry would ever come and take us away.

I wasn't much of a sailor; the ferry over to Ireland was only the second time I'd been on a boat. The first time I'd begged not to go, desperately trying to avoid a school trip to France, a torturous week with classmates I despised. Jennifer Spencer was the worst of them. A rich bitch with amazing clothes and attitude. All the boys fancied her and she flirted with them outrageously, dangling them on little sticks from her place at the front of the pack. I hated the stupid posh school, my exclusion enhanced by my status as a scholarship kid and Jennifer's continuing refusal to even acknowledge my existence. I signed up for the trip with purpose, slamming the headmaster's door when I grudgingly tossed my deposit across his fine oak table, cursing the fuckin world. Until I realised she was different.

Jennifer – Jenny – started to talk to me a couple of weeks before we left for France, encouraging my cheeky retorts in class, smiling as she tumbled past me in the corridor surrounded by her many disciples. On the ferry she startled me, grabbing my arm and pulling me behind a massive capstan on the middle deck. She was slurping enthusiastically from the neck of a bottle of red wine. I listened to it slip noisily down her thin neck before she passed it in my direction. 'The rest of them are fuckin idiots, I've always liked the look of you,' she said.

I welcomed her into my heart that afternoon, her drunken

confession ripping me apart. Her father was over attentive, taking more from her than he should have been taking. I needed to take care of her, to draw her close and protect her, yet the first time she kissed me I was stunned into silence, pulling away sharply, her soft lips staggering into retreat before breaking into laughter.

'For fuck sake Elizabeth, don't look so shocked, I was only noising you up.'

But she wasn't and she persevered, striking it lucky with me on just the second attempt. We didn't stop after the kiss, spending the night together, our inhibitions quashed by a yearning to explore the raw nakedness of our individual lives.

I was fifteen and instantly I loved her with all my heart. She was soft and kind, never hurting or threatening, just warm and loving, like the Mary that had once upon a time entered my life and then left it again in the blink of an eye. She urged me to take control and at first I shied away only understanding how to be led, only knowing how to give, never before having had the desire to take. Her tenderness fuelled my confidence and finally I grasped the opportunity, my love spilling into a fervour I never knew existed. I shared my story with her, and she with me. My circle with Mary became a triangle. For six months we breathed the same air and she shared my evening prayer.

The last time I saw her she stroked me passionately, teasing me, gently running her fingers between my legs, kissing my breasts and then letting her lips linger on mine, our bodies clinging together as shaking knees struggled to keep us upright. She pulled away eventually and took a necklace from around her neck. She placed it around mine, lingering for a second to steal a glance, her hand clutching my hair, her fingers caressing my shoulders as she let it fall against my bare skin. I pushed my chin against my chest and smiled at the upside down Virgin Mary pendant. She knew I loved it.

I saw Mary once. I had told her about it as we lay entwined in bed. *Whatever*, she sniggered from under the covers when I described seeing the Virgin in the flesh. Jenny fell onto her back and laughed, deep chortles thrusting her large breasts into the air. They bounced freely until I grasped them in my hands and her girlish giggling evaporated into short passionate breaths.

I ran my fingers around the chain and took the medal in my hands. 'I can't possibly have this Jenny, you love it, you said it keeps you safe.'

'Yes', she laughed, 'but Mary's your pal, isn't she? She's never bothered to visit me.'

It was meant as a parting gift, a sweet sorrow. Jenny was going away for the weekend with her father and I didn't want her to uncurl her fingers from mine and share her softness with a monster. She kissed my eyelids, urging me not to forget her. I should have listened properly to what she was saying. *See you Monday* I had hollered as she climbed into her father's car. I hung about waiting for an encouraging wave that said see you soon, but it never came. Jenny's father had captured my life, his thick fingers stroking the side of my lover's beautiful face.

Jennifer Spencer killed herself that evening. Her father Larry found her in the garage. She was hanging by the neck from a rope tossed across the rafters of the ceiling, her fifteen year old body still and quiet, all its vibrancy dissipating into cold air that swirled around the room, trying to flee the tragic landscape that surrounded her.

I pictured the scene often, a swell gathering around her dangling feet, the soft arms of time holding a snapshot of her former existence, waiting to lay her to rest, allowing her to escape to the only place she believed she was able to go. I tried to see her face, my eyes squinting through the pain so I could trace the outline of her lips with my fingertips, but an almighty barrier always prevented me from embracing her soft skin. I tossed countless sketches in the bin, my mind forcing me to remember my lover as she was and not as she had become.

Jenny didn't leave a note, no hastily written plea for help allowing her pain to spill like dripping blood on plain white paper. Yet there was no denying that her message was blatant in ensuring that it was him, her father Larry Spencer, and not anyone else that found her young skin, naked and on display, devoid of anything resembling life. I made a pact as I glared in his direction at the funeral, that one day he would know that I knew, that I was well aware that he had strangled her tiny heart with all his woeful might. I hadn't forgotten that promise, never, not for a second. Knowing I'd made it ensured I survived Patrick and everything he threw at me because one day I knew I'd need my strength for something else. I'm glad Mary reminded me of that, throwing her porcelain skin in my direction at the grotto, crashing the scene at the most opportune moment, delivering the sign I craved.

Sadie was hollering something and it took a few seconds to let go of Jenny and decipher her words.

'That's the boat nearly in Elizabeth, jump up on the wall and you'll see it.'

I accepted her hand and clambered onto the wall shaking the tears away from my eyes harshly. Sadie assumed my tears were of uncertainty and I went with that notion, not willing to share what little I had left of Jenny.

'Are you awright hen? You're no having second thoughts about going over are you?'

Sadie's boyish toughness softened as she placed her hand onto my necklace. She grasped the medal of Mary, holding it between her fingers before placing it on the palm of her hand. I said nothing, feeling the bond that she was creating, Sadie's energy finding its way into my soul via the golden frame. I closed my eyes remembering Jenny's touch, her caress as gentle as a butterfly, her touch so different to Bananarama Girl.

'You know . . .' Sadie paused to breathe, placing the medal back on my chest, her fingers dwelling for just a second before she drew them away, thrusting her hands into the pockets of her coat, ' . . . there's a gorgeous grotto at the chapel over on Carravindoon. It's dead peaceful, I used tae love sitting down beside it wae my granny. She's pretty mental though; she talks tae the Virgin as if she was joining her for a cup of tea.'

I laughed, joy puffing my chest in the knowledge that Mary wasn't just coming with us, she was already there. Sadie smiled, her vowels splattering into life as if she was spraying a wall with a can of colourful paint. She pulled her right hand and a packet of cigarettes from her pocket, her left hand catching up and arriving a few seconds later clutching a lighter. She placed the long white wand on the edge of her mouth and puffed noisily until the stick ignited, smoke billowing from her lips when she turned away from the wind.

'The boat's nearly in E, it'll be here in ten minutes. Ah'm gaunae run over tae the phone box and gie my ma a quick call. Ah just want her tae know ah'm awright. Dae you want tae call anyone before we head o'er to Carravindoon?'

There was no-one to call, a trip to the phone box was pointless.

'No you're all right Sadie, I've nothing to say to anyone.' I screwed my mouth to the side wondering about her call. 'You're not going to say anything to your mum about where we are, are you?'

I traced my fingers around my neck, feeling the life choke from me as I imagined the world closing in on our escape. I grasped Mary in my fingertips, the medal warm and inviting against my cold skin. I dropped it quickly, Jenny creeping back into my thoughts and stealing me away from the moment. Sadie interrupted like a woodpecker on speed.

'Oh for fuck sake Elizabeth she knows we're here, she wiz desperate for me tae come over, she knows this is the wan place in the world where me and Laura will be safe. Ah just need tae tell her Laura's awright, she'll be missing her like crazy. And don't worry, ah'll no mention that you're wae me.'

She jumped off the wall turning with an outstretched hand to help me down.

'E hen, I just want tae tell her that ah'm still doing awright and I'm off the smack and trying tae make her proud. Ah'll no be a minute, honest.'

I nodded, watching the smoke from her cigarette make for the sea, its grey cloud setting sail without us. She grasped me tightly around the waist, her fingers avoiding my broken ribs with care. She lowered me down and kept hold, our toes touching, her face so close I could feel her warm breath.

'Keep a wee eye on Laura for me will you?'

'Of course, I'll see you in a minute.'

I shouted to the girls drawing them towards me with the loud exclamation that I'd seen a whale. They giggled, clambering alongside me as their bright eyes scanned the horizon. Sadie wasn't gone for long. She came out of the phone box minutes later, her arms thrusting forward as she walked quickly, trying to propel her legs to work faster. Her face was pale, her lips a bloody red in contrast, her fingers shaking as she fumbled with the buttons on Laura's coat. She grabbed her close, hugging her as if there might not be a tomorrow. I pulled her aside as the boat swished into the little pier, loud voices hollering something and nothing as thick ropes thudded onto concrete shelving, a ridge between us and the choppy sea below.

'What's happened Sadie?'

I grasped her arms tightly, my fingers struggling to feel flesh under the thick layers of protective clothing. She shook me away.

'Stop fuckin nagging me will you, I told you ah've got stuff tae face when I get over there. Gie me a fuckin minute tae try and get it all straight in my head will you, you're not the only one with fuckin issues tae deal with.'

She was lying. There was something else. I could see it in her eyes, they were flashing the kind of fear that I'd seen in the mirror, many many times.

Oilskins and blankets

Sadie's pale features were worrying me. Something was going on but instinctively I was aware that the news would cut me in two. She said she was okay and I chose to believe her. I could stop time when I needed to; I'd had plenty of practice. I gently encouraged the panicked knot in my stomach to relax and concentrated on examining the boat.

It wasn't a ferry; it was a glorified rowing boat with a filthy black engine gripping its back, slipping in and out of the water like a giant fish. There was a lot of crap lying around on the deck.

'When we set out you'll need to sit down there and don't let the youngsters near the edge.' The ferryman was pointing to the boat, showing me something I could quite clearly see.

'You'll need tae hold ontae them youngsters tight when we get out in the channel, she's blowing a bit of a gale out there and we'll need tae move quickly to get her in at all.'

The seating he referred to was a series of wooden slats across the breadth of the hull; four or five of them which he repeatedly impressed upon me was where we should sit. He was small and round, his back bent over. The skin surrounding his eyes was dark, black pools swirling from his inner lids to his eyebrows. He wiped one eye harshly, thick fingers waving at me as they rid his sight of whatever it was that was causing irritation.

I took a small step back; it was probably me. I had the habit of bringing the worst out in everybody. For all their bleakness though the man's eyes didn't appear tired or weary. When he let his hand fall back onto his hip I noticed how brightly they shone, deep and green like a winter sea. I felt my grip on Collette's shoulders relax but I remained close, pushing my knees into the small of her back to keep her within reach. She was looking at the boat, her feet tapping enthusiastically with a splurge of go go go, her eagerness willing me to hurry her on to it.

I scoured the rest of the interior of the vessel. The wood on the slats was cracked and worn, patches of moments past ingrained into the surface, like a series of hidden messages. I could read the one written for me. *Help, my fuckin life's a mess*, but I erased it from the beam letting the negative feeling pass, reminding myself that I was moving on. The boat was small, maybe twelve foot in length, six or seven feet across, the faded white paint of the main body only visible when it rolled away from me on the pier, the large swell threatening to take the entire object into its gigantic throat and swallow it. The rim was bright green, a thick perimeter that would push against the horizon.

Sadie bumped past me and clasped her hands around Laura's waist. Picking her up in one giant swoop she slung her over the edge of the pier and into the arms of the boatman with the emerald green eyes. Laura squealed in delight and Collette tugged at my fingers urging me to let her go next. I passed her hand to Sadie, who passed her on to the boatman.

Sadie stepped on to the boat and the green eyed man hugged her tenderly.

'Welcome back,' he said, 'it's great to have you home again.'

Sadie dropped her eyes and he jumped in quickly with a retort, their conversation suddenly quick and intense. I couldn't hear it all, the wind was snatching sporadic syllables, but eventually they moved towards me and I was able to eavesdrop.

'Your granny will be thrilled te have ye back, she's been awfy down since your da . . .' Sadie butted in quickly, refusing to let him finish his sentence.

'Missed me, Seamus? She's more likely tae want tae curse me.'

'But she's not seen you since what happened tae your daddy and she's had it tough as old boots. She always looked forward to her favourite wee lassie arriving fae Scotland.'

'Aye and then I grew up, turned intae what I am, drove ma dad tae a fatal heart attack and then she tellt me she hated me at the funeral.' She pulled her hands from her pockets and wrung her hands. 'I doubt she'll have been pining after me Seamus but I dae want tae show I can make her proud. I'm trying tae make it right, for aw of us, not just me and Laura.'

She pulled the hood of her jacket tightly across her face, pushing the Velcro strap firmly to say that her talking was done. In silence Sadie and Seamus helped me on to the boat, taking great care, Seamus touching me ever so gently despite his strong hands. I suppose it was obvious that I was struggling; the bruises were deepening in colour, my face a depiction of modern art. Sadie organised the seating, sandwiching the two girls inside us so we acted like rudders.

'Here, watch, you're gaunae need tae have that buttoned right up, it'll get freezing wance we're out in the channel.'

Sadie pulled my zip up to my chin and pulled the bobble hat she had bought me down over my ears. I let her do what she needed to do; for a brief second I didn't feel the need to be constantly fighting for survival. Yet there was still something going on, a dark secret that Sadie was shouldering. I could see it, feel it strongly when she urged Seamus that we should be moving on. She blamed it on the tides, reckoned if we left now we would miss the worst of the weather.

'Ah Sarah you know the score so ye do. There's no been a boat in o'er a week; we've had force nines for days. You're lucky te be getting o'er at all and auld Sarah will no have had a drop oav milk . . . sure she gave up the cattle when your da
. . .'

He stopped and looked away, Sadie's head turning in the opposite direction simultaneously.

'Sadie what's going on, what happened to your dad? And why does he keep calling you Sarah?'

'Ah'm Sarah ya numpty, ah shorten it tae Sadie when ah'm trying to run away fae myself. Ah thought it would make it easier tae keep running away and no go back.'

'And your dad? What happened?'

'Look hen, ah don't like tae talk about it. Ma da died a couple of years ago, he had a massive heart attack no long after ah got myself saddled with Alan and the smack. Everybody said it was ma fault, it was aw the worry that did it.'

I pulled my body upright.

'Fuckin hell Sadie, I'm really sorry, I didn't realise your dad was dead.'

I thought of my own parents, their interest in me long since forgotten, their demand that I forget my *'fixation'* on Mary or forget them. I didn't see them again after the hospital. I was sixteen by the time I left. I didn't need anything anymore, well not until Patrick. But even then I didn't think I needed him, I most certainly knew I didn't want him but he told me different and I followed his lead because that's what I'd been taught to do.

'Ah well, there's a lot you don't know about me, ah've only known you for fifteen minutes Elizabeth not a fuckin lifetime.'

'I'm just asking Sadie. I'm not judging you, believe me, but I am risking a lot to bring my child into your life, we both are. If there are things we think we need to share with one another then we should.' I pressed Mary into my breast knowing that I wouldn't be making the mistake of sharing my relationship with her. I'd had enough of Piggy to last me a lifetime.

'Actually hen, ah think you'll find ah don't have tae tell you anything, but seen as you're such a fuckin nosey cow ah'll tell you. Ah couple of years ago ah got myself arrested. Aye, ah said arrested, there's no need to drop your fuckin jaw. Alan had spent aw our money on junk and ah needed nappies for the wean. Ah stole some, got caught, got let off by the cops but they phoned ma da tae lift me up fae the station as that's the number ah stupidly gave them so Alan wouldnae find out. He found out, slapped me so hard he nearly broke my jaw and at the same time managed tae break my dad's heart. The end.'

She slapped her hand down on the wooden bench, a dull thud escaping into the air.

'There. Happy now? Boat's not left yet so plenty of time to piss off and escape the bad woman responsible fae killing her father.'

I swallowed hard, seeing for the first time how awful her life had been. Like a fool I'd been too wrapped up in my own to even begin to understand anything about her.

'Jesus Sadie, I'm not wanting to run away from you. I care about you and I'm really sorry about your dad but bloody hell it wasn't your fault, he could have had a heart attack any time, people have dodgy hearts that just pack up. You're not to blame and your granny's bound to have been upset, she was burying her son, can you imagine how you would feel if anything happened to Laura? Why would I judge you for being you Sadie, I'm your friend. I care about you, even after just fifteen minutes.'

She slumped down on to the bench, sighing hard.

'Thanks, that means a lot.'

I leaned closer, making sure the kids couldn't hear.

'So, does this mean you and I are officially sailing off into the sunset together?'

She laughed, an outrageous guffaw that sounded like a seagull in flight.

'Aye, seems like it right enough. You getting scared that ah'm gaunae jump you once ah get you alone in the tent?'

The pleasure hit me like a bolt of thunder, passionate feelings rippling through me as I imagined Sadie's fingers exploring my body. It'd been a long time since Jenny but I'd never forgotten. I flirted back.

'Now you're talking. But maybe you are all talk, you've had plenty of chances to make a move already and you've no bothered your arse.'

'How dae you know I've no been bothering ma arse, you've been pretty wasted these last few nights.'

Another wave flushed from my stomach and I squeezed my legs together. I blushed, remembering Jenny, ashamed that someone else could create the same physical feelings. Sadie saw my discomfort and smiled. The moment passed but its possibilities lingered between us.

The boat pulled out from the harbour. The sky was a shrill blue. It was cloudless, giving it a natural beauty so rarely seen it appeared false, like a backdrop to a movie set. The air was chilled, but the wind had dropped taking the sharp cold of yesterday with it. The sun was climbing in the sky and might have warmed our cheeks if we had been directly facing it. The boat rocked gently from side to side and the girls gasped in excitement. The island was to the north of us, its tall cliffs calm and inviting, the long finger of the south side of the L shape welcoming us to its shores. I sucked the air in deeply, swallowing two little pills as the boat trundled noisily towards the channel, the first of the cold waves tossing into the boat and furnishing us with a lick of salt. I rested my head on Sadie's shoulder, my mind racing as I challenged it to quickly imagine our new and safer life. A world without Patrick and his violence and memories of a childhood I constantly tried and failed to forget. Sadie kissed the top of my head and I felt her intake of breath before she spoke.

'Elizabeth darling, ah wiznae sure how tae tell you this but seen as we're almost live-in lovers it looks as if Alan knows where ah am . . .'

I didn't lift my head and I could hear my own words clearly as they spilled the short distance from my lips to Sadie's ears.

'Looks as if he knows, or knows?'

'He fuckin knows Elizabeth, I'm gaunae have tae come up wae a plan and fuckin pronto as this might get a little bit messy.'

I stayed where I was, a selfish streak I didn't know I possessed bursting into action. *Thank fuck it's not Patrick* was all I could hear myself say, the words buried carefully inside my head.

The Long Way Round

Painful folds on Sadie's face dragged out the agony as we sailed, a series of dismayed glances to the south sitting as evidence for the prosecution as she constantly revealed her hand, searching for Alan's imminent approach behind us. I followed her gaze, her anguish bobbing up and down in my peripheral vision, her chiselled features faintly visible as the spray evaporated into the air alongside us, mirroring the nothingness our sorry little lives dictated. I reached for her hand, her cold fingers resisting for just a second before curling around mine, a second hand joining the fray moments later, pressing against my knuckles, anxiously seeking the kind of comfort that neither she nor I were in a position to offer.

I said nothing, preferring instead to watch as Sadie's story unfolded, her eyes normally large and frivolous suddenly withdrawn and edgy, her lids flickering, her cheeks withdrawn and tense. She'd spoken about Alan, a little, and then some more, her comments sporadic and confusing, her emotions obviously distracted by a sentimentality that said she cared about him just a little bit more than she let on. I could see that, but I could also see that she needed to be free of him. It was the only way she stood a chance of sinking her past; severing the line and letting it anchor on the bottom of the ocean.

Our eyes locked just as an almighty wave crept into sight alongside the boat, its height hovering in our direction, twitching impatiently, like a killer whale anxious to swallow its prey. In preparation we urged the kids to duck and then it was upon us, its shoulders full and green, its long arms white and heavy as it saturated us loudly, roaring with laughter as it meandered its way through the boat, stealing its way into every available nook and cranny. The kids squealed and we laughed with them, freezing water dripping from our ears and our noses, Sadie's fingers peeling from mine, gently wiping a drip of salty water from my eyelash. I closed my eyes and let her touch me, forgetting the pain of my cracked face and my wretched jaw. Instead I welcomed her own anguish, receiving her pain as it washed over me like the salty wave. I stirred, remembering the vulnerability of Jenny, imagining the determination she salvaged from deep within herself to overcome that weakness and find the strength to throw a heavy rope over the rafters of the garage wall and make it strong and safe enough to swing her to her death. The sadness was overwhelming, knowing that she didn't have Mary to save her.

Sadie traced her fingers along my forehead and I used the moment to wonder if Jenny had thought of me, if *us* had meant anything at all as she slipped the noose around her oh so beautiful neck, an enchanting throat that had cried out time and time again as we lay stitched together, reminding ourselves that love and tenderness really did exist. I spared myself the shift towards anger that often followed memories of Jenny, a selfish trait that wished she had endured him as a means of staying with me.

'Sadie, let's try and put some kind of positive spin on this whole thing. Alan's coming, but so fuckin what, that's a bloody good thing; it'll give us a chance to sort this out and then we can just get on with our lives.'

I watched her shiver, her thin body moving with the rhythm of the small boat. Her fingers gripped the side of the vessel, her pale pink knuckles now a sheer white, the colour blending with the massive cliffs that were emerging ahead of us, tall mountains of muscle that would form a circle of strength between us and our invaders. I watched them grow as the boat sped nearer, the throb of the tiny engine now more apparent as we left the more violent waters of the channel behind, fingers of calmer sea passing us from palm to palm, guiding us closer to the icons that would protect us. The rippling waves handled us gracefully, the long fingers curving and then straightening as they stroked the edge of the cliffs tenderly, tickling as they rolled forward, brushing the milky white surface with a tender kiss.

When we stepped off the boat a crowd had gathered, several people staring, gazing at the unexpected arrival of winter life. Their faces were as muffled as their voices and my world began to spin. I felt my knees weaken as consciousness threatened to leave me, the immense pain of my body reminding me with vengeance that it was for real. I fought the dizziness, the darkness that was stealing me away but I wasn't strong enough to win. My senses slowly left me, loud inaudible voices finally giving way to silence as I fell heavily to the ground.

When I came to I didn't move. I tried to work out where I was lying, who was standing nearby with kind yet indecipherable voices. After a few moments I opened my eyes, my vision blurred and confused by my surroundings. I was inside a house, the flames from an open fire crackling to my left, soft pillows gently supporting my head.

Sadie emerged from a room to my right, followed by a tall woman, her hair long and loose and wild as if she'd been hanging it to dry on the pulley. It was losing its colour but still shone, thin strands of grey intermittently apparent, trundling down her shoulders like a sprinkling of pale white heather nesting amongst bright primroses. Her face was long, matching the tall frame that gave her a height I'd never seen in an older person. In Glasgow their bodies seem to curl, both ends striving to meet the other like a tortoise curling inside its shell. She stood as high as Sadie, her shoulders curving slightly. I smiled at her and full lips responded as soon as the message reached her face. Her teeth were straight, pale yellow like hay in a field. Her lips were smothered in lipstick, the polish on her nails a deeper shade of the same burnt orange.

She was dressed in blue, almost like a uniform, a navy blue crew neck jumper just visible under a long pinafore in the same colour that was buttoned up the front. It fell to just below her knees, American tan tights visible above old black wellington boots that were smothered in dried mud. A long blue cardigan completed the outfit, swinging below her hips, draping large breasts that hung heavily on her chest.

I crept slowly to my feet, embarrassed that I was lying lazily uninvited on this woman's settee.

'Ah you're awake then, you're obviously no used to the sea air are you, you've been in the land of the wee people for hours.'

Her accent was gentle, Irish like Seamus but more subtle, like an announcer reading the news, drawing us to sit up and pay attention. I glanced towards her, grinning in response to her warmth.

Take me to River

Paddy threw his cigarette into the sea in disgust.

'Are you gaunae tell that prick that he's taking us over to that piece of shit out there or am I gaunae have to break his fuckin legs?'

'Aye, its sorted mate, he's just waiting on the tide shifting or something like that, don't worry, we'll get there.'

Alan spoke quickly, tugging the collar of his jacket closer to his neck to try and stave off some of the chill. He had the silly notion that talking more quickly would buy him some time to think of a plan but the problem was that he wasn't a thinker; he didn't really do ideas that brought any advantage to a situation. His single talent was in fuckin things up. So he dug a little deeper, still pulling at his clothes, placing himself uncomfortably beside an angry Paddy who was vociferously chucking rough edged stones into the ruffled water from the harbour wall.

'Ah was thinking Paddy mate, if Sadie's got the cash oan her then maybe we can whip it off her and just dae a quick u-turn?'

He paused, but without a reaction from Paddy he carried on, babbling with a little more confidence in the misguided belief that no news was good news.

'It's no as if she won't have learned her lesson and it'll gie you a chance tae get back tae sort out your own bird and aw that mess between her and the Boss.' He murmured an exaggerated *ouch*, pawing his balls, separating them from the uncomfortable lining of his jeans.

'But it's not just that Paddy mate, it's the wee one, ah don't want my wee lassie seeing her ma getting hurt.'

Paddy examined his fingernails and then rubbed his palms

together, gently at first and then more emphatically as if he'd had a revelation.

'Aye right enough Alan, ah should have thought about that. You're right, of course you're right, I don't want the wee lassie seeing me break her ma's scrawny neck any more than you do.'

Alan exhaled sharply, his emotions thrown into disarray as he celebrated his victory whilst swallowing the news of Sarah's fate.

'We'll blindfold the wee brat. How will that do?'

He grabbed Alan by the waist of his jeans and tugged them up harshly, mouthing *poor you* as Alan screeched with the sheer pain in his balls. Paddy's laugh was that of the pantomime baddie, deep and exaggerated and unnatural but he wore it like a name badge as he dropped his hold and then approached Alan sinisterly, his right arm outstretched, his hand raised. The end of his middle finger was resting on the edge of his thumb forming a loose representation of an 'O'. Alan followed the letter as it drew closer to his face, his pupils' gyrating as they tried to absorb Patrick's message.

You're a fuckin arsehole it said as Paddy flicked the end of Alan's nose sharply, the action sending him cross eyed as he meekly accepted the delivery with a pathetic cry of *ouch*. He rubbed his nose softly, thankful that his balls were still intact. He sat quietly, instinctively knowing that additional words would only dig him deeper into the shit. He searched for his reflection in the water below but his image wasn't there. He sniffed, understanding that he couldn't even manage that.

Paddy spat on the wall, the vile green syrup catching the edge of Alan's right hand as it fell heavily. He didn't move despite an urge to pull away and vomit. He was thinking about Sarah. In his own way he thought the world of her, but it was hard, he was a nobody, the kind of wee prick people just took a kick at for fun so he tried hard to be something else, somebody people would listen to. He didn't mean to take it so far but as soon as he'd got into the smack that was it, he couldn't get out. He wasn't entirely blameless; even when deep in the shit he still searched for the positives in his lifestyle, reminding himself that one day he'd be as respected as Paddy, maybe even the Boss Umberto, and when that happened Sarah would know why, she'd understand and love the sacrifices he'd been making.

He did love Sarah. Being with her had been fun at first, before Laura and the junk, and in his deluded mind he was sure it would be harmonious again. He dragged his foot along the ground wishing that he was smart enough to think of a plan to stop Sarah's impending pain. He glanced at Paddy and the anger on his face told him that unless he could outwit him he was going to have to go through with it. Sarah was fucked. He wrung his hands in dismay, already trying to rid them of her blood.

The moment was tempered by the arrival of an elderly man who hollered that it was time to sail. It wasn't the usual ferry man. The ferry boat was over on the island and wouldn't be back until the next afternoon at the earliest. This man, Bosco, who had been untangling nets beside his boat in the wrong place at the wrong time, was taking them over. Alan nodded at him, understanding what the glare meant, a lingering glance delivered to the back of Paddy's head saying he was acting under duress. Alan had no idea what Paddy had said but he knew it wouldn't have been pleasant, he'd seen him smashing Sarah's mother's face in, delivering a heavy blow without the remorse of a heavy heart. He hung his head in shame and dragged his feet heavily as he walked forwards, hopeful that Bosco would believe he was cut from a different cloth than Paddy. But he wasn't, he was one and the same, leading a monster to its prey.

The Arrival

Sadie ran her skinny finger along her father's name, erasing his untimely death from the memorial stone. She was kneeling, matchstick legs bent at the knees, her bum hovering just above her trainers, the outline of her knickers visible through her grey cord jeans. Her jacket was tied tightly under her chin, the spindly faux fur of the hood's rim shielding her face. I couldn't see any tears but I knew they must be there, spilling silently into the folds of her neck.

After a few moments she grasped the top of the stone with both hands and hauled herself to a standing position. In my head her knees groaned like an old oak tree, the low drone of a maturity beyond her years. She stood in silence and I stepped back in similar vein, unsure where the moment was taking us. Suddenly she turned and prodding me in the stomach exclaimed that her granny wasn't a bad old soul for feeding us when I'd woken up. She wanted to keep the conversation she had just had with her father to herself.

'Not bad? Bloody hell that dinner was amazing. Mind you your granny's not exactly backwards in coming forwards, she gave me a right old lecture on standing up for myself.'

Ignoring me Sadie blew a kiss and catching it in the palm of her hand caressed the perimeter of the stone with her fingers, imprinting its loving mark on the marble before dropping her arm to her side and marching into the distance, her pace quick from the off. I stumbled along behind her, watching my feet carefully as we zigzagged our way across the cemetery floor, thick trundles of autumn grass cushioning our path. Stones carved in an assortment of shapes and sizes were placed in a seemingly haphazard order, but I understood that the positioning was deliberate, that I was uncovering the carefully calculated pieces of a long drawn out game of chess.

The rooks and pawns dictated Sadie's next move as we left the sheltered arms of her father.

Joseph MacLean's resting place was elevated, standing on a vertical mound to the right of the church, the ancient building's strong stone walls protecting him from the north-westerly winds. His headstone jutted from the belly of the hillside as if he was upright and standing guard, a lighthouse, keeping a constant watch on the shoreline below.

The shore-side church that housed the cemetery was old but not foreboding, the main body of the building broad and long, the accompanying tower tall and alluring as if it were hiding the mystical Rapunzel. An uneven track pebbled with broken limestone separated it from Carravindoon's vast green-blue sea, its soft waves congregating rythmically in a sheltered bay beyond the narrow road. Large beach boulders saturated with seaweed prevented the water's edge from spilling onto the road and swallowing the island's past into its deep cavern.

I followed Sadie to the low slung cemetery gate and I closed it carefully behind us, its gentle creak mirroring a pair of busy oyster catchers chatting incessantly on the shore, picking at treats they teased from the seaweed. Sadie turned right and kept walking. I hurried to keep up, glancing at the tiny play park where the girls were flying in mid-air, chirping like winter robins on bright red swings. Sadie was heading towards an old stone pier that was lying quietly forgotten on the sea beyond the church's gable wall. Still proud and defiantly walking on water its perimeter was crumbling into the depths, the once solid frame bullied into submission by wind and waves. In parts the pier was exposed to the elements on both sides. Sections of the supporting breakwater wall had surrendered to the depths, its mix of shingle and cement reclaimed by nature and now thick with green and brown moss. An old boat, hauled from the water and drained of its purpose, lay upturned and rotting at the entrance, tiny flakes of white and green paint barely visible on the bow and stern, a fleeting memory of an existence once more vociferously lived. It was sad yet symbolic, an appropriate partner for the collapsed pier.

Sadie marched to its precarious edge and I held my breath for just a second, wondering what I would do if she were to leap into the depths and disappear from my life. But she sat down, dangling her feet over frothy water that murmured gently as it relentlessly kissed the coarse yellow stone. I relaxed, bundling my body beside her. She loosened her hood and shook her hair into the wind, tossing her head in the direction of her father, his black marble stone shining like a beacon behind us.

Her eyes were red and crisp, her tears as real as I had imagined.

'I told my granny everything. We cannae try and work things out unless ah'm honest with her so that meant telling her about the drugs an' the money and Alan and all the rest that comes with it. Ah needed her to know how much ah really miss my dad.'

She stared vacantly out to sea, her attention stolen by its vastness.

'Don't worry, it's fine, it's a relief and let's face it, if Alan does arrive it'll be no bad thing to see your granny knock him out with her rolling pin.'

A wave crashed violently against the stone and Sadie raised her voice, bringing it lower when the white froth ceased charging and began to hiss softly.

'Aye, and the rest hen, she's got two shotguns and she knows better than most how tae use them. If that prick is daft enough tae try and threaten us she would be mad enough to take a pot shot at his balls.'

A large gull squawked violently overhead and its song rang deep in my ears long after it had flown into the distance. Sadie pulled her knees towards her chest so her heels clipped the edge of the harbour, her feet poised on a platform like an island bird ready to dive underwater for cover.

'Ah'm serious Elizabeth, my granny says she's not gaunae let Alan take me back to that crazy world we ran away from.'

I said nothing, reacting only when we heard the girls calling us from the play park. Silently we helped each other to our feet and walked with them along the main beach of the island. The crescent shaped strand crunched underfoot as we circled its shoreline, giant arms of seaweed creating a path as we walked towards Doon, a quiet bay that Sadie promised held a surprise for the girls. Collette hollered to Laura and they stopped by a rock pool giggling and poking at something that had captured their interest.

Sadie dropped her bag onto the shore and huddled down beside it, hauling her knees towards her chin before wrapping her arms securely around her shins. I joined her, the chill from the shingle racing from my coccyx to my head the instant I sat down on the damp surface. I picked up a piece of hard seaweed and used it to draw on the cold grey sand. I drew a sheriff's cell from a cowboy film, sketching the cartoon characters Snoopy and Deputy Dawg on either side of the thick bars.

'That's your life with Alan.'

Sadie laughed at my warped interpretation, physically closing my own giggling gob, her cold fingers patting my cheek gently when my teeth chattered in response to her icy touch.

'Hey it didn't look exactly like that; Tom and Jerry lived with us as well you know.'

She smiled, a sweet calm sweeping across her face, her tenderness reminding me once again of Jenny. A familiar anger washed over me when I thought of Jenny's father, but remembering my promise to her the pain sank like a stone, a sudden desire for revenge providing the anchor I needed to keep me going. It was a small but important victory.

'So what's with you and Alan then? How come you stayed with him?'

'Ah know you must think this is mad, but in ma own way I do love him, well ah think it's love, whatever love means. He's all right Elizabeth, he's not a bad person really, he just, fuck, he just cannae be himself you know, he's always got tae prove he's bigger and better than he is. The mad thing is he'll always be a fanny cos that's whit he is, he's no the sharpest pencil in the case but he loves the wean and ah suppose that's got tae count for something, ah didn't want Laura not having her dad around, ah know how crap that feels.'

She glanced in the direction of the graveyard but its view was hidden by the breakwater protecting the harbour.

'Bloody hell Sadie, I thought he was a maniac, he let you down big time and you're running away from him! How the fuck can you sit there saying that you love him?'

I shook my head failing to see the irony of demanding to know how she could stay with a man who abused her.

'But he's no that bad really Elizabeth, he's just guilty of being thick as two short planks. Fuck, in his daft wee mind he probably thinks he's daein the right thing getting mare gear so he can make mare money tae get us a new start. But ah just needed tae make the break and good luck tae him, ah hope he does sort something out wae his life but it's no going tae be wae me.'

'And here we both are.'

'Aye Elizabeth, here we both are and before long we're going tae have tae deal with him arriving at the front door.'

'What are you going to do then? It sounds as if he's going to be easy enough to sort out.'

I eyed her hopefully, praying that the whole mess was drawing to an anti-climax.

'You're absolutely right, ah can deal wae him no bother. Trouble is, this other guy is involved because oav the money I took and although ah've never met him ah know he's a bad bastard. He's the right hand man tae Umberto and let me tell you that bloke is really fuckin nasty, a real evil bastard. A few of the lassies talked about him in the homeless unit. He diznae stop at anything, he's killed folk for less than stealing a couple of grand.'

The name struck me as odd.

'What did you say his name was?'

'Umberto. How? You don't know him dae you?'

I shook my head, freaking out as my mind struggled with the shock of the synchronicity.

'It's totally weird, I've never ever met anyone with that name before and yet when I was sent down to the homeless flat I met this really flash prick and he was called Umberto. Jesus Sadie, you don't think it's the same guy do you?'

I swallowed hard, remembering my stupidity, fleetingly believing he might be a source of warmth when all he wanted to do was gorge on me like a piece of meat. The wind blew my hair into my face and I struggled to disentwine it.

'Whit, some rich bloke renting houses tae the council? There's no chance it's the same guy, this bloke's a gangster, he has people do his work for him. But listen ah'll tell you something, he's not the type of bloke you want tae mess wae, neither of us do. He's fuckin crazy, thinks nothing about doing whatever he likes and leaving everyone else tae clear up his mess. Ah don't know him hen, ah've never even met him, but ah know he's evil, he really is.'

I shivered, thankful that the Umberto I'd come across was just a regular user who saw the chance of a shag and took it with not so much as a thank you very much. But the real Umberto was still exactly that: real.

'Jesus Sadie, if Alan's mixed up with him then we're completely out of our depth. What if this Paddy guy has already called Umberto in?'

I could hear my voice screech, grating painfully.

'Calm your jets Elizabeth hen, the last thing we should dae is start freaking ourselves out. Look, ah know this must sound crazy but there's no way Alan will have let it get that far. He might be totally fucked off wae me but he'll have told Paddy he can get the money, he'll have made sure there's no need tae involve anyone else.'

'You sure sure, absolutely sure sure?'

She nodded convincingly and then we let it go, both keen to toss the fear to the wind. We stretched to our feet, shaking the chill from our cold behinds, and headed towards the girls, our talking carrying on inside our own minds. I walked more quickly than I had been; easing myself away from the conversation, the pain of the past few days beginning to lessen as I stretched my stride, my bandaged ribs jagging a little less than before.

The girls were yards ahead of us so they saw them first, their shrieks of delight not loud enough to frighten the mass of seals they had discovered lounging lazily on the rocks. Sadie urged the girls to keep their distance, explaining that the seals would come to them if they were patient. She was right and before long curiosity got the better of them, the seals ceremoniously flopping from the rocks into the cold sea, their heads quickly reappearing in the water in front of us, their long black noses exhibiting handsome whiskers that twitched rapidly as they bobbed playfully in the clear water. Sadie had her granny's camera with her and grasping it from around her neck I snapped Collette as she stared at the seals, capturing the moment of awe on her face. Sadie clip-clopped noisily along the white pebble beach and with each footstep the stones parted, sliding in several directions, creating mini avalanches as she crackled towards the girls. I clicked repeatedly, stealing the scenes before anyone else could.

As we climbed the hill home, we stopped a couple of times to gather our breath and snatch another glance at the beautiful view. Our pace was steady until Laura shouted that there was a boat coming in. Without looking at it we knew. We raced towards the house, the children believing we were playing a game; the more we encouraged them the harder they tried to come first, their brightly coloured clothing loud and present on the hill above the harbour. We ran into the house and the kids sailed into a little room off the kitchen, quietly closing the door as instructed so they could play a game.

Sadie's granny grasped her tightly by the shoulders and, ushering me to follow, she steered us towards the kitchen, its window a picture perfect view of the route from the mainland to the harbour. A little boat was bobbing just below the edge of the kitchen blind, floating in the distance its perspective smaller than the thumbnail I held in front of me.

'That ferry's still miles away, will they not be ages getting in?'

I sank onto a wooden chair, gulping down two pills before offering the bottle to Sadie. She pushed my hand away.

'Get a fuckin grip Elizabeth, Alan's gaunae be getting off that boat in all oav fifteen minutes, it's not the right moment to drop a downer.'

I shrugged, reluctantly following them both back into the living room. I was out of the loop, excommunicated from the mission. Sadie thrust a bag into my hand.

'Here hold that will you and shove the money fae under the dresser intae it. Ma gran is away up the stair to get us the rest from her own money.'

I dutifully fell to my knees, stopping to fix my belt, the angle of the leather digging into my bruised belly.

'Fuckin hell E, dae it the day will you, he'll be here soon and ah want to make sure that he's out of here before he's even come in.'

She wasn't really making sense, not literally, but I knew what she meant. I delivered a metaphorical salute.

'Aye, okay, give me a second.'

I picked up my pace, catching the wad of cash that Mrs MacLean tossed at me from the open staircase above. The girls ran past, tugging my hair, shouting *bbbyyyyyyyeeeee*.

'What the fuck, where are they going?'

If I was a cartoon character I would have been tripping over my lip, sorry sorry me, nobody tells me anything.

'Fuck sake E don't look like that, Seamus is outside he's taking them for a spin, ah don't want Laura seeing that prick, it'll only upset her and ah don't suppose you want Collette tae hear what ah've got tae say to him?'

I nodded, huffily. I wasn't upset with the plan, it was grand, it made sense to have the girls out of the way but it would have been nice to know. It was all moving so fast, so very much out of control. I didn't really know who any of these people were. It wasn't anything to do with me.

The money thrust into the blue cotton bag we stood quietly, waiting, beady eyes scanning the horizon from the porch. As soon as he came into sight I knew it was Alan. He looked exactly as I expected him to, his limbs thin and fragile, years of junk having decimated his muscles. The recognition made me feel part of the unfolding story; in an instant I was back in the gang, one of the trinity. He raised his eyes towards the house, scanning his target, skinny fingers drawn to his forehead, shielding the brightness of a sun slipping quietly to the west of the island. Automatically we drew away from the window, feet rooted to the earth, clipped wings allowing only our torsos to bend, pushing backwards against gravity, three puffin chicks cowering from the raven.

Alan stopped at the bright red gate and pushed it. When it refused to budge he pulled it and then stood gravely still, perplexed when it didn't open. He scratched his head oblivious to the fact that Sadie was calling him a prick. I watched her for a second, wondering what emotion was flickering in her eyes. She tutted and I turned my attention back to Alan. He was burrowing closer, grasping the frayed rope which was tied securely to the iron railing and then around the tall concrete post. Wearily he tugged at the knot, shaking the gate in frustration with his left hand before realising that he just needed to slip the noose up and over. Triumphant at last he swung the gate boldly into the foot of the hill, bending his body at a right angle, using a force his limbs didn't appear to possess to push the gate through knee high gorse and bracken, its thick arms splayed without uniformity, the north, south, east and west winds having dragged sections in their own unique directions.

Alan pushed the heavy gate back on itself, the iron clattering profoundly off the opposite concrete post, its chime escaping and scurrying up the hill. It disintegrated outside the window as if its glistening tone had been captured by an opportunistic magpie.

'Nothing like closing the gate behind you, you'll need to give him a wee row for that Mrs MacLean.'

'Ach, we'd only be opening it again soon enough to get rid of the idiot, don't you worry about that.'

She folded her arms across her chest, huge breasts resting on her wrists like a newborn babe in arms. We followed Alan's journey, tempted to laugh when he stopped and stamped his foot angrily, shaking wet cow shit from the sole of his shoe. He carried on, following the traces of a path created over hundreds of years, its history lost on his lack of imagination. The trail meandered back and forth in broad sweeps from left to right and right to left, its carpet thick with bracken and shit. Alan kept his eyes fixed to the ground, his hands hunched deeply inside his pockets, narrow shoulders sheltering his ears. He looked weak, almost nothing, as insignificant as a cardboard cut-out.

It took a few seconds to recognise the person walking behind him and just a second to say his name, my puzzled tone heavy with confusion and disbelief.

Carravindoon

Sadie caught me by the hair, her right hand pulling my head down to my chest, her words spitting into my ears.

'Fuckin answer me Elizabeth, dae other folk call your man Paddy?'

I wriggled away, but my shoulders were suddenly snared, an old woman's wrinkled face in mine.

'Is this the Paddy fella Sarah's been running away from?'

What Paddy? Sadie had never mentioned anyone called Paddy. There I was again, kicked out of the circle, no idea what the fuck was going on. Sadie flew in between us sidestepping from foot to foot. She dug her nails into my scalp, hissing. I tore her hands from my head and watched as she shook her fingers, tresses of my hair falling to the floor like frayed ends of a rope. I imagined Jenny at the end of it, wishing I was with her, swinging to a different world.

'Fuck fuck fuck,' Sadie was screaming, over and over, fumbling in the dresser drawer, her pale face red with rage. Finally she thrust a white box into her Gran's hands, bullets spilling into her palm on impact.

'Fuckin hell Sadie what the fuck are you doing? This is crazy!'

I tucked my hair behind my ears, the action useless, devoid of any fuckin sense but I needed to do something with my hands, take them out of the mess that was being created around me. I couldn't get it, couldn't understand why Patrick was here. It wasn't my fault, it couldn't have been.

'Get that fuckin innocent look off your face hen. This is aw because oav that animal that you've brought here. Ah don't know how you did it, ah don't fuckin know why you fuckin did it but all ah know is that you're wan evil cow and ah'll never forgive you for this, never.'

Her eyes, black with hatred, burned through me as she turned, her disgust pulling her towards her Gran, away from the clutches of the enemy she didn't know she had. I stood on the spot, broken glass spraying onto the linoleum when Alan and Patrick crashed into the house, the door imploding in protest, shards falling from above like snowflakes. A random fleck drifted to Sadie slicing into her forehead, a solitary trickle of blood escaping but travelling no further than her eyebrow, already bored with the journey or clever enough to know when not to make an entrance. I screamed at her, pointing to her head, my words lost under the noise of the shards of glass that were exploding underfoot as the intruders charged towards us.

My husband, the man that I promised my life and love to on the altar, made straight for Sadie's gran, raising his right arm high above his head. She was cramming fat red shells inside a long brown rifle, square pegs in round holes, their reluctance to succumb painful to watch. I watched the drama as if on the set of a movie, eavesdropping on the penultimate scene, my presence invisible to the performers. The satisfying click of the bullets slotting into place seemed deserved of a live audience round of applause.

Believing my invincibility I snuck closer to Patrick, intrigued to see what he was clutching above Mrs MacLean's head. I asked myself the question, instantly chastising myself for being so stupid. Why on earth would my husband have a candlestick? I had all this time for thinking and yet it was all happening so quickly. Sadie and I realised what he was holding at exactly the same moment, both of us lunging towards him and the metal baseball bat.

The blood trickled at first, like a garden sprinkler when the first drop of water has escaped from the nozzle, that moment when you know not to raise the hose to your face, just to check if it's working. We were calm for a second, it didn't look too bad, but then it burst into life, spraying high, the blood jetting from her head, a vertical route that suddenly fell and crashed to the ground like a water feature in a town square. She tried to stay upright, her back buckling, her arms outstretched, her fingers flexed and pointing at Patrick, the rifle clattering violently to the floor. I tried to catch her but I couldn't move.

'What the fuck, get off me you prick!'

I tugged my arms, my shoulders threatening to tear from their sockets. Alan was holding my arms, his face pale with shock, dark shadows of blackness skulking into the hollows of his cheeks. Despite the chaos I remember thinking at that moment that Laura shared his grey eyes, only hers were alive. I struggled to break free, panic giving me a strength I didn't know I possessed but despite his gaunt appearance he held me strongly and I roared, losing the air from my lungs as I fell to my knees.

Alan was crying out to Paddy that he shouldn't have done that, he shouldn't have hit the old lady. His shout wakened Patrick from his rage and even though I was looking at Sadie's gran I could feel his eyes burning through me. Patrick had found me.

I raised my eyes just as the recognition washed over Patrick's face. Bizarrely it had taken this long to register with him. I was out of context so maybe he didn't think it could be his dutiful wife. He was holding Sadie tightly, one large hand pulling her hair, his grip so tight it was tearing her scalp. His grasp was changing the shape of her face, her eyes were long and narrow, her forehead perfectly taut. She was deadly white, shock silencing her despite the pain. With his other hand he pinned both of her arms behind her back.

Her right shoulder was hanging uncharacteristically low, his wrench having pulled it out of its socket. He kicked Sadie's gran like a dog and she remained perfectly still, her silence more painful than an excruciating scream. Sadie opened her mouth and a noise escaped, an eerie tone that chugged like a train from her lungs, the shock stealing snippets of audio from her voice box.

Patrick laughed as he dragged her across the room and I

glanced longingly at the floor, hoping for a delayed reaction, a hand reaching up and knocking the bold man off his feet but it never came. She lay still, like a corpse. I pleaded with her to get up, my tears fuelling Patrick, his adrenalin rising with each whimper.

'See you ya fuckin wee bitch, ah'm gaunae kill you, don't ever, ever think you can steal from me and get away with it.'

He soaked Sadie's face in saliva but she stayed defiant, raising her foot to kick him in the balls. He dodged out of the way and laughing, grabbed her by the throat and tossed her on to the long settee. She drew her knees towards her chest, her feet turned upwards and pointing in Patrick's direction, her will still strong and determined.

Alan released his grip on my arms, screaming to Paddy that enough was enough. I took it as a chance to make a move, on my feet in a split second and aiming a punch, my thumb pulling my fingers towards the palm of my hand. I didn't get close, he got me first, Patrick's fist landing cleanly on the jaw he had already broken. I fought to stay conscious and lunged towards him but his retaliation was too much. His head landed perfectly on my nose and I heard the bone shatter as my world went black.

When I awoke Alan was counting the money, sobbing, meek whimpers escaping alongside tears and snot that he soaked up with his sleeve. Patrick, or Paddy, the creature he had now become, was on the floor on top of Sadie holding the baseball bat between her legs, laughing. His zip was undone, his belt flapping open, his tools poised and ready to hurt her.

'Leave her alone Patrick, I swear to God I'll kill you if you don't stop right now.'

I tried to stand up but couldn't, the room was lit up like a disco, everything spinning in an anti-clockwise direction. He jumped upright and placed his foot on Sadie's throat. Her eyes were black and swollen, her lip burst, red blood splattered on her face and t-shirt. She didn't move.

'See you ya fuckin whore, shut the fuck up cos you're

getting this next.'

He swiped at my head stopping the hard metal just millimetres from my ear. It made a flapping noise, just like the wings of a bat.

'You see tramp, because that's what you are, a fuckin tramp, you're gaunae die because you're just filth now. You shouldn't have done it.'

'I'm sorry Patrick, I am, we just got scared and ran away, it was stupid. We've got all the money, every penny, just take it please, we'll work out something to tell the police, just leave us alone, please.'

His raucous laugh startled us. It shouldn't have surprised me though, he always did it when I begged.

'You fuckin daft wee tart, it's no about the money, it's about you being a slag and shagging the fuckin boss, there's no going back fae that. How am ah supposed to have any respect for Umberto ever again now that my wife's had his dick up her cunt?'

He hammered the bat between my legs, the metal crashing off my pubic bone. The impact was agony. I screamed and fell to the floor, collapsing in a heap beside Sadie. He lunged alongside us like a giant cat, punching Sadie full in the face. Her eyes rolled upwards and then backwards inside her head. Alan dropped the money and eased her head on to his knee.

'Fuck sake Paddy, give it a rest, please man, we've got the money, let's just leave the lassies alone now, you're gaunae end up killing Sarah. Please mate, gie it a rest.'

Paddy laughed unashamedly, loving the pain, the violence, the control.

'Shut it wee man, it's not our fault the old bird fell off the wall out in the garden and done herself in, don't you go worrying about that. And don't you go getting soft on this wee fanny.'

He kicked Sadie hard in the ribs.

'She got you into this shit. She's due every fuckin thing she gets, just like this other piece of scum.'

He grabbed me by the hair. I heard it rip from my scalp.

'So tell me my lovely little wife, how the fuck do ah manage tae find you here? Tell you what, I didnae think a nobody like you would ever surprise me so you've got me there.'

I answered him, doing as he told me to, just like I always did.

'I met Sadie at the homeless unit, we just got talking, I didn't know the money was anything to do with you I promise.'

My voice was unrecognisable, even to me.

'And what about opening your legs for Umberto eh, did you forget that you were married ya fuckin cow.'

He slapped me hard and my tongue ripped off my back teeth. I let the blood spill down my chin. Alan was shouting, it was time to go and get the boat. Patrick ignored him and grabbing me by the hair he pushed me face down, his other hand ripping my jeans from my hips. His belt was still undone so I knew it was coming but I didn't expect the sheer pain, the agony of something violently tearing my anus. The baseball bat was saturated in blood when it fell on the couch beside me. It took me a moment to realise that the blood was mine, to understand that this was the source of my pain. Alan picked it up and violently thrashed it across Patrick's back, the bat slipping from his fingers on impact. Paddy's face was contorted as he fell to the floor, his features a mix of shock and admiration for the fact that Alan suddenly had balls. For a second we thought it was over, the respite making us lax, long enough for Patrick to lunge to his feet. He squared the bat up in front of Alan's face, mocking, laughing, Alan pulling his eyes shut in preparation for the impact. But he laughed and turned away, roaring as he smashed it across Sadie's head. The silence of the moment was deafened by the clank of the metal as it crashed off her skull.

I didn't think about it, the action was instinctive, essential. The gun exploded almost as soon as I picked it up. There was absolutely nothing left of his face. One pow and my husband's life was obliterated. I looked across at Sadie and smiled, but she wasn't moving. Her eyes were tightly closed, her head buried in a plump cushion. Its softness should have been caressing her but her neck was stretched across the blue fabric at such a weird angle. I called over to her, *that must be so uncomfortable the way you're lying*. But there was only quiet in response, the silence only broken by the hum from Alan's lips, hands in face, weeping like a child.

Mary

The helicopter had landed in the little rose garden next to the chapel on the hill and the doctors rushed towards the metal body as the blades began to slow and quiet. Elizabeth was on the stretcher, her body still and quiet. Before they went to the island Sadie had spoken to Elizabeth about Mary's grotto, the little place where her gran would pass the time in conversation with the Virgin. As the rescue team raised the stretcher into the mouth of the giant bird the grotto came into Elizabeth's line of sight. She screamed, her cry pushing through the confines of the oxygen mask. Her arm was broken but she managed to push it towards her face, dislocated fingers grasping the cold plastic and forcing it away from her lips. Her words filled the frame of the expansive sky, its mood heavy, dark grey cloud giving into lashing rain.

'Fuck off Mary. You're nothing but a callous murdering bitch.'

1993; Collette

'What time's it sister? Should she not have been here by now . . . ?'

I waited for the reply, my body as close to the nurse as protocol allowed, my stance intense.

'She'll be here soon enough, try not to get too excited, it'll not be much longer.'

Sister. I wasn't allowed to address the nurses by their first names, especially not this one. She was called Mary. I'd heard the doctor shout after her in the corridor one evening, the softness of the syllables gathering in my tongue as I remembered a time I craved another Mary's attention. A time when I was a little less sane.

Even after all this time I hadn't got used to the formality of using titles, it was like being at school, yes miss no miss three bags full miss. I hadn't changed that much, Piggy was still Piggy and I called him nothing. His therapy was monotonous and repetitive, his treatment as useless as the flight of an emu. A glare sufficed when he collapsed in front of me but I had learned to play the game, to give them what they wanted and that was a farewell kiss to any memories of the Virgin. It was a fair trade, I was glad to see the back of her, happy to fill my nights with sketching instead of hundreds of fruitless prayers. Today, though, wasn't a day for rebelling. I muttered an *okay,* my voice high and shrill, a train speeding through the platform without stopping.

Sister, Mary, was standing by the door, the monotonous shuffling feet giving notice of an impatience that embodied my own. She was clutching a set of keys, unpolished metal that sang when she moved, the moulded notes chiming like church bells, the curled fingers of her right hand orchestrating repetitive music. The key ring was connected to her waist by a chain that stretched and retracted. I turned to her just as the shackle extended, her knuckles travelling from hip to lips, a violin bow caressing its strings, the crisp cotton of her uniform murmuring in a gentle response that on a different stage might have been a lullaby. I remembered that I should treat the people around me with caution. The doors in my ward were unlocked, they had been trusting of my runaway status for months and I could come and go as I pleased, but they always held the power to hold me in if they decided to. This was a time for escape. I swallowed hard hoping I'd never have to hear the clink of another lock.

'Sit for goodness sake. She shouldn't be too long, she's not even technically late yet.'

Sister answered in an east coast twang, the dialect singing to me as audibly as the keys she orchestrated in her hand. I listened and then quickly moved on, fixing my gaze on the window, my eyes searching beyond the metaphorical bars that hugged the outside of the glass.

I sat down and stroked the book. The motion was tentative at first, like a fragile old lady offering her hand to love for the first time in a long time, the moment of mystery before remembering that shagging was like riding a bike, slightly easier on the knees but just as physical on the heart.

'Do you think she'll like it?'

I wasn't interested in the response; my own opinion was the only one that was relevant. Gaining some gusto I rowed my elbows across the exterior, my arms ironing the surface, carefully expelling the demons. I drew back the cover, the title page surprising me for the umpteenth time, its soft cream paper unveiling her beauty as if she were an apparition from heaven. I caressed the colour photograph, softly, my fingers only just making contact with her face, Collette's brilliant eyes shining as brightly as the new moon. It was an old picture. She was three years old and amazed by the sight of her first seal. She was hunched low on the ground, the happiness racing across her face but hanging around long enough to imprint a perfect smile that stayed and shone.

I'd snapped the picture just at the moment of discovery, her reaction capturing a moment in time, a raw honesty I wondered if she had long since forgotten. It was the only photograph in the book; the rest of the images were creations of memory, sketches of our short history together, a life in charcoal and pencil, something to remember or to help her forget. The choice would be hers, if she were ever compelled enough to make it.

I picked myself up again, the physical action a determination to urge my mind to take some control. I walked to the door, searching for something on the other side that would offer an alternative to the unhappiness that lay ahead. My vision was narrowed by the thin glass panel that was cut into the door frame. The glass was cloudy, not smudged by fingers or the passage of time but by the thin veins of metal encased between the layers, a spiders web that held me as captive as a wanton fly. I felt weak, the emotion of what lay ahead burning a hole in my heart, but it was a physical pain too.

It had been four months since the last dragon had roared inside me yet still the desire to experience the numbness smothered me every day. It reminded me of Sadie yet all the while it helped me to forget. I collected the pills I didn't swallow, prising them into the fabric in the hem of my turned up jeans, its crisp whiteness hiding my deceit. I sat down again, my constant uncertainty unleashing a jack in the box comment from *sister*. I smiled as vociferously as I could because today was a day in the making and I had to take control of it. *Sister* Mary was okay. She was one of the good ones, despite the fact that she was the keeper of the keys.

'You okay, Elizabeth? Do you not think you should have taken the doctor's advice and had some valium? This is not going to be easy for you. You do understand that, don't you?'

She sang as she always did and her words sailed across the room and settled on my shoulders offering a way out, an opportunity to revert to type. She didn't touch me, but I could feel a sentiment that was as genuine as it could be from someone who couldn't possibly understand. But I wasn't going to take the medication; I wasn't going to take any drugs full stop. Enough was enough; once my baby was gone I had to let the pain in my heart fire me. I needed to be sharp, focused, driven. I didn't even lift my head, avoiding her eyes and a possible route to a blissful high. I wanted to tell her to fuck off and mind her own business but I didn't. Being sweet, sorrowful and repentant was all part of the long term plan. The better the disguise the sooner years of planning could come to fruition.

'I'm fine, I don't need anything. I'm keeping a clear head for leaving tomorrow.'

I sounded cold but I had to curtail my emotions, convince them that the old me that had clung on to the memories of apparitions had long since gone. They had gone, but they did happen, she did choose me, but only for a moment in time. Like everyone else she took whatever it was she needed from me and moved on. Bitch. I smirked, wondering why I'd craved the Virgin's pathetic assistance for so long. If she came back to see me I'd most likely punch her in the face.

Despite the flux of my emotions I stayed still, watching silently as I allowed *sister* to leaf through the pages of my carefully constructed book. It was a surreal moment, watching my story unfolding from a tiny cloud above another's shoulder. The images flickered by quickly, the movement bringing them to life like a cartoon. After a few moments *sister* Mary stopped, her finger and thumb sliding from the corner of the page to the centre, her gaze lingering on the sketch of Collette and Laura on the boat, their thin arms entwined around Sadie's waist. Sadie was holding them close, like a mother suckling twins, her warmth evident in the smile I had drawn and redrawn, the repetitive action more of a desire to make her laugh, to hear her voice for one last time.

I remembered the moment so clearly the figures lifted from the page, the charcoal giving way to rich colour, the air suddenly heavy with the smell of the sea. Then I thought of Alan's tears and Sadie's stillness, the acknowledgement that like Jenny she would never wake up from that uncomfortable position she held on the couch. The memory of Patrick's obliterated head did nothing to ease the pain.

The image sank when a car distracted me, the fan belt screeching ever so gently as it scurried into the car park. A Volkswagen Beetle was emerging through the gates, its unyielding wheels like wings, its strong back a suit of armour, the roaring engine intensifying the image I had of an amphibian that harvested power on land and sea.

Instinctively I knew it was Collette and yet I asked the question, turning to *sister* Mary and demanding to know if I was right. As I uttered the anxious words my little angel bounced from the car, the door the rudder for her rig, her vibrant actions as bold as the purple dress that sailed to just below her knees. Her long blonde hair was in plaits sealed with ribbon that matched the dress and fluttered in the midday breeze. She skipped and arms outstretched she tacked towards the entrance zig zagging towards the door, her lips in flight, the corners of her mouth turning in the direction of the sky as she hummed and giggled her way through her journey. I smiled, remembering a rerun of *Little House on the Prairie* that Sadie and I had watched with the girls in a different place, a different world from so long ago.

In some ways it felt so much longer than four years, like I'd only ever known the heavy door that slammed shut in my face and held me captive, a prisoner in life and in my life. But today would be the worst of them all, the day I would be saying goodbye to my beautiful baby girl. I had to do that before I could find the strength to say a final farewell to the fuckers that had destroyed me and my friends.

Elizabeth

Elizabeth knelt down in front of her. There was nowhere else to go. The room was little more than three feet square, like an upright coffin. There were walls on either side of her and if she reached out she could have caressed either wall without unlocking her elbows. They were smothered in sallow paint. There was a large wooden cross hanging to her left depicting the son of God at his crucifixion. Elizabeth turned her head towards it. Jesus Christ's feet were level with her mouth and she nervously gnawed at her lower lip, piercing the skin with her tooth as she examined the nail that was penetrating his little bare feet.

There was a velvet curtain on the wall straight in front of her but Elizabeth knew it wasn't concealing a window. The curtain was slightly ajar revealing an iron grid which was sheltering a pale yellow light. On the floor below was the narrow kneeler, encased in plum leather. It was sticking to Elizabeth's knees, squelching as she wriggled back and forth trying to find a more comfortable position. She could feel its damp chill on her bare knees and it sent shivers pumping up her thighs. The vibrations congregated in a heavy pulse that sat deep within her pelvis. She clasped her hands tightly together in response, her fingers drumming. She laid her elbows, supporting her throbbing hands, on to a little ledge at the berth of the curtain and waited.

She was frightened. The door was shut and it reminded her of being with Andrew. Then she jumped, startled by a voice emerging from within the light.

'Let us pray together my child, in the name of the father and the son and the holy spirit.'

Elizabeth completed the sentence for him in a quiet, unassuming voice.

'Amen.'

Then she continued, this time her voice quaking.

'Bless m'faither, fir ah've sinned.'

She lowered her head and paused. *Suffer little children that come unto me, for thine is the Kingdom of Heaven.* The words swamped her head as she swam in the filthy waters of her sins. She spat them out, quickly. Getting rid of them as fast as her tongue would allow her to. But it didn't have the desired effect. No weight was lifted. It was like playing ball against the school shed wall. *Wee Sam, piece an' jam, went tae London in a pram* . . . Every time she let it go with force, it came back again, and with each thump its potency was harder and deeper.

Father Brennan didn't respond immediately. He said absolutely nothing in the face of her wicked transgressions. The silence was suffocating and Elizabeth prayed for the strength to open the door and escape.

When he finally spoke his words came in the form of an invitation to the Chapel house for a wee cup of tea. To give them both, he said, 'time for reflection.'

Elizabeth noticed a cross on the wall. It was unusual, but she was familiar with the style. It was made from used matches, regimentally placed alongside one another, the fragile sticks encased in a coat of varnish, sealing the symbol of the Son of God behind a thin veil.

Elizabeth had made one exactly like it, seven years before, the summer she began spending time with Andrew. As a seven year old girl she had announced to her family that she wanted to be a nun, to go and live in a convent and give herself to God. Her mother arranged for Elizabeth to spend some time helping out with the chores at a local convent, confident that a few days running for the messages for the sisters would give her aspirations to go into medicine, dentistry, fishing, farming . . . anything but the convent. The plan backfired and Elizabeth looked forward to spending her time there. Every Monday Elizabeth was allowed to go to the convent straight after school. She created her cross while she was there, the nuns being kind enough to say they believed her when she told them about the Virgin Mary's visit to her bed.

The convent was a big red sandstone house. From the outside it looked no different from any other home in the street, but above the porch there was a large grotto. Sitting on its roof was a statue of Our Lady. Elizabeth was always telling the nuns that when Mary came back she was going to wrap herself in the shelter of her pale blue cloak. She watched and waited, never for a moment giving up hope.

When Father Brennan walked into the room clutching two cups of tea Elizabeth wondered if this was the beginning of something new in her life. She might have been just fourteen but she knew precisely what people expected from you. It wasn't necessarily always a give and take thing. *Always* it was about taking, but there wasn't *always* a lot of giving.

She accepted the cup of tea graciously, conscious of the fact that you should never bite off the hand that feeds you. Misty fumes steamed from the tea and the liquid kissed the gold brim as it rocked in gentle waves in time with the Father's steady pace as he crossed the room towards her. The porcelain was painfully thin. Elizabeth politely raised her lips to its outer edge but was scalded by the ferocity of it. She attempted it twice in quick succession, each time her bottom lip bonding like superglue to the rim. She fought to retain her graciousness.

Mary was watching from the corner of the room but it didn't concern her in the slightest. She worshipped Mary.

After struggling with the molten liquid for the second time she carefully placed the china cup onto a white doily on the three legged table. The handle burned the index finger of her left hand and it was still hot when she drew it towards her face to wipe a solitary tear which trickled slowly from the damp corner of her eye. She caught it just before it leapt from her cheek.

Mary was still watching. Elizabeth toyed with trying to avert her gaze, but she was drawn to her and cautiously she raised her eyebrows upwards, the movement dragging her sunken eyes in the direction of the Virgin Mother of God.

Mary was clad, as always, in a long, pale blue cloak. It flowed from the nape of her neck to the floor; its folds dispersed around the circumference, perfectly balanced like a theatre curtain, the window to an untold mystery. Beige hands emerged from its crevices. Her outer layer of clothing gaped open slightly, revealing a white cotton undergarment. It too gushed towards the floor revealing Mary's bare feet. Her head was partially covered by a white mantilla that rested on her temples uncovering locks of long flowing dark brown hair which fell to just below her shoulders. Elizabeth felt safe. Mary would be able to look after her this time. After all, she was in the priest's house.

Father Brennan had other ideas and the violence of his voice shook her so hard she juddered. If she had been holding the little china cup it would most certainly have smashed to the floor.

'There's no point in gazing over there,' he bellowed in her direction. 'I KNOW what you're thinking and let me tell you this before your disgusting, impure thoughts get any more sinful, you can't compare HER to YOU. Not for a second!'

With his words the tears began to flow. He was right. The child growing inside of Elizabeth, unlike Mary, had nothing to do with divine intervention.

The here and now; the Elizabeth and Mary Chain

She really was the last person I ever expected to see.

And I mean that as I say it. Mary, the Virgin Mother of God, was the very *last* person I *ever* expected to see. Or wanted to see. At one point in my life I'd prayed for it, but then when I got over her I prepared for it, but only as the ultimate eventuality, at that final defining moment when you realise that, shit, your mission on earth is finally finished because you're stone dead. Then, and only then, I had decided I would let her know what I thought of her.

But I wasn't dead. I had a pulse. I knew that because it was racing, thumping loudly between my ears like a marching band but there she was, the Virgin Mary, bold as brass, standing at the bottom of the fire exit stairway, in front of the door. I was alive, and she was back. I curled my fists, hoping that it was nothing more than an apparition, an affirmation that the doctors had always been right. I was insane as the mad March hare.

If it wasn't so funny I might have laughed. I mean funny *odd*, funny *strange*, or funny verging on *spooky* but definitely not funny *ha ha*. Funny *ha ha* would have been Mary waving a flag shouting 'Come in, your number's up.' I liked the idea that God might be as capable of taking the piss as he was of taking the biscuit.

But there wasn't any time for fairy-tale endings. My number *was* about up. I was executing the perfect murder, its delivery coming together assertively, shackled securely within the confines of my shit-hot master plan.

By murder I mean m*ur*d*ur*, emphasising the 'ur', holding both pivotal letters in a barrel in the centre of the tongue before unleashing rapid-fire rounds of 'muuuuurrrrr' and 'duuuuurrrrr', short, sharp and directly on target. The ignition is crucial, as is the delivery, driven all the more sweetly by a Scottish accent.

My patter isn't original. I borrowed it from the TV show 'Taggart'. It was like a red rag to a bull. It sealed Larry Spencer's fate. The minute I said it out loud I knew I was going to actually do it. I'd thought about it, I'd definitely *thought* about killing Larry Spencer, but once I'd uttered the cute little phrase for myself it was always going to happen.

'There's been a m*urd*ur.'

It was easy enough to say, but it wasn't going to be as easy to conceal the smile that would tease my tongue. I knew it was a potential problem, a stumbling block, a stuttering, stammering interlude that could fuck the whole thing up for me so I made some time for me and the phrase in front of the mirror. Believe me, even practising saying it was nothing short of magnificent.

The plan was a belter. And not just because I had chosen the 31st of October for its delivery, the day of guises and deceptions, but because I had carefully allowed for every potential disaster. Well, I thought I had, with one *obvious* exception. I had forgotten to add an important footnote to the agenda:

'*N.B. in the case of Our Lady popping down from heaven on a social call, prepare an alternative plan of action.*'

It was mental. When you least expect it, you run in to an old friend from school, or the neighbour's cat, not Mary the Virgin Mother of God.

Maybe I shouldn't have been that surprised. It wasn't the first time I had come across the lady in blue and white. She'd been in my bedroom. I was seven years old at the time and in bed fighting tears. She arrived just before my nightly battle with the demon that would descend with sleep. She didn't say a word, just sat on the edge of my bed and smiled until I fell asleep. I slept right through, dry bed and not a monster in sight.

When I gathered my wits on seeing Mary again at the bottom of the stairs, I noticed the same smile. But I didn't want to have to be bothered with it. It wasn't a good time for me. I was deep in thought, focusing on my escape down the fire exit. I needed to get outside pronto, before anyone noticed I had gone AWOL during the fire alarm. But my absence had been vital, the annoying screech of the evacuation message more design than accident. It was all systems go in more ways than one, giving me the heads up to put a key stage of my plan into action. Fat, evil, disgusting Larry Spencer had even provided me with the bait and now he was *just about* captured. What a tit. A quick trip upstairs was enough to grasp hold of his despicable little world and now I was holding it in the palm of my hand. I shivered in glee; I was enjoying possessing a God like quality.

Larry Spencer wasn't aware of the fact that he was a total fanny. Being clued up wasn't one of his better qualities, if indeed he possessed such a thing. No, his fall from grace was a wee surprise that I was saving for his benefit after the charade of the office Halloween party. A precursory bullet before I finished him for good. The party was just the start of the fun and games.

It would appear though, that the entertainment was about to kick off early, what with Mary the Virgin Mother of God's surprise appearance. Talk about calling round to see someone at an inopportune moment. But there was no hiding behind the curtains. She was tapping her feet impatiently and now only inches from me as I thumped my way down the stairs.

My mind started whirring and I was thinking about a hundred things at once, reflecting on far too much whilst I gawked right at her, a glaicket mist settling on my irises as if the windscreen had all steamed up. I was in too much of a hurry, thundering down the stairs in leaps and bounds, hurdling imaginary obstacles, adding as much drama as I possibly could. Today was special, years in the making, so I had to give it a bit of an edge. Seeing Mary knocked me off balance though, chucking the momentum out the window. I'd let the rhythm take over but I should have known better. I didn't have any.

I'd been singing since I'd walked backwards from Larry Spencer's laptop. Mission accomplished I started to bounce, finding a gleeful spring in my step that I hadn't possessed since I was six years old and skipping to the ice-cream van with a shiny ten pence piece in the palm of my hand. My lips joined in, my tongue yack, yack, yacking with every beat. The loud vocals were wholly inappropriate, considering I was on a secret mission, but I was excited.

I was going to commit a m*ur*d*ur*.

Larry Spencer was going to get it.

The first song was childish, but it was quite funny. I giggled in between the verses. I'd only bothered to make up one, but I kept repeating it over and over again.

Ah'm gaunae get ye

Ah'm gaunae get ye

Ah'm gaunae get ye

It was good but the repetition got to me quite quickly. Bored, I improvised, my route taking a new twist as I staggered from side to side in a series of zig zags, each angled whhoooosssssshhhh complementing my new childish chant. But what the fuck, after all I'd been through, I was entitled to a bit of fun.

In and out those dusty bluebells

Larry Spencer thinks he's doing well

In and out those dusty bluebells

The dick's so wrong.

I was just working out how best to use hell with bluebell when I first saw her, at the foot of the 39th step. Robert Powell, A.K.A Jesus of Nazareth maybe, but Mary? I stopped on the second bottom step and instinctively covered the left hand side of my chest with my right arm. I didn't want Mary to see it. See my soul.

Exactly as I remembered her to be, she was radiant. Trendy in her long flowing dress and cloak, she could have just stepped off the catwalk. I flirted with the idea of borrowing the outfit for the Halloween party. The cloak was a fabulous blue, its rich colour striking another chord. Not many people had a colour named after them.

So what colour's your new coat then?

Oh, do you like it? It's Virgin Mary Blue.

I wasn't seriously toying with borrowing the outfit. Despite possessing a filthy lump of coal for a soul I wouldn't have dared to kill Larry Spencer while disguised as Mary. But I had dressed up as Mary before, for the school Nativity play. I was six, but it was different then. My soul had been white.

Mary was standing perfectly still, just inside the door. She didn't really look much different from the wee blue and white statues. Her cheeks were a little rosier but that was probably down to the freezing cold. This was Glasgow in October, also known as *fuckin Baltic.* It was blowing a gale outside, the wind cackling, hissing and bubbling like a witch's cauldron and stealing in through the gap in the frame. It was gathering momentum at Mary's feet, forcing the bottom of her frock to sway gently. Despite my bravado I hedged my bets and decided to retain some caution, my right arm switching from enshrouding my chest to encasing my Mary medal which I pulled out from under the collar of my shirt. Mary didn't flinch, although those annoying little toes of hers were still drilling the floor intensely, tip tapping like a forgotten leak in the kitchen sink. If there was one thing for sure, she was going to do my head in. I know I'd promised to punch her if I ever saw her again, but murdering bitch that I was, I couldn't sink that low. I uncurled my fist.

Scanning her in more depth I spotted her shoes, tan leather Jesus sandals. That said everything. The vast majority of devout Catholics had had the good grace to avoid being captivated by the brief resurrection with fashion that Jesus sandals toyed with in 1979. All apart from my mother who to my eternal embarrassment had made me wear them to school, whilst I was recovering from a swollen broken foot. By the end of a week's torture in the playground my toe was mended, but my heart broken.

I was still staring at her little brown toes as I navigated my way towards the bottom step. It was all her fault. She unnerved me. I missed the stupid thing completely, coming down like a pack of cards, in embarrassing instalments. My shoulder crashed to the floor first, then my wobbling arse and jelly legs.

I landed by her feet, my lips close enough to kiss them. What a welcome that would have been, straight down to a bit of toe sucking before Mary the Virgin Mother of God had a chance to say *bless you my child*. I tried to conceal my shock and embarrassment with humour but she didn't laugh.

'And the Oscar goes to . . .'

There was an awkward silence. I got up. Trying to ease the nerves I added a drum roll.

'Deee rrrraaaaaaaa.'

She said nothing, slinging me the dreaded rubber ear. No response. Not a word. I panicked, wondering if she wasn't there at all. Maybe I'd actually always been mental. I was off my trolley, away with the birds and the fairies. The *stupid girl* I'd been called so many times as a child. I took a deep breath and got myself square in front of Mary, shimmying my weight from side to side. Then I just went for it. I lifted my right leg up so my knee was aligned with my hip and then I dropped it down.

Ccccrrrrrruuunnnnncccccccccchhhhhhh.

I slammed down as hard as I could on to the vision's foot. As soon as my heel was touching flesh I knew it was going to be one of those days.

'Ayyyyeeeeaaaaaaaaaaaaaahhhhhhh!'

I shook my head. I might not have been completely mental but I certainly wasn't the sharpest tool in the box.

Bringing it all back home

Assaulting the mother of Jesus wasn't one of my better ideas, but maybe Mary should have been counting herself lucky. There was a wee second back there when I'd considered going for the jumping front kick. Still, the toe crunch wasn't going to do me any favours either, not with the way Our Lady was rubbing her foot. Point proven though, I wasn't seeing things, sanity was still with me, for the time being at least.

I said a quick in the name of the father and of the son and the holy ghost into myself and prayed.

Dear God, give me a fighting chance will you? I'm in a hurry to get out of here. You know, the big murdur thing I've been telling you about . . .

Is it appropriate to ask for God's assistance when you're about to commit a m*urd*ur? It was a rhetorical question of course, but knowing the answer hadn't stopped me praying for the delivery. Maybe that had been my first mistake.

Dear God, please may I have your guidance and the guarantee of no impromptu interruptions during the execution of my murdur plan. All the best for now, hope the family are well.

But at the end of the day what the fuck did it matter? Larry Spencer was toast, burnt black toast, falling on a manky kitchen floor, butter side down with an almighty splat. Thinking about it sent shivers of excitement up and down my spine. I was getting ready to suffocate his filthy mouth and thoughts of watching him take his last, pathetic, dirty breath kept me focused. Knowing he would be found splattered on the ground, finally unmasked, was my glass of wine with dinner, my two squares of chocolate instead of one, and most importantly my prayer before bed. The next stage of my plan would successfully unveil him to the world. But, and there always seems to be a but, the next stage of my plan depended on Mary disappearing just as quickly as she had appeared. I stared at her, my mind whirring as I wondered what to do.

She had slipped down onto the floor, her thin back square against the wall, her knee drawn tightly towards her chest. She was clutching her foot, skinny fingers kneading her skin, doing what they could to massage the pain. Her long, thick hair straddled her face, bright blue eyes peering through the strands, Audrey Hepburn cheekbones sculpting lips that portrayed a wry smile. She was stunning, a beautiful apparition.

I thought about the impact of my first meeting with Sadie, all those years ago when she had appeared just as dramatically as Mary, the connotations of that day changing my life forever. In a sense, that moment was the very beginning of the ending I now had in sight. Meeting Sadie had defined my thoughts on everything.

I hunched down on the second bottom step, keeping my distance, my feet pointing firmly towards the exit.

'Mary, I'm really sorry. I was totally out of order there. That shouldn't have happened, no excuses. Please don't go all huffy on me, not tonight of all nights.'

She drew her hand away from her foot and wiped the dust from her palm, the wry smile broadening into something more forgiving.

'Don't worry about it, ah might have been tempted to lamp me one as well if ah was you.'

I was blown away. Mary could talk. Well of course she could speak; there shouldn't have been any surprise in that. It was how she spoke that was overwhelming me. She had a salt of the earth Glasgow accent. I might have expected a deep south American drawl, something with a bit of drama. I popped the index finger of my right hand into my right ear and gave it a rigorous rub, toying again with the theory that I'd lost my marbles. The Glaswegian accent suited her wee peely wally face. My own Glasgow accent was long since gone. I'd lost it. Not physically. An accent's not something you can leave on the bus.

Shit, ah forgot tae lift ma accent. It'll be fuckin well gone by now, somewan will be away wae it.

When Patrick and I ran away to London when I was sixteen I did my best to leave behind what I could of the pathetic creature I had been as a child. I enhanced my private secondary school tones with one of those wishy-washy Anglo-Scottish accents and it had stuck like glue. Why talk when you can sssiiiiinnnnngggggg the words in the middle, at the beginning, or even at the end of your sentences? My voice was all that betwixt and between way, a little of something, but mostly a lot of nothing. But it's the way I liked it. There was absolutely nothing left of that wee Glesga 'me'.

Mary's accent was dead nice. Homely, I suppose. I wondered if it was a statement of politeness and if she landed in Moscow she would have blethered away in Russian, or if she was in Paris, she would *par le vous* quite the thing to an equivalent murdering, conniving bitch in French, rolling her 'r's and doing that strange thing with her diaphragm and throat, all *çavas*, *bonjours* and *pardonez mois?*

Mary held out her hand and beckoned me to help her to her feet. I ignored it, remembering Carravindoon and my vow to keep her callous face out of my life. I stood up taking two steps backwards up the staircase. Disappointedly or disdainfully, I didn't know her well enough to assess which emotion she was throwing at me, she reached across to the handrail and hauled her body to its feet.

'Look, ah know you're in a mad rush. Ah've been keeping a wee eye on you. The thing is, I just wanted tae make sure you knew exactly whit you were daein. There isn't any going back from this one you know. And by the way, hello, it's nice tae see you again.'

I dropped back down onto my hunkers, my deep sigh supposed to be a sign that said, *don't you think I know that.* I had taken the decision with pride and conviction, there being no going back making the plan all the more special. It would show Jenny how much I loved her and what I was willing to do to protect the others.

'Look, Mary.'

I relaxed my shoulders, my words in turn coming across all quaint and twee. I listened as I spoke. It felt weird hearing her name out loud, not simply the sound that it made, but the sweet connotations. It was its own music, much more defined than the well versed Ave Maria. Her name got me thinking. I had no idea what her surname was. I'd only ever known her as Mary 'The Virgin Mother of God'. God forbid, she couldn't have been lumbered with that mouthful. Obviously not, Joseph was her husband and he must have had some kind of surname, some identity other than that of Joseph Carpenter. Joseph and Mary Carpenter. The Carpenters. On top of the world, looking down on creation.

'This isn't some knee jerk reaction. I want to do this. I have to do this, there's too much at stake not to. So thanks, thanks for caring, but I really think it would be better if you just left. Please. Please Mary, just go will you, you had your chance and you blanked me then so I'm not meaning to be nasty or anything but it's my turn to blank you now . . .'

She jumped up onto the first step and grasped my arm, gently. Her fingers felt warm and strong, her smell the sweet perfume of freshly blooming white roses. I let her tease me to the foot of the stairs, a horse being led to water.

'Ah'm going soon enough Elizabeth, but there's no way ah'm missing out on this Halloween party of yours. Have you any idea how far I've had tae travel to get here?'

The Virgin had sarcasm down to a fine art. This day was getting more mental by the minute. Still, it would be different in all that it delivered so I shouldn't have expected it to pass without some extraordinary happenings. She took two short steps towards the door and I fell silent. Her Jesus sandals gently brushed the floor, the wooden sole of her left foot making contact with the ground for just a split second before gliding through the air as the right foot made similar, brief contact. Mary was grace personified. I looked at her closely and it struck me that for the moment, hanging about with my pal Mary might not be such a bad thing. I was late; Larry

Spencer might have noticed that I was missing. Bumping in to Mary was the perfect excuse, she was the perfect alibi. I followed her towards the fire exit door. She stood aside to allow me to take the lead.

'All right Mary, you can come but if you win the prize for the best outfit I'll be well pissed off. And by the way, what do you mean with the *nice tae see you again* comment? Was that really you sitting on my bed all those years ago?'

No response, just the smile.

And they'd all told me I was a complete head-case.

Life wasn't like that

The rain had finally stopped cascading from the dark, low sky. The cold air was damp, a moist cloak that clung to your shoulders, penetrating deeply inside your bones. It was instantly chilling, but Mary didn't seem to notice. She squelched through the puddles in her sandals, pools of water smothering her sockless feet with every stride, washing them with a stark Glasgow welcome before splashing onto tarmac polished with rain. It reminded me of a childhood memory, red wellies, a clear plastic brolly and a smile as a wide as the Clyde. A stupid tear wasted the moment. There wasn't any time for sentiment. Life wasn't like that.

I directed Mary towards the front of the building, my pace urging us to get to the door quickly, my heart once again furiously pumping, its urgency reminding me of the important job I had to do. The car park was packed but there wasn't any sign of life. The emergency was over. Larry Spencer was back in the building. He was where I needed him to be. I could set the wheels in motion. I could kill him.

Saying kill instead of m*u*rd*u*r sounded harsh and an unexpected attack of conscience gripped my throat. I coughed and spluttered, struggling to spit it out. Mary reached over and rubbed my back, gently massaging the deep groove between my shoulder blades, her fingers instantly sending a wave of heat searing into my lungs. I knew she was real, I 'd always known. For a second the pain left me, and my knees buckled with the impact, the sheer force of wondering if I was doing the right thing. I know I finished Paddy off but that was different. I didn't know I was going to do it. I'd never planned to kill anyone before. Well, not many people had, you don't get up in the morning and just decide to *get the Bastard* instead of having your cornflakes.

Although for me, it happened like that. I decided I needed to avenge Jenny's death. His touch had killed her. For years I lay awake in my hospital bed, staring at the ceiling, wondering what I should do about it. Confronting him or phoning the police didn't have the same impact, neither seemed punishment enough.

It was too risky, taking a chance that he might do it all over again. I was stirring my black coffee with a spoon, round and round and round the cup when I realised that it was just a vicious circle, it would never stop until he was stopped. Killing him was the only way to do it. And as soon as I decided I was going to do it, to finish the fucker off, I knew that soon, very, very soon I was going to get my life back. Most of the time, I tried to forget that it had ever existed.

Mary kept her hand on me, even though the coughing fit had passed. I let her touch me, a school of piranhas swimming inside my veins. When I looked at her eyes I even smiled. They matched her coat.

'Are you up tae going inside now or dae you want tae wait another few minutes tae get your breath?'

She placed her other hand on my shoulder and stood quietly, waiting for an answer.

I want to go home. I want to never have to think about Larry Spencer again. I want all this to be over.

I nearly said it. And I would have done, I would have caved in if the kids hadn't run past, giggling and skipping. There were four of them, little girls, about six or seven years old. They were in their Halloween costumes, three of them dressed as witches, their innocence making mockery of their attempt to be dark and scary. They stopped when they saw us. Not for the first time in her life, the Mother of God was the centre of attention.

'Ma look, there's the Virgin Mary.'

There was a woman with them, looking harassed, trying to keep up with their exhilarations. Another of the little witches shouted.

'Ah really like your outfit Mary, ah'm gaunae dress up the same as you next year.'

She smiled sweetly, waving at Mary with one hand whilst using the other to hold tightly onto the little black cape which was sheltering bony shoulders. The mother tried to hurry the girls on, shooing them like a character from a story book.

'Sorry hen, they're just that bloody excited cos we're on our way to a wee party, we didnae mean tae bother you.'

The woman unintentionally knocked one of the little girls in the back of her head, swinging her pointed hat over her face so the brim hung precariously around her neck. The girls giggled and gathered round, helping her retrieve her features. Mary edged towards them, moving her hand away from the glowing embers of my back leaving a sharp nip in the air in its place.

'It's no bother missus, they're fine. The kids look great.'

Mary turned from the woman to the girls, her voice soothing yet expectant.

'Well then, are yous going to do me a wee turn for your Halloween?'

She stood patiently, waiting for a performance. She got it from the little girl dressed as an angel. She looked just like Collette. The moment would have broken my heart if I'd let it. She was about the same age the last time I saw her. She would be seventeen now, a woman, safer in a world soon to be bereft of monsters like Larry Spencer. I tried to stay calm, listening, the wee girl's voice driving my mission forward.

'Aye Mary, ah've got a joke fir you. Whit dae you call two robbers?'

'Eh . . . Let me think . . . No hen, I don't know this one, you're going tae have tae tell me the answer.'

'A pair oav knickers.'

They all laughed, their gentle beauty crippling me. It made my blood boil. It was my duty to protect them. I dragged my right hand across my shoulder and onto my back so I could brush the remnants of Mary away. I poked her in the arm, my urgency making me drill my finger into her flesh more ferociously than I needed to.

'Are you coming, or are you going to stand there gawping at the kids for the rest of the day?'

I stormed off in the knowledge that she was following, her Jesus sandals splashing rhythmically behind me, each spiritual step a reminder that I was planning to commit a murdur under the watchful eye of the Virgin Mary. At the front door I called to security.

'How you doing Kenny, everything all right?'

He barely raised his head.

'Could be worse, could be better . . .'

He buzzed us in, pissing me off that he did so without acknowledgement. He wasn't in the least bit curious about who was with me. It was a moment of high drama; I was standing in front of him with the Virgin Bloody Mary. I tutted loudly and pressed the button for the lift pushing Mary inside when it arrived at our floor, dragging her away from the television screens in the entrance that always excited visitors, wowed them with the knowledge that this was a building that made telly. The doors closed and I rubbed my eyes, weariness sinking in even though I had still achieved nothing. Out of the corner of my eye I saw her stumble, her tiny frame thrown off balance by the sudden movement up the shaft. Mary grabbed the handrail tightly, big yolky fried eggs for eyes revealing her fear.

'Jay-zus.'

'Tsk, tsk Mary,' I responded immediately, licking the salty sarcasm from my lips.

'You really shouldn't take the Lord's name in vain, it's not big and it's not clever. You'll go to the big bad fire if you keep that kind of nonsense up.'

She tutted in retort, her pale cheeks blushed with a soft pink. I had embarrassed Mary. I felt a tad guilty, but not *that* guilty. It was still game on; I was still going to kill Larry Spencer. I was *this* close to finishing him off. At the office door I grabbed Mary by the hand ensuring I was making an entrance, covering my back, creating an alibi for my earlier misdemeanour whilst everyone was outside.

Her entry created the desired effect. An impromptu round of applause and a healthy bit of Glasgow banter, an unrecognisable figure in a Star Wars mask mumbling that Mary's costume was a belter.

The office was full of wankers, none more so though than Larry Spencer. Reputedly he was Scotland's answer to Jeremy Paxman. It must have been true, because he had created the strap line himself. He'd been given his own TV show, 'Spend Sunday with Spence,' his weekly programme about politics, a fat poisonous slob lounging on a leather couch with a dog tooth suit and pointed, black patent shoes. Hating him so much made me feel better.

'Mary, come and meet my boss Larry Spencer.'

I pushed her in his direction but as she stretched out her hand to shake his I panicked and then tried my best to intervene. I didn't want her touching that filthy stinking shovel. *God* knows where it had been.

I wasn't quick enough and Mary offered her pearly white, Virginal hand to Larry Spencer. He held on to her hand for an eternity and I swallowed hard as she introduced herself.

'How are you doing mate? Ah'm Mary.'

He fell into a frenzy of laughter which curdled like bubbling custard in his throat, his dog collar bulging out sharply with each round of 'hhhhhaaaaaaaaaaaaaaaaa, hhhaaaaa, hhhhaaaa, hhhaaaaa' until it finally stopped, dead. Unfortunately, he wasn't. He was alive and flirting with her, the thick yellow fingernails on his right hand scaling up her forearm, trying to worm their way in to her flesh. There was blood on her hands; it was supposed to be on mine when I killed Larry Spencer.

He was stuck to her, flirting and laughing, his breath covering her in a film of filth. He was dressed as a Priest, the manky bastard, and in doing so he thought he had a God given right to paw Mary. I raced after them when he tried to guide Mary towards his laptop. This motion filled me with panic, not because I knew he was going to show Mary the photograph of his creepy pal dressed as a nun for Halloween, but because if he went near that computer alarm bells might ring. Thick as he was, it would just be my luck that he would notice something was out of place.

I grabbed Mary, wrapping my arms tightly around her waist. It was tiny, childlike. Gently blowing the hair away from her left ear I whispered quietly.

'You really don't want to go there'. I kissed her lips, lingering on their softness for a fraction longer than was necessary to make the point. Their softness stunned me. I fell into them head first. I was kissing a cloud.

Mary edged her chin back, peeling herself from me, my lips suddenly missing something they'd only just met. She searched for something in my eyes and I blinked repeatedly, hoping that she wasn't going to find it.

'Whoa ho, would you credit it Elizabeth, Mary's no a wee lamb after all . . .'

My instinct was to punch Spencer's fuckin fat face, but I didn't.

'Larry calm your jets. Mary's going to give me a hand to get changed, so why don't you chill out and go down to the studio? It's time we got this party started.'

My words were finished by an echo of song as my colleagues delved into Pink. I led Mary away by the palm of her hand. It felt incredible. I was holding something safe, something totally fabulous. So I let go. I dropped the nicest thing in the world like a hot potato, rubbing my hand furiously up and down my jeans just in case there was any remnant of niceness left. Fuck her. I had a m*urd*ur to commit. The pretty little Lady with the lips had to go. And so did Larry fuckin Spencer.

Apparition

Mary was walking slightly ahead of me but I was keeping my eye on her. Anything could happen in the company of a woman whose usual status is 'apparition'. At the end of the corridor I skipped in front of her, opening the door to the ladies' toilet, stealing a glance at her long robe as it swished around the frame like a cat's tail, its fabric purring as it tickled the tiled floor.

Inside she gazed around inquisitively, becoming familiar with new surroundings. I needed to use the toilet, I hadn't been all afternoon, the business of my day pushing the demands of a full bladder firmly to the side. I was definitely in the right place for it, but I didn't feel comfortable peeing in the same room as the Virgin Mother of God. Murd*ur* yes, having a pee no. I decided to keep it in.

'Mary, what's the chance of you staying out of trouble and waiting there for a few moments whilst I get changed?'

I nodded encouragingly, emptying my bag onto the floor and gathering my belongings into my arms, swaddled safely until I was ready for them.

'And keep talking will you? I want to know that you're still there. No sneaking off to try and save the world.'

Ridding the world of filth was my job. I squished backwards into the cubicle, determined not to look in the direction of the toilet pan. It was the only thing standing between me and a humiliating experience. A big inviting loo seat was singing.

I can make you feel good . . .

The need to pee was making my forehead burn and my lower back ache with a dull, throbbing pain. I turned away from the toilet trying to focus on the thin partition between myself and the Virgin Mary. Pressing my forehead against the cold door I sighed deeply, relieved that Mary seemed happy to engage in diversionary chit chat.

'Here, whit's all the mystery about whit you're putting on? You still havenae said whit you're dressing up as.'

I still haven't said.

How bizarre. Had she forgotten that we'd known each other for about half an hour? Obviously by now we should be acquainted with each other's families, swapping addresses, planning summer holidays on the Costa del Sol. Mind you, I was already on first name terms with her family.

Jesus, Mary, and Joseph.

The Father, the Son, and the Holy Ghost.

Mary was strike three in the holy trinity but for the time being at least I needed her. I had to hang on to her, before I could lose her and find myself. I answered her calmly.

'No, sorry Mary, it completely slipped my mind. Have a little patience and all will be revealed.'

All will be revealed.

I shouldn't have said that. It coincided with taking my trousers down. My pants thought they were next for the off so the urgency got increasingly urgent. Desperation set in, as did the paranoia. The toilet pan started singing again, the lid lifting, a big pair of wet lips reciting the chorus. It was pathetic. Everybody has to go to the toilet. Well, everybody apart from Mary. I hated admitting it but there was probably nothing but goodness in the Mother of Jesus, even if she had let me down again and again.

I didn't give a shit about such things in the mental hospital, neither when I was fifteen nor when I was in after Sadie. Dignity wasn't part of the package. I had more to worry about than someone hearing me pee. Back then I just wanted to die. I missed them all, Collette especially and Sadie, and even Patrick. I was on my own, there was no-one there to tell me what to do, demand things of me. I was terrified. I pined for Jenny, but pining for her eventually made me strong. Strong enough to know I had to kill her father. Not strong enough though, to use the bathroom in the vicinity of the Virgin Mary.

But I was bursting. And I mean *buuurrssstiinnn.*

I tried crossing my legs, squeezing my thighs together tightly whilst jumping up and down on my tiptoes.

It wasn't enough.

I tried biting my lip and thrusting my hands between my legs.

That didn't work either.

Then I began to move around in circles, the heel of my left foot digging into my right calf like a contortionist. But the low concentrated 'hhhhhhhhhhhhhhhmmmmmmmmmmm' that was escaping my exasperated lungs was causing a nosey Mary some considerable concern.

'Whit's the matter hen? Ah'm getting worried out here, have you got a zip stuck in an awkward place or something like that?'

That's when my bladder decided, FUCK IT. My naked behind was on the pan in seconds and I sighed deeply waiting on the relief.

But it refused to come. The psychology beat me to it.

Oh oh, it's pretty quiet in here. She'll be able to hear everything. And I mean everything.

I sat there, motionless, with my knickers at my ankles praying that my pee would depart from this world both slowly and gently, but more importantly, silently. It was as quiet as a chapel on confessional day, everyone outside, ears wagging, hoping to hone in on the length of penance.

I could hear me breathing.

I could hear Mary breathing.

I pushed my head into my hands, digging my elbows into my knees, trying to divert the pain from the intense cramps deep inside my stomach. But it was at its most vociferous inside my throbbing head.

I tried to remind myself what I was doing, but it was no use.

I couldn't hold my reserve for a second longer. My temperature was beginning to rise, I had to let go. Clenching my bum cheeks and gritting my teeth I used pelvic floor muscles to try and push the wee, and absolutely nothing else, out.

In the end all my controlled efforts were useless. Desperation pushed dignity out the *wind*ow and I pee'ed like an old carthorse. After a short recovery period I dressed quickly. I was barely out of the door, having finally changed into my Halloween outfit, when she started.

'You're no thinking of going down tae the party dressed like that are you?'

I had a wee look up and down, firstly from my own vantage point and then in the mirrors when I moved over to the basin to Mary's right and my left.

'How?' I queried, the Glaswegian coming back out on me as I ran my hands up and down my outfit. 'What's wrong with it?'

It was a genuine question. I thought it was really good. 'I'm pretty pleased with myself here. Nothing like spoiling the moment, Mary.'

Her comments were delivered with the same sentiment as a boot in the balls. With a ten foot runny. I hardly knew the lassie, but when you've taken a lot of time to pick out an outfit you hope that the effort's appreciated. But one thing was for sure; I wasn't going to get any plaudits from the Virgin Mary.

'Can ah gie you a tip?'

'What? Don't hang your washing out when it's raining?'

'Aye, very funny hen.'

She shook her head before continuing, her hair fluttering in the breeze from the hand dryer that was gently buzzing beside her.

'Listen, I know you're angry, ah get it, but let's just get something straight here - you aren't God Almighty, so stop trying to act as if you were. It's no big and it's no clever.'

She stood in front of me, tutting, like a kid who wasn't

getting her own way. She just wasn't getting it. I had no time for playground antics. I had a courier coming at five thirty and there was no way Mary's little tantrum was going to stop me from meeting my messenger.

'Oh for fuck's sake Mary, give yourself a rest, you sound like an old fishwife. It's just a daft costume that's supposed to be a bit of fun.'

I glanced at the mirror again, affording myself a second to throw a satisfied smile in my own direction.

'What's worse in the grand scheme of mortal sins? Killing someone, or wearing a dodgy outfit when you stick the knife in?'

I drew in air quickly, my outburst leaving me a little disorientated. I opened my left hand to check if the pink bullet was still there. It was. I still had him in the palm of my hands. It was all that mattered to me now. It was everything. It would get me out of bed in the morning and give me a reason to want to sleep at night. Mary wasn't on quite the same level though. She stared straight at me, through my hand, and into my soul. A solitary tear trickled from her eye, skydiving to the tiled floor.

It was a useless tactic. Tears never worked. The pain followed regardless. But I kept an eye on her anyway, curiosity making me wonder what would happen if she let her guard down. I followed the droplet closely, waiting cynically, almost ruthlessly for the next tear, but it never came. Releasing a big sigh, the kind that a toddler delves out when it's coming towards the end of its tantrum, Mary moved her hand across her face and wiped it dry. It shook my resolve; for a split second she looked like a frightened little child, terrified of what might be coming next.

Instinctively I put my arms around her and tried to console her. But I didn't want to squeeze too hard. She might break. Not because she was so skinny, but because it had happened to me before, back in the days when I was a silly little child. Waking from a nightmare I had crawled over to the makeshift altar on the windowsill beside my bed. There were two statues, the Virgin Mary and the Pope, 'guarding me' my mother said.

A framed black and white picture of John F Kennedy sat between them. I was never sure if they were protecting him, or they were beholden in some way to the President of the United States.

I picked Mary up and carried her across the room, placing her on the pillow before climbing in to bed and pulling the covers back up over us both. Tiny Tears was relegated to the bedroom floor. I eventually dropped off to sleep but I woke up some time later with the Virgin gawking at me with cold, piercing blue eyes. As bad as that shock might have been, seconds later there was worse to come. The bottom had cracked off the statue and Mary's wee feet were lying in a jagged lump, snake and all, about an inch from her head.

At seven years old there was no consoling me. I had broken the Virgin Mary. My dad said not to panic, it was only sacrilegious if her head fell off. But I knew differently. It was a mortal sin, my second at such a young age. Dad tried to help but he just made it worse. He glued Mary back together, but she was all squinty. Her feet were heading for the altar, but her body was already coming back with the Communion host. She got her revenge though, the life-size statue in Ireland nearly throwing me over the cliff and into the sea below. She seemed to remember.

'Hoi, steady on, watch you don't flippin break me. Ah'm delicate so ah am.'

We laughed and I took my chance.

'C'mon Mary, let's head down to this party. I don't look that bad and it could be worse. I could have dressed up as the grim reaper. Now, that would have been taking it too far'.

She took a step back and smiled, her warmth radiating, a pleasant feeling catching me unawares.

'Aye, all right then, but ah'm keeping my eye on you. Don't forget that I know whit you're up tae.'

She nudged me gently in the ribs. Little Mary, getting tough. But all I could do was smile. I think it must have been contagious.

When worlds collide

'You go in Mary and I'll catch up with you in a few minutes, I just need to go and meet someone first.'

The party was being held in the main studio and we were standing outside the door, music and laughter hitting us hard in the face.

'You can't be planning oan leaving me wae that lot?'

She turned her head, encouraging me to do the same. Spencer was on the dance floor, doing the dad dance, a middle aged woman I didn't recognise arching her back and drunkenly teasing him, large round breasts bouncing from a Wonder Woman costume that was better suited to someone two stone lighter. I nodded, understanding her apprehension.

'I see your point but I won't be long. Just stand out here if it makes you feel more comfortable.'

'That seems a daft idea. Ah'll tell you what, I'll just come wae you.'

She was smiling but there was defiance in it. I didn't want her to come, she couldn't be part of this, she was the Virgin Mary for God's sake. I sat down on the sofa in the foyer beckoning Mary to join me. I rubbed my face with my hands.

'What *are* you doing here? This is crazy. I can't possibly be sitting in work having a conversation with the Virgin Mary. I've gone completely mad. The happy pills the doctors gave me to make me sane have actually driven me completely off my trolley, haven't they?'

I rubbed my forearm. Mary followed the motion of my fingers, her eyes dancing back and forwards.

'Dae you still miss her?'

I didn't answer.

'It's fine, you don't have tae talk about it.'

It was more than I could take.

'Miss *who* Mary? My mother? My primary school teacher?'

She hadn't earned the right to question me about anything.

'You're going to need to be a bit more specific if you want to engage in grown up conversation. And quite apart from that you've still not answered *my* question. What the fuck are you doing here?'

I shouldn't have raised my voice, shouldn't have sworn, but she was getting inside me. I actually didn't know who she meant. Jenny? Collette? Maybe she was even talking about Sadie. I pushed myself back in the seat, my movement echoed by Mary who did the same, straightening her back and pulling her legs together so her knee bones protruded through her robe.

'I meant Sadie, but only cos she passed away and since her death you've decided tae kill Jenny's dad in the vain hope that his death is somehow gaunae help. Ah didnae mean tae pry. Ah'm no here tae dae that.'

'Is that supposed to be the understatement of the year?'

I concentrated on keeping my voice low. The anger helped, the sheer shock exasperating my vocal chords into submission. Mary looked across at me quizzically.

'Why? What are you talking about?'

'*Why?*'

I leant into her face, my words spitting through clenched teeth.

'Let me see, could it be the fact that Sadie didn't pass away, she was kicked and punched and battered with a steel baseball bat until her fuckin brain exploded, there was no passing away about it but what do you know because guess what, you weren't there! No, you only turn up when you're so *not* wanted, which brings me back, for just the *third* time in succession, to my question.'

I sighed deeply, I was exhausted, the sudden stillness

reminding me how tiring life since Jenny had been. All the angst and pain and the constant planning, decisions made and changed, scrapped then altered then abandoned again in favour of something more explosive or dramatic or downright tragic.

'What are you doing here? Why can't you just leave me alone to get on with things? You did plenty of that over the years, that's for fuckin sure.'

The words cut like glass but it was true, I'd prayed for her to help, countless times.

'Things . . .' Mary curled her fingers into her palms before carefully locking her hands together and placing them on her thighs. Her tone was quiet but her voice was trembling, a tiny stutter revealing her uncertainty.

'Things just arenae that simple Elizabeth, believe me they aren't. But ah'm here now and I want tae help you. This plan, this murd . . . ach I can't even say it, it's not going tae make you feel any better, trust me.'

They all said trust me, that's what they do. Jenny trusted her father.

'Tough, it's a done deal. I've come this far and don't get me wrong, my dear, sweet, all forgiving, innocent little Virgin, I'm not doing it without an understanding that it's technically wrong but I'm happy to live with the consequences. It's a small sacrifice to make, believe me.'

I straightened my shoulders, drawing them back defiantly, my aching body in a hurry to get to its next destination.

'Now, here's what's going to happen. I'm going to flirt with Larry and then go and meet a courier. You can do what you like.'

She followed me into the studio. Larry Spencer was smirking when I reached him but I didn't care, not long now and he would be laughing on the other side of his face. He was giggling crudely, his words heavy with the vapour of alcohol, his cruel side at the forefront of his drunkenness. Sometimes he could be kind and funny. I'd worked for him for years, getting close, gaining his trust so he could confess his crimes against Jenny and there were moments when I had allowed myself to forget, moments when I might have convinced myself that it wasn't true, that Jenny had never been at the mercy of this monster. She loved him, she loved him dearly, she told me that many times, but it was the wrong kind of love. I knew all about that type. But it wasn't easy, people like Larry Spencer know how to get deep under your skin. To climb inside and grasp a firm hold. They become part of you, like an organ, that's what makes it so difficult to walk away. You can't live without your liver.

He had Jenny's nose. It had a bump in the middle that would drive her to distraction but I would tell her to love and accept it, it was part of her character. Part of who she was. Part of who he was.

Spencer leaned into the side of my face, our familiarity with one another giving him the freedom to invade me.

'Did you and lover girl have a wee tiff? You two keep that up and she'll still be a Virgin tomorrow you know.'

He was watching Mary, her youth and vulnerability undoubtedly attractive to him. A wave of annoyance grated inside and I recognised it almost immediately, its intensity growing with the recognition. Jealously slapped me hard, its sting lingering on my cheeks. My teeth ached as I watched him flirting with Mary with drunken abandon.

I quickly took myself somewhere else, pushing thoughts of him wanking over obscene images on his computer screen into my mind. It wasn't irrational. I knew he did it, he must have. He was so protective over his laptop. He let me have access to everything on his desktop in the office, his emails, his confidential files, but the laptop was a no go. I opened it one afternoon. I couldn't find notes on his office computer that he needed for his show and he was under pressure to get to rehearsals so I assumed he had made a mistake and it was stored on his laptop that he had brought in from home. He slammed the lid down when he saw me, my fingers narrowly escaping his wrath.

'Touch that fuckin computer again and you will seriously regret it.'

He meant it, I could recognise the anger in his eyes, it was complicit with the monster I knew he was capable of being. When he calmed down he apologised, his anger coming, he said, because the computer was where he stored pictures of his daughter. Jennifer, he finally told me, died when she was fifteen. He refused to be drawn on why. It was the first time he had even acknowledged her existence. The most beautiful creature on earth and he didn't even talk about her. I was glad; hearing him say her name made me physically sick.

I knew then that he must have filth on the machine and I would use it to kill him. To commit my murdur.

'Elizabeth should have dressed as a cat eh Mary, trying to stick her claws into an innocent wee thing like you.'

I intercepted their purring conversation, getting myself back in from the outside so I could assert control, put the plan back on track.

'You shouldn't talk like that Larry, its blasphemy.'

'Aye and you'll be denying Mary three times before the cock crows in the morning.' He laughed, his tone suddenly warm and friendly, an act to impress the pretty young Virgin.

'How long's this been going on with the lovely Mary then, you wee dark horse you?'

He placed his arm around my shoulder like he always did when we were having a laugh, when I was doing my best to crawl under *his* skin. But this felt different. I didn't want him touching me in front of Mary so I dipped my knees and slid from under him, throwing my arm instead around an unsuspecting Mary who flinched when I accidentally on purpose let my hand rest on her breast.

'It's not like that you big daftie,' I teased. Prodding *him*, imagining dragging a blade in and out of his chest. 'Mary's an old friend who's come to visit for a few days, that's all.'

I smiled sweetly, feeling dizzy in the process. But I had to keep on top of it if I was to be sure of winning my fight with him.

'But here listen, I was wondering if you fancied catching up later, there's something we need to talk about.'

His eyes lit up in response.

'Oh there is is there? Sounds interesting. I shall of course provide you with my undivided attention. What do you fancy?' he drawled slowly, thinking the innuendo was flirtatious, cute even, as he rolled his eyes up and down before finishing his sentence. 'How about we go for a wee bite tae eat? Café Mao's nice. I'm not planning on staying here for too long so I'm happy to meet fairly early. About nine?'

What a dick, I was going to kill him and he wanted to go for dinner. But it wouldn't happen in the dining room with the carving knife and red roses and scented candles on the table. I laughed.

'No, listen, what I want to talk to you about is much more appetising than that. I'll call you and maybe I can come up to yours? Should be tennish, or round about then.'

Of course it would be convenient. He would be desperate to know what I wanted, whilst all the time convinced that it would be him.

'Right, I'm going to head off just now, Mary's been on a long journey and she's shattered. It was sweet of her making the effort to come along but I'm going to take her back to the flat and make her something to eat before I head out to meet you.'

I walked away without waiting for an answer but stopped when he shouted, his words a lasso grasping me firmly around my throat.

'Hey, you might be a dark horse or even a wee sneaky cat, but what the fuck are you supposed to be dressed up as tonight?'

I was stunned, devastated. I'd spent as long thinking about what I would wear whilst committing my *murdur* as I had planning it yet Larry Spencer had no idea what I was. I quickly concluded that he must be at it. He was taking the piss.

'Aye right, very funny. Hands up, you got me.'

'No listen, seriously, I've got absolutely no idea what that rig-out is all about, it's way over my head. So spill then, what is it?'

I glanced over at Mary and gave her a look. I'd been warned about this particular look in school. It was spiteful and intimidating, so I used it when I could. Despite Mary's whinging in the toilets about the inappropriate nature of my costume not a soul knew what I had dressed up as for my Halloween. I gritted my teeth tightly.

'Tsk, tsk,' I whispered, the index finger of my left hand waving pointedly from side to side, right in front of Spencer's face. 'I thought you were a wee bit more astute than that but don't worry, I shall unravel the mystery later, after I've sorted Mary out.' I dropped my finger and moved closer to him, angling my body so that I could whisper quietly in his ear.

'Do me a favour will you, don't mention to anybody that I'm coming up, I don't fancy everyone gossiping about us, you know what they're like in here.'

God how bad would that be, people thinking that I was getting down to it with Larry Spencer? I'd sooner die. But I also had to be practical. When his body was discovered it would be crucial that no one knew I'd been at the flat. He replied instantly.

'Of course, don't worry about it, we're friends aren't we? But listen, if you're really not having a tête a tête with the lovely Mary put a wee word in for me, will you?'

Ignoring his comment I left him to it, hurrying instead to meet the courier, the message that he was outside buzzing in my pocket. Mary held her balance in the lift, watching me whilst I addressed the jiffy bag.

'Whit wiz that all about then?

'What Mary, what is the fuckin problem now?'

'You're no still planning tae go through wae all this are you?'

'No Mary, I've just spent the best part of ten years planning it for nothing. It was a crap idea.'

'Sarcasm's the lowest form of wit,' she said lifting her hand from her chin and tutting loudly. The *diinnggg* of the door opening almost swallowed her words but I heard her clearly enough.

The courier was at the entrance so I shouted to security that it was someone for me. It was freezing yet the courier was wearing shorts. He had a really hairy leg. The other leg was partially sheathed in a knee sling that covered the bottom half of his thigh and the top of his lower leg. He was wearing climbing boots, his mountain bike resting on the wall beside the front door. He tried to pass us but I stopped him in his tracks.

'Excuse me mate, are you here to pick up the Spencer package?'

'Yeah, G'day.'

He was Australian. How weird I thought, two folk from different worlds in the one day. You just never know the minute. His voice was deep, a fraction away from sexy. He reached out his right arm and tried to grab the door.

'Do you know where I've to pick it up?'

I edged him gently away from the handle.

'Aye, come here out of the wind, I've got it.'

I flashed the jiffy bag in front of his eye, excitement welling up inside me.

'Is there something I have to sign?'

He handed me a clipboard. I handed him the package, keeping my eyes firmly fixed on it whilst he took it from me and carefully placed it in the rucksack shackled to the back of the bike. I picked up the pen. It was tied to the clipboard, its string fraying. I used it to write *L Spencer*. He jumped on his bike and was away, the strength in his legs ensuring that he didn't sway in the wake of the wind. I nudged Mary gently.

'You've not taken the huff have you? Look, it's not your fault, some people just aren't for saving.' I was calm, the pain in my chest less intense than it had been in a long time. 'I'm not saying I'm not grateful, because I am. I feel really privileged, but I've got to do this. So, what do you say to coming back to mine and getting yourself out of those Halloween clothes? I'll even make you dinner; get something inside before you go back up the road.'

I jumped up and down in front of her playfully. Spencer would be at the party for a while longer so I still had plenty of time to pull everything together. Mary linked her arm through mine, rain suddenly bursting from the heavens, violent in its intensity.

'Aye, all right hen, whatever. But ah'm choosing whit ah wear. You've got previous for dodgy outfits.'

'What do you mean? This costume's what you would call very clever, Mary.'

'Clever? Tell me this, will ye? And we're going wae your version of the legend, right? If the last thing that somebody hears before they kick the bucket is the screams of the Banshee then how's anybody supposed tae know what one looks like?'

'What?'

'Eh, think about it. It's no rocket science. Nobody gets the chance tae see the Banshee. The lights go out afore she appears. Know whit ah'm saying?'

'Ah for fuck sake Mary. Don't be such a bloody know it all, it's not becoming. And anyway, it was good enough for you to know what it was supposed to be. But granted, it was a pish part of the plan. I hope that makes you happy.'

It didn't matter. The revised plan was so much better.

Taxi

'I think we'll walk tae yours Elizabeth, it'll dae us a power of good.'

Mary snuggled in, hunching her shoulders so the side of her face was pressed against mine. Even though it was a command, the warmth was exciting and the sweet smell of roses invigorating. Finding strength I pulled myself away from her sharply, cracking the shell of the shiny toffee apple.

'Walk . . .?'

I stopped dead in my tracks. Sighing, I raised my head to the sky, my arching eyebrows indicating that even if she wasn't immediately aware of it, it was still pissing down. I waited for the slap on the back of my neck.

Ach ah'm only winding you up hen, we'll jump a taxi.

I might have heard the words but they never came from Mary. The taxi rank at the train station was mobbed, lots of little black cabs winking at us seductively, their orange signs flirting from under the filthy rain, teasing us with the promise of a hot ride. Drawn to that side of the road I grabbed Mary's hand and tried to pull her.

But like most she was stronger than me. She pulled me towards her and as we turned the corner I looked back and greedily glared at the taxis, trickling all over the road, like a big burst bag of my favourite liquorice allsorts.

'Mary this is absolutely stupid, we're getting soaked. We need to get a taxi. Jump into this doorway for a minute and I'll order one from the app on my phone.'

'No need,' she said, laughing, raising her eyebrows skywards. The rain stopped, its absence leaving an empty silence in the air. I tutted and walked on, edging in front of her so I didn't have to talk. I didn't want her clearing my head of its morbid thinking.

I stopped anyway, the heavy scent of wet autumn leaves drawing me to the bridge. I closed my eyes and imagined bobbins of red and gold sailing down the Clyde, spinning and weaving whilst dark grey water gave chase, paving the way for winter. Breathing deeply, I inhaled the last few moments of *green*, the final remnants of a passing season.

'Come here you, I suppose you should see this too.'

I nudged Mary gently, inviting her to join me and we turned round, drawn towards the water beneath us. We hung precariously over the bridge, on tip toes, wiping our soaking hair away from our foreheads, watching the world swoosh underneath our feet.

'This must be a bit mad for you, Glasgow a bit of a culture shock after Bethlehem I imagine?'

'I dunno hen, it was a rare wee place in its day you know. Ah couldnae even find anywhere tae stay it was that popular.'

I burst out laughing, the noise suddenly drowning in another downpour which thumped onto the ground ferociously, the rain bouncing back up as high as our knees. We ran quickly, the pavements forming another river, debris sailing colourfully down the street.

'This is crazy,' I shouted over the sound of the water crashing off the pavements, 'we're getting a taxi no arguments, there's a private rank just across the road.'

Mary was shouting something back to me over the lashing rain, a wet hand pointing at a silver Mercedes sports car parked outside the office. I couldn't hear her. Cars were hurrying past, their wheels swooshing up waterfalls.

The engine of the car she was pointing at was roaring loudly, the lights on full beam, the wipers thumping back and forwards across the windscreen obscuring the view of the figure hunched inside the driver's seat. We were across the road yet even in the dark I thought there was something familiar about him. The traffic calmed affording us a moment of silence to speak.

'What did you say a minute ago? I couldn't hear you with all that racket.'

'Ah was just saying that's a nice motor but ah see you've been looking at it yourself anyway.'

I looked at it again, straining to see why it felt important to me.

'Yeah, it's lovely but I doubt it's a taxi Mary, think it's more likely that we'll be climbing into a Skoda.'

Mary was shivering with the cold. A car flew past and splashed a puddle over us both. She climbed under my arm, but searching for warmth under the armpit of a chilly murderess probably wasn't the best place for the Virgin to seek comfort.

'Ah'm freezing hen, I hope that bloke's no getting the last taxi.'

She was staring at the man emerging from the taxi office door, her lips quivering. There wasn't a taxi on the rank, just the silver merc.

'Doubt it; he must have just got fed up waiting. There doesn't seem to be a taxi about but it's warm in there so I think we should wait.'

The man stopped in his tracks at the door. He had his back to us, his broad frame struggling with the narrow surroundings as he tried to release his arms from his coat. He kicked the doorframe angrily and threw the heavy coat over his head, sheltering his body from the rain as he jumped across a puddle and into the passenger seat of the waiting car. I caught a glimpse of his shoes as he slipped into the car. I stopped, drawing to a halt in the middle of the road as the car sped past. It couldn't be him.

'What's up? You look like you've seen a ghost, hen. Dae you know that bloke?'

Mary, like I, was watching the car as it disappeared into the distance.

'No. Well at least I don't think so.' I couldn't be sure.

The receptionist in the taxi office looked us up and down, her glare nonchalant, lingering on Mary as she threw herself down on a plastic seat beside a little one bar electric fire. She was a solid girl wearing clothes that were too small for her.

'Any chance of a taxi?'

'Aye, well it is a taxi office, that's whit people come in here for.'

I gritted my teeth.

'Well that's a stroke of luck because that's exactly what I'm looking for.'

She grunted, swinging her chair so her back was turned away from us.

'There's wan oan it's way, it'll be about ten minutes, you'll need tae wait.'

She didn't look up.

'Thanks. Did that guy have to wait long?'

'Whit guy?'

'The guy that just bailed out of here as we came in. Was he in here looking for a taxi as well?'

She got up off her chair and stuck her head through the little glass window. Red lipstick stained her two front teeth. She pointed her finger at me, her hand pushing past her own breasts, their heavy mass propped on her frame like a sack of spuds.

'Get yourself tae fuck. Naebody comes in here and starts playing fuckin Colombo. You and the Virgin there can walk and ah hope tae fuck yous get fuckin pneumonia.'

Oh Little Star of Bethlehem

Mary was freezing, her nose shining as brightly as the star of Bethlehem when we got to my flat. We gathered in the hall like strangers at a wedding, both of us unsure what to do, stationary, as if the music had stopped. Mary moved first, rubbing her hands above the radiator, drawing the heat into her long spindly fingers. Satisfied with the recovery in her hands she turned around and transferred her skinny body to its helm, resting her lower back on the wall above the searing heat.

She stood quietly but her trembling limbs were almost audible. She looked like a child, her scrawny arms and legs splaying like the branches of a budding rose bush, her soft red cheeks the fruits of a premature blossom. I wondered what it had been like for her as an innocent child suddenly 'chosen', the special one, thrust unexpectedly onto a different path. The real child had been stolen, buried deeply under the sands of time. We weren't so different, Mary and I.

But I had to get moving.

'Right c'mon, let's see what I've got that you can wear. Although I'm not so sure that anything I've got will fit you. There's not a lot to you.'

Looking Mary up and down I smiled, beckoning her towards my bedroom. I had four of them. My bedroom was the first door on the right hand side of the big empty hall, nearest to the exit. The ceilings in the ground floor of the flat were tall, the walls forced to climb a magic beanstalk just to meet them. The tenement was split into two levels but I almost never went upstairs. There were two additional bedrooms up there but they were cramped and stuffy, the attic skylights providing little in the way of light and freedom. The rooms lay empty, a dark void that I didn't want to have to deal with.

Next to my bedroom was my living room. I had painted it raspberry so it was always summer, somewhere bright to keep me motivated, help me remember that there was a light at the end of the tunnel. Across the hall was the other bedroom, caked in blueberry like a giant muffin. The bathroom was next to the blue room. It was shocking pink although the only person it had ever surprised was me. A large kitchen took centre stage at the end of the hall but the only thing I really liked about it was the pulley that hung voraciously above the big oak table. I loved hanging my wet clothes on it and dragging them to another place, tying them in the wilderness.

'Whit have you got then?' Mary looked up and down at her robes, tugging at the blue fabric whilst wrinkling her tiny nose. 'Ah only ever really wear this dress so ah've not got a clue about fashion.'

But she was certainly excited about it and within seconds she was alongside me, raking though the rails of my wardrobe, giggling at the prospect of sampling something different. I quickly grabbed a pair of faded blue jeans and a red jumper.

'Here, try these, they're a size eight, but I've got a belt if they're too big for you.'

I chucked the trousers and jumper at her and she almost fell over reaching for them.

'Brilliant, these look smashing, but ah'm soaked right through. Ah don't suppose you've a pair of knickers ah could borrow an'all?'

I rolled my eyes; just how bizarre did things have to get? I opened the top drawer of the dresser in front of the window and pulled out a pair of red thongs. I threw them across the room to Mary. I also grabbed a red bra, tossing it after the knickers, its fabric stretching across the room, taking flight for a brief moment in time.

'For flip sake, whit on earth is that wee scrap of fabric supposed tae be? Ah'm no exactly gaunae cover much wae the likes of that.'

She held the pants up in front of her face, yanking the string and dramatically pushing her arm through the leg hole.

'Fuck sake Mary, take it or leave it. I'm busy. I need to get changed as well. If you don't want to wear them don't and if you do, then DO. Just sort it, I need to go out.'

She was upsetting my focus, trying to take my mind off the things that I needed to do.

'Aye, all right, keep your flippin hair on, ah'll wear them. Ah'm just pointing out that they're a wee bit different tae whit ah'm used tae.'

I left her to it and headed into the kitchen. I stretched up on the balls of my feet, pulling my combats and a black woollen polo neck off the pulley. I had to bounce on my tip toes, extending my muscles up again and again before I managed to grab a pair of black pants from the wooden pole. I swept the bundle into my arms and rushed into the bathroom to change.

I dressed quickly, getting ready for action, my skipping heartbeat registering my excitement in a series of energetic palpitations. Once I was ready I drew my body in front of the mirror, taking one last look at myself. I touched the reflection of my cheeks in the misty glass and shuddered, a tremble falling from the nape of my neck to my toes. It was exhilarating. I knew that the next time I stood in front of a looking glass I would be different.

I opened the door and bumped straight into Mary. She still wasn't dressed.

'Elizabeth, when's this going to stop? Ah wish you could see that you're making a huge mistake. Let's sit down and talk this all through, see if we can get aw this nonsense out oav your system.'

Fanny. That's exactly what I was doing.

'No. You look, Mary. I've said it again and again so this will be the last time. Final, finito, end of. I've got something to do and I'm going to do it.'

I grabbed my jacket from the hook on the wall and pushing past her, opened the door.

Larry Spencer

I was on my way to kill him. I could hardly breathe. Excitement gripped my gullet. It was an incredibly intense emotion, physical and thrilling, exhilarating even. And yet somehow it was menacing and for a few seconds I stopped and questioned my actions, a voice inside my head telling me to pack it in and get back up the road.

I stood hen-toed, my knees knocking together. I wrapped my arms tightly across my upper body, my right hand squeezing the big bone which was bulging under the lean flesh on my left shoulder. Touching it made me think of the moment that Mary had filled with her warmth and for a second I let her make me smile, but it was never going to be enough to make me stop.

A workman wolf-whistled at me from behind the security of his big, fat, steering wheel and I spun back into action.

'Fuck off you stupid prick.'

He gave me a much needed boot up the arse, a timely reminder that there was no room for fear, or contrition. Larry Spencer was an impostor. He was living a big fat lie. He was a vicious, malevolent deception. The instant his image was back inside my head - not that he had ever been gone, he'd just been hidden beneath the moment - I knew I was doing the right thing. There could be no room for doubt. The guy was a fuckin monster.

I closed my eyes. Jenny was hanging from a rope and I gasped, the blood rushing to my head, the shock as harsh as being tossed into the freezing Atlantic. I rubbed my face furiously, but her bulging eyes were still there, rippling in front of my eyelids, the memory of her loss dancing the death march.

Fuck you Larry Spencer.

Reinvigorated I took to the road, my pace once again vigorous and defiant. I knew where I was going, the route was etched carefully in my head, tattooed like a satellite navigation system, the streets precisely mapped, a bright illuminated runway securing a perfect landing in the path of Larry Spencer.

It was so straightforward it was beautiful. When I got to the corner of his street I knew that all I had to do was turn left at the off sales on the corner. But I stopped at the top of the road. I had to adjust my clothes; I wanted to look measured when I committed my murdur. I tugged on the belt holding up my combats, pulling myself in, ready for active duty. I hauled the neck of my jumper towards my chin, jamming it briefly on my curving jaw line before dragging it higher, the fabric gradually concealing my lips and mouth before chaffing the bottom of my nose. My nostrils flared and instinctively I drew breath. Long, hard and intense, I sucked the air in slowly before coughing sharply.

I tried to calm down, ease my way into the next step. I'd waited so long for this I didn't want to blow it by fainting. That would be so typical of me, to go down like a pack of cards, peeing my pants in the process, lying like a wounded dog in a pool of my own piss.

Therapeutically I drew on the loose strands of hair straddling each side of my face. Twisting them I felt each grow from a carefree strand of idle nothingness into thick woven ropes, strong enough to draw around someone's neck and pull tightly. Calmly, feeling the strength under my fingertips, I placed them carefully in the hollow between my head and the back of my ears.

Almost ready I clicked my heels together sharply. Only one more street, one final obstacle standing between me and Larry Spencer. I allowed myself a moment to wallow in a timely reminder of his crimes, and as usual my thoughts were laced in guilt. They all flashed before me, Collette, Jenny, Sadie, Patrick, even little Elizabeth, who I hadn't allowed myself to think about in a long time. I had destroyed her too. They were all there, yelling at me with different instructions, each competing to be the loudest, the most important, encouraging me to get on with it, to become a do-er, or to stop it, to fuck off and crawl back into my hole. They were all screaming at me, their voices snatched by one another, chewed up and spat out like some vulgar fungus. In the end it was the child who had the strongest voice. *It's time,* Elizabeth mouthed in a soft calm voice. I smiled at her and moved on.

I turned the corner but it was chaos that greeted me head on. There were two police cars on the main road. They were parked precariously, their noses kissing gently at ninety degree angles, the vehicles no longer occupied. Spectators were gathering, unclear of the reason yet intrigued regardless. Blue beams radiated succinctly from the roof of each car, flashing rhythmically, the ample rays penetrating the muffled faceless comments of the public.

The lights blinked in tune, accentuating their delivery by sweeping inordinately, slightly out of sync, like a professional dancer carrying a novice round the floor, one striking shaft of light followed moments later by an incoherent, out of pace stutter. The blue brigade waltzed without music, the car sirens quiet, still, listening to the beat which penetrated the air without any audible accompaniment. Yet the scene wasn't entirely silent. Observers in the crowd were mumbling, possible theories bouncing around the air, each stimulating another potential angle of conversation.

As I got closer I could taste the carnage. The stench of alcohol was compelling yet overpowering, precipitating a wave of nausea that rose and then fell inside me. A figure lay motionless on the pavement, covered loosely in a dark blanket but I could still make out the outline of the body. I joined my wrists together in front of my chest threading my fingers together before pressing them tersely onto my knuckles in a symbol of prayer. I took a deep breath and prayed that the heap of nothingness on the ground wasn't Larry Spencer.

I looked up towards his window. It was occupied. I could see two police officers standing behind the glass despite their outlines being partially obscured by a Roman blind which had been hastily discarded to one side of the window. The window was open. The edge of the blind was rippling in the chilling wind.

'He probably didnae mean to dae it,' one observer declared assuredly, satisfied with her explanation. 'Aye, wan of they cry for help thingymajiggerys,' another figure mumbled from under a head scarf, 'you're right so you are, mibbae he probably definaiiiitttttttely didnae want tae dae it.' The remainder of the mob nodded, their 'hhhmmmms' rumbling across the street excitedly rather than sympathetically.

Definitely-maybe, open seven days a week except Sundays, totally-almost. Just another of life's little inconsistencies. I wanted to kneel down and cry, right there and then, absolutely definitely for sure, no maybes about it.

Yet instinctively I turned around, suddenly sensing Mary was with me. I could feel her presence surround me like she'd cast a net and was preparing to reel me in. Saving her the trouble I succumbed, falling into the red jumper, collapsing like a dying swan. The wool was wonderful, but I knew that the heavenly feeling came from being encased in her arms.

When the ambulance arrived I perked up, willing them to bring him back, glancing towards Mary with a beseeching glare, demanding a miracle. The irony didn't pass me by; I'd spent years wishing him dead and now that he was I wanted him to rise like a phoenix. The paramedics' arrival was routine and they did nothing. Seconds later a fourth car arrived, its appearance signifying the point of no return. The vehicle was black, a transit van, its purpose a trip to the morgue.

An influx of thin lipped policemen hastily arranged a blue tent so they could obscure Larry Spencer from our view. That embittered me. Undoubtedly the most satisfying image at this precise moment would have been that of his pathetic crumpled body, as they squashed it into a black bag, a zip scrunching past his hollow head, covering the last remnants of his fat greasy face. I was deprived of even that.

I tried desperately to piece together the events that were unfolding, without Mary knocking me off course.

'I didnae know hen,' Mary muttered, shaking her head repetitively, 'but even if I did ah couldnae have told you this was gaunae happen.'

I sneered at her; she knew all right, she knew everything. The fucker was going to die anyway, with or without my help. The first of the journalists arrived on the scene. Not surprisingly, Larry Spencer was one hell of a story. I cooried into the circle of knowledge, shuffling into the carnal fountain of journalists who were spilling over from behind the blue line, drenched with news of the weapon that had killed him. Just as I got close enough to decipher the muffled whispers I was forced to change direction. I tried to smuggle my haggard figure out of view and into the background. But I was too late.

He'd seen me.

The clock strikes twelve

I feigned a quizzical look, not ready to admit my existence to him even though he was right in front of me, his stance exactly the same as the first time I had seen him. He repeated himself.

'Elizabeth? Now there's a fuckin turn up for the books. I didnae expect tae see you again.'

I took a step to the side and he moved with me, his thin image bouncing in front of me like a fairground mirror.

'Look, there's nae point in throwing me a happy daftie look. There's no way ah'd get this wan wrong, that fuckin face of yours is not one am gaunae forget in a hurry.'

I wanted to say no, don't be mental, I've not been me for a long time but there wasn't much point. I swallowed deeply, glancing from the kafuffle around the body bag to his face, searching for the passage of time. It was there in abundance. He was even skinnier, his features fraught with age, thick lines pulling his eyes low in his face. His cheeks were protruding sharply, finally losing themselves in a cracked top lip that was savaged with cold sores. In contrast his clothes were smart, an expensive wool coat partially hiding a grey suit and purple open neck shirt. He was clean shaven, folds of excess skin hanging around his neck like a tiered necklace. He was different, and yet all the while still the same man whose jeans had been soaked in her blood.

'Ah take it you're still using smack, Alan? That forever-ever-bottom-of-the-soul promise didn't last very long did it?'

I shuffled my feet, taking a moment to check their place on the pavement, anything to avoid the cold stare penetrating my forehead. I'd believed him when he cried, screaming about his love for her, promising her floppy corpse that he would change, he would do anything for Laura. Eventually I'd had to take her from him. I prised his fingers from her still warm cheeks, her skinny arms swinging without purpose as I laid her on my chest and wrapped my scarf around her sullied head until they arrived.

'Fuck off Elizabeth, at least ah didnae just abandon *my* wee lassie.'

His words were strong but he delivered them meekly, even though he was right.

'For fuck sake Alan, you are still as thick as you were back then,' I spat tensely, keeping my sharp tongue out of the earshot of the journalists behind us. '*Your* wee lassie would still have had a mother if you hadn't single-handedly ensured she was found and slaughtered.'

I hadn't seen him since the court case. Piggy had blamed my actions on a mixture of self-defence and diminished responsibility and, due to my fragile mental state, had taken me (willingly) back to the same psychiatric hospital he'd secured me in before, when Jenny died and they wouldn't believe me that it was just a matter of time before Mary would come back and help me through the sadness.

When the judge described Sadie's injuries I said the carnage had been my fault, that Alan had been an innocent passenger, as much abused by Patrick as Sadie and I. I knew if I did they'd let him look after Laura. He was a prick but I couldn't forget Sadie saying that she didn't want Laura to grow up without her dad. And it was my fault. I might as well have killed Sadie with my own hands. I was the guilty one. It was Patrick's anger at me that made him kill her. He was doing it to hurt me. And so Alan was right. I didn't deserve to be a mother. I didn't know how to protect my child.

'Like ah just said hen, ah didnae throw my wee lassie tae the wolves, can you say the same thing? Nah, don't think so . . .'

I knew it, and everyone else rightly understood it, and yet I still slapped Alan, hard, my hand burning with the force of the impact.

I didn't expect the punch but it came almost immediately,

landing with force on the back of my head. I fell in slow motion, baffled to see that Alan stood still, his hands fixed firmly in his suit pockets.

'What the fuck?'

Mary grabbed me but she tripped, yelping as she fell awkwardly on the pavement, her ankle buckling beneath her. I fought to stay on my feet but I couldn't see what I was fighting until she spun me round to face her, smoking grey eyes boring into my face.

'Touch him again and ah'll fuckin break your face.'

She ran her finger down my cheek like a gangster from a movie.

'Sadie . . .?'

The word burst from between my teeth, I didn't mean it to, I knew it wasn't her but she was her double, the hair, the shape of her eyes, her lips, her skinny limbs all fired up as if she owned the world. I deserved the slap that came in response.

'Da, who the fuck is this arsehole and what the fuck is she daein talking about ma maw?'

I curled my fingers around the hand on my face, understanding who she was.

'Laura, it's me, Elizabeth, do you not remember me?'

The follow up slap was justified and it stung fiercely, blood from my tongue trickling down my throat.

'Fuck sake, you've aged, and you're not looking the best for it, eh? But listen, ah might not have recognised you but it's not as if ah'm about tae forget that you and your prick of a husband were responsible for killing my mum.'

I looked at Alan and he shook his head in a *just leave it* motion. I let it go, relieved that the crowds and journalists were still focused on the body and not my unfurling life.

'No sorry, of course you've not forgotten, I know you'll never be able to. I think about it all the time too. I just didn't think you would remember me.'

She said nothing in return and we stood looking at each

other, the three of us, a triangle of glances as each examined the other, assessing how we'd changed. There was nothing left of the little girl who screamed in terror when she ran into the house with Collette, tearing towards Sadie, begging her to get up, tugging at her limp limbs and pushing me away as she tried to ease her mother's broken head from my chest and onto her tiny innocent lap. Laura was a little bit older than Collette. She would always remember.

'Eh, sorry to interrupt, but I'm Mary. Do you no think it would be a good wee idea tae all go somewhere for a coffee? Just to gie yourselves a wee chance tae catch up?' Mary was pale and tired. She was nursing her sore ankle yet still had the energy to be so unbearably sweet and naive.

Laura thrust her hands on her hips responding to Mary in the same *fuck you* tone her mother had mastered so well.

'Even if we wanted to give that boot any of our precious time we cannae, we're going tae meet my da's boss.' She turned to Alan, her pride in her father squaring her shoulders back, pushing her chin high. 'He's taking us tae some new posh restaurant up the town, isn't he da? As a thanks for the job you were doing the night.'

Her tone was gallus, determined in her delivery to show me, that despite my efforts they had survived. It was a bittersweet moment. I was happy for Laura but it was Sadie who should have been earning her plaudits, not Alan. I tried to relax the tightness in my throat.

'Oh aye Alan, you've got yourself a job then, that's good news. What are you up to then?'

'Right enough Da, you never said what you were daein the night, wiz it something tae dae wae one of the taxi offices?'

Laura turned to me.

'My dad's the manager oav the biggest taxi company in the city, not bad for the *thick guy who didnae turn up for school and didnae have the brains to know what he was doing.*'

I blushed. She was drawing on the statement I'd delivered in court. The words were paraphrased but Alan must have told her that I'd run him down, leaving out the part that it was to give him a chance to let him and Laura live together. I glared at his skinny little features but he couldn't keep my gaze, his eyes glancing towards Spencer's corpse for a second longer than they should have. It was long enough to let me know that there must have been a connection.

My unfounded suspicion turned to an explosive rage in seconds, the force of it firing from my toes, at the other end my fingers grasping his neck, searching under his skin for the answer his tongue was keeping secret.

'C'mon then Alan, let's hear it, what was the job you were doing tonight?'

The policeman grabbed me from behind, Mary's loud protestations that I was upset and didn't know what I was doing enough of a diversion for Alan and Laura to disappear into the crowd.

'For fucks sake, he's not just my boss, Larry Spencer is my friend, I'm upset that I wasn't here. I should have been with him.'

After the third time I screamed it he let me go. I showed him my work I.D. and he apologised, taking down my details. Larry's suicide, he said, must have come as a tremendous shock.

The photograph

I helped Mary up the stairs to the flat. *I* was helping Mary the Virgin Mother of God. Why couldn't she just conjure up a wee miracle and wave the pain away? It flummoxed me a little, but I could only assume that she wanted to make a point, endure all the drama of having to do the human thing.

Been there, done that, worn the flippin t-shirt.

A Mary t-shirt would be great, Our Lady in a tight top, her own image across her breasts above the words 'human and hurting'.

She leant on me heavily, struggling to keep as much weight as possible off her left ankle. She felt warm. Her face grimaced with every hobbled step and she paused when we reached the last flight of stairs. I did nothing to encourage her to continue and instead placed myself at her side, a crutch between her skinny frame and the wall. She stood slightly off balance with her hair magnifying her lop-sidedness. Her perfect hair was now chaotic and locks of silky hair were gate crashing on the wrong sides of the parting. They were a beautiful imperfection.

She smiled. It was a broad smile, a humbling image and I swallowed hard, lost in everything. It was all crazy, everything was a mess, a thousand things climaxing at the same time, their stories entangled, their messages confused. But she'd come back, like I always knew she would.

'Hey missus, don't you go worrying yourself about this, ah'll be right as rain once we get inside and ah can get a wee seat.'

'Are you sure? I feel bad considering you hurt it trying to help me.'

'Look ah'm no telling you again, ah've got a wee bruise on my foot from your crunching tackle earlier and then I twisted my ankle because ah'm not used to these shoes, it's no big deal.'

She raised her foot in front of me, the red and white Nike trainer held aloft for observation and comment. The bruise was entirely down to me. Welcome back I had said with a bang as my foot crashed down on her little tiny toes. My own wee Glasgow Kiss.

I tested the water with my elbow and put the basin down in front of Mary. I grasped her calf in one hand and gently began to edge the shoe off her foot with the other. Despite my tentative approach she still winced and I saw why when I peeled the shoe from the sole of her foot. Her sock was wet, glazed with an orangey substance that had seeped into the fabric. It was Mary's blood. I was torn between guilty tears and voyeurism, a yearning to know if inside she was exactly the same as me. Her blood had an eerie look about it though; a pale syrupy residue that had never quite given birth to life.

A drop seeped from the sole of Mary's foot, slipping through her sock into the water, a diver freefalling from a springboard. Its entry was sleek and sharp, the impact barely creating a splash on the surface. I watched the shape as it spun underwater, spiralling quickly in various directions, swimming and kicking, determined to last forever. It was soon submerged, the cloudy puff disintegrating as if it had never existed. Mary and I glanced at each other briefly, wondering if the journey had been a figment of our imagination.

I made a tender attempt to peel the sock away from her foot, praying that the blood hadn't solidified and crusted together in a gluey substance, sealing the fabric to her soft brown skin. A sharp cry informed me that it had and I opted to slowly submerge her foot, sock and all, into the warm water. She sighed, and we both watched in silence as the water changed colour from that of absolutely nothing to a powdery red.

Her foot was a mess. And I was a mess. I was thinking about Larry Spencer and Laura and most of all Collette. The first tear that fell dripped silently. It landed so weakly in the water it didn't even register an onomatopoeic entry. The rest fell like a rain storm crashing off a caravan roof.

Mary lifted her foot clean out of the swell and I grabbed it and submerged it again, desperate that the moment wouldn't be about me. With the sudden movement my hair slipped from behind my shoulder and plummeted into the water smothering Mary's toes in an auburn coloured seaweed. Still silent, she clasped my head between her two hands, her bony fingers suddenly strong, drawing my puffy face in her direction. Slowly she leaned back in her chair, dragging me with her, her manoeuvres short and sharp as if she was parking a car. With our eyes level she drew her left leg out of the water and placed it casually over her right knee. A shower of water dripped from the sole of her foot, pitter pattering back into the basin. Unable to keep my back straight I curved my spine and rested my head on Mary's knee. Spirals of my hair swung forwards and caressed her foot. I laughed as a scene from *Jesus of Nazareth* came to me.

'I might have known if I ever got to play the role of Mary again it'd be the bloody Magdalene, not the Virgin.'

I looked up in time to see a smile flash across Mary's face, but it was distant; it had lost its durability.

'Ah hear whit you're saying hen, but it's hard to think just now. I'm totally exhausted. Would you mind if ah had a wee sleep?'

She looked tired. Part of me wanted to push her away, propel her brazenly back to wherever she'd come from. But a bigger part of me wanted her to stay. Her warmth was precious. She was finally real, and part of my life. She curled up on the sofa and was asleep in seconds.

I wandered into my bedroom, opening the wardrobe nearest the window, kneeling down on my knees as if I was about to pray. I had hidden the bag under two rows of shoes, holding it down, making sure it had nowhere to run to. The bag was made of mesh, a deep blue like the sky at twilight, but the colour didn't suit the contents, it should have been black, a little black book of memories holding details of the past. I packed the bag when I was sixteen, just before I headed south. I was in, and then out, like a sharp snap of the fingers. When Patrick and I took the midnight bus to London the bag was at the bottom of my suitcase, my memories and my communion dress enclosed inside.

The dress was beautiful. It was so small, yet so symbolic, the purest, Virginal white. I pulled it out from under the tissue paper swiftly, the entire dress swooping into the air effortlessly, weightless, but so incredibly heavy. I held it up against me, stroking the silk and lace with my free hand. I pulled the neck up towards mine and turned towards the mirror, shocked that the hem barely passed my waist. I was such a tiny little girl back then, on my communion day, as I strolled down the aisle, pulling my blue velvet cloak in towards my body so that it stretched tightly across my shoulders.

I wondered why they decided to stop protecting *me*. When Mary and Jesus had decided enough was enough.

I'm bored with that wee lassie now, c'mon we'll ditch her and find another wee wean to heap our love and praise upon.

I peeled the dress from my chest and placed it on my bed, folding the delicate sleeves so I could put it back in the bag along with my childhood. But suddenly she was there, the photograph face up when it squeezed out from under the neckline of the dress. Her beautiful eyes were staring lovingly in my direction, soft baby white teeth gaping from under the lips of a broad happy smile. I had put it there when I got out of hospital, tucking the photograph inside the dress. Seamus had developed the film in Sadie's grandmother's camera and sent me two copies of the picture I had taken of Collette on the beach. I had glued one copy into the book of drawings, the memory trail I had given to Collette the last time I saw her, the day she visited me in the ward, her plaits swinging through the door, her embrace as warm as the summer sun. She was happy then, excited to flick through the pages, torn between looking at my sketched stories and sharing her wee happy stories, her excited lips telling me all her news. She was staying, she told me, with a really nice lady, but only until I got better and came home.

But I never did go home and I don't know if she had looked at the book since. She probably wanted to forget that I had ever existed. Seeing Laura was crippling me, knowing that my daughter was also a woman, beautiful and yet so full of hate for me. I crawled under the duvet, pulling the photograph and dress to my chest, pushing them against my aching heart. I let go, unable to control the pain. I don't know when Mary arrived but she did, climbing under the duvet beside me, prising my arms from the dress and redirecting them towards her. I slotted in, without a battle. I didn't want to fight her anymore.

All Saints Day

I was sleeping. Yet in the thick haze I could hear the constant menace of a telephone. Not ready to face reality I tried to turn the annoying *bbbrrrrrrr bbbrrrrrrr* into a soothing melody that would rock me gently back to sleep. It was pointless. A split second of consciousness was enough to engage my conscience, and the crushing weight on my chest returned, rendering escape in dream impossible.

I covered my ears, wishing that my entire life would fall into silence. But someone answered the phone and I lifted my head from the pillow, straining my ears, picking up one side of a conversation from the hall.

'Listen son, like ah said, she's not coming in the day and that's all there is tae it. Ah can say it again if you want, but it's not gaunae sound any different.'

I drowned my head with the duvet and tutted loudly, my reaction saying Mary's still fuckin here, when I really meant *thank God she's here* . . . She must have been talking to work. No doubt they were searching for answers. They weren't the only ones. I'd completely lost the plot. I didn't have a fuckin clue what was going on anymore.

I stretched my aching legs and my toes edged out from under the duvet. I drew them in quickly, the chill of November pinching me sharply, a harsh reminder that today would have a wee nip in the air. It was All Saints Day so perhaps it wasn't a coincidence that Mary was visiting here, now.

I edged myself up slowly, stopping when my shoulders touched the chill of the wall behind me. Seconds later the door edged open. Mary peeked her head inside, checking I was awake. I tried to screw my eyes shut but she was nobody's fool.

'Ah saw you looking. It's high time you were up and out of that bed. C'mon, shift it, ah've run you a nice hot bath.'

She breezed over to the bed and stood beside it, clutching a glass of water. She was wearing my pink dressing gown. I was really pleased to see her but rather than tell her that I looked her up and down, determined to make her feel unwelcome. Being defensive was the closest to emotion I was prepared to get.

'Make yourself at home why don't you.'

'Aye, cheers, nice wee comfy robe, what I would have done for this on a chilly December night in Bethlehem.'

She rubbed her hand up and down her skinny hip, her long brown hair falling into her face and catching in her teeth as she laughed.

I did a double take. It hadn't really struck me that Mary was *that* Mary. S*orry, there's no room at the Inn* Mary. I sighed deeply, wondering what the fuck I'd gotten myself into as she stretched out her arm, handing me a drink.

'Here, I brought you a glass of water hen, figured you might be a tad dehydrated after all that greetin last night.'

She smiled sweetly, the glint in her eye ensuring I didn't throw it back in her face.

'Thanks.' I didn't lift my hand to take it. 'When did you get up?'

'Ach ages ago hen, ah couldnae really sleep. All this is a bit strange for me. Ah don't think ah've ever gone tae bed wae another woman before.'

There wasn't even the slightest trace of innuendo in her response. She was too perfect for anything like that. I tutted, and leered towards her, examining her face for any evidence of a lack of sleep. She looked tired, dark circles surrounding her eyes. I had managed to fall asleep whilst she walked the floorboards of my worry. I couldn't even do depression right.

'Was that my work on the phone? What did you tell them?'

I sat upright, pressing my spine firmly against the wall,

drawing my feet up to my bum. I pulled the duvet towards my shoulders, waiting on her answer.

'Oh aye, ah should have told you about that when ah came in. I said tae some guy fae your work that ah wiz the Virgin Mary and ah had popped down from Heaven to try and stop you from killing Larry Spencer.'

She flopped on to the bed beside me and tapped the duvet.

'He was cool about it, said you were just tae give them a call when you were up tae going back in.'

I watched Mary puff out her chest, chuffed at her humour. She squared her shoulders in a mock act of bravado and a bare breast threatened to escape the pink terry towelling. It distracted me and I pushed her hand away from my leg whilst wondering what the hell she'd done with my bra.

'Mary, you're a fuckin nutcase.'

I diverted my eyes and gazed through the tiny gap in the curtains. Naked trees twitched on the skyline, long brown fingertips peering over the houses across the street.

'Dae you want tae talk about the dress, Elizabeth?'

Mary shimmied backwards on the bed, hauling herself up beside me.

'Talk about what?'

I pretended that I couldn't understand what she meant. I glanced at the sideboard. Mary had folded the dress neatly. The photograph of Collette was face down on top of it but I could still see its image clearly; my baby girl was always in my eyes.

'Ah'm really sorry, ah don't mean to put you under pressure. I'm not exactly a dab hand at face to face heart to hearts, but ah am trying my best, I promise.'

'I don't know what you're talking about Mary so how's about you just change the flippin record.'

'Aye nae bother, it's up tae you, whenever you're ready.'

Mary smiled, sliding up the bed and stroking my shoulder, intimacy offered without consultation. I didn't want her to do that. I was too scared of what it would make me feel.

'But whit about what happened with Alan and Laura last night, dae you want tae talk about that?'

Fuck sake, she didn't mind pushing it. I sniggered at her audacity and hit the back of her head with a pillow. She toppled forwards, plunging onto all fours on the carpet for dramatic effect. The glass tipped, spilling onto the floor beside her. The pillow fell last, slowly, thudding with a loud belly flop into the pool of water. Mary laughed but I stared at the carpet, speaking absently.

'Do you know what?' I raised my eyes, making sure Mary was watching me. 'I wish that was a brick and I'd just whacked it right off Larry Spencer's nut.'

Take that you Bastard . . .

Mary frowned.

'Ach don't say that, he's a wee soul.'

I couldn't believe my ears. She must have been taking the piss. I invited her to make amends.

'Fuck up Mary, I think what you meant to say *was* . . . he's a complete asshole.'

She got up from the carpet and, turning round, leant her skinny arse against the dressing table, taking the weight off her feet in a moment of fuckin chaos.

'YOU can think whit you like Elizabeth, but ah'm telling you, Larry Spencer's a wee soul.'

I tried to stay calm, watching her incredulously as she slipped down off the dressing table, bending her legs so she could kneel back down on the floor. Screeching, she jumped back up as soon as she hit the ground, rubbing her bare knees, wet from the damp patch on the carpet. I said nothing, gazing disinterestedly at an anonymous shadow, wishing I was alone. Mary turned away from me, her image stealing into the corner of my eye. I watched her as she pulled the curtain aside and peered out the window, a ray of sunlight enveloping her silhouette in a smoky frame of dust. She stood still for a second, a squeaky noise finally escaping from her finger when she stroked condensation on the glass.

'Ah get a sense that you're no really wanting me around Elizabeth but ah'm afraid you're stuck wae me for the time being.'

She turned around to face me, shrugging her shoulders apologetically.

'I'm stuck with you? Are you having a fuckin laugh?' I drew breath. 'I spent my entire life begging for you to help me and what did you do? Absolutely fuckin nothing... And then you turn up at the door like the long lost relative from Australia. No fuckin way. Too little, too fuckin late.' I paused, wiping the saliva from my lips.

'And do you want to know something else? You were a hell of a lot more appealing when you were a daft wee statue with its lips painted on. At least then I had some hope and you didn't spout a lot of shite. *He's a wee soul.* You make me sick.'

'Whit are you talking about Elizabeth?' She spat my name in anger. 'Have you ever considered thinking before you open your big gob? Is there *any* flippin chance you might listen and wait for the whole bloody picture?'

I jumped out of the bed, squaring up in front of her.

'Fuckin hell Mary. Is it not about time you wised up? It's not me that's got a problem. Hello . . . are you listening? C A N Y O U H E A R M E?' I pointed to my ears, speaking in a slow, sarcastic voice.

'It's like this Mary. Spencer was a fuckin animal, he repeatedly raped his own daughter and she killed herself cos she couldn't take it anymore. He deserved to die and in a hell of a lot more pain than he fuckin did.'

I flew towards her, finally snapping, *so* close to belting her with the clenched fist that I was thrusting into her face.

'If you had fuckin helped *me* when I needed you then none of this would be happening now. Can you not see this is YOUR fault, yet you've got the fuckin cheek to stand there and blame me? Just get out . . . MOVE! . . . GET TO FUCK

OUT OF MY HOUSE!'

She jumped back, frightened. Exhausted I crumpled into a heap on the floor. I uncurled my fist and thrust my fingers into my forehead, trying to release the pressure that was building up behind my eyes.

'Can you not understand that by coming here you've spoiled the only chance I had to make amends for Jenny?'

The doorbell rang. I raced to the door, opening it violently demanding to know who it was as I crossed the hall.

'What the fuck do you want?'

I pushed the handle towards the floor, my angry scream startling Alan.

Elizabeth

Elizabeth covered her stomach, protecting her unborn child from the bellowing rage of his voice. She was fourteen. The Virgin Mary had been about the same age when it had happened to her. Elizabeth was well aware of this fact and every day she asked Mary what she should do, until her silence told her she should probably tell someone who would be able to provide her with the answer. Andrew's only response was to slap her and remind her of the consequences of revealing their secret as he announced that he was joining the navy. Confession was different, it wasn't telling tales.

'Child, are you listening to me? To anything I've said to you?'

Father Brennan's words physically hurt her head. Of course she was listening to him, she couldn't hear anything else.

'Aye, ah heard you Faither, ah just didnae know if ah was supposed tae say anything back tae you.'

Father Brennan threw himself in Elizabeth's direction and she felt powerless to avoid him. As he got closer her skin dampened; timidly touching her cheek she realised that a film of his spit was spraying directly onto her face. A drop of it landed directly on her lip and she shuddered. The fluid was warm and smelled like sick. It was disgusting, but she didn't dare say that. Maintaining silence Elizabeth glanced quickly in the direction of the Virgin's statue, hoping Father Brennan wouldn't notice that she was once again seeking Mary's divine intervention. She was too slow, her gaze lingering for just a fraction of a second longer than it should have. Although expecting his roar, it still startled her and she jumped like a startled animal.

'What do you honestly think you are going to gain by

looking over there?'

He tutted loudly and smirked, a wry calculated smile wiping across his face in a malicious attempt to discredit her.

'She's the incarnate Virgin, Mother of God. But you? You Elizabeth, you'll be going straight to hell.'

He glared at her before roaring the pivotal word again, ferociously, just in case she hadn't realised its significance.

'Hell!'

Elizabeth had heard it all before. There was a very vocal 'hell' demonstration every other day in school. You could always tell if it was a Monday, Wednesday or Friday. Most of the time she took it with a pinch of salt but the odour of stale garlic hung so heavily in the air today that it was like a cloak of filth. Father Brennan coughed violently, and his putrid breath travelled in a series of twisting tornadoes towards Elizabeth, its stench making her feel even more nauseous. He began to shake, but instead of cowering in fear Elizabeth collected his arm gently from where it clawed his chest, and spoke to him calmly.

'C'mon and sit doon Faither, you're gaunae dae yourself an injury wae all that coughing.'

She helped him onto a seat, a big old armchair that swelled under a bright floral fabric. The greens and browns were worn in patches, revealing frequent visitors. Large lace doilies, once white but now tinged with a hint of yellow, fortified the angular arms which slanted upwards, pointing towards heaven.

Despite Elizabeth's temperate guidance Father Brennan fell on to the chair like an elephant and the impact shook the cups on the table, the china singing before settling back into a respectful silence. The grumbling priest's anxiety decreased as the pain in his lungs retracted. Calmer but still impatient he instructed Elizabeth, with an irritated wave of his right hand, to pass him the remainder of his cup of tea. Suitably cooled it soothed his acid tongue and his temper waned as the contents sank medicinally to his gullet. As he drank Elizabeth bent down to pick up the remnants of her own cup, the china parachuting from the table when the priest threw himself on to the chair.

'Child,' he said. 'Come and sit beside me whilst I talk to

you.'

He patted the arm of the chair, indicating where he expected her to go. She obliged because that was the way of the world, when an adult asked you to do something you did it. But it didn't really matter. Sure she would go along, but she was never really there.

Slowly she walked the four short steps across the floor to his chair. Stalling momentarily she was hurried on by a defiant pat on the arm of the chair. It was delivered with such conviction that a cloud of dust puffed skywards, billowing towards her and congregating thickly in the back of her throat.

Coughing she looked behind her, a bolt of instinct telling her to retreat, but the decision was taken from her when her right hand was grabbed and used to spin her body on to the arm of the chair. Immediately it was uncomfortable; the edge was rigid and a metal spring was forcing its way to the surface, pushing against the cheeks of her thin bottom.

'Will you stop fidgeting!'

It was an order, not a question, and she responded swiftly. Wriggling free she found solace at a more comfortable spot; her back now resting on the main body of the chair, her right arm quiescent on Father Brennan's left side.

'Aye, sorry about that Faither ah just couldnae get comfy. Ah think this chair has seen better days.' She tried to force a laugh, hoping her flippancy would lighten his mood. It did.

'That's a good girl,' he cooed serenely, but his tone was tainted with a sinister edge. 'Now,' he said, pausing briefly to run his thick red tongue over the jagged perimeter of his cracked bottom lip.

'Let's get nice and cosy and we can have a little chat. There's nothing to be scared of, I'm sure we can work out something to make sure you don't have to go to hell. A pretty little girl like you shouldn't have to be condemned forever. Isn't that right, pet?'

Elizabeth nodded, confused, but keen to please.

'Definitely Faither, ah didnae mean to cause any trouble

or anything like that, ah've been praying tae Mary and ah thought that seen as she'd been through the same thing and a' that maybe ah should talk to God about it.'

Elizabeth stared into his eyes, searching for absolution but he ignored her. His gaze was fixed firmly on the door, his breathing frenzied, a panting dog shading from the summer sun. Turning towards her he playfully slapped her leg, the second time his hand accidentally on purpose pushing her skirt up her thigh towards her pants.

'Be a good girl pet and run over and pull the bolt across the lock on that door.'

Elizabeth looked at the big heavy door, with its round wooden handle and silver bolt that stretched from the door to the frame at the left hand side. He carried on talking.

'This is to be a very private conversation, an important conversation. We don't want to have anybody listening in now, do we?'

Elizabeth turned to face him, unclear as to whether that was a question that required an answer. It was irrelevant anyway, she knew the routine. There wasn't any point in protesting, if she didn't get up and lock the door he would. Just like Andrew always did. But there was some comfort. If she locked it herself she would know how to open it. She would know how to get out. She wouldn't have to stay there forever.

So she obliged, pulling away from a playful slap on her bottom as she climbed down off the seat, a slap that made her face singe with a red glow. She might have been a child but she knew she was way too old for that. When she got back from the door Father Brennan was perched on the edge of the armchair with his legs spread-eagled, his elbows dispersing the weight of his arms onto his thick chubby thighs. He urged Elizabeth to kneel down in front of him.

Elizabeth, with her knees pressing into the carpet, wasn't expecting any surprises. She knew what happened next. She shivered but the Priest spoke to her in a quiet, unassuming voice.

'What happened to you pet, what silly thing did you do to get yourself into this state? You must only have yourself to blame, you know that don't you?'

He pointed towards her belly and her hand smothered it in a mark of protection whilst her head fell to her chest. He gently raised it before caressing her blushing cheek. She said nothing, feeling guilty. Yet the warm hand on her face soothed her. It was Catch 22. Draw her in, push her out.

My aggressor, my confidante. My enemy, my friend.

'Ah'm no supposed tae say anything about what happens cos my mum and dad will end up hating me if ah dae. They'll send me tae some crazy children's home if they find out.'

'And do you honestly think I don't already know everything, that God hasn't told me exactly what's going on?'

Elizabeth thought about it for a second. Did he already know? Out of all the people in the world had God really taken the time to speak to Father Brennan about her? She decided she couldn't take the chance.

'Aye, ah suppose so Faither. Ah, um, ah just have tae be good and that and dae whit ah'm tellt and then I get a wee present for being so nice tae Andrew. But ah've got tae make sure I don't tell a single soul.'

But she got herself prepared to tell him everything. Elizabeth sold her soul because she thought she had to. When she finished talking Father Brennan roared again, his mouth bulging like a rattlesnake harvesting the carcass of a small deer.

'You can't have secrets like that from God you stupid, stupid girl, he knows everything, he can see everything, he knows exactly what you've done. The only way you can get forgiveness is to listen to me and do exactly what I say.'

He hissed at her, his forked tongue laced with the venom he had spat at her earlier. Elizabeth was scared, battered into submission, up down, round and round, swings and roundabouts. She imparted the rest of the story. He listened intently, savouring every last word as she explained the things that made her special. Minutes later he pulled her on to his knee and softly kissed the back of her head. She could feel the growth in his lap underneath her.

Here we go again.

He parted her legs and his fingers, escaping the evasion of her pants, slipped deeply inside her. Pushing her slender frame on to the floor he turned her round so she was facing him. She never spoke; she knew it wouldn't be worth it. In one movement he removed her pants, mumbling something incoherent as he worked away at his objective. Then he spread her legs. She didn't feel the need to watch the rest. She closed her eyes as he covered her mouth with one hand before locking both her hands behind her head with the other. With the vision of Mary sheltered beneath her eyelids she did as she always did. She prayed.

Hail Mary, the Lord is with thee. Blessed art thou amongst women and blessed is the fruit of thy womb Jesus. Holy Mary Mother of God pray for us sinners now and at the hour of our death. Amen.

And there she continued, over and over again until it stopped and the door was opened.

The Past

Alan was on the welcome mat, my angry scream as I opened the door anything but that. He was anxious, his left eye twitching nervously as he thrust a letter into my chest.

'Here, take it, it's yours, well at least ah think it might be, ah'm no sure.'

I took a step backwards ignoring his hand and the letter.

'How the fuck did you find out where I lived?'

He stretched his arm out further, pushing the letter even closer. I scanned behind him, searching to see if he was alone.

'Laura doesn't know ah'm here, she's away tae meet a pal.'

'That's great, it's nice to know that she's having a day out but fuck off Alan, I'm having a bad day and seeing you again is making it worse rather than better.'

He didn't budge, the letter still waving in front of me, the dark circles under his eyes boring into me.

'Look hen, ah'm no supposed tae be here, just take the fuckin letter and if it's meant for you then great and if it's no then let's put it down tae a wasted visit. You did something for me wance and ah'm just wanting tae do something in return. No big drama, just a gesture that may or may not mean something.'

'A gesture?' I snorted sarcastically. 'How weird, I don't hear a peep from you in years, not so much as a fuckin card to let me know how Laura was doing whilst I was in a locked hospital ward taking the heat for a scene of carnage which incidentally you played a part in, and then not only do I see you twice in twenty four hours you suddenly want to do something wonderful for me. Nice style Alan, I'm touched.'

He shuffled his feet, his head hanging low, his thin neck straining under its weight as he raised it to talk to me.

'Fuckin hell Elizabeth, it's no that fuckin simple. Ah had tae keep my head down, it was pretty mental for me too you know, ah didnae have an easy time of it explaining tae Sarah's ma that her daughter was deid cos ah'd chased her across the country wae a class A nutjob in tow. And wee Laura, man, she was in a mess for a long time. You know what she saw, she didnae sleep properly for years after.' He paused, swallowing loudly, speaking again quickly so he didn't have to linger for too long in the past.

'And ah didnae have my troubles tae seek with the Boss either that's for sure. You blew his right hand man's head off. That's no an easy thing tae explain over a pie and an' a pint.'

I remembered my loving husband, his obliterated head blown inside out. His name ticked off the list. 'Right okay, fine, I'll take it, whatever the fuck it is.' I grabbed the letter from his hand, partly out of curiosity and partly to get rid of him. 'Maybe we'll run into each other in another decade but until then let's just do our own thing.'

He said nothing, turning on his heel and skipping down the stairs, his foot reaching the bottom step of the first landing just as I noticed the writing on the envelope. It was Jenny's. I raced after him, grabbing him by the shoulder when he reached the second landing.

'Stop the bus Alan. Where the *fuck* did you get this letter?'

My lungs were strangling me, my heart snared inside, the erratic vessel being dragged backwards and forwards across my chest with every sharp intake of breath.

'I told you, ah cannae say anything about it, just take it and forget you ever saw me.'

I fell to my knees.

'Alan, I need to know, *please*. Don't forget what I did for you, Laura's still yours because of me. Tell me, please . . .'

The after match

Alan was sitting on the very edge of the couch, his constant glances at the door confirmation that he knew the means of escape. He looked worse than earlier, his eyes as black as coal, his body skinnier than I would have thought possible, spider thin legs pushing against the fabric of his trousers.

'Elizabeth, ah cannae tell you everything, it's no safe for Laura and most of it isnae even relevant.'

My breathing was still intense, sharp. There was a band of steel gripping my forehead. I pushed my fingers along its rim but it wouldn't budge.

'I understand that but tell me what you can, it's important. I can't for the life of me work out how you got your hands on this letter.'

I clutched it tightly, turning it over and over, not brave enough to open it and reveal its contents. I could feel Jenny's pulse from within, her soul seeping through the pale pink envelope. I had bought her the writing set, craving the silly notes she left under my desk or in my schoolbag. She sometimes addressed them *To, The magnificent, outstanding, highly talented Ms Elizabeth Reilly*. I glanced at my name on the envelope, feeling her fingertips, soft hands curled around the pen as she created the elaborate sweeping letters. I could hear her voice, her elongated vowels when she sang them from over my shoulder as I opened the precious notes that she sent with regularity. Mary settled on the seat beside me, her arrival pushing me to my feet and over to Alan.

'Just tell me what you can. For fuck sake Alan I'm at the end of my tether here, the last ten years or so haven't been easy for me either. This letter is a crazy blast from the past and I need to know how you of all fuckin people managed to got a hold of it. It doesn't make any sense whatsoever. Did you even know Jenny?'

Alan's eyes fell to the floor, his attention drawn to his shoelace. His shoes were polished spats, my only previous experience with footwear like that a nauseating one.

'Son, do the lassie a favour and tell her whit she needs tae know, she's been through enough and it's no fair tae keep her hanging oan like this.'

Her tone was older than her face, a wise and caring woman's voice emerging from a youthful apparition. Alan nodded at Mary, tying the lace tightly before running his fingers through his hair.

'Aye all right, ah'm just getting tae it.' He coughed, his Adam's apple bursting from his throat like a frog.

'Look, ah've got no idea who *Jenny* is, ah didnae even know the letter was fae someone called Jenny. Ah was daein a job with the boss. A journalist that does a few turns for him got a hold of a hard drive that was supposed tae have evidence about a TV presenter being a paedophile so we paid him a visit.'

I jumped to my feet. 'Which TV presenter?'

'The boss thought we might be able tae get a few quid out oav him to keep it quiet.'

I bent over, my face pushing into the air that Alan was claiming as his own.

'Aye, whatever, but which TV presenter Alan?'

I glanced over at Mary, knowing she understood the connection. Alan looked at her too, a quizzical look on his face as if he'd only just realised she was with us.

'Just fuckin speak Alan. Mary's all right, you can say what you want in front of her, she's going to work it all out sooner or later anyway, believe you me.'

He stared at us both for a few seconds then carried on.

'You know fine well who ah'm talking about Elizabeth, ah know you work for him, ah know what you've been doing for years, ah've seen you in the town loads of times.'

'What are you talking about?'

'As if you didn't know, it's your boss, Larry Spencer. Ah don't suppose it wiz a coincidence that you turned up at his flat as well? Ah know it was you that sent the drive to that journalist bloke Neil Connolly, you left some oav your own files on the drive.'

I fell on to my knees, the rug catching my fall as I tried to understand what was going on. I was confused. I was exactly what Piggy had been telling me all along. Unclear, muddled, not too well in the head.

And stupid. So much for my master plan. I must have used the drive at some point and then forgotten about it. I was a fuckin idiot. But it didn't really matter. The important thing was trying to work out what Alan had done to Spencer and why I suddenly had a letter from Jenny.

'So what the fuck happened when you got to Spencer's? Did you kill him Alan?'

I concentrated on swallowing my anger, raging that a pathetic loser might have been more able to capture the moment I'd been working towards than me.

'No, give me some fuckin credit, ah'm no a murderer, ah've got my lassie tae look after, ah'd never risk doing a life stretch.'

I'd shooed my daughter away like a fly, anything to give me time to plan my murdur. Puke raced to the back of my throat, tickling my tonsils with its vile taste. 'Then what?' I said it quietly but the bitterness was still apparent. I could feel it as slipped back down into my stomach.

'We went up to the flat wae the wee hard drive thing and the boss was quizzing Spencer about some letter he had scanned into his computer fae his daughter, saying he would take it tae the papers if he didn't give him a wad of cash. And no, before you ask ah don't know what it said, he diznae tell me everything and neither dae ah need tae know everything.'

He cleared his throat again, each tiny interruption an agonizing wait as I searched for the truth.

'Next thing Spencer says he cannae live wae everyone knowing the truth and he pushed the fuckin window wide open and dived out. Ah couldnae dae a thing. It was fuckin horrible, he didnae even scream but the noise when he fell, man, it was mind blowing, like being back oan that fuckin island again.'

I shook my head. Nothing would ever compare to that day.

'Anyway the boss said that we better get tae fuck out of there and as we were hurrying out the door ah saw this letter oan the table wae your name oan it, well your name from before, ah know you don't use Reilly anymore, you started using Paddy's name again when you got out the hospital, didn't you?'

'Who are you, Jessica fuckin Fletcher?

I had changed it, again. Elizabeth Shaw. It reminded me of Collette. She had her father's name, poor kid, but at least she didn't have her father, I'd made sure of that. But it wasn't just that, I couldn't run the risk of Larry Spencer remembering me, Elizabeth Reilly, the wee lassie who almost spat hatred at Jenny's funeral.

'Aye, whatever. It's a small world Elizabeth, nobody just slips into the woodwork when they've blown someone like Paddy's head off, there's always going to be somebody wanting to know what you're up to. Anyway, I thought ah better take it in case it really was for you and it was anything that would get you intae bother with the polis. Ah'm sure you're not in any hurry tae end up in the jail.'

I pushed the letter to my lips hoping to smell her perfume but it was long gone. Whatever message Jenny had left me it was enclosed within.

'I was going tae just chuck the letter away once ah got home, ah would have done if we hadnae bumped into you. I guess it wiz some kind oav a sign fae above.'

Alan rose to his feet and nodding he opened the living room door, its low creak the only sound as he shuffled to the hall. I followed him out, thanking him.

'You've done a great job with Laura, Alan. When I saw how you were with her, that day, you know, when Laura came in and saw what Paddy had done to her mum, I could see a kindness in you. Sadie said she didn't want her growing up without you. I couldn't take that away from you as well.'

He shrugged his shoulders, embarrassed.

'Nae bother.'

'Can't believe you beat me to it with Spencer, I wouldn't have minded pushing him out that window himself.' Another understatement, delivered understatedly.

'So who's your boss these days, Alan? I'm glad you got away from Patrick but it sounds as though you're not exactly the clean living type.' I tried to laugh but a strange noise came out in its place.

'Aye, ah did try believe you me, but I had Laura tae look after and I wanted tae get her intae a good school, one of those fee paying schools that gies you a posh voice like yours.'

'I take it you thought better of it then.'

I smiled, recalling Laura's broad accent, her syllables singing at me in Sadie's warm tone.

'Nah, she's just a rebel, says she prefers to talk in a real voice that reflects her natural surroundings, whatever the fuck that means. But she's as smart as fuck, she got five A's in her Highers this year and she's going tae Glasgow uni tae dae medicine so I guess ah'll need tae keep working for the boss for a few years yet tae pay for it all.'

Alan's chest visibly puffed. I closed my eyes for a second, scribbling behind my eyelids, rewriting the scene so it could be me talking with pride about my daughter Collette. But she was long since gone, in another world, with another mum. A sane mum who wouldn't expose her to the bastards that seemed to sit alongside my life. I opened my eyes.

'Fuckin hell, that's brilliant, she's amazing.'

'Ah know, ah cannae believe it worked out like this, she's

going tae be able tae do whatever she likes. Doctor Laura, eh?'

'Like I said Alan, you've done a brilliant job, you should be proud of yourself.'

Not like me, I'd no idea how my little girl had turned out. The social worker had promised me she would be well looked after; I had to force myself every single day to believe it. She was better off without me.

'Aye, I am. And it's not like you said hen, ah've no touched the smack in years, ah wouldnae go near the stuff, Laura deserves better than that. Wan of these days ah'll go totally legit but it's no easy working for Umberto. He diznae let anybody leave his service in a hurry. Paddy was lucky, you did him a fuckin favour.'

He walked down the stairs, my eyes boring into the back of head, the vision in the silver Mercedes now clear. It was Alan and Umberto fuckin Donati. I shut it out, closing the door firmly behind me so I could concentrate on the letter.

The end of the road

I hurried to the bathroom and shut the door tightly behind me, for once enjoying a closed door. I allowed my legs to collapse and collecting my body weight on the edge of the bath, I placed my heavy head carefully on my knees. My left hand plummeted into the bath, hitting the waiting water like a dead weight. The splash forced me to raise my weary eyes and I watched my fingers ripple across the surface. I followed the warm water as it lapped to the sides, trying to escape the confines of the tub.

'Dae you want me in there with you, hen? You don't need tae tell me what the letter says, ah'm just offering a hand tae hold in case you need it.'

I dried my hands with the towel and picked the letter up from the windowsill needing nothing apart from my connection with Jenny.

'No, I'm all right, just leave me will you? I'll shout you if I need anything.'

I placed the toilet seat down and sat on the lid, my hands shaking as I turned the letter over to open it. I slipped my right hand thumb under the seal and then stopped, turning it over once again to run my finger over the ink, checking for the umpteenth time that it really was addressed to me. I opened it slowly, trying not to tear the paper, to desecrate anything else of her memory. I pulled the pink paper out, two folded pages slipping into my hands.

Dear Elizabeth,

This is the hardest thing I've ever had to do but I'm going to do it and one day you'll be glad I did because you would hate me even more otherwise. I can't bear the thought of you hating me and not just you, my whole family hate me, or at least they will once dad reads the letter I've written to him. I can't keep lying anymore, it's driving me mad, the pain in your eyes breaks my heart and it breaks my heart even more knowing that you think I'm sharing your pain. I'm not making any sense I know but I'm doing my best to explain. I'm explaining cos I love you Elizabeth, you're the most amazing person in the whole world and that's why I can't go on hurting you like this.

He didn't do it to me, he never has, never did. Dad has never touched me. I made the whole thing up cos I'm stupid and I like being dramatic and causing a stir. I didn't expect you to believe me and then when you shared what had happened to you with Andrew and that fucked up priest I couldn't bring myself to tell you that I wasn't really sharing your pain. I'm so sorry but you know what I'm like, always being dramatic, trying my best to shock. Oh fuck Elizabeth I was just trying to wow you, I would never have said it if I thought you'd believe me. I just wanted you to like me, maybe help you think I wasn't so posh and shallow, that I was real just like you. I'm so sorry, I wanted to tell you the truth but I thought it would make you feel better if you thought it had been happening to me too but now that you want to tell the police on my dad I can't let him get hurt like that. They probably wouldn't believe me and he'd go to prison and he'd just hate me and I know you're hating me right now but I don't know what else to do. I've written a letter to my dad, telling him what I've done just so he knows that I love you both. I'm sorry Elizabeth, I know I said I'd never tell another living soul about Andrew and that prick of a priest but I needed to tell dad in his letter so he can understand that I was just trying to protect you. I can't live anymore, not with you hating me cos I lied to you and dad hating me for making up something so evil about him.

I'm sorry Elizabeth I really am. I love you, always and forever,

Jenny xxx

I felt an overwhelming panic. I'd killed Jenny too. The girl I loved, the girl that made me feel safe and kept me from the monsters that had shaped my past. I felt myself slipping back there, to that dark place I had fallen to when she died. There was numbness at first and then it all went black. I didn't know how to speak anymore and then when I remembered it was just to call out for Mary. Over and over, screaming to the Virgin to come back and take me too, take me to Jenny. She didn't come then and all they did was take me away. Lock me up in the hospital with Piggy and the pills and the black tunnel that became my home. I didn't give up believing though, I knew she'd come back. For a split second I had the desire to Facetime Piggy and show him that Mary was here, but I let it pass. It was pointless given what I had decided to do.

I stared at my reflection in the mirrored cabinet door, failing to recognise the image that faced me. I opened the door sharply, acting quickly whilst I was at my most assured, moving a razor and a ten pack of Tampax out of the way so I could reach my prize. The bottle was almost full and as I tore at the lid I struggled with the child proof holster. I'd saved four months worth of tablets, the little fuckers that Piggy would give me to wipe out my memories in the hospital. It was ironic, given he had no fuckin idea what my memories were.

When I was released I picked the pills from the hem of my jeans, carefully extracting the little balls of fluff before tossing some vitamins down the toilet pan and resealing them in the empty bottle. I'd kept them safe for all these years. Originally I'd planned to use them after I killed Andrew but I didn't have the heart to carry on and initiate that plan. I couldn't wait that long. Not now, not when I knew what I'd done to Jenny.

The bottle lid was being stubborn, slipping round and round as my fingers tried to loosen off the cold hard plastic. But I was patient. I felt the strangest emotion, no tears, no drama. I shook the contents out, slowly at first and then greedily, cupping my right hand so that it created a deep hollow. I smiled, knowing I was ready to go.

On your marks, get set . . .

The green light. The first pill slid down my throat with ease. I continued with grace, resisting the temptation to ram each pill into my mouth avariciously. I sealed the end dramatically, holding the last tablet on the centre of my tongue.

In the name of the Father, and of the Son, and of the Holy Spirit.

Amen, was the perfect climax. It was the beginning of the end. I sat down at the edge of the bath, remembering the night when I was fifteen, remembering some of the things I'd stupidly shared with my darling Jenny. She must have hated every moment of my pathetic tales. I thought I was sharing them with someone who understood. She had held me close and kissed me softly on the cheek when I told her about the baby.

Elizabeth

The water was warm, far too hot to be in but I had to get under the water. I needed tae do something tae try and ease the pain. I thought I was going to die. It was that bad, part of me was hoping I was going to die but ah was so scared ah prayed that it wouldnae have tae come tae that.

The pain attacked me every few minutes, waves and waves of intense fury as if someone was rubbing a red hot poker up and down inside my body, tugging at my insides, ripping and pulling, in and out, in and out.

Then it would stop, just as suddenly as it came, meaning I could get up off all fours. During the attacks I was spread-eagled, the muscles in ma skinny arms holding my weight as I pushed down, my pelvis scraping off the floor as I dipped with each deep pant. I was panting heavily just so I wouldnae scream. But ah wanted tae scream. Ah wanted tae tell the whole world about my pain. When it stopped the heat would seep away from my body, disappearing like a puff of smoke, a cold sweat on my brow replacing it whilst ah leaned over the bath, my arms resting on its edge as I tried tae gather a wee bit mare strength from somewhere. Cos ah knew it was coming back. It wiznae about tae leave me alone.

And ah was right, it was only ever respite, a chance tae catch my breath and wipe the sweaty strands of hair off my face and pull the clumps off my teeth that had congregated in my mouth. Then it was upon me again, the force of it thrashing my body down onto the cold lino. I tried counting the diagonal shapes, then fitting my hands and feet into the little squares. But nothing stopped the pain. I couldnae take ma mind off it, it wouldnae let me. And it got worse and worse, until the panting wasn't enough to keep myself fae shouting.

I grabbed my dressing gown and shoved the sleeve intae my mouth, ramming it in, muffling the agony that was bursting tae come out. I retched, the thick cotton making me want to boke, to choke it back up and spit it out. I couldnae breathe, ah really couldnae breathe. It was like somebody was holding my head under a pool of water. It was like as if somebody wiz on top oav me, holding me down. Ah wished ah was dead.

Then it stopped again. I breathed quietly, relief sweeping through my aching muscles, my fingers uncurling as the message circulated through my body. I laid my head oan the edge of the bath again and started greetin, dead quietly. The last thing ah needed was anybody hearing me, knowing what ah'd been up tae. I knew what that would mean, ah'd been told often enough. It was etched inside, right at the forefront oav my mind.

If you tell anybody, a single soul, your life will be hell. You'll spend the rest of your life wishing you'd kept your mouth shut. Now you don't want that do you, my little special Princess . . .

Ah dipped my hand in the water. It was roastin. Ah pulled it back out thinking ah'd probably boil alive if ah went in. But the pain started again and ah just went for it, gathered my taut body, rigid wae the torture and ah threw myself intae the water. The shock hit me right away, but ah went with it, hoping it would take my mind off the pain in ma back. But it didnae, all it did was make ma skin go bright red. I watched it sizzle, burning wae the Dettol soaked water that was spiralling up my nose and catching in the back of my throat making me want tae vomit.

Ah looked at ma skin closely, but it was just another useless diversionary tactic. Back on all fours the water had forged a strict line of demarcation across ma body. Ah was red and white, ma arms bright pink right up to past ma elbow, ma swollen belly and hips stained with the heat. When the pain intensified again ah thrust forwards, bending ma elbows so ma hair plunged intae the water along wae ma swollen breasts. Ah looked down at them, all round and firm, and questioned the boys in school who called me names, said they wouldnae touch me wae a barge pole cos I had no tits.

Ah didnae like them being touched. They were aching; they'd been sore as anything for weeks, pulling at me, pain ripping through ma body if ah moved too quickly. It felt like ah had two big heavy boulders hanging off my chest. I tried pulling ma bra tighter but it didnae really help. Nothing helped. Everything hurt. Even Father Brennan. But that ah hadnae expected.

I screamed, ah couldnae help myself, the pain got worse, so bad I thought ma whole insides were trying tae burst out of my stomach. Ah could feel them pulling down, ah could feel myself wanting tae push the whole of my insides out. I leant over and grabbed the dressing gown again, shoving it back in ma mouth, the screech tapering off tae a stifled murmur.

But ah wiznae stupid. Ah knew. Deep down ah knew that it wiznae my insides coming out. It was my baby.

Suffer little children who come unto thee for thine is the Kingdom of Heaven.

Ah didnae know what tae dae, but I sort of did know what tae dae. Ah knew ah couldnae keep it in there any longer. Ah knew it had tae come out.

Ah climbed out oav the water, stopping tae wipe a trail oav blood away that was trickling down my legs. Ah wrapped reels and reels of toilet roll round ma arm and stuck it between my legs, wiping it without looking at it, touching it without feeling it. Ah stretched over and placed it in the toilet pan, and gravity pulled me wae it. Ah sat down, ma chin pushing against ma knees, ma knees pushing against ma chin. And me pushin and pushin and pushin. It didn't take long and ah heard it through the pain.

There was a thump. I jumped up quickly and turned around. Ah didnae have a clue whit ah was going to see. But ah couldnae see anything. Just a big pool of blood. Ah just stood there, blood flowing down my legs, my back arched, ma hands covering ma mouth, pre-empting a squeal. But there was no time; ma ma was oan her way up the stairs, shouting.

I think ah panicked. Or maybe ah wanted tae dae it, ah don't suppose ah'll ever really know. Ah flushed the toilet. And it was gone. Ma wee baby was gone. Andrew's baby was gone. Ah leant over the sink and puked.

Ah cleaned up as best ah could and delved deep intae the bathroom cabinet for a Doctor Whites. They were massive, but today ah wiznae caring. Ah got ma nightie and dressing gown on and went intae ma bedroom and laid down oan ma bed, drifting into a hazy sleep almost immediately. But ah woke up wae a start. My ma was screaming in my face about the mess. My new pink dressing gown was covered in blood. Ah don't think she ever forgave me for that.

As gentle as a swan

I shut the toilet door behind me. Mary's head was collapsed on her forearms, resting on the kitchen table. I could see from the movement in her shoulders that she was crying. I don't think she was aware that I had moved so close. I stood quietly, wishing I could lift her head up, scrape the thick brown hair from her face and hold her in my arms while I wiped the salty tears away from her cheeks.

But I couldn't make a commitment; the overdose was going to kill me. I'd never see her again. I was going to the big bad fire, for sure.

The left side of her face was crushed in the creases of her crestfallen arms, whilst the right side was clearly visible. Her long black eyelashes were batting a constant flow of tears. I watched them stream down the side of her face, trickling under her jaw line before congregating on her sleeve in a damp pool. She looked vulnerable, her skin soft and her face uninterrupted by the rigours of age. A deep shadow darkened the hollow of the socket under her eye, but even that was becoming.

Her lips formed a cartoon cupid's bow, as if the rich red colour had been swept liberally across her face with an artist's brush. My heart skipped a beat, thinking how kissable the velvet arches were. I reached out, my finger hovering over them, so close that I could feel her hot breath wrapping around my skin. Temptation was burning in swirling waves in the pit of my stomach. It was too much. I pressed the soft pad of my finger onto the curve in the middle of her top lip. Then I waited, not sure what I should do next.

'Oh for the love of God, hen. Ah think ah'm gaunae whitey big time. Any chance you can gie me a hand tae the toilet, ah don't think ah can make it oan my own. Ah feel so flippin sick.'

Mary shot to her feet, as if I'd just shoved a cattle prod between her teeth. She ran across the floor, retching, holding her skinny little hand over her mouth like a horse bag. I pushed her towards the bathroom where she vomited violently into the toilet pan. I stayed calm, focused. I held her hair from her mouth and stroked her back, ever so lightly, remembering how annoying it is to have someone touch you when all you want to do is puke. I ran my hand across her forehead. She was clammy, that indecisive way between roasting and freezing that makes you want to hug the toilet pan whilst you wallow in self-pity.

She settled into a pattern. Anxious panting and deep heavy breathing before shooting upright onto her knees, head hanging over the bowl whilst she vomited intensely, coughing and spluttering, only searching for a piece of toilet roll to wipe her mouth as she edged towards the end of the cycle. With her hot head cooling she would lean back, her body resting heavily on mine, relishing the few minutes of relative calm before it started all over again.

I sat behind Mary on the floor, and during the moments of respite she slumped wearily on top of me, entwined, the base of her spine pushed inadvertently against my pubic bone, her elbows resting on my thighs whilst I sheltered her in a human cocoon. She was heavy, not burdensome, yet I tried to shimmy my body weight from side to side. My arse was freezing, the tiles cold on a bum only protected by a thin layer of clothing.

We sat quietly, both frightened to move and risk another frenzied spell of puking. I glanced at my watch. Forty minutes came and went and I scratched my head, searching for the muzzy feeling that would signify my own ensuing death, the 'nod' that it was time to go.

Gradually Mary began to fidget. I imagined the life draining from me and transferring to her wee bones. Maybe I could save her. Instinctively I kissed the back of her head, happy that she seemed to be through the worst of it.

'For fuck sake Mary, where did that come from? I didn't

think Our Lady could vomit. Is this because of me?'

Everything was my fault. Jenny, Sadie, even Larry fuckin Spencer.

'You do if you're having a wee holiday as a human.' She craned her head and smiled.

'Thanks a million for being there for me, it's a horrid feeling being sick, ah kept thinking ah was going tae choke.'

'Don't be daft; I wasn't going to leave you to go through that on your own. Although . . . You *do* know what I was doing in here earlier?'

It wasn't really a question. I budged her out of the way and drew myself in front, my bum squeaking awkwardly along the tiles. I paused, waiting for a few moments, allowing her to find her balance.

'You do know that I'm leaving?' I spoke tenderly, but forcefully enough to make my point. I needed her to know that I wasn't messing about. I'd made my decision, I was ready to die.

'Aye hen, ah know that was your intention . . .'

'Is my intention, Mary. Nothing's changed, the game's still a bogey. I just wish it would hurry up and happen.' I rubbed my forehead, wondering what the fuckin hold up was.

'So what made you sick, have you eaten anything since you got here?'

'Ah'll tell you later hen, first things first. Ah wouldnae mind having a wee wash. Stick your hand in that bath will you, and see if the water is still warm. If you're not having it, ah may as well.'

I got up slowly and sank my hand into the waiting bath water. I drew it back quickly, reaching across to grab a towel. I dried my fingers whilst examining the little hairs that were standing to attention on the back of my hand.

'There's no way on this earth you're diving into that, unless you want to catch pneumonia on top of everything else.' Mary looked up towards me, disappointed.

'Mary, I'm not trying to do you out of my bloody bath, it's fuckin freezing. If you had balls they'd shrivel up and fall off in there. I'll need to run you another one.'

I watched her struggling to her feet. I offered her my arm.

'Are you okay?'

'What's there to say hen, everyone has crap tae deal with in their lives, ah'm no different, there isnae any Virgin Mary immunity. Anyway, forget the bath will you, ah honestly don't think ah can be bothered waiting for another one to run.'

'But some of it Mary, it's just not right is it? I'm sorry, I really am, but I guess I never thought about what you've been through. We're brought up thinking Mary's just a nice wee wifie who didn't mind anything at all that happened to her because she was up for it big time. It wouldn't have been me though. I'd have told the Holy Spirit to go and take a flying fuck to itself. But I suppose you were a brave wee lassie to have made that decision for yourself.'

'Who said ah made the decision?'

Mary lifted her heavy eyes. She looked like shit.

'Well . . . the priests and that in school . . . And the entire flippin Catholic Church. They tell us you fell pregnant and then skipped all the way to the stable in Bethlehem. How, is that not what happened?'

'Aye hen, you're right enough. Ah'm just tired, ah shouldn't have opened my big gob, ah'm just talking nonsense. It must be the fever; it's getting tae me.'

'Look Mary, I know I'm a bit of a head-case but you can talk to me, I wouldn't break your trust or anything like that. I'd take it to the grave. That's a promise, cross my heart and hope to die.'

I crossed my chest in a sweeping movement, smiling, knowing that it was just a matter of time. Mary just shivered, her entire body suddenly contorting in a series of violent shakes.

'What the fuck's the matter?' I grabbed her tightly. 'Look, stay there a minute, I'm going to call someone.'

I pulled the dressing gown tightly around her neck, trying to capture some warmth before I leapt to my feet. Mary called after me as I sidestepped between leaving her and going to the door, not having a fuckin clue whether I was coming or going. I had no-one to call.

'No, here listen hen, don't go bothering anyone else with this, ah'm just no well, ah don't suppose there's any chance of putting on a fire or something like that?'

I jumped back down beside her and grabbed her hand.

'Of course, you should have said. Let me help you into the living room, I'll put the gas fire on and get you a duvet. Don't worry, I'll look after you.'

She stared into my eyes and I had to pull away. They were swimming in guilt. How the fuck could I promise to look after her? I was in the process of going and never returning. I was waiting on the Banshee. But she didn't speak, and I helped her to her feet, letting her lean her body weight on me as we shuffled our way from the bathroom to my raspberry room at the front of the house.

'Here, sit down there for a wee minute, I'll go and get you a cover and a pillow.'

Directing her towards the floor I helped keep her steady while she folded her legs and sat on her bum in front of the fireplace. Weakly she drew her knees up to her chest. I ignited the gas fire, checking that its flames had erupted before kissing her gently on the forehead. Patting Mary's head encouragingly I swept past her, heading to the bedroom. When I came back she was facing the fire, warming her long spindly hands against the living flame.

'Here, put this around you, it'll warm you up.'

She obliged, grabbing the cover whilst pushing backwards so she could rest her spine against the leather chair. I lifted a pillow and puffing it up, placed it carefully behind her head, making sure the duvet stretched over her completely, leaving no stone unturned, no part of Mary unprotected.

'Thanks.'

She said it meekly but her smile was warm.

'It's no trouble. Will you be all right for a minute whilst I go and put a jumper on? I'm freezing with you hogging the duvet for yourself.'

Mary laughed and, patting her hand on the top of the duvet, made me an offer I had craved for what had felt like a hundred years.

'Dae you want me to budge up? There's plenty of room; we could always coory in thegether?'

'What and risk getting your lurgy? No offence Mary but I want to go out in style, in Bette Davis fashion, with a dry martini and a cigarette. I don't want to be retching all over the living room carpet. Which reminds me, do you need a bowl or do you think you've puked enough for one day?'

I laughed, teasing her with a colourful vomiting motion.

'Na, ah think that's me for the minute, ah could really dae wae brushing my teeth though. Any chance you could gie me a hand with that. If it's not too much trouble that is . . .'

'Oh shut up will you, of course it's not too much trouble. Give me two minutes and I'll sort it.'

I went into the bedroom and picked up the pile of clothes lying in a heap at the side of my bed. My *mur*d*ur* clothes, the outfit I'd prepared for killing Larry Spencer. I suppose it was both ironic and fitting that the carefully chosen clothing would share in my own death, in the role of shroud. I shoved the black jumper over my head quickly. With a little warmth secured I slipped out of my joggies and pants and put on a fresh pair before pulling on my Spencer killing combats. I kicked the discarded pants across the floor, remembering that sometimes Andrew had to keep the old ones, because of the mess they were in, he said.

'Things just seem tae disappear in this house,' my mother would say. 'God knows where half oav Elizabeth's underwear gets tae.'

Mum . . . Don't ask God, ask me. Ask me, I'll tell you. Ask me, ask me.

I buttoned my fly then refocused on Mary, filling a bowl of water in the kitchen before grabbing some toothpaste and a new toothbrush from under the bathroom sink. It was a replacement brush I was keeping for myself; I'd certainly never intended to have anyone staying over with me, least of all Mary the Virgin Mother of God.

'Right M, do you want me to put the toothpaste on the brush for you, you look as if you've got about as much strength as a new born sparrow.'

'Aye could you hen? Ah'd really appreciate it if you did.'

I squeezed some paste on the brush and handed it to her. She brushed softly, her wrist slowly pushing her hand back and forth across her mouth.

'Oh cheers, that's so much better, ma mouth felt clatty. Ah don't suppose it would be pushing my luck too much if ah was tae ask you to get me a drink of water?'

She smiled, precipitating with kindness any excuse I might have had for a wee moan at her.

'Aye, but fuck's sake Mary what are you like? What did your last slave die of?'

I went to get it anyway, glad to be able to do something wholesome in my final moments. I ran the tap and then changed my mind, kneeling down and reaching into the cupboard to find the bottle of brandy that Spencer had given me for Christmas. For the second time in a day he was redeeming himself. I unscrewed the lid and poured it liberally into two tumblers, enjoying the hypnotic music as the nectar gushed from the bottle.

'Here, get that down your neck. You'll be feeling right as rain in no time.'

Mary raised the glass to her lips. She recoiled as soon as she tasted it, the sticky liquid spilling from her chin to the front of her dressing gown. She jumped to her feet.

'Oh no, will you look at the mess ah've made oav your dressing gown. Ah'm really sorry, ah'll go and wash it the now.'

Elizabeth, what the hell's been going oan, will you look at the mess oav your new dressing gown, this is an absolute disgrace. You should be ashamed of yourself.

I turned away. She was forcing me back. Dragging me down a road I didn't want to have to travel. Mary stood at the junction, directing the route.

'Elizabeth honey whit's going oan in that heid oav yours and please don't say *nuttin* . . .' She turned her hand over, one palm facing the ceiling as she carried on.

'You've wasted too much time saying nothing, it's time you gave yourself a fighting chance. Ah'm here if you want tae talk about it.'

She settled back down onto the floor, folding her legs into a cross, dragging her body like a crab across the carpet until she was facing me. Reaching out with both hands she grabbed mine, rubbing my knuckles reassuringly. Her warmth was inside my heart in an instant. She was where I'd always begged her to be.

'Where the fuck do I start Mary?'

'Wherever, whatever, say the first thing that comes intae your heid. It diznae matter, not one iota.'

'I think that was the worst day cos it put everything into perspective.'

I nodded my head at Mary, peeling my hand from her grasp to touch the wet fabric of the dressing gown.

'It let me know that there was nobody out there for me.' I dropped my arm and it fell wearily to my side as if it didn't belong to me.

'They just pretended they were, but the reality was they were taking the fuckin piss. But I was too scared and too fuckin stupid to know any different. And to be honest Mary, you weren't much fuckin help were you?' I ran my fingers through my hair sharply, aware that I'd said more than I'd wanted to.

'Okay hen, ah deserved that, but come oan, ah cannae take the blame for aw oav it. There were other forces at work.'

'Aye, getting to fuckin work on me. Have you any idea what that's like?'

'No hen, ah don't suppose ah have, that's why it would be better if you tellt me.'

She looked at me, saying nothing. I guess that meant she was willing to listen but we both knew that she already knew it all. She was always there. Every single time it happened I'd be praying, giving homage to the Virgin, until I made it through to the other side.

Elizabeth

'Whit dae you mean ah look like Mr Potato Heid? That's no very nice Elizabeth, especially when ah've goat you such a nice prezzie. Ah've a good mind tae take it right back so ah have.'

Ah looked at Andrew, worried that ah'd upset my pal. Ma ma always said you shouldnae ever go upsetting your pals. They're the people that you know you can trust. Ah didnae really care about the prezzie, he could take it back as long as he didnae fall out wae me.

'Ah wiz only joking Andrew, you look nothing like a Mr Potato Heid, they're all ugly and squidgy, you're nice. Here, you can have the book, ah'm no bothered.'

Ah picked my prized possession up and handed it over in his direction; it didnae look aw that special anymore anyway. Ah shimmied along the bed so ah could get closer tae him, close enough so he wiz touching my arm. Ah could feel his warmth right through my jumper but it wiznae burny hot, it was nice hot, like the hot water bottle when it's cooled down enough so you can take it out oav the cover and hold it oan tae your leg when you're having a growing pain. Ma ma always lets me dae that, she says it saves me having tae come away out oav my bed and come through tae her an ma da's room and get them out oav bed when ah cannae sleep for the pain. Andrew nudged me and smiled an ah felt a whole lot better.

'Don't be daft, ah'm only kidding you on, ah don't want the book back it's yours, ah bought it for you cos it's perfect for you. Anyway, Mr Potato Heid's better than calling me a big ugly troll, now that would have us falling out.'

He moved the arm that was touching mine and used his fingers to stroke ma arm, pushing my jumper up tae my elbow. His fingers were all light and fluffy, tickly but not tickly, annoying but nice.

'You know what Elizabeth, you're such a skinny little thing ain't you, just a wee skinny wean.'

Ah pulled my shoulders back. 'Ah'm no that wee, everywan says ah'm getting bigger each day. Ah'm the tallest lassie in ma class by a mile and that's saying something cos that Michelle McLaughlin's like a giant.'

'Ach ah know, ah'm sorry hen, ah didnae mean tae upset you.'

Andrew took his hand fae my arm and ruffled my hair. My ma had let me wear it down the day. She let me dae that a lot in the summer but ah always had tae tie it up for school in case ah came back wae nits. Ma brother did wance and ma ma nearly had a nanny roony. Ah didnae fancy going through aw that drama again over a few beasties.

'Now listen tae me Elizabeth. There's no way you and I are gaunae fall out, dae you hear me?'

Ah blushed wondering if he was just saying that cos he thought ah wiz about tae start greetin or summit like that.

'Ah know, we're best pals, we'll be pals forever, no matter whit.'

Andrew's face went aw serious and he didnae say anything for a couple of seconds but then he grabbed me by both shoulders and pulled me round so ah wiz sitting in front oav him, facing him oan the bed. He was quite rough and ah nearly let out a cry but ah kept it in just in case he got annoyed wae me and fell out wae me after all. But it wiznae sore when he started tae stroke ma hair. It was just nice. Nice and soft, like the way ah brushed ma doll's hair, being extra careful so ah didnae hurt her. Ah looked at his face expecting a smile but ah never found wan. He was looking aw serious like the way ma dad does when he's about tae tell me something really important.

'Elizabeth. You and me, we're no gaunae fall out, we'll never fall out, no if you're a good wee girl and dae whit ah tell you all the time. Remember whit your ma said, ah'm the boss no matter whit, the decisions are always mine, even if you think that they are wrong. Mine's is the last word.'

'Ah know that Andrew, ah'm no daft, ma ma tells me that every morning afore we leave the front door. But ah'm no a wee girl, ah keep telling you that.'

Ah threw ma arms down ontae my knees, fed up that he still wiznae listening tae me. Adults seemed tae be like that. They were always right and didnae listen if they didnae want tae.

'Ah know, sorry hen, you're a big girl now and ah'm gaunae treat you like a big girl fae now oan. Ah just didnae know if you were ready to be grown up but if you're sure you are?' He paused, staring at me, waiting for an answer. Ah looked at him, shrugging my shoulders wae excitement.

'Aye, oav course ah am.'

'Good, that's whit ah like tae hear but as long as you remember that ah'm the boss, even though ah'm treating you like a grown up. And you cannae tell your ma that ah think you're a grown up cos then she might think you're big enough tae look after yourself.'

Ah closed my eyes thinking about how horrid it would be being in the house on ma own every day. Ma brothers were older and they didnae need looking after ma da said. Anyhow they were never in; ma da says they were like soldiers going out every day fae dawn tae dusk, coming home filthy like they'd been fighting in a war. Ah wouldnae want tae have tae hang about wae them, an ah wouldnae be allowed anyway, girls couldnae be in their gang. Ma answer tae Andrew wiz simple.

'Ure the boss.'

We didnae talk for ages after that. Andrew just let me get oan wae playing wae my tracing book. It was magic, and ah raced through it determined tae savour every moment oav it afore the day was finished. But ah never goat tae finish whit wae Andrew tugging at me telling me it wiz time for lunch.

'Ah don't want anything Andrew, ah'm no hungry, ah'll

just eat some mare crisps.'

'Eh, whit were you saying earlier about daein everything that ah tellt you? Now c'mon, we're gaunae eat something then ah've goat another surprise for you.'

Ah was a sucker for the word surprise.

'How, whit is it?'

'Ah'll tell you in a wee minute, first things first though come an' help me make the rolls and banana.'

Ah gave in without moaning. Ma da had always said there wiznae any point in moaning cos if an adult says you were tae dae something then they wanted you tae dae it. Nae amount of greetin about it was gaunae make them change their mind. Me and Andrew ate our rolls in silence. But he kept looking at me, all funny, just like Mr Potato Heid again but ah didnae dare say it in case ah goat intae any mare trouble like the last time. There wiznae any point in upsetting him. He was the Boss.

'Are you done wae that plate and cup?'

Ah didnae answer Andrew in words, ah just handed him the stuff and then waited for him to speak. He looked like he wiz about tae say something else. And he did.

'Gies two minutes till ah take this stuff through tae the kitchen and then ah'm gaunae gie you another surprise. But this wan's a secret, you've got tae swear oan your mammy's life that you'll never tell a soul, if you dae lots oav very very bad things'll happen tae you and you'll end up getting taken away an you'll never see your ma and da again.'

He looked serious, like the priest when he wiz daein the magic bit in Mass when he hid tae concentrate really hard cos he wiz turning the bread and wine into the actual body and blood of Jesus.

'Oav course ah'll no tell anyone, you're ma pal.'

'Aye hen, ah'm your best pal, the best pal you'll ever have.'

Ah wiz excited and then dead disappointed all at wance

when Andrew came back intae the room. He didnae have anything in his hands, not a brass farthing ma da would say. Then ah decided ah should jump up anyway as he could have hid it in his poacket. Ah imagined a diamond hairclip. Like the wan ah'd just traced oan my tracing book, the wan entwined in the Princess's hair. Something like that would be heaven.

'Hoi, whit's up wae your face? You look like you've just had tae swallow a cold brussel sprout.'

Ah thought about that for a second and ah felt sick. Ah hated sprouts, everybody did, except my ma who thought that just cos she wanted about fifty oan her plate that the rest oav us should want the same for our Christmas dinner. Ma da wiz dead funny though, he used tae grab them oaf our plates when ma ma wiznae looking and hide them in a napkin until he could get rid oav them for us. He was good like that ma da, a bit mental but no in a getting carted off tae the loony bin kinda way, in a good way. Every year my ma was clueless thinking we were all just dead happy whilst we were eating our dinner but every time she turned her back we were all giggling trying tae shove mare turkey in our mouths so she wouldnae hear us.

Ah just told Andrew that ah wiz fine even though ah wiznae really. Ah didnae know whit ah could say to lie so ah just didnae bother saying anything about it. It wiz best no tae look too greedy. Naebody likes a greedy child. The priest always said that every single time he came down tae the school.

'Good, well you'll be feeling up tae getting your wee surprise then. Your special surprise.'

Ah went skipping across the room tae him right away. The diamond clasp wiz inside his poacket, ah just knew it.

'Hoi you, where dae you think you're going? Just get yourself back oan that bed pronto and turn your back tae me.'

Ah did exactly whit he said, closing my eyes tightly shut when he said that if ah didnae ah wiz getting nothing. Ah waited for ages though and nothing happened. Andrew didnae come near me, but ah could still hear him, ah could hear him breathing so ah knew that he wiz still there. Ah wiz just about tae turn around, he must have known cos ah shrugged my shoulders as ah got ready tae move, when he put his hand oan my right shoulder pressing down hard so that it wiz nearly sore. But ah didnae mind, at least he hadnae forgoatten about me.

'Are your eyes still shut? Tight shut?'

'Aye, ah promise, ah can only see black.'

That wiznae really true ah could see orange ripples flashing behind my eyelids but ah didnae think he needed tae know that.

'Okay then, turn around slowly. WITHOUT opening your eyes.'

His voice was firm and he raised it tae make sure ah wouldnae open my eyes and look at whitever it wiz he had fir me. It wiz all right, he didnae need tae shout at me, ah would have done it anyway, he wiz the boss. Ah did whit ah wiz tellt. It wiz as simple as that. So ah turned around, guided by Andrew's hand and he pushed me intae position, which ah think wiz right in front oav him, then ah knew for sure that ah wiz right in front of him when he pushed ma legs apart and stood in between them dead close, his hand oan ma left shoulder, ma legs open wide. Ah felt embarrassed and wondered if ah should be sitting like that. My ma wiz always shouting at me when ah wiz daein cartwheels in the front garden cos she said it wiznae right tae let anybody see my pants. Ah thought about pulling away but then ah didnae cos Andrew wiz the boss and he didnae seem to mind me sitting like that.

'Can ah get ma surprise now Andrew?'

Ma voice sounded all squeaky, like ma pal Theresa McCartney's wee kitten when she'd just goat it and it wiz all wee and scared and just cried aw the time like wan oav they dollies that you take its dummy out and it just greets and greets until you put it back in again.

'You can, but you've goat tae remember that this is a

special surprise and that you're no allowed tae tell anyboady about it.'

Andrew squeezed my neck and it wiz quite sore. Ah didnae feel as if ah wanted the present anymore so ah tried tae get up, keeping ma eyes shut in case ah goat intae trouble.

'Hey, little girl, sorry, ah didnae mean tae dae that, ah just get scared that ah might have tae stoap seeing you and ah would hate that. Ah would miss ma best friend mare than anything else in the whole wide world. Ah didnae mean tae be so rough.'

He bent down and kissed the top of ma head softly, nuzzling his nose intae ma hair like the way ma dog Misty used tae. It felt nice, and tickly so ah laughed. Ah didnae want tae lose ma best pal either.

'Right, now we're friends again ah want you tae wait until ah say it's okay and then you've tae open your eyes. Open them wide and have a good look at your big prezzie. Okay?'

'Okay Andrew, but can we hurry up now, ah'm dying tae know whit you've goat for me. Is it a diamond hair clasp?'

'No hen, it's no, it's much better than that. Now open your eyes.'

Ah just sat there looking right at it cos ah didnae have a clue whit it wiz. It wiz like nothing ah'd ever seen before. Well it wiz a wee bit like something ah'd seen before but ah knew it couldnae be that. It couldnae be. Ah know ah looked disappointed but ah tried dead hard not tae be and ah laughed, hoping that it wiz just a joke and Andrew had ma real prezzie hidden away behind his back.

'Whit are you laughing at, dae you no like it? Well that's fine if you don't, ah'll just phone your ma at work and tell her that you don't want tae be ma pal anymare and that she'll have to gie up her work tae look aefter you.'

Ah goat a shock by whit he said and it made me get all panicky like ah do sometimes if ah lose my ma's hand in the middle oav the Barras an there's just hunners and hunners oav folk in the way and ah'm scared ah'll never see her again.

'My ma cannae gie up her work, she needs the money so we can all go to the game oan a Saturday. Ma da says the season tickets cost loads and loads and we need the extra money tae help pay for them. And ma brothers would go mental, they always come tae the games as well.'

'Aye well it's your choice hen. Now dae you want your present or no?'

Ah looked at the big thing in front oav me and wanted mare than anything tae say no but ah knew whit saying no would mean, ah knew all the trouble it would cause and ah didnae want tae be the wan that messed everything up. My ma would have been so sad, and ah've only ever seen her sad wance, the time when we all goat sent to stay wae my auntie cos she'd lost her baby. Ah never understood it, ah didnae even know she had a baby that she wiz able to leave anywhere. Ah asked ma auntie where she lost it but she told me no tae be cheeky and tae stoap asking questions or ah'd get myself in trouble wae God. Grown-ups were confusing, an Andrew wiz confusing me an all.

Ah looked at ma prezzie. It was pink, but it was purple. A purpley kind of blue like the handle oav my brother's tennis racket. But ah knew it wiznae a tennis racket cos it wiz moving aw by itself.

'Is it alive?'

Andrew laughed. 'At this moment little wan, as alive as it's been in a long time.'

Ah wondered where it'd been, where he'd been keeping it all day. It can't always have been in his poacket, it would have been uncomfortable when he sat down.

'Here, come a bit closer tae it and you'll be able tae see it better.'

Ah did whit he said and leaned forward and when ah did it jumped right up in the air, pinging up and down like it wiz a big tongue wagging.

'Look Elizabeth, he's goat a wee face and he wants tae talk to you. That's whit he's trying tae tell you.'

Ah looked right at the end tae where he wiz pointing and he wiz right, but it wiz a funny face, he had just one eye, or maybe it wiz a mouth. Ah wiznae sure at all, but then ah knew it wiz a mouth cos it started tae drool and Andrew rubbed his finger over it tae soak it up afore it spillt oan the flair. But he didnae wipe his finger, he just held it out in front oav me.

'Here, that's for you. Lick my finger.'

Ah didnae know what he wiz talking about. Whit did he mean it wiz for me?

'He wants you tae have it. He's gieing you a wee drink of his special juice.'

Ah didnae want a wee drink oav his special juice. Ah was thirsty for Irn Bru.

'No thanks, can you tell him that ah'm no thirsty.'

'Ah would if a could, but ah can't so ah won't.'

Ah laughed cos that's what everybody says when they are trying tae act smart in the playground. But Andrew wiznae being smart cos he tellt me that he couldnae tell it ah wiznae thirsty cos it needed me tae tell it all by myself.

'You're a big girl now, you keep telling me that. Now come here and tell him that you don't want a drink.'

'What will ah say, will ah just say ah'm no thirsty?'

'No hen, he cannae hear if you talk tae him like that, you have tae dae it a special way, you have to put him right inside your mouth and then he'll read your mind. He's not just magic he's dead clever an all.'

Ah didnae like the look oav it. Ah didnae want tae touch it. Ah didnae think it wiz right. Something wiz telling me it wiz wrong. Ma brothers had wee tiny things like that in their trousers and ma ma always went mental if they touched it. She said they'd go tae the big bad fire if they didnae take their bloody hands oaf it. She said if she caught them daein it she would definitely tell Father McGonigle and that would be it. And that would be it for me an all if anywan found out about this. Ah looked up above; the priest had said at ma first confession that God wiz watching me every minute oav every day and that he'd know right away if ah was committing a sin. Then the Virgin Mary would be sad. Sinning made her very sad and people whistling made her cry.

Ah didnae want tae dae anything tae upset her. Ah looked over tae the door. The door tae the secret room. The snib was drawn right across the lock and ah didnae think ah would be able tae unlock it myself. But ah had tae go. This wiznae right.

'Andrew, ah want tae go outside now ah don't want this present, ah don't feel well.'

'Fine, oan you go, ah'll see you later.'

'Thanks, sorry about the present.'

Ah stood up, but he wiz still standing right in front oav me so ah couldnae move away. Ah didnae like it, it wiz a horrible feeling like ah couldnae breathe right or something like that.

'Can you open the door for me please?'

'No hen, sorry ah cannae, ah'm busy the now. You'll have tae get it yourself.'

'But ah cannae get it, it's too high up for me. Please Andrew can you let me out, can you just open the door for me please?'

Ah wiz getting dead scared, ah just had this really horrible feeling that ah needed tae get out. Ah couldnae breathe right. Ah'd felt a wee bit like it before, wance, when ah'd got ma head stuck inside ma polo neck jumper and ah wiz in the room myself and ah couldnae get out. Ah didnae think ah wiz ever gaunae get out until ah screamed so much ma da came running in and goat the jumper off in a split second. Ah wanted ma da now. Ah wanted him tae come and get ma head out oav the hole.

'Here calm down you, don't forget ah'm your pal, your best pal. Ah'll look after you, don't you worry about that. Of course ah'll open the door for you. Ah promise, cross my heart and hope tae die.'

Ah watched closely as he crossed his heart, trying tae concentrate on what he wiz daein and saying and not oan the locked door. 'But first oav all Elizabeth, ah need you tae dae something for me. Ah need you to dae something and then promise tae keep it tae yourself cos if you tell anybody your ma and da will throw you intae a home an' they'll lock the door oan you and toss away the key. Now, does that seem fair pal? You happy tae help me out and ah'll help you out?'

Give and take, ah'd heard ma da saying that hunners oav times. Friendship's all about give and take, if your pal does something fir you then you've goat tae make sure that you dae something for them in return. Ah wiz still swaying when Andrew reminded me that he wiz the boss oav me anyway.

'Aye, all right then, whit dae you want me tae dae?'

Ah figured it didnae really matter just as long as ah could get outside intae the warm summer air. The secret room wiz cold and dark and it didnae smell very nice. Ah wanted tae smell the roses and pick daisies and buttercups and feel the sun soak intae ma back as ah bent over the grass.

'Well for starters, ah need you tae give this wee guy a kiss. A proper kiss now, so you need tae put him right intae your mouth.'

Ah looked at it. It looked even angrier now and ah wiz just wondering if it would hurt me when Andrew said it wouldnae.

'Don't worry it's no gaunae bite. He's friendly; he likes you better than me. Now c'mon hurry up, as soon as we get this over with the sooner we can go oot and make some daisy chains.'

Ah was still pondering, my lips just centimetres away but all puckered like they were wae the brussel sprouts. But ah'd rather have had a plate oav them than this. Then Andrew just made me dae it, ah think he wiz in a hurry oar sumthing like that. He held ma hair at each side oav ma head and pushed ma mouth ontae his thing. Ah kept ma lips and ma eyes closed and when ma skin touched his ah juddered. It wiz all wet but smooth and soft. Ah didnae dae anything though, ah just sat there wae ma eyes closed.

'Elizabeth you have tae open your mouth now. He wants

tae go inside and he won't take no for an answer, just like me? Remember ah'm the boss.'

Ah didnae want tae but ah did. Ah just did it cos he wanted me tae. Give and take. It felt as if ah had a big massive gobstopper in ma mouth. Ah nearly choked and ah coughed but Andrew just laughed, he seemed tae think it wiz funny, but ah didnae, ah didnae think he should be laughing at me. Then he just kept telling me that ah wiz a good girl, a very good girl. He wiz moaning. Ah wondered if ah wiz hurting him but ah couldnae speak tae ask him. There wiznae any room for my tongue tae move. So ah opened ma eyes. Ah goat a big fright. There was a big mass of ginger curly hair at each side oav the thing. Ah didnae like it. Ah didnae like any oav it so ah started tae pray to the Virgin Mary that he would stoap. Ah'd only said two Hail Marys when he did, he stoapped. Ah thought it wiz over. Ah thought it wiz all over but it wiz just beginning. It wiz just the beginning when he told me tae lie down on top oav the bed and take off ma pants.

Sinners and saints

I got up off the floor making straight for the bay window. I stood by it, breathing as calmly as I could, even though my heart was racing ten to the fuckin dozen. Mary followed me. I didn't doubt that she would.

The view from the window was sensational. It was a crisp November evening, the sky clear and black. I put the fingers of my right hand on the window, my knuckles bent and my joints splayed, my fingers curling like a spider's legs. The glass was cold. I moved my hand up so I was holding it in front of my eyes, a human telescope through which I blinked sharply and waited for the hundreds of different coloured lights across the city to wink back at me. For a second I felt trapped; they were laughing at my self imposed imprisonment, sniggering because my shield was as clear as the glass and they could see right through me.

'It's a pretty impressive view from here Elizabeth, ah can see for miles and miles.'

Mary put her arm loosely around my waist and then squashed her nose against the window, trying to get closer than me. The view stretched as far as the eye could see and forever beyond, the city lights eventually consumed by the vastness of the dark Campsie Fells which came into their own in daylight.

The air was clear, not freezing cold, but chilled. I could feel it lift the hairs on my arms as it snuck its way in through the cracks in the old timber windows, smell and taste it as it engulfed the rest of my senses. It surprised me. I couldn't hear it, I couldn't hear November. The local kids were slacking, normally they were lighting their bonfires and setting off bangers and fireworks for days and days before the 5th, the night when the air was thick and matted, smouldering deeply into your lungs, making you cough and splutter yet tempting you into parks and gardens all the same. The mere taste of it meant you were still alive.

I turned around and laughed at Mary's wrinkly nose, squashed against the pane of glass, turning upwards like Tabitha from *Bewitched*.

'It is a great view but I can't believe it's that impressive for someone like you. This can't be a patch on what you can see from the pearly gates.'

I pushed my finger into the side of her nose and it squeaked loudly, her flesh shimmying across the glass. I made a mental note never to do that to her if she had a runny nose. She looked from left to right and then to the left again, assessing what was in front of her before she made her judgement.

'Kind of, but kind of not. It's hard tae explain, but only cos ah cannae explain, I'm no meant tae say anything about what happens and that.'

'Aye, so you keep telling me but you may as well, it's not as if you aren't in a whole load of trouble already and it's not as if I'm going to be around to tell anyone anyway, I'm in the throes of suicide.'

'Ah know exactly whit you're saying hen but ah'm not falling for that. Ah'm no stupid, I managed to get a first class degree in psychology and a PhD after I got settled into life in heaven. I'm not just some daft wee lassie from the desert you know.'

'No way, turn it up Mary, did you really?'

'Eh . . . no . . . Ah thought you were supposed tae be the quick witty one here. Ah'm taking the piss Elizabeth.'

She smiled, but not just as sweetly; there was a certain sense of devilment about her.

'Aye very good Mary, do yourself a favour though and keep your crap jokes to yourself in future.'

'Aye ah will, ah'll save them for someone who cares. You're too stubborn tae laugh at anything I've got to say anyway.'

'Right enough, I've got such a lot to laugh about right now.'

I turned around to look at her and she covered her mouth, ashamed.

'Sorry hen, ah got carried away trying tae take your mind off what you just told me. That Andrew was evil. I understand how much he hurt you, ah really do.'

Her hand was wrapped around her own throat, her grip so tight that her knuckles were white and knobbly, the bones protruding from her skin like little ski slopes.

'Let's forget the rules Elizabeth, he cannae get away with the way he's treated you. We need tae come up wae a plan, a good plan, good enough tae sort him out once and for all. He's evil, it's time he had a wee taste of his own medicine.'

I was shocked. I had expected a pull-yourself-together-he'll-get-punished-in-the-afterlife type of reaction from Mary. Not this.

'Mary have you lost the plot all together? The very reason you came down here in the first place was to stop me doing something stupid to the now seemingly innocent whiter than white Larry Spencer. Have you gone completely mental after just one sip of brandy?'

'Look, ah'm not suggesting we kill him, just sort him out. I think we need tae put the frighteners intae him, make sure he knows that he hasn't got away with what he did tae you.'

'And how exactly do we do that, tell him he's been a naughty boy and that he's not to do it again?'

I laughed. Mary's idea of redemption was sure to be different from mine.

'Don't be so sarcastic Elizabeth, ah'm not thinking about asking him to pop down tae confession, ah'm talking about making him understand that what he did was unforgiveable and that at some point in the no too distant future he'll need tae pay for whit he did tae you.'

'Jesus Mary, by doing what exactly?'

'Have patience my dear little Elizabeth. Ah'll tell you whit we're gaunae dae once we get there.'

'When we get . . . *where* . . . exactly?'

'To Andrew's *obviously*, how else are we going to deal wae this? Got tae go straight tae where the action's happening hen.'

'Mary it's after midnight, not exactly the best time to be planning an expedition. Anyway, I don't have a clue where the fucker is. I've spent every fuckin day since I toddled off to London at sixteen years of age trying to pretend that he doesn't exist. And maybe he doesn't. He could be dead for all I know. Let's just leave it for now, until we calm down at least.'

'Na Elizabeth we need to do something the now. C'mon.'

She clapped her hands loudly then rallied her fists together in front of my face like the big daft bear from the Jungle Book.

'The sooner we get started Elizabeth the sooner we can deal with this. Ah'll need tae borrow some more of your clothes.'

I snorted loudly.

'What, as opposed to turning up with your Virgin Mary robes on? Here that's an idea; wear them, that'll scare the shit out of him so much you'll not even need to say anything to him.'

'Elizabeth, is it any wonder that none of your plans actually work?' She shook her head as if I'd just told the teacher two twos were five.

'Thankfully with me in charge this plan will deliver exactly what we need.'

I shuffled my feet.

'What do you mean *this plan*? Does this mean you've got one already?'

'Aye, although ah'm still working on the final details. But this'll be a good one, not like any of your pathetic attempts so far.'

I sat down on the settee. I was hallucinating; the overdose was finally coming to fruition. I was dying and spiralling downwards into hell, home to Mary's devilish alter ego. I'd fallen asleep in the arms of an angel and woken up on the wrong side of the bed. Mary was full of anger, seething at what he had done. But she'd known all along; my outburst shouldn't have been a big surprise.

'Mary this is great, you supporting me like this but I don't really understand it. You're acting as if this is the first you'd heard about it. I know this was a big secret that I'd kept from the world, but not from you, you're supposed to know everything that goes on and I prayed to you every single fuckin time he came near me. There can't have been a communication error all the time.'

Mary grabbed my hand and lowered herself onto the seat. I sat uneasily on the edge of the cushion, not really sure what to do with myself. After a few moments she tugged on my hand and turned me round to face her. I realised that she needed a moment and I gave it to her. But it felt like a long moment the way she was looking into my eyes, reading the last page of the book. I was exposed and as a consequence she'd turned into the evil twin.

'Elizabeth. Ah've got something tae tell you. Ah really shouldnae be opening ma big gob but ah've got tae. There comes a time when the least thing you have tae worry about is the consequences.'

'So what are you saying, you're a fuckin rebel? Big fuckin wows Mary. Congratulations.' I created a wee respite in the conversation, long enough to pull my hand away from hers. 'Don't look so worried, I know you're in loads of trouble, but you're the bloody Virgin Mary, they're not exactly going to banish you for having a couple of days off your work. Do they not do sickies in heaven then?'

Mary sighed deeply, the air she finally exhaled stirring the hair resting over one side of her face. She answered, removing the hair from her eye and tucking it behind her ear.

'Ah don't know about that Elizabeth. I'm not even

supposed tae still be here, never mind talking tae you about . . . *things*.'

'Good code name Mary, I suspect anyone listening in on the conversation won't have a clue what you're going on about.'

'Aye your dead right hen they probably can't understand a word ah'm saying wae this Glesga accent . . .'

'Very funny.' I smiled at her. 'Thanks for lightening up a bit. I'm the one who's supposed to be upset. Don't forget that it was me that was reliving my childhood traumas fifteen minutes ago. I'm tired Mary, I just want to get this over with. I need to move on, to go to sleep and let myself go. Enough's enough; it's been one fuck of a week. One fuck of a life. Come on, please, lie down with me whilst I go to sleep. Hopefully it won't take too long.'

'You know whit hen, ah don't think ah could sleep a wink, not wae all this on my mind, it's driving me nuts. Ah cannae believe it was so bad for you and ah know you havenae even told me the half of it. And the worst thing about it is that it's aw my bloody fault. If it wiznae for me not being there for you then none of it would have happened.'

'Mary, I'm not sure if I picked you up wrong there, and please God tell me that I did, but did you just say that it was *all your fault*? You are actually sitting right in front of me and admitting that you could have stopped it all?'

My voice tapered off to a whisper, the audio snatched by my fingertips pulling harshly on my bottom lip. My nail ran coarsely across the soft bit in the middle and I winced. We both stood up, our bodies square in the middle of the room.

'MAAARRRRYYYYY! I'm fuckin talking to you. What's the story, what are you talking about? How the fuck can it be all your fault?'

'Calm down, please Elizabeth.'

She reached out to touch me but I backed away forcing her to continue.

'You're no understanding whit ah mean. Aye, ah knew it

was gaunae happen, ah could see whit Andrew was gearing up tae do so that's why ah snuck down tae your bedroom. Ah just wanted tae gie you a wee sign that ah was thinking about you. Ah'm no in charge of Andrew, or that prick Brennan for that matter. Ah'm only in charge of you so ah couldnae stop them fae daein anything but ah could gie you a wee visit tae let you know ah was close by and then intervene if you strayed intae something unforgiveable.'

'Oh right, so I plot tae kill Larry fuckin Spencer and you ride in oan a white horse tae save him. Nice one. Aye right enough Mary, I feel incredibly wanted.'

'For goodness sake will you listen tae me for a flippin minute? Ah wiz saving you, no him. Ah wiz saving you from being a killer. Look ah tried tae help you but it's no like that, ah'm no allowed tae just interfere wae everything that's going on doon here. I wiznae supposed tae say anything tae you when you were thinking about running away and leaving Collette in Ireland but ah did. Ah knew you needed tae be on Carravindoon to save Laura.'

I stretched in front of her, pushing my heels into the warmth of the carpet.

'Mary what the fuck are you talking about? Ah prayed tae you all the fuckin time in Ireland and you did absolutely fuck all tae help me.'

'Aye ah did, ah threw a fuckin life-size statue of myself in your face at that wee grotto so you would know ah wiz real and stop being such an idiot. The lassies aw needed you, even Sadie. She had tae know when she was dying that you'd find a way tae make sure Laura wiz all right. She couldnae have known that if Paddy had killed her without you there.'

I knelt down on the floor.

'Ah'm sorry Elizabeth, I really am. Ah should have insisted that we saved you from those fuckin monsters, or ah should have just taken it upon myself tae come down and dae something about it but it diznae work like that, everything's part oav a bigger plan and sometimes they're as complicated as yours. Ah might have given birth to the son of God but ah'm not equal by any stretch of the imagination. My role in life is as fragile as yours. Ah'm sorry hen, ah really am, but ah'm making up for it now that's for sure.'

'And how exactly are you doing that then Mary? It's a bit late anyway as for the hundredth time I'm not going to be here much longer, I'm going down.'

'Well, ah'm going tae see what ah can dae to deal with Andrew and ah've already gone tae work on saving you hen, there will be no imminent death, aw that puking in the toilet was me transferring all the poison fae your system intae mine. You're not going tae die, there are a few years ahead of you yet.'

She smiled triumphantly. I punched her under the chin. She fell in instalments and instead of running I stayed to watch, riding high in the pleasure of watching the bitch get what she deserved. She drifted in slow motion, her upper body flopping backwards before spilling over and folding in half, the motion propelling her forwards then backwards, her shoulders gravitating to the reverse, her knees finally buckling as consciousness left her. Like Zebedee. Her hair was the last to fall and when it did it settled on her face, its length caressing her exposed chest, the pink dressing gown now finally resigned to where it belonged, in a heap on the floor.

The whole episode was silent, except at the very climax. I had expected a thud, and it arrived on cue, but I wasn't expecting the crack. That was a total surprise.

Cccccrrrrrrrrrrrrrrrraaaaaaaaaaaaaaaaacccccccccccccccccccckkkkkkkkkk

Then the sound was eerie. I was in a wide open field, the rain thundering down in torrents and the wind howling so loudly that the only sense I could acknowledge was hearing. All that intense noise and then nothing, as if God had suddenly switched the volume off.

Cccllliiiiiccccckkkk

There was nothing, not even the noise of my own breath or my thumping heart. It stayed like that for a few seconds and then it was as if God had turned a tap on. I could hear a little stream trickling by in the distance.

Tcchhhhhh tcchhhhhh tcchhhhhhh

I was drawn towards it, enticed by a desire to see where it lapped the shore, lacing shingled lips in tranquil recurring motions. I went without reluctance, wandering softly to the water's edge, my feet shuffling in long wet grass. I could feel the moisture under my toes. I wriggled them. The water was warm. I looked down, hoping to catch sight of a shell. But all I could see was red.

The water was red. I looked at it quizzically for a few seconds. I didn't understand it. But then I did. It was blood. It was Mary's blood. Her head had cracked off the marble fireplace.

I jumped high in the air with fright, leaping from the ground before landing back in the thick sticky mess. My feet slapped onto the floor, stomping in the puddle as if I had my red wellie boots on. My hands were covering my mouth but they couldn't hold in the scream. Nothing would have held in this scream. It could have come from Mary as she fell to her knees at the foot of the cross. I paced round and round the room urgently, my senses obliterated, my mind melted by the explosion.

I scurried across the room, darting from side to side and then running around in mazy circles, my hands shifting from my mouth to my neck to the back of my head. Each time my mouth screamed the same stupid thing, my lips stammered that I'd killed Mary. I knelt beside her, trying not to touch any of the blood on the floor but I slipped, covering myself in the very essence of the Virgin Mary. I lifted my hands up to my face. They were red, like I'd been dabbling in a game of finger paints. I didn't want to play anymore.

Mary

She was lighter than I thought she would be but even still I was out of breath by the time I placed her carefully on the bed. My combats were saturated in blood, a thick red soup that had soaked into the fabric when I placed her head on my knee, my fingers stroking her cheeks as if they held the miracle touch of Jesus. She was breathing, softly and slowly but regularly enough to tell me that she was alive.

I placed the duvet over her and climbed under it, lying on my side and placing my arm on her chest, being careful not to rest my hand on her breast, understanding that everything about that kind of thinking was wrong. I kissed her forehead. She stirred and I drew breath sharply. I wanted to die before she woke, I didn't want to have to say goodbye. I rolled on to my back and thought of Jenny, the terror she must have felt when she pulled the noose around her neck and stepped away from her horrible world.

I slipped out from under the cover and smoothed it around Mary, pulling the edge up to her chin. I checked to see if the towel on her head was still stemming the flow of blood. It had finally slowed, almost grinding to a halt. The cut was small, the blood way out of proportion, but it would hurt all the same. I stroked her cheek praying that on waking she could simply banish the pain away.

The scissors were in the drawer in the kitchen and I took them out, opening and closing them a few times in quick succession to confirm that they were capable of doing the job. I pulled a chair from the table and moved it across the floor so I could reach the slack rope from the pulley. I cut it forcefully, the scissors slicing through the bind with ease. I threw one end of the rope out so it lay in a long line across the floor and then I hauled it in, doubling and then tripling it to give it strength. I tossed an end up and over the pulley, pushing it through the metal frame, looping it and tying it tightly before forming a noose with the other end.

I checked on Mary again and then reached for the phone. I remembered the number from our visit the previous night.

'Can I have a taxi please?'

'Where tae?'

I sat down on the seat in the hall keeping an eye on the noose hanging from the pulley whilst all the time listening intently to the voice on the phone. It was the same girl that was in the office last night, with the tits and arse.

'It's for number 11 Hampden Quadrant but listen, I need to ask you a favour. I . . .'

'We don't dae favours hen, just send out taxis. Dae you want wan or no?'

I almost sniggered, imagining her face puckering in annoyance on the other end of the phone.

'Yes, I'd very much like a taxi but I'd like to request a driver.'

'Are you mental hen, like ah said we don't dae favours. Ah've no got time tae cherry pick drivers, you'll get what you're given or you can go elsewhere, it's nae big deal tae us, there's plenty wanting any taxi that comes.'

I cleared my throat realising that this part of the plan wasn't going as well as it should. I needed to be sure that someone would find Mary and make sure she was all right. The only person I could trust to keep their mouth shout was Alan.

'Listen, sorry for bothering you, I'm not meaning to create any hassle it's just that the taxi's for Alan Findlay's granny, she's not feeling well and won't let me call an ambulance, she says the only person that can take her to the hospital is Alan.'

There was a moment of stillness at the other end of the phone, the dull echo finally interrupted by a loud tut.

'But he's no a driver, does she no realise that?'

'Absolutely, I know, she's forever going on about how he's the boss but she still wants him to drive her and she's all over the place and can't remember his mobile number. I can't even find her phone to call him myself.'

'And who are you, her guardian angel?'

I almost reprimanded her. I was a customer, her telephone skills were appalling but I let it go, I needed to get on. I giggled, squeezing the rattle out convincingly.

'No, if only. I'm her neighbour, I live next door.'

'Right, ah'll see what ah can dae but ah'm no promising anything. Alan might not even have his phone oan at this time, he's been working aw day you know.'

'Thanks, I appreciate your help, I'm sure Alan will too.'

'Aye whatever. Whit's your name so ah can tell him who's looking after his granny until he gets there?'

'It's Elizabeth Shaw. Can you tell him it's urgent and to come as soon as he can, and listen, can you also ask him to come right up to the top flat, I'm not going to be able to get her downstairs myself.'

The tut was slow and deliberate. I could feel that she was torn between helping and telling me to fuck off. I gave her the address again, although technically if it really was Alan's granny's flat he should already know it. Fortunately she wasn't smart enough to work that out for herself.

'Aye all right, ah'll send a car along but only cos we're talking about a wee old lady, ah wouldn't normally bother Alan at this time. Ah'll dae what ah can.'

A purr at the other end of the line told me she had hung up so I placed the handset down and opened the drawer in the hall dresser. The notepaper was pink; I still hadn't got out of the habit. I scribbled quickly.

Alan,

Sorry for the story about your granny, I don't even know if you still have one but it's the only thing I could think of to get a message to you. Can you make sure Mary's all right? I think she is but I'm a bit worried that she might go into a coma or something so can you keep an eye on her until she's awake? She's in the bedroom. I can't explain but she's important, I'm sure that one of these days you'll be glad you had a chance to help her!!! I'm in the kitchen but just leave me be, don't call anyone, there isn't anyone anyway. Thanks, and give my love to Laura, I can only hope that Collette turned out to be just as amazing as her.

Elizabeth.

PS, the door's on the bloody latch, no need to kick it in!!

I opened the front door and pinned the note in the centre just above the letter box. He couldn't miss it. I clicked the lock onto the latch and closed it over, content that Alan could get in and check on Mary, take her to the hospital if he had to, but she would be okay. She had to be.

I stood outside the bedroom door, fingers curled around the handle, bouncing from heel to toe, toying with the idea of going back in to say goodbye. I decided against it. Her heavenly features would wreak havoc on my forthcoming mortal sin. I went into the kitchen and closed the door.

Climbing onto the chair I slung the noose round my neck with gusto. I rocked gently from side to side, readying myself to kick the chair into touch. A few more seconds and I would be with Jenny.

I had never noticed it before but my kitchen clock's tick is incredibly loud, its incessant clunk bouncing between my ears, not even trying to escape, more content to torture me than free me. It was directly in my line of sight, on the wall beside the cooker, tick tick tocking, its crazy language hurting my head. I found myself blaming it for keeping me still, *hypnotic* I called it to its large round face, out loud, challenging it to stop when it suited me better when it was ticking, distracting me from the drop.

After a while its rhythm grasped me and I found myself slipping into old ways, my tongue circling my mouth and finding the words of the Virgin's prayer, licking the letters over and over in my diversionary trick of the past, when the words swept through me, accompanied by Andrew's dick as it forced itself inside, tearing, his knees pressing down on my thighs, my legs spread wide and his tongue outstretched and flicking as if it and not his prick were en route to such a tiny place.

The Hail Mary was more like a song than a prayer with Andrew. I could recite the first five lines slowly and deliberately, like a violin introduction in a concerto, his dick pushing up gradually, content to feel its way before pulling back at the same leisurely pace, a soft murmur escaping periodically from deep at the back of his throat. He always kept in pace with my prayer for the first verse; it was as if his prick could hear it. A smarter seven year old would have called it a rhythm stick.

But he always needed a chorus; he needed the backing of the entire orchestra, a round of fucking applause, the beat faster, louder, harder for every second verse, *the blessed fruit of thy womb Jesus* a signal that I would have to up my pace and deliver my next line with a great deal more urgency. He liked a lot of choruses, pulling back for his slow solo each time I hit *Hail Mary full of grace*, savouring each note, each word, each ticking second before his audience encouraged him to move on with vigour.

And then there was the priest. The prayer was quicker with Father Brennan, his thrusts more direct and urgent, the whole of Mary's prayer always recited dramatically as the words rocked in tune to his crescendo. He beat a fine tune did the priest, never stopping until he delivered the climax, racing to get to the final sentence, crashing out on me by the tenth recital of *at the hour of our death amen*.

I never made eye contact with either of them; Mary just kept me to time until I could slip out from under them and open the door. Once though, Andrew made me look. He startled me, pulling out of me mid prayer, bouncing his knees from my thighs to my arms, pinning them by my sides, the weight of his legs pushing down between my elbows and shoulder, his prick in front of my face. As soon as I saw it I closed my eyes and fought to place myself back in the prayer but he grabbed my hair, screamed at me to watch and I never did find my thread again, not even when he spurted all over my face, his thick fingers forcing the stuff onto my tongue, rubbing it onto my teeth, ripping Mary's words from my lips. By the time I lost the baby it had happened 298 times. Umberto made it 299 and Paddy, the lovely Paddy, sealed the deal on 300 with his metal baseball bat. I was glad I was going out on an even number.

I glanced at the clock. Ten minutes had past and I could feel Andrew's spunk on my teeth. I jumped high, thudding back on to the chair. It didn't move, not the first time or even the second time. But on the third stroke it fell to its knees and I crashed down with it, the rope grasping my throat, tearing at me, ripping my horrible world from my soul.

I didn't think of Jenny, not even for a split second.

Susan

'Susan hen, you're still my number one girl, even after all these years. What would ah dae without you eh?'

A high screeched giggle rolled from the phone like a smoke signal. Alan feigned a cough being careful not to let Umberto catch him eavesdropping on his conversation. He dug his own mobile from his hip pocket and texted Laura about meeting for dinner later, signing off with a smiley face that made him do exactly that.

Umberto hung up and placed his mobile in the cup holder in between the two front seats of the car.

'You're looking pretty pleased wae yourself there Alan. Who's that you were texting?'

'What? Eh, Laura, just checking on what time tae meet her later on. How?'

'Laura. Ah see, and there was me thinking that it might have been that wee boot Elizabeth Shaw.'

Alan gulped, heat rushing through his body from the soles of his feet. He ran his fingers through his hair using the palm of his hand to try and hide the red flush that was firing a deep colour into his cheeks.

'No man, it wiz Laura, here check.' He pulled his phone from his pocket and opened the text holding the screen in front of Umberto's face.

'Fucks sake Umberto, ah don't even know Elizabeth's number and even if ah did ah wouldnae be contacting her anyway, you know that.'

'Aye sorry mate, ah know you wouldn't try and take the cunt out of me. If you had been in contact with that wee boot you would tell me, ah know that. Sorry man, it was just a fuckin shock for her tae turn up in the thick oav that plan tae fuck over the TV presenter guy. But ah shouldnae be surprised, she always was wan for sticking her oar in. Tell you whit though, you better no get in touch wae her cos if she finds out about the wean ah'm gaunae hold you directly responsible. You know whit happened tae Paddy an' you'll no get off as lightly if ah'm holding the gun instead oav that wee *cunt* Elizabeth. Dae you hear whit ah'm saying or dae ah need tae spell it out for you a wee bit mare directly?'

Alan jumped, a text message arriving in his inbox startling his already agitated state. It was from Laura. He showed it to Umberto whilst speaking quickly, his words racing to leave him behind.

'No way man, ah wouldnae dae that to you, ah know how important it is tae make sure naebody finds out about you and the wean. It's all a bit weird though, Elizabeth popping up again after all these years. Dae you mind if ah reply tae Laura?'

Umberto glanced at the phone. 'Aye, fire away. By the way, tell her that tonight's the night.'

'Eh?' Alan asked the question without lifting his head, his eyes darting across his iPhone screen as he typed his message to Laura.

'Ah said tell her tonight's the night.'

Alan placed the phone on his knee, looking at Umberto inquisitively.

'The night for what?'

'The night ah take down her pretty little panties and fuck her senseless.'

Alan felt the colour drain from his face. He cleared his throat, unable to say anything.

'Your wee lassie's not a wee girl anymore mate, she's eighteen now, and before you start moaning at me ah wouldnae normally have waited this long, sixteen's the legal age in case you've forgotten but ah was being loyal tae my mate. Ma mate Alan.'

He opened the glove box and took out a pair of black leather gloves. He looked at them carefully before slipping them on to his hands, his fingers working to pull the leather tightly into place. He waited an agonising few moments before pulling the car alongside the petrol pump just vacated by the car in front.

'In fact, ah wouldnae have gone near her at all, not ever, she's my daughter's best pal after aw, but when you find out that your trusted mate has bitten off the hand that feeds him by lying through his teeth then you have tae come up with something that hurts more than physical pain. Dae you not agree Alan?'

Reality sinking in, Alan began to fight to save his daughter.

'What are you talking about Umberto, ah don't understand. Ah know you mate, ah know you wouldnae do anything tae hurt Laura. Ah've seen you wae Collette you've always treated that lassie like a princess, you're great tae her and you've been like an uncle tae Laura, she thinks the world oav you man, like you're family.'

'You see Alan ah might have listened tae a plea of mercy if it hadnae been for the fact that Susan's just called tae tell me that your granny's no well and she needs you tae go tae hers right away.'

'Whit? My granny's been deid for fifteen years Umberto. What the fuck's she talking about?'

'Now that's what ah had been thinking you would tell me but it seems that she's still alive and her neighbour *Elizabeth*, *Elizabeth Shaw* tae be precise, is looking for you tae get over there and help her right away. Now how dae you suppose that happened if you've no spoken tae her?'

'Ah don't know man, ah really don't.'

'You know, you might be forgiven for thinking that Susan in the office is no the sharpest tool in the box but you've got tae hand it tae her, she says as soon as she came off the phone tae some lassie called *Elizabeth* she thought it was all a bit weird.'

'It is weird boss, ah don't have a fuckin clue what she's talking about, ah honestly don't.'

'Well, weirder and weirder. Susan was saying that just after the mystery call from the mystery caller called *Elizabeth* that Laura phoned the office looking for you and when Susan asked her where her great granny lived it was a bit oav a surprise to her to hear that apparently you've no got a wee granny anymore. Imagine that eh?'

'Fucks sake mate ah know, that's whit ah'm saying, my granny's been deid for donkey's years. There must be some sort oav mistake Umberto, ah promise you mate, ah don't know what she's talking about, ah havenae got a granny ah told you that.'

Alan spoke with conviction; this bit was true. He didn't know why Elizabeth had said something about his granny.

'Ach well if it's going to be like that ah guess we'll just head over tae see Laura the now, ah'm getting pretty hard here at the thought of getting stuck intae her. She's still a virgin Al, did you know that? Aye, she let it slip tae her uncle Umberto a wee while back, seems she wants tae save herself for the right guy. What dae you reckon mate, think ah fit the bill?' Umberto laughed. 'Here text her and tell her ah'm oan my way over and ah've got a surprise for her . . . unless of course you want to try and make amends for the situation by telling me what the fuck is going on with that boot Elizabeth.'

Alan wrung his hands, the sweat making them squelch loudly.

'Do you know what Umberto, ah think I might know what the fuck might be going on, ah can try and explain.'

'Think? Think hard you little prick cos every second you continue to take the cunt out of me your wee lassie just gets it even harder.'

'Aye, ah right, ah know, fucks sake just leave Laura out oav this, she's done nothing wrong. Elizabeth lives over on the south side but its gaunae take us ages tae get there at this time, the traffic's mental the now. Ah'll fill you in oan the way.'

'Excellent young man, good tae see there's a wee slither

of sense in you after all.'

Umberto slapped Alan sarcastically on the back, grinning menacingly as he drew his fingers from his shoulders to the nape of his neck.

'Now, get out of this fuckin motor and fill up the tank and let's be on our merry way. Chop chop.'

Alan texted quickly at the kiosk ensuring his hands couldn't be spotted from the car. He deleted the message as soon as he sent it and stepped back into the car. As he pulled away Alan reminded Umberto, as he always did, to put his seatbelt on. This time though he wished he had the bottle not to bother. Umberto ignored him, as always.

Umberto

I would have sold Jenny's soul if I could have. I didn't give a fuck about her struggle, or imagine falling into her arms like a dutiful lover. I wanted to be as far away from her as possible but I couldn't stop it, the rope was taking me away, squeezing what little bit of life I had left from my bones.

When I kicked the chair over Jenny was nowhere to be seen, just Sadie, her soft hands moving with manic speed as she tore at the rope, her fingers flicking quickly when she spotted the scissors, the sharp metal slipping with ease through the rope, the tension snapping and sending me plummeting to the floor.

'Sadie . . .'

I coughed, struggling for breath whilst reaching out my hands to touch her face. It was warm and clammy.

'I think you must have been starved oav oxygen tae the brain, either that or you just want tae make a habit of thinking that ah'm my mother.'

I pulled the rope from my neck and rested the makeshift noose on my knees. I was on the kitchen floor, my deep breaths long and cavernous. Laura was beside me, her cheeky retort doing little to disguise the look of sheer panic on her face.

'What are you doing here?'

My voice startled me. It was so deep and hoarse I barely recognised it as my own.

'Never mind that the now. Are you hurt somewhere else? Where the fuck is all that blood coming from?' She was looking me up and down, her eyes searching for the source of the blood on my trousers.

'We're going to need to get some ice on your neck tae stop

the swelling whilst ah get you tae the hospital.'

I clutched at my throat, feeling it constricting.

'I'm fine, it's not blood, it's just an old paint stain and I'm not going to the hospital. What the fuck is going on anyway? I thought I was dead.'

'Nah, not yet anyway but ah'll tell you what, you're lucky I was only down the road when my dad texted me or you flippin well would be. You sure that's no blood, looks awfy like it tae me?'

I coughed, moving out of reach of her approaching hand. It wasn't easy; an intense pain was gripping my windpipe as if the rope was still squeezing my throat. I circled my hands around my neck, double checking it was really gone.

'Did you just say your dad? Why did he ask you to come up?'

'Bloody hell, ah find you dangling like a puppet fae the washing line and you expect me tae know what's going on? Ah've no got a fuckin clue, maybe he thought a bit of resuscitation would be good practise for me before ah go off tae medical school.'

I felt the tears when they reached my throat, the salt stinging the fresh graze from the rope. I clenched my fists, hating that I was crying.

'Listen, all ah know is my dad sent me a text with this address saying ah should get here ASAP and get you out of here before he and Umberto arrive.'

I coughed again; this time it stayed with me and I buckled, the weight of the attack pushing my chest towards the floor. Laura waited patiently for it to stop before handing me a glass of water. I swallowed it slowly, the first sip squeezing painfully into the narrow channel of my swollen pipe.

'Is Umberto coming here?'

'Fuckin hell man, did ah not just say that? Jeezo, are you sure you didnae buy that degree?'

Laura was pointing at my graduation photograph, its centre

spot on the notice board catching her eye.

'No, it's real all right but I guess this isn't my smartest hour.'

'Some might say that wiz a bit oav an understatement. You sure there's not something else going on here, ah cannae believe that aw that blood just dropped down fae heaven.'

She squinted her eyes, examining my trousers again, suspicion causing little lines of distrust to roll in like a wave along her forehead. I shook my head and looked away.

'Well are we at least over this suicide shit cos my da didn't say anything about babysitting a nut job.'

She smiled Sadie's smile, her mouth gaping wide, her tongue running cheekily along her teeth in exactly the same way her mother's had.

'Jesus hen, you're the double of . . .'

'Aye, my mother, ah know, ah get it but its not exactly remarkable is it, a daughter looking like her mother, ah'm sure it's happened before in other families. Shock horror, in fact Collette's the image of you but ah guess you don't give a fuck about that.'

I clambered to my feet.

'Of course I give a fuck, I think about her every fuckin day in life, just because I gave her up doesn't mean I don't love her and if she knew me she'd understand that.'

It was only then I really heard what she'd been saying.

'Collette, you've seen her . . . ?'

She threw her head back and shook it slowly, sarcastically. Her long hair fell on to her face. I could feel her eyes glaring at me angrily through the unruly strands.

'Listen Elizabeth, it's not a great time ah know but Collette's my best mate and she knows all right, she knows fine well that you didnae give a fuck about her. Umberto told us he tried tae make a home for the three oav you thegether but all you were interested in wiz finding money for your next tenner bag. Fucks sake Elizabeth, fortunately Collette diznae know this bit, but I know that you even made him pay you for sex when all he wiz trying tae do was look after you. You're fuckin pathetic.'

I struggled to speak but she refused to let me butt in. She had an agenda, and the filth was all ready to roll off her tongue.

'But dae you know what the worst fuckin thing was, the thing I cannae get my head around even now? Ah cannae work out why you pretended tae Paddy that Collette wiz his and then dragged us all tae Ireland when he found out Collette was someone else's. Nae wonder he wanted tae kick the shit out of you, that's the fuckin lowest of the low doing that.'

My head was spinning, I could feel the world closing in but I clambered through it, trying to get her to listen to me.

'Laura, hen, listen to me, that's all lies, it wasn't like that I promise.'

I grabbed her shoulders but she pushed me away. I fell to the floor like a sack of potatoes.

'Fuck up the now will you? Ah've waited a long time tae say this and if it wiznae for my dad ah'd have laid into you the other day when we met you.'

She pulled a chair across the floor, its legs grating noisily on the timber boards, like chalk grinding down a blackboard. She placed it in front of me and sat on it, her knees in line with my chin, her upper body towering oppressively over mine.

'Ah'm no daft. Despite the fact that my da seems tae think there's some good in you ah know the real truth. Umberto told us everything, the lot, and let's face it, it's no wonder you've kept your head down all these years. Ah would too if ah'd been responsible for killing someone and destroying not one but two wee lassies' lives.'

'What? What do you mean, Laura? I tried to save Sadie, I promise you I did, Patrick was just mental, he was totally out of control, I couldn't stop him. I was in the intensive care ward in hospital for three weeks after Patrick and your mum died. Please Laura, you need to talk to your dad, he'll tell you what happened. I did what I could to help him too, and you. I helped make sure Alan got to keep you, ask him.'

'Look Elizabeth, ah know what happened and that's that. If it wiznae for your fuckin lies my mum wouldn't have gone away with you, she'd be alive. She'd have spent her life loving me and maybe, just maybe, her and my dad would have been happy.'

I tried to push myself up but a finger on my shoulder was enough to keep me still.

'Wait the now will you? Ah'm talking and believe me ah've got plenty to say. Listen, ah'm no gaunae get all dramatic about it cos ah've done all my crying over the years but tae be perfectly honest ah wish it wiz you that had died. But no, instead you managed tae get my mother killed. Ah don't know why ah bothered cutting you down off that rope, ah should have let you swing sister.'

I grabbed her arms, pulling her towards me, panic not pain trying to snatch my voice.

'These things you're saying, they're all mad, it's just crazy . . .'

'Fuck off, let me go Elizabeth, ah don't want tae hear any of it. Now, let's just get tae fuck out of here like my dad asked. Ah don't know why he's always stuck up for you, but me and Collette wised up quick enough that's for sure.'

'But I don't understand, how do you know so much about Collette? Do you know where she is?'

'What, the wee lassie that you couldnae be bothered wae and wanted packed off to the orphanage when you decided your ma and dad couldnae have her anymore? Of course ah know where she is. Thank fuck her da wanted her, at least he was willing tae give her some sort oav life and ah'll tell you what she's had a good one, a million times better than if she'd been wae an evil cow like you.'

'Her dad? Laura, what the fuck, Collette's dad is dead, Patrick . . . I . . . He hurt your mum, I picked up Sadie's granny's gun and shot him in the fuckin head. I was there, I fuckin did it, I killed him with my own two hands Laura. He died on that island. There was nothing they could do, he was already gone by the time the medical people got in from the mainland. I don't want tae put too fine a point on it but his head was like a pumpkin. He *definitely* died.'

'Not that stupid prick, ah'm talking about Collette's real dad. Aye, Umberto, the one you forgot tae tell anybody about. It's just as well your psychiatrist handed over the letter to your ma and da wae you telling the truth about who Collette's real dad was or Collette would have been sent to some god awful home. Fuckin hell, you couldnae even dae that for her. Just cos you didnae want her didnae mean she had tae go without her da as well. Tell you what though, Umberto's been amazing, Collette's done all right without you. She's better off as it happens.'

I couldn't believe my ears. It wasn't true. I certainly hadn't written any such letter. Piggy must have been in on it with Umberto. They all knew, even my mum and dad. Ah thought they were happy wae me giving Collette up for adoption because they wanted me out of their lives. Us or Mary they kept saying, we cannae have Collette listening tae that crap when you get out of the hospital. We put up wae it for years and we're no daein it again, they said. I chose a safer life for Collette. They didn't protect me from Andrew. Collette was the same age, prime for the taking. I wasn't going to let that happen to her under their care. But the bastards all conspired behind my back, handing my angel to the devil. Piggy even offered me a tissue when I signed the formal papers to relinquish her from my care.

Laura picked up the rope and scathingly tossed it to the other side of the kitchen. I fell backwards against the wall and she picked me up like a rag doll.

'C'mon Elizabeth, it's time tae hit the road. Ah'll leave you at the airport, but make sure you take the longest journey out of here cos ah'm no really in any rush tae see you again.'

We both turned when we heard the kitchen door open, creaking like an old man yawning his way into another early morning.

'Mary, is that you, tell her will you, I can't understand any of this.'

I saw the shoes first, the pointed toes, the Italian leather.

'Not Mary, just your old lover Umberto. It's been such a long time since ah've seen the mother of my child. Hmm, have tae say though, you're not looking your best. Did the loony bin not serve you well hen?'

The scissors were the first thing I saw. I was like a magpie, the little glint of silver on the worktop enough to make me want to capture them and thrust them deeply into Umberto's neck. I was quicker than the rest of them, but once I had them I didn't know what to do with them, until I tried to turn them on myself.

I didn't realise the screams were mine until I looked around me in the stairway, the hollering bouncing off the walls as they carried me down in the little red chair, the oxygen mask doing nothing to hold the pain inside. I guess it was just ready to all come out.

A life remembered

The room was cold and I couldn't stop shivering, not even when I wrapped the duvet around my shoulders and tucked myself firmly inside. My hands were blue, my feet so numb I didn't feel as if they belonged to me anymore. I looked down at them, recognising them as something I was once familiar with.

I drew them back under the covers and touched their icy surface, mildly enjoying the sense that they were someone else's, that maybe I wasn't really me. It had been a few days, maybe a week. Definitely a week, my period had come and gone and it was like clockwork so eight days must have passed. Or was it the second time I'd bled? I couldn't remember. Maybe it was the tenth, or the eleventh. Or even the twelfth. They all seemed the same now, the days that came and then went away without leaving anything different behind.

On the first day he'd taken my clothes, all of them, but he didn't touch me. Not like that. He always made me think he was going to. Every time he came into the room I was ready for him pushing me into the corner, making me bend over beneath him but he'd just dig his hands into his pockets and smile.

It wasn't Piggy. Piggy was gone. He'd moved on to a different hospital. I was disappointed and pleased at the same time. Disappointed that I wouldn't get the chance to look him in the eye now that I knew what he had done, pleased that he'd gone and that I didn't have to kill him.

I didn't call the new one anything. Just in case. I knew that smile; I'd seen it all before. I understood what was at the other end of it so I stayed quiet. I didn't speak, not to anyone. My words were all mine, I'd given enough to everyone else.

The white walls somehow made it feel colder, the heavy

blue curtains like a permanent winter sky. Sometimes I sketched the sun and a rainbow on the walls, just in my mind, I didn't have the energy to do it for real, but most of the time the bare canvas was like a cinema projector screen, playing the whole damn thing back, my life in pictures, staring me in the face.

They tried to get me to go outside into the sun. Come and feel the warmth on your skin Elizabeth, he without the name would say, but I ignored him. There was nothing for me out there anymore. Anything that was left was trapped inside, racing around like a rollercoaster, nudging and budging and stopping me from getting into any kind of decent rhythm, crashing in and out so I couldn't concentrate on Mary's prayer.

It was an intentional act. They wanted to interrupt my flow; the pills they were feeding me and watching me swallow with water were supposed to cut me off from Mary. They were confused. The new Piggy seemed to be of the opinion that Mary's visit was just in my imagination. The whole visit, he said, was a creation of my mind. There was no-one in my bed with a fractured head, I was having a relapse of the illness I'd had before. He slowly talked me through it, his tone gentle and seemingly authoritative (even though I knew his words were as crazy as he believed mine to be). Twice before, he explained like he was reading from a big armchair in that ancient TV show *Jackanory*, when Jenny died and then when Sadie was murdered in cold blood in front of my bleeding ass (he didn't use quite the same sentence structure) I was having some kind of delusion. I could see why they would think that. It was a logical, medical, conclusion to come to but we weren't dealing in science, we were dealing in actuality.

There were moments when I laughed about their incompetence and then there were the quieter stays of execution, the days when I had to swallow the anger in long sustained gulps. It was extraordinary to think that they were being that shallow, that they really believed that my mind was so crazy I could invent an entire being, a relationship with a mystical person at the age of seven and then keep the untruthful narrative in tow for the rest of my life. No matter how many times he said it, and don't get me wrong there was a certain kindness in his eyes when he was saying it, repeating it over and over in case I hadn't heard him, *there was no Mary, Elizabeth, she didn't actually exist*, I didn't choose to believe it.

I suppose it was kind of them in the sense that they thought they were helping me, but cruel in that they were trying to resign me to nothing. If I was to believe them, no-one had ever wanted to save me. I scowled and coughed when he told me, the closest I'd come to making a sound in a long time. They thought I had developed an imaginary friend. Their gross inability to comprehend the complexities of the world they lived in shouldn't really have come as any kind of surprise. People fell into two brackets. Them, and me and Mary.

I took the pills, not because I believed him, just because I hoped they'd help me find my prayer. Everything else was gone for good. I knew that. I could see that.

My room door opened slowly, the curtains of night sky rising into the room for a moment before giving up the ghost and settling back on their launch pad. I resisted the urge to look in its direction but I took my hands from my freezing feet and clenched my fists under the duvet. I was ready, always ready for the moment he would reveal his true self. It was coming, it was just a matter of time. I turned to him when he said her name.

Collette.

At least I think that's what he was saying.

Collette and Laura

Laura sat back down on the sofa beside Collette, having checked for the third time that her dad was still huddled in front of the live football coverage on the telly in the kitchen. The match commentary was booming, indecipherable tones of excitement racing into the living room via the narrow crack under the door. A loud roar from the kitchen indicated a goal for the *wrong* team and Laura pulled back again, raising her eyes to the ceiling like a dog trying to place the movement of a stranger in another room.

Despite the chaos Laura kept her voice low, her body curling with purpose next to Collette as she whispered that it should be okay to talk. She pushed closer and their shoulders touched, the bare flesh of their upper arms gelling with the same tackiness that characterised their relationship. Laura peeled away when Collette asked her if she would prefer to sit on her knee.

'Sorry, ah'm acting like a total dick, ah know I am, but dad's bound tae think it's weird that ah'm not watching the game wae him . . . and by all accounts it doesn't sound as if it's going that well. He'll probably fire in here in a minute tae tell us how he could dae better than the lot of them.'

Collette nodded sympathetically. 'I know and I'm sorry for spoiling his night but I need to talk about this now, right now, otherwise it's going to drive me insane as well. You know what Alan's like, he hates me even mentioning my mother but for fuck sake Laura, I may have spent the last ten years hating her but she's still the only one I've ever had. And let's face it, Alan only hates talking about it because he was complicit in the whole Umberto charade.'

Collette paused to run her finger along Laura's forearm, responding to the way Laura's features had crumbled. 'Look

Laura, please don't look at me like that, I'm not blaming him, I know he didn't have much of a choice but jeezo, it's my life that is fucked up by it all, not your dad's.'

Laura nodded silently, catching Collette's finger as it circled her wrist. She held it for a moment before letting her friend continue, watching her arm as it stretched beyond her and on to the coffee table. Collette lifted a glass and drained the wine from it, gulping slowly with her eyelids tightly closed.

'I guess there can't be many friends out there who've been through all that we have. God, it breaks my heart to think about what happened to your mum but at least you've got a dad that cares about you Laura, both of the fathers that I was lumbered with were complete and utter psychopaths. No wonder my mum finds herself two sandwiches short of a picnic.'

Collette pushed beyond the now empty glass and reached for the bottle of wine. The ring on the index finger of her right hand arrived at it first, the clash of diamond and glass sealed with a high-pitched clink. For a moment it sang, its shrill tones a snapshot of melancholic birdsong. She examined the ring for a moment and then tutted, peeling the expensive piece of jewellery from her finger as if she was discarding the skin of an onion. She tossed the yellow metal onto the table in front of her, the circle falling almost perfectly onto an aging knot on the blonde wood.

'Umberto gave that ring to me on my sixteenth birthday, remember?' She carried on talking, drawing breath quickly. 'I never told you this before but he said that he'd bought my mum a similar one when she was sixteen but that she'd sold it to buy drugs. He spouted all this shite about how he just knew that I would never treat him with the same lack of respect that my mother had. *What the fuck* was that all about?' Collette raised her voice and the pinkness faded from Laura's face. This time her unease didn't soften Collette's tone. 'God, how absolutely fucked up was that? He made the entire thing up and I believed him because he was *my dad.* I thought he was my guardian angel. He was a fuckin head-case Laura, *he*

didn't even know my mum when she was sixteen. What a fuckin dick
I am, never mind you.'

It was Laura's turn to draw breath and she did it sharply,
saying the same words she'd said over and over to Collette,
repeatedly searching for some kind of clarity in the deceit that
had unfairly latched itself on to her life.

'Hardly Collette, he was your dad, or at least we thought
he wiz your dad. Of course you were going tae believe
everything he told you. Bloody hell, I swallow everything my
da is telling me even though we both know that most of it is
total bullshit. But it's different when you're a kid. What they
say goes, we both believed it and tae be honest we didnae
have any reason not tae.'

Collette nodded her head and swallowed some more wine.
This time she kept her eyes open, her gaze fixed on the
photograph on the mantelpiece. Collette and Laura were
young in the picture, the photograph taken on the day Alan
and Paddy had arrived on the island and made sure that their
worlds would never be the same again. Collette picked up her
glass and stretched to her feet, her tall shoes pushing her high
like a forest of foliage. She pulled her green cardigan close to
her chest, throwing the long flowing edges over her shoulder
like a scarf, her milky white hair falling down her back like the
flowers of a hawthorn. Laura watched Collette as she paced
the floor, wondering what she would do until she realised the
path she was carving was leading her to the oak fireplace.
Collette stepped on to the marble hearth, her heels clicking
noisily like Dorothy's, the fingertips of her left hand clasping
the mantelpiece and pulling her lean frame towards the wall.
She placed her wine glass on the wooden shelf and grasped
the photograph tightly, the glass squeaking as she rubbed the
surface, her disappointed eyes searching for a life she had
spent a decade being persuaded not to remember.

Collette couldn't recall the picture being taken; she and
Laura had been too engrossed in new discoveries to
understand the day's enduring prominence at that particular

moment in time. She didn't know who had taken it, but in her mind's eye she suspected it was her mum as the perspective slightly favoured her over Laura, her toddler curls sweeping across her face as she glanced in response to Elizabeth's excited call that she should look in her direction. That's how she preferred to see it, at least on the rare days when she remembered her mother with affection rather than anger. There was little else about the day she had forgotten, although she had chosen never to tell anyone she was still processing its horrifying outcomes.

It was the day that Laura had lost her mother, her pain stirring the spirits as she crawled over Elizabeth's shoulders and begged her mummy to wake up. It was also the day that Collette fell silent, seeing what was left of the man she believed to be her father on the orange lino floor, his once perfectly shaped head blown to smithereens. It was a moment she always denied she could remember.

'I guess we've got tae look on the bright side Laura, any one of us could have ended up in that mental hospital with all the crap we've both been through. Who knows, maybe I'm going to end up like my mother and I'll be having imaginary visitations before the night's out.'

Laura began to speak and then paused, understanding that the bellow from the kitchen was about to signal a visitation of another sort. Even though she was expecting it she still jumped back when the door burst to life. Alan charged through it with all the excitement of a kid at Christmas, his football top looking out of sorts on a frame as far removed from athleticism as the imagination could stretch. He was bouncing on his stocking soles, the balls of his feet pounding the bare floorboards as he pressed into the room with purpose.

'Yous have just missed the best goal ever tae have been scored. Ah cannae believe you're in here gossiping when the game of the season is oan.'

Alan looked at Collette and smiled, his cheeks burning slightly at the excuse he had used to venture into the lounge. Every moment Collette spent in a room he shared gave Alan hope that she could forgive him for lying about Umberto. Collette placed the photograph back on the mantelpiece and spoke quietly, the 'Hi Alan' she muttered shadowed with sadness. She tried to smile, pulling her lips together to disguise the disappointment that she was struggling to contain, fighting it not to reinvent itself as a bitterness she would have been unable to run away from. ' . . . You can have your football buddy back in a minute, I'm heading out to do a couple of things anyway so she's all yours.'

She paused, looking to Laura to find a quick end to a conversation she wasn't really ready to have. Laura jumped up from her seat and wrapped her arms across her father's narrow shoulders, her long fingers gently nudging his skinny frame, a short sharp push to encourage him to turn back towards the door he had just pushed through with such aplomb.

'Dad, you're missing half of the game standing here gabbing a lot oav nonsense. I'll be through in a wee minute.'

Alan stood still, his eyes avoiding everyone's gaze, his shame palpable in the way his toes pointed inwards. Laura stretched open her eyes and glanced towards the door, her will pushing Alan back to the kitchen.

'Aye, what am ah like, ah wait aw week for the match and then miss the best of the action because ah'm blethering tae you two like a wee lassie. Right, ah feel another goal coming on.'

He raised his eyes to Collette, his tiredness apparent in the folds of wrinkles that stretched from his lashes into his temples, disappearing into a head of greying hair. He paused for a second, hoping for a sign but Collette gave him nothing back and he left, the door creaking noisily as he closed it purposefully behind him. Laura picked the audio up as soon as the room fell back into something resembling silence.

'Sorry hen, ah know this is awkward for you but he's trying, he really is. He loves you as much as he loves me. I'm angry too, but he's just a fuckin idiot, you know that.'

'Aye, well we don't need to talk about that just now, we're

supposed to be trying to figure a few things out about my mother. So, are you going tae put me out of my misery and tell me what you found out at the hospital?'

Laura rubbed her hands before responding. 'Collette for fuck sake, don't go repeating that in front of anyone, the nursing team has no fuckin idea that ah know you and if they did ah would be in the shit.'

Collette sat on the edge of the sofa. She rubbed the palm of her hand onto her chin, her fingers covering her nose for a second before she pushed her hand down on to her neck and let it settle on her throat.

'Aye right enough, I'm going to go and tell my mum's psychiatrist that you told me some tea room gossip, bloody hell Laura, get a grip, I know how important being a shrink is tae you. I think you're nuts right enough, but obviously ah support you.'

Laura nodded and sat down, the moment of panic passing as her shoulders dropped into a less tense position.

'Okay, but listen, like ah said in my text, ah didn't actually see Elizabeth in the hospital, ah only overheard a couple of the nurses chatting in the tearoom. Ah shouldn't be repeating it.'

'Aye, I know Laura, jeez, you're building this up into something it's not. I just asked you to let me know if you heard anyone talking about my mum. You're the one that texted me tae come round because you had something to tell me. All I've heard so far is a doctor telling me that Elizabeth is totally bonkers and she might give up all this imaginary friend stuff if she gets her daughter back.'

Laura glanced at the door again, the drama in her face causing both her and Collette to laugh.

'Aye, ah know I'm a tit. Look, the doctor obviously knows his stuff, fuck I'm training to dae the same thing but ah don't know Collette, just listening tae some of the nurses talking about your mum makes me so pissed off. Ah'm no sure that they're giving her a proper chance. Don't get me wrong, to be honest it aw sounds completely and utterly scatty but I just don't know, mibbae it isn't necessarily all crap.'

'How, what do you mean?'

'Well, ah don't believe she was imagining everything and if some of it is true, then fuck knows Collette, stranger things have happened. This is maybe going tae sound a wee bit crazy but she was definitely there the night me and my dad bumped intae your mum outside that guy Larry Spencer's place.'

'Hoi, stop the bus. Who was where? I'm not following.'

'What dae you mean who was there? You're the one that's been asking me to find out about your mum's delusions. That Virgin Mary lassie was with your mum, for absolute definite. She seemed really nice tae be honest. She even asked us did we all want tae go for a cuppa coffee.'

Collette slipped off the arm of the chair and squeezed beside Laura on the sofa, their thighs slotting together like spoons in a drawer.

'Laura, what the fuck are you talking about? Have you lost the heid, my mother was with the Virgin Mary? This is as wild and wonderful as the *Umberto is your real dad* story. Aye good one, keep it coming.'

'Oh for fuck sake Collette, don't start acting like an idiot. Look, the doctor has told you that Elizabeth is having some kind of delusional episodes hasn't he?'

'Aye, I told you that last week after he phoned me. He said that she had treatment for it years ago as well, the first time when she was about fifteen and then again when your mum and my dad were killed. She must have been getting treatment for it when I was visiting her in the hospital after she blew my dad's brains out. Oh for those heady days before Umberto rode in on his fuckin white horse and made it all better, eh?'

Laura paused to rub Collette's hand, her touch gentle, her eyes fighting off the memory of the tears that had stung her face when she saw the carnage that had left her mum and Paddy dead.

'Well, according to the tearoom chat your ma has been

saying that the Virgin Mary was living with her before she was brought into hospital. She also says that when she was a wee lassie the Virgin Mary visited her and then kept watch over her.'

Collette placed both hands on her knees and looked straight ahead, her eyes drawn back to the photograph. 'Aye, I can see that Laura, her good pal Mary was obviously keeping a right good watch over us that day your mum and Patrick had their heads smashed tae a million pieces.'

'Don't shoot the messenger Collette, you asked me tae see if ah could find out anything and ah'm telling you. But listen, call me nuts if you want but she's right enough, Elizabeth definitely had somebody called Mary wae her that night me and my dad saw her in town.'

'God, I actually think you are spending too much time in that hospital Laura. Even I can work out that the woman that gave birth to me is completely and utterly insane. I mean come on, we were both brought up in all this Catholic shit but we didn't for a minute think that the wee lassie with the baby had a closed hymen, never mind an inclination to visit my mother. The only thing we know about my mum for sure is that she abandoned me and gave me to a psychopath.'

'Aw come on Collette, ah know some of the things she's been doing don't make a lot of sense but you cannae pin that oan her. She says she didnae know that you had been given to Umberto and tae be honest ah believe her. She seemed genuinely confused when I was saying tae her that ah knew Umberto was your real dad. She wiznae making that look in her eyes up. Ah know they're saying she's mad but that was genuine, ah'm telling you. Whatever happened to make it happen we can be sure that your ma wiznae involved in you being brought up by your dad.'

Collette turned to face Laura. 'He's not my dad. Umberto was absolutely nothing to me, there's not even the slightest hint of a connection. He was just an evil cunt who wanted to hurt my mother. What I'm trying to work out is if she deserved hurting. If she is mad or evil or stupid or just really

really unlucky. I've got no idea. I didn't even know she was in Glasgow until a few months ago. Thanks, of course, to you and Alan hiding the fact that you'd seen her in town that night. Ah but don't tell me, any best friend would have done the same thing.'

'Collette, I know I deserve that but come on, we've been through this a million times. Your dad, Umberto, whoever the fuck he was, he would have gone apeshit if we'd told you. He said it wiznae worth the hassle of hurting you and we believed him, we didnae have any reason not tae.'

'No Laura, you didn't have any reason not to disbelieve him, but your dad did. Alan knew fine well that they had deceived my mother. I know she killed Patrick but did she deserve to lose her child as well? Alan knew that bastard Umberto wasn't my dad. I just can't get my head around any of it. It's like a fuckin waking nightmare.' Collette placed her hands on her knees and pushed herself to her feet. 'Look, I need to go. I need some air and some time to decide if I'm going to visit my head-case of a mum. The doc says he's run out of ideas so maybe I can help. I don't know, maybe I will and maybe I won't.'

Collette stretched her spine and Laura pulled up beside her like a reflection. They stood silent for a second and then embraced, the hug warm and cloudy like a murky summer day. They parted silently, Collette mumbling quietly when Laura asked her to let her know what she was going to do.

The visitor

The rain was lashing off the pavement, but undeterred Collette marched towards the river. She walked quickly, her pace steady despite her high shoes, the tall heels clip clopping musically along the concrete, her mind focused on feeling the rush of the water beneath her. She tracked its meandering path, funnelling underground in darkness until it and she emerged at the riverbank, the sweeping flow chasing her yesterdays with the same determination she had. She leant across the bridge, her feet pushing on to their tips as she pushed her breasts up onto the cold stone, her fingers stretching towards the air that circled between the water and her wet clothes. The cathedral commanded the bank directly across the river and Collette closed her eyes to its presence. A voice interrupted her train of thought and she opened her eyes to it, turning her head to catch the conversation with her soul.

'Not so long ago your ma and I were here, and it was pishing down that night an' all. Ah guess that means ah'm no exactly what you would call a wee ray of sunshine.'

Collette dropped to the pavement, her feet firmly fixed on earth.

Elizabeth and Mary

'Collette is here to see you Elizabeth. Is it okay if I let her in?'

I wrapped my arms around my neck, pulling at my ears, staring and staring until he said it again so I could know I was hearing it for sure.

'Is it okay? She really wants to see you. She says she really needs to talk to you. Maybe it will do you a bit of good to see someone other than all us medical folk for a wee change. I can stay with you if you like?'

I shook my head. No. No. No-one else should be here.

'Does that mean she can come in? There's no pressure, you don't have to do anything you don't want to do.'

That was a first.

I nodded that he should let her in and I held my breath whilst he left the room. Their voices were hushed but audible, I could hear them talking as they walked along the corridor, their steps humbled by the long syllables of a gentle voice that sang like Keats's nightingale. I covered my ears, not wanting to believe it was real until I could see her.

She looked just as I had always imagined she would, like the sketches I'd drawn over and over again as the years passed and the pain refused to budge.

Her hair was the first thing that struck me. Her little blond curls had grown up. She had Patrick's hair, the colour intense, its brightness dazzling my eyes. She had his skin too, golden brown, permanently tanned. I didn't need to feel it to know it would be velvet to the touch. Her fingers were long, slender and thin, just like his, a silver watch circling the wrist of her right hand.

But it was my face. Everything about it was mine. Especially her eyes. I could see my reflection in them as soon

323

as she entered the room. I pulled back, expecting the mirror in front of me to swing in the same direction but it carried on walking, stopping at the end of my bed, smiling. She gestured that she was going to sit down, her words quiet. I had to strain my ears to hear them, to let myself believe that they were real.

'Mum. It's me, Collette. Is it okay to come and talk tae you for a bit?'

The tears fell, both of our faces saturated with salt and yet still I couldn't utter a sound. I couldn't begin to speak, not to her, not to the baby I had destroyed. She kept talking, my eyes, her eyes, our vision locking, our lids slowly fluttering, dancing around our past like butterflies.

'I've missed you mum. I've missed you every day of every week of every month of every year. I would have looked for you but dad . . . Umberto . . . he said you didn't want me. I used to beg him to find you, when I was little, before I believed him that you didn't care. I shouldn't have believed him. I know I shouldn't have but he was all I had.'

She, *Collette*, took my hand from my neck and held it, her fingers soft and warm. I curled my pinkie around hers, like a child would do.

'Mum, please don't cry, it's okay. I'm okay. I know what happened, Mary told me everything. I'm so sorry about everything you've been through. I wish . . . oh Mum, you're amazing, you're the most incredible person I've ever known. You're so brave.'

She pulled her head to the side, looking behind her, checking he was gone. I looked at her, scared to swallow any of it in case it disappeared. Did she really say *Mum* or did I imagine it like every other day? Collette, Mary, both of them visions in my little squished brain. I heard her name just as I was thinking it. *Mary*. The word was coming from Collette.

'Mary came to see me. You remember Mary don't you?'

I didn't say anything. Maybe she was crazy, or trying to trick me. I said nothing, just in case Piggy was back on the scene and about to give me my daughter back before stealing her away.

'Hey, don't look at me like that.' She smiled, a laugh threatening to escape from behind her teeth.

'Aye, I know you remember her, she's not the type of visitor you forget in a hurry is she?' She allowed the laugh to burst to the surface and I almost felt an emotion inside, a ripple of something pinching sharply at my insides.

'Anyway, Mary . . . well, Mary said to say to you the headache's finally gone. She was laughing when she said it; she said you'd know what she meant.'

She, *Collette*, looked at the door again, her gaze lingering around the room before she returned it safely to me.

'Mum, I'm so sorry, I want to help you. I need you so much, I need you to get well. Can you do that for me? Please? I want my mum back.'

She stroked my hair and I bristled. Not because it was horrible but because it was beautiful. I was scared it would suddenly end.

'I've still got the book. You remember? The one you made me when I came to visit you that last day I saw you? I didn't know I wasn't going to see you again, if I did I would, well I would have been different with you. I've always treasured it, even though I thought you didn't love me anymore. Maybe deep down a part of me knew that you wouldn't be so cruel.'

I threw my head back, the tears becoming too much, my shoulders collapsing and swallowing my neck.

'It's okay, please don't cry. I'm going to take care of you, I promise. I'm going to take care of everything, it's the least I can do for you.'

She smiled but I didn't dare to do the same.

'It's just me now, Umberto's gone. Alan crashed the car when he left the flat that day . . . the day you came in here. Alan, he, well he smashed right into a tree at the bottom of the road. The impact sent Umberto through the windscreen. It was pretty horrific. He was in excruciating pain. Alan was always telling him he should wear a seatbelt, that he might

325

end up wearing the windscreen one day. It was all over for Umberto in a matter of hours but the minutes were long for him, very long. Alan was fine, he was well strapped in . . . It was a terrible *accident*.'

Her teeth were gritting together, her cheeks gnawing from side to side. I moved my body towards her. She had learned to hate him. It was in her eyes.

'I've been living in a flat around the corner from Laura ever since, quite liberating for a seventeen year old tae have her own pad but dad . . . Umberto . . . left it to me so I don't need to worry about money. Just my exams, and you . . .'

She stopped for a second and looked around, her lungs drawing breath and consuming our surroundings greedily. I shuddered, hoping that my hopelessness wasn't going to give her answers.

'I'm going to need to get myself used to hospitals. We both are. Laura has started studying medicine and I'm going tae do the same next year. All those years at school together and now we're still in each other's pockets. You'd have thought we would be sick of the sight of one another by now but we're best friends, like sisters really. We're just like you and Sadie would have been, friends for life.'

I felt the tears cascade down my cheeks. Collette wiped them away, her touch gentle, like an angel.

'Don't worry mum, Laura knows the truth too, she's really sorry about the way she talked to you in the flat. She didn't know, neither us of did. She's working things out with Alan, she's finding it hard to deal with knowing he lied about Umberto for all these years. She's angry but she knows that he thought he was doing the right thing. He genuinely believed that Umberto wanted the best for you. You know what he's like, he's not the smartest kid in the class. He didn't understand Umberto was enacting some sort of sick revenge on you for Paddy . . . Patrick. I can't say dad, I think I'd rather have none than the two I had. Anyway. Some joke eh, Umberto was one evil prick. But listen mum, we've got the last laugh cos we're together now and he's fuckin rotting in hell. I've got you back and I'm not letting you slip away again. Do you hear me?'

She wiped my cheek, her hand slipping onto my chest and picking up my Mary medal.

'By the way, Mary said to tell you that Larry Spencer knew who you were, he always did. She said you would know what that meant. I take it you know what she's talking about?'

I nodded.

'Well she says he was trying his best to look out for you, because of what Jenny had told him in a letter. He thought you needed someone you could think of as a friend. I guess that's good news?'

I bristled again and she drew closer, lowering her face.

'Mum, please don't pull away, all I want to do is help. Mary says you've not to worry about it, that you didn't do anything wrong.'

I pulled the duvet around my shoulders, folding my hands back inside the covers.

'Laura and I are not long back from somewhere you might like to go to. Carravindoon. Yes, that Carravindoon. Dad . . . Umberto . . . bought Laura's great granny's old house, Sadie's granny's place. Well you know, obviously you were there. He left it to Laura in his will. At first she didn't want anything to do with it but Alan thought it would be a good idea to go out there and spend a bit of time with her mum. Sadie is buried with Laura's granddad, in a beautiful little graveyard on the seafront.'

I nodded my head, I knew where it was.

'Laura and I were hoping that you'd come over to the island with us, once you're feeling better. Would you like that?'

I came close to smiling, my heart thumping like a rampaging bull. My little girl said nothing for a few moments and then opened her hand.

'Look mum, I've got something for you.'

It fell on to the bed, the dandelion clock glistening, the

little cotton heads catching the fingers of sunlight seeping in through the window.

'It's time to fly mum, to spread your wings and say goodbye to the past. Mary told me about Andrew, about everything. She told me where he was too. The dandelion clock told me how to deal with him. It told me it was time for me to fly too.'

Andrew

Collette took the flower from her right hand and carefully transferred it into her left, blowing the dandelion clock very very carefully.

Big breath in, out and bllooooowwwwwwwwww

He dies

Big breath in, out and bllooooowwwwwwwwww

He diznae

Big breath in, out and bllooooowwwwwwwwww

He dies

Big breath in, out and bllooooowwwwwwwwww

He diznae

Big breath in, out and bllooooowwwwwwwwww

He dies . . .

Big breath . . .

Collette moved around with every turn of the clock, the bell tolling, changing time's direction this way and that. She moved slowly, squeezing the winder, making sure he could feel every click, see every little second slip slowly towards the next. The first time she looked up from the clock she realised that she was facing him so she smiled the sweetest smile. His eyes twitched. He could see Elizabeth, remember what he had done to that little loving child. Her eyes were exactly the same. Like a mirror. The only disappointment for Collette was that her mother wasn't there to see it, to see her take to the clouds.

But Andrew could, and she showed him, stretching her arms high into the air, her toes pushing towards the sky . . . *'guess what the time is, Mr Wolf.'*